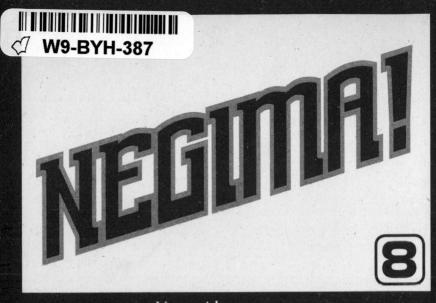

NEGIMA!

8

Ken Akamatsu

TRANSLATED BY
Toshifumi Yoshida

ADAPTED BY
T. Ledoux

LETTERING AND RETOUCH BY
Steve Palmer

DEL REY

BALLANTINE BOOKS · NEW YORK

A Word from the Author

It's all set—*Magister Negi Magi* is going to be animated! Without the continued support of you readers, this would never have happened, so, *arigatō gozaimashita*!

My hope is, as they come to life across your TV screen and on DVDs, that you'll keep an eye out for Negi and his 31 classmates, just as you've done in the manga. (Please check your local listings for airtimes.) You can go online and visit my home page for more details, or maybe even visit it by cell phone!

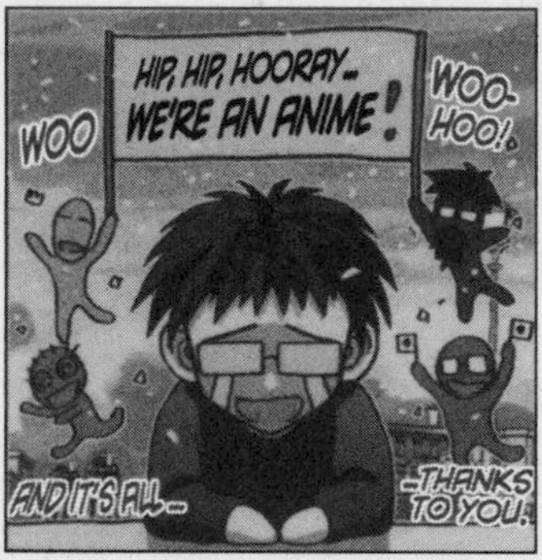
WOO-HOO!
HIP, HIP, HOORAY... WE'RE AN ANIME!
WOO
AND IT'S ALL...
...THANKS TO YOU!

This is now the third time an animated version has been produced from something I've created. The first, of course, was *Love Hina*, followed by *Rikujō Bōeitai* ("Ground Defense-Force") *Mao-chan*, for which I was credited with "original story concept." I've gotta say, it's a great feeling. (^^) With this as encouragement, I'm going to have to work even harder. Can you *imagine* how crowded it's going to be in that voice-over recording studio...?! (Heh.)

Ken Akamatsu
www.ailove.net

2005 Del Rey Trade Paperback Edition

Published in the United States by Del Rey Books, an imprint of The Random House Publishing Group, a division of Random House, Inc., New York

Originally published in serial form by Shonen Magazine Comics and subsequently published in book form by Kodansha, Ltd., Tokyo in 2004, copyright © 2004 Ken Akamatsu.

ISBN 0-345-46540-7

Printed in the United States of America

www.delreymanga.com

Library of Congress Control Number: 2004090830

1 2 3 4 5 6 7 8 9

First Edition: January 2006

Translator —Toshifumi Yoshida
Adaptor—T. Ledoux
Lettering and retouch—Steve Palmer
Cover Design—David Stevenson

Honorifics

Throughout the Del Rey Manga books, you will find Japanese honorifics left intact in the translations. For those not familiar with how the Japanese use honorifics and, more important, how they differ from American honorifics, we present this brief overview.

Politeness has always been a critical facet of Japanese culture. Ever since the feudal era, when Japan was a highly stratified society, use of honorifics—which can be defined as polite speech that indicates relationship or status—has played an essential role in the Japanese language. When addressing someone in Japanese, an honorific usually takes the form of a suffix attached to one's name (example: "Asuna-san"), or as a title at the end of one's name or in place of the name itself (example: "Negi-sensei," or simply "Sensei!").

Honorifics can be expressions of respect or endearment. In the context of manga and anime, honorifics give insight into the nature of the relationship between characters. Many translations into English leave out these important honorifics, and therefore distort the "feel" of the original Japanese. Because Japanese honorifics contain nuances that English honorifics lack, it is our policy at Del Rey not to translate them. Here, instead, is a guide to some of the honorifics you may encounter in Del Rey Manga.

-*san:* This is the most common honorific, and is equivalent to Mr., Miss, Ms., or Mrs. It is the all-purpose honorific and can be used in any situation where politeness is required.

-*sama:* This is one level higher than "-san." It is used to confer great respect.

-*dono:* This comes from the word "tono," which means "lord." It is an even higher level than "-sama," and confers utmost respect.

-kun: This suffix is used at the end of boys' names to express familiarity or endearment. It is also sometimes used by men among friends, or when addressing someone younger or of lower station.

-chan: This is used to express endearment, mostly toward girls. It is also used for little boys, pets, and even among lovers. It gives a sense of childish cuteness.

Bozu: This is an informal way to refer to a boy, similar to the English term "kid" or "squirt."

Sempai: This title suggests that the addressee is one's senior in a group or organization. It is most often used in a school setting, where underclassmen refer to their upperclassmen as "sempai." It can also be used in the workplace, such as when a newer employee addresses an employee who has seniority in the company.

Kohai: This is the opposite of "sempai," and is used toward underclassmen in school or newcomers in the workplace. It connotes that the addressee is of lower station.

Sensei: Literally meaning "one who has come before," this title is used for teachers, doctors, or masters of any profession or art.

-[blank]: Usually forgotten in these lists, but perhaps the most significant difference between Japanese and English. The lack of honorific means that the speaker has permission to address the person in a very intimate way. Usually, only family, spouses, or very close friends have this kind of permission. Known as *yobisute,* it can be gratifying when someone who has earned the intimacy starts to call one by one's name without an honorific. But when that intimacy hasn't been earned, it can also be very insulting.

魔法先生 ネギま!

MAGISTER NEGI MAGI

8

Ken Akamatsu

赤松健（あかまつけん）

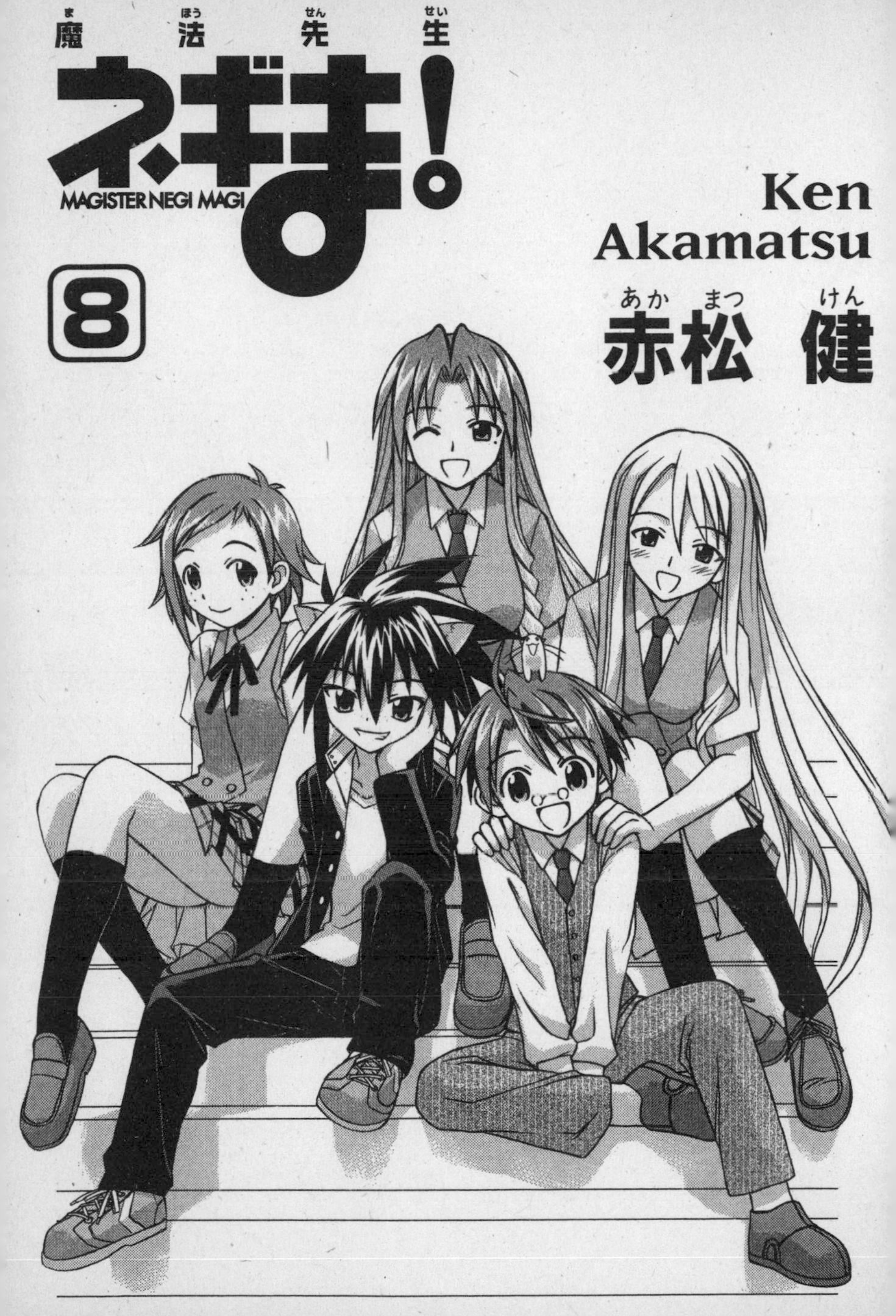

CONTENTS

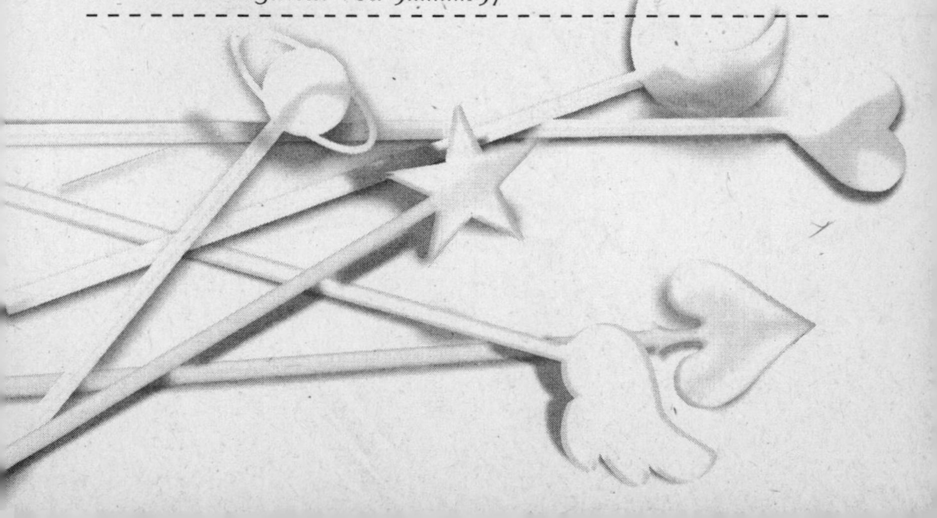

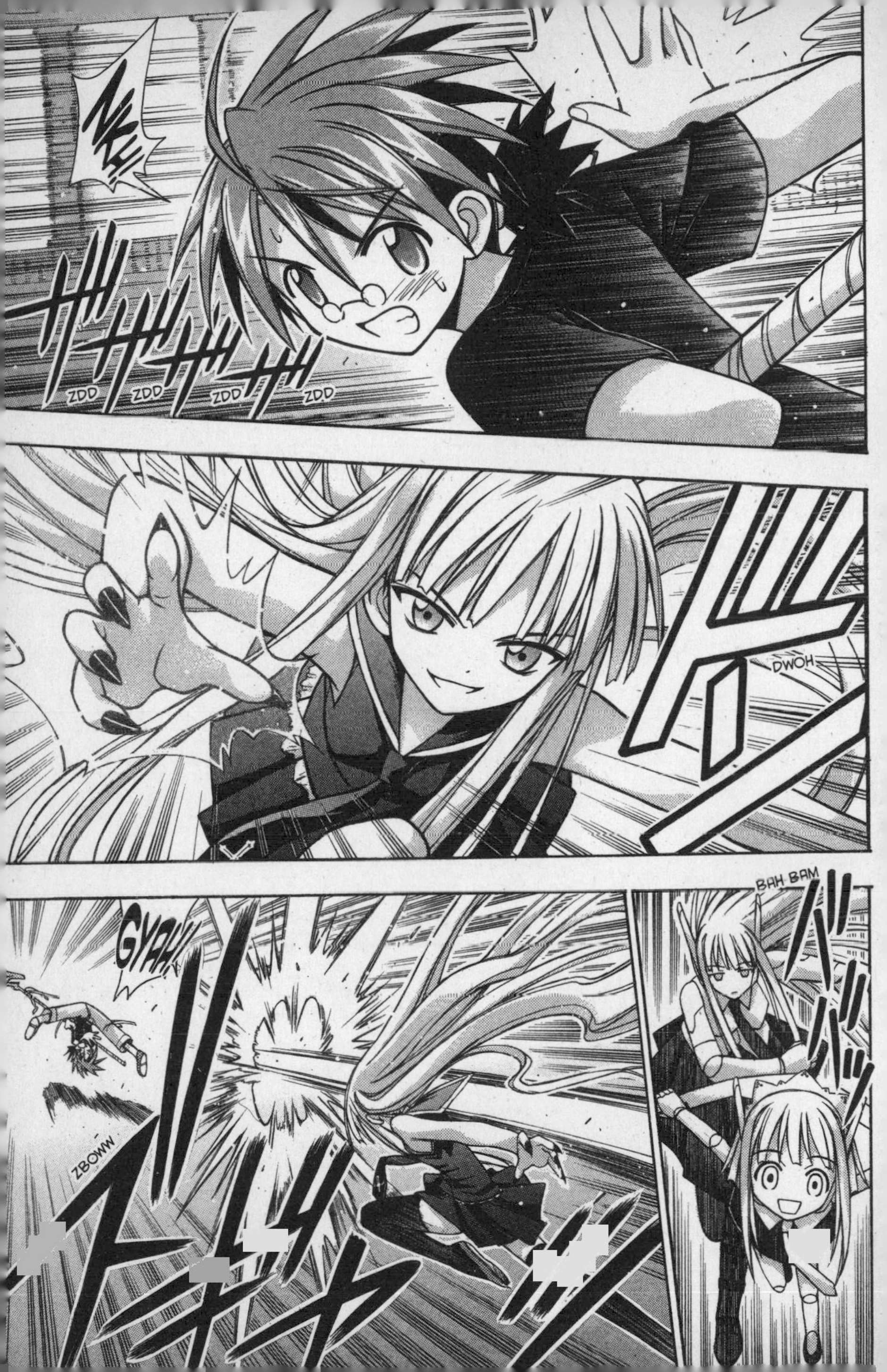
NKH!!
ZDD
ZDD
ZDD
ZDD
DWOH
BAH BAM
GYAH!!
ZBOWW

SIXTY-THIRD PERIOD: (SECRET) TOWER FOR TWO ♡

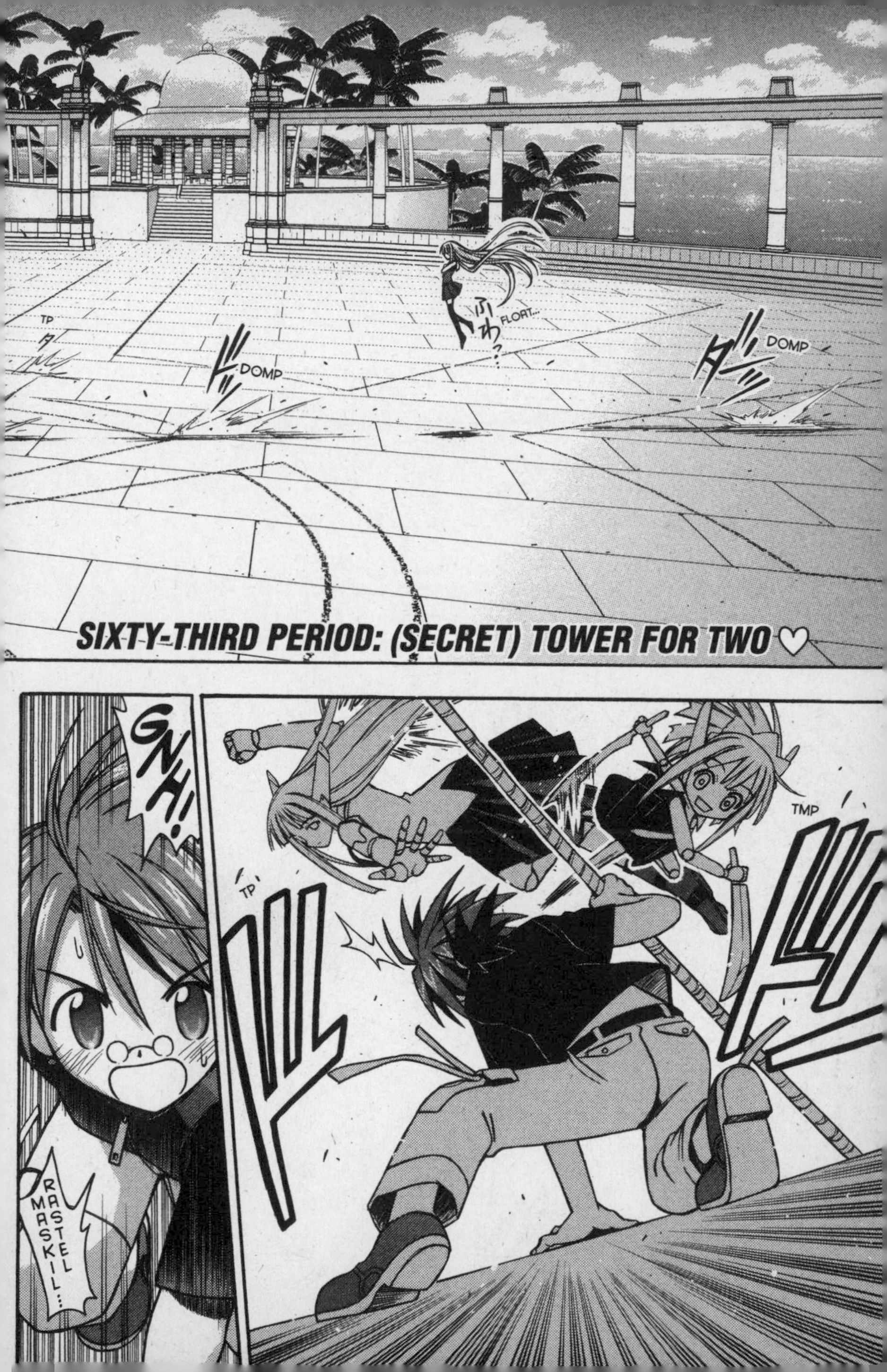
DOMP
ふわ
FLOAT...
DOMP
TP
TMP
TP
GNH!
RASTEL MASKIL...

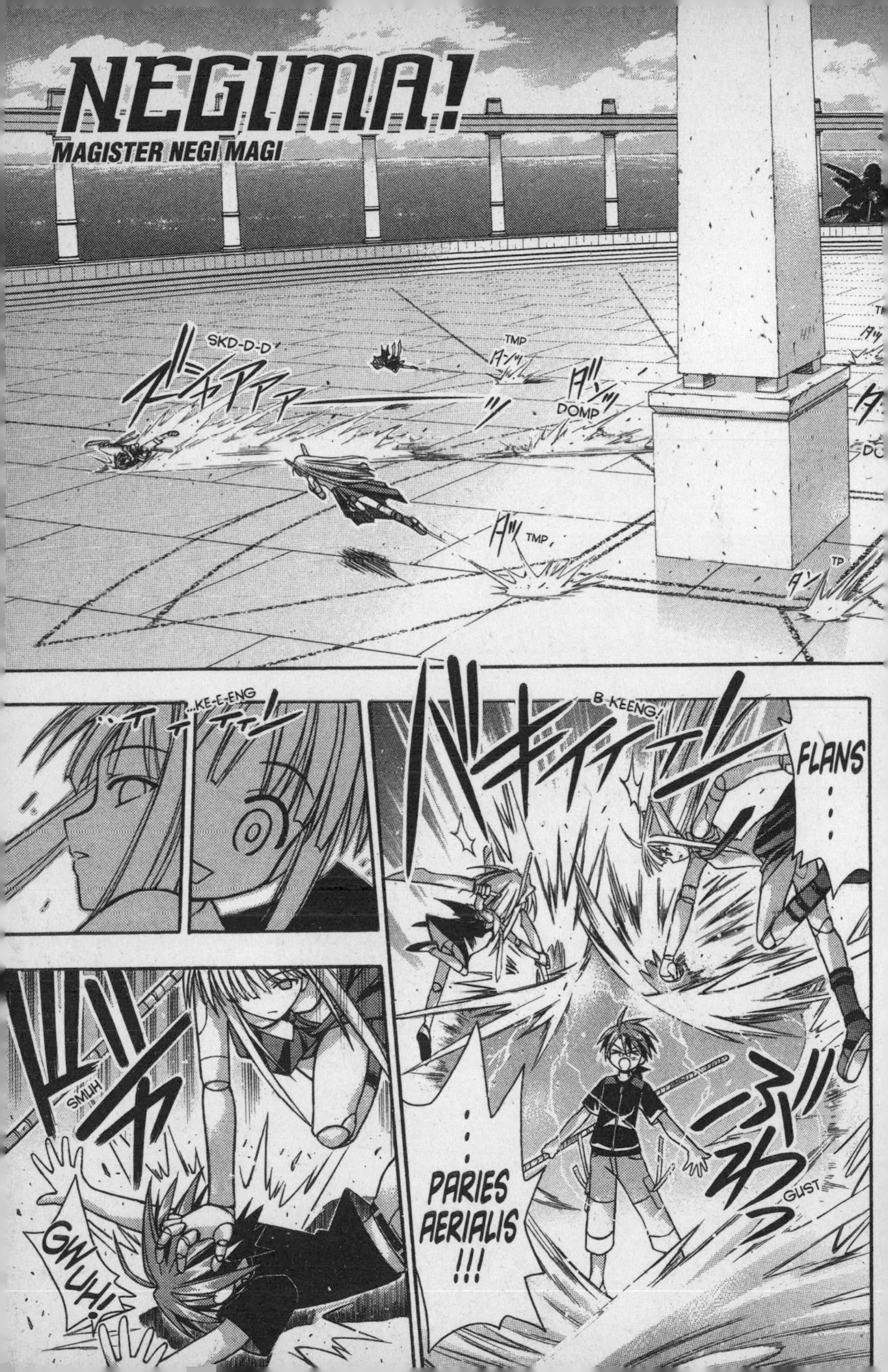
NEGIMA!
MAGISTER NEGI MAGI
TP
TMP
DOMP
TMP
SKD-D-D
FLANS
B-KEENG!
...KE-E-ENG
PARIES AERIALIS !!!
GUST
SMUH
GWUH!

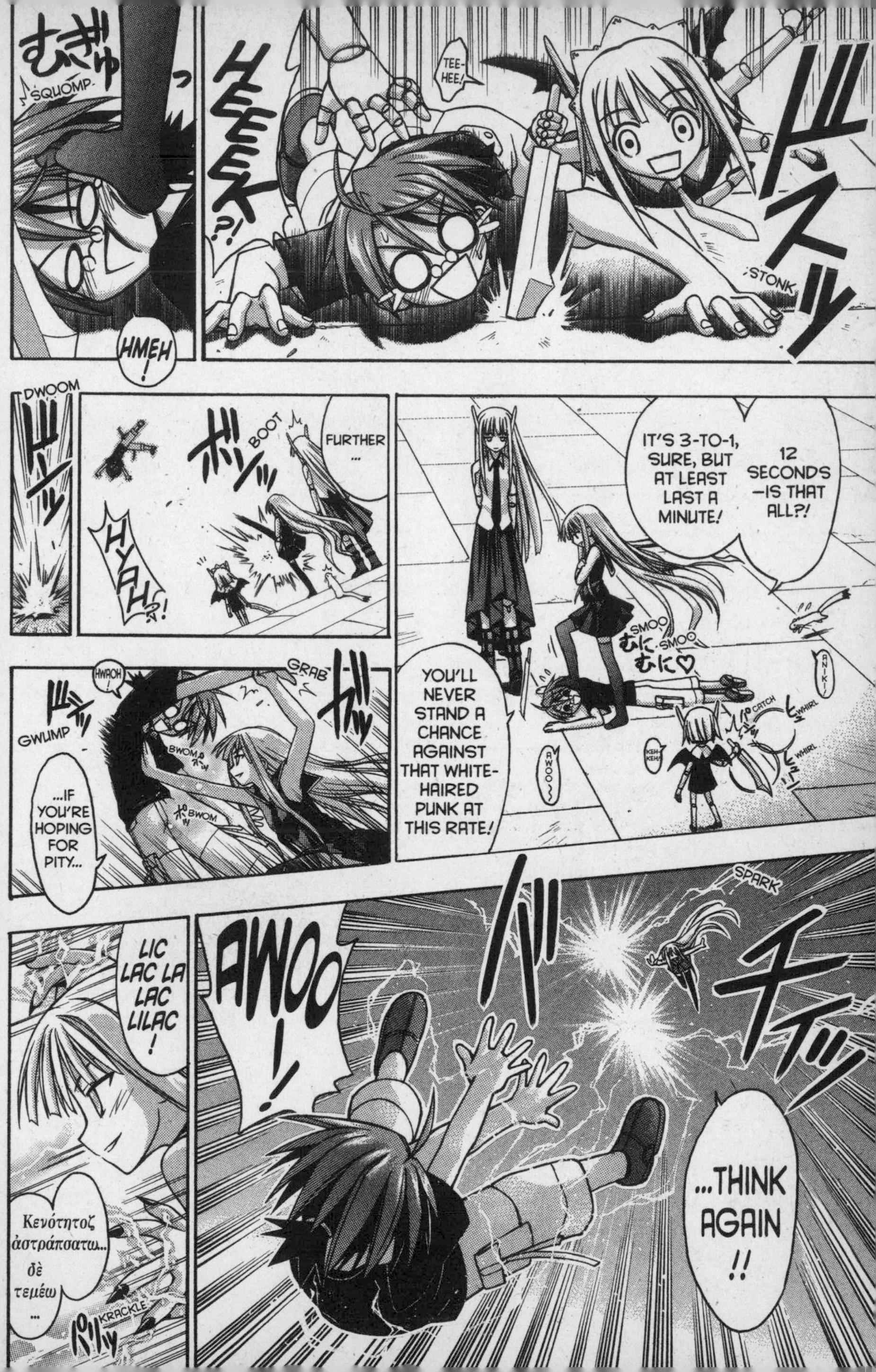
TEE-HEE!
HEEEEK?!
ドスッ
STONK
むぎゅっ
SQUOMP
HMEH!
12 SECONDS—IS THAT ALL?!
IT'S 3-TO-1, SURE, BUT AT LEAST LAST A MINUTE!
SMOO むに SMOO むに♡
ANIKI!
CATCH
ヒュ WHIRL
ヒュ WHIRL
KEH KEH!
AWOO~
YOU'LL NEVER STAND A CHANCE AGAINST THAT WHITE-HAIRED PUNK AT THIS RATE!
FURTHER...
ボッ BOOT
HYAH?!
ドンッ DWOOM
ガッ GRAB
HWAOH!
BWOM
BWOM
GWUMP
...IF YOU'RE HOPING FOR PITY...
バチッ
SPARK
AWOO!
...THINK AGAIN!!
LIC LAC LA LAC LILAC!
Κενότητοζ ἀστράπσατω... δὲ τεμέω ...
パリッ KRACKLE

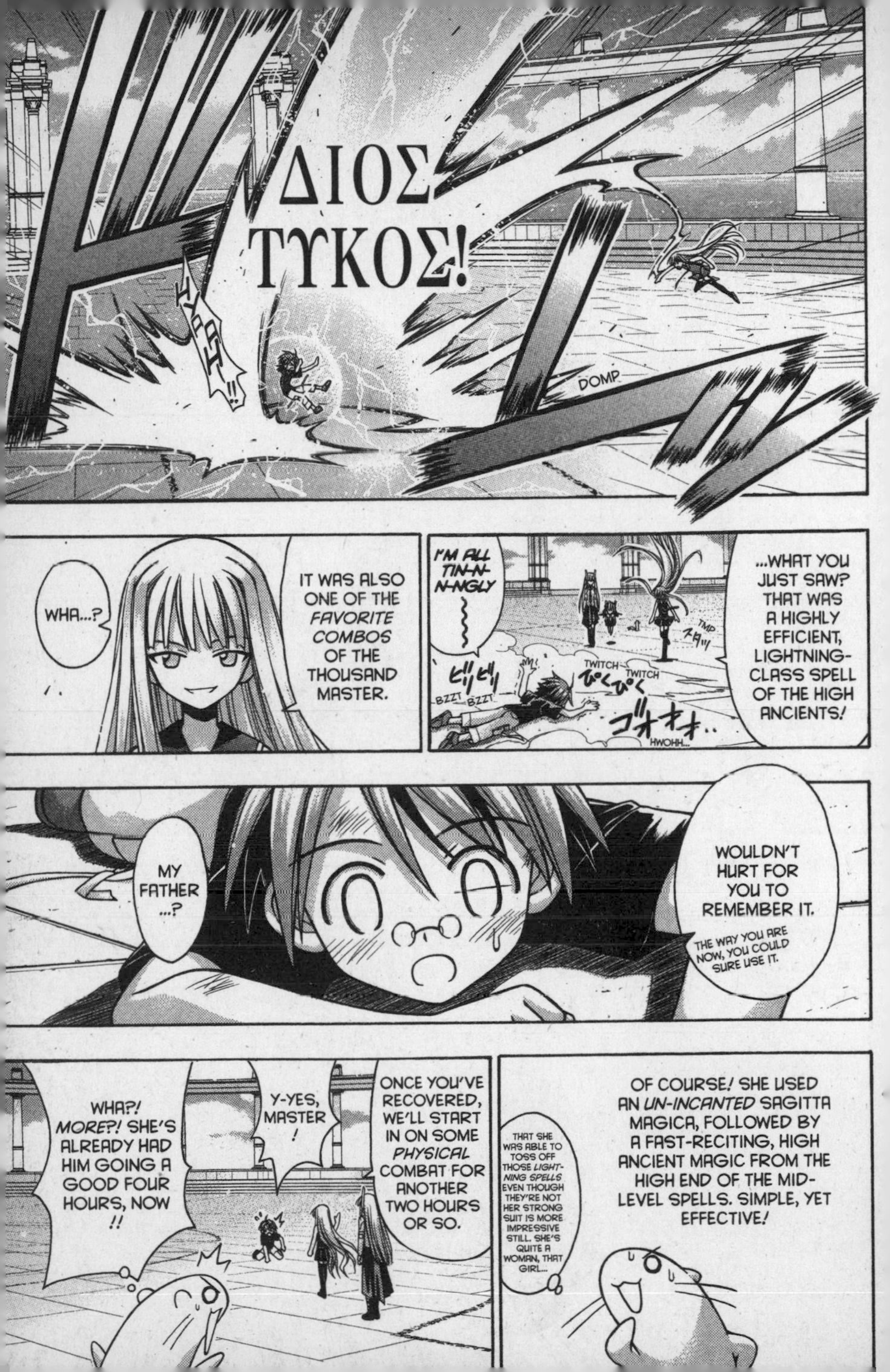

ΔΙΟΣ ΤΥΚΟΣ!
DOMP
...WHAT YOU JUST SAW? THAT WAS A HIGHLY EFFICIENT, LIGHTNING-CLASS SPELL OF THE HIGH ANCIENTS!
TMP
I'M ALL TIN-N-N-NGLY
TWITCH TWITCH
BZZT BZZT
HWOHH...
IT WAS ALSO ONE OF THE *FAVORITE COMBOS* OF THE THOUSAND MASTER.
WHA...?
WOULDN'T HURT FOR YOU TO REMEMBER IT.
THE WAY YOU ARE NOW, YOU COULD SURE USE IT.
MY FATHER ...?
OF COURSE! SHE USED AN *UN-INCANTED* SAGITTA MAGICA, FOLLOWED BY A FAST-RECITING, HIGH ANCIENT MAGIC FROM THE HIGH END OF THE MID-LEVEL SPELLS. SIMPLE, YET EFFECTIVE!
THAT SHE WAS ABLE TO TOSS OFF THOSE *LIGHTNING SPELLS* EVEN THOUGH THEY'RE NOT HER STRONG SUIT IS MORE IMPRESSIVE STILL. SHE'S QUITE A WOMAN, THAT GIRL...
ONCE YOU'VE RECOVERED, WE'LL START IN ON SOME *PHYSICAL* COMBAT FOR ANOTHER TWO HOURS OR SO.
Y-YES, MASTER!
WHA?! *MORE?!* SHE'S ALREADY HAD HIM GOING A GOOD FOUR HOURS, NOW!!

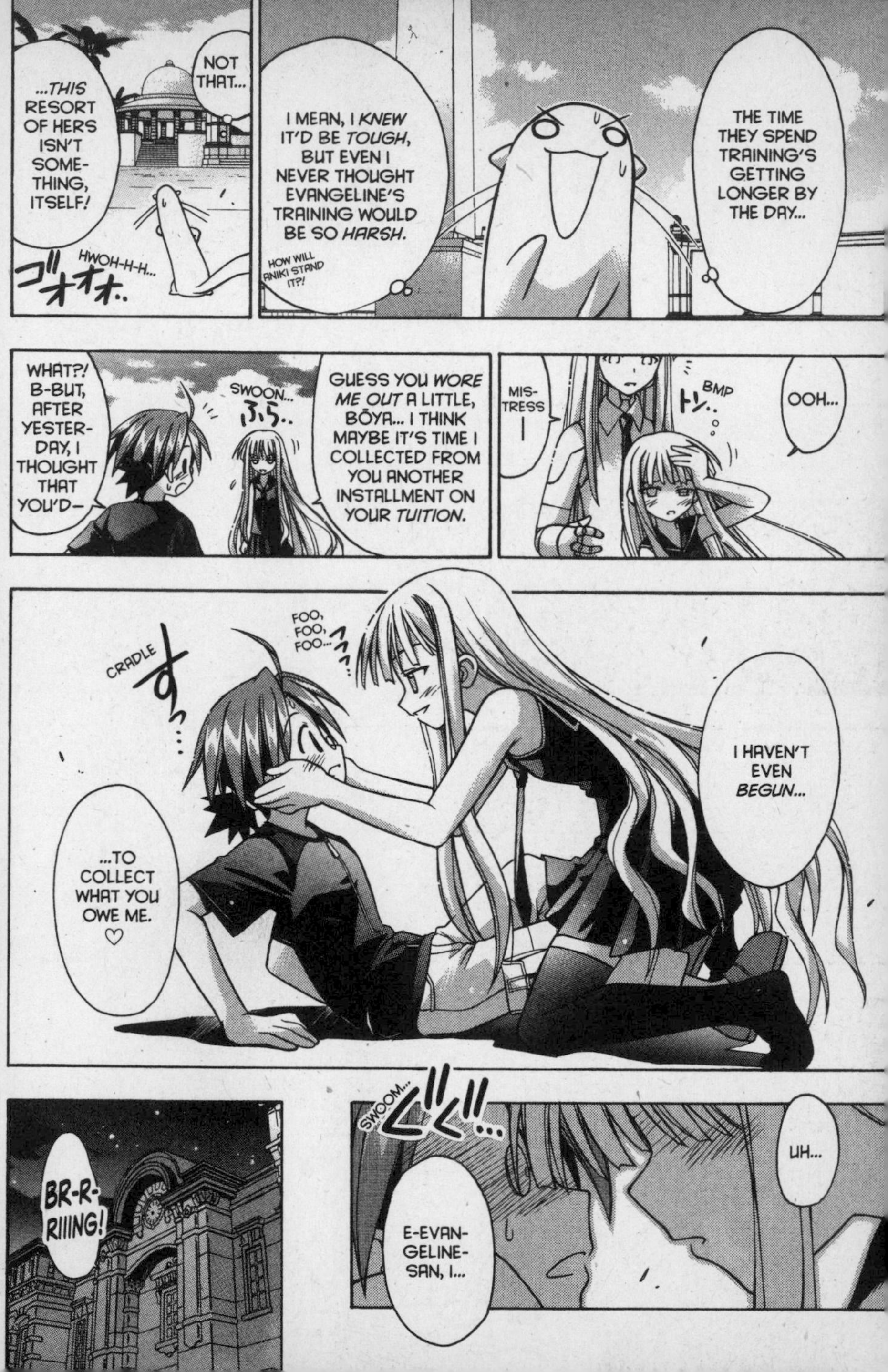
THE TIME THEY SPEND TRAINING'S GETTING LONGER BY THE DAY...
I MEAN, I *KNEW* IT'D BE *TOUGH*, BUT EVEN I NEVER THOUGHT EVANGELINE'S TRAINING WOULD BE SO *HARSH*.
HOW WILL ANIKI STAND IT?!
NOT THAT...
...*THIS* RESORT OF HERS ISN'T SOME-THING, ITSELF!
HWOH-H-H...
ゴオオオ..
OOH...
BMP
トン..
MIS-TRESS
—
GUESS YOU *WORE ME OUT* A LITTLE, BŌYA... I THINK MAYBE IT'S TIME I COLLECTED FROM YOU ANOTHER INSTALLMENT ON *YOUR TUITION*.
SWOON...
ふら..
WHAT?! B-BUT, AFTER YESTER-DAY, I THOUGHT THAT YOU'D—
FOO, FOO, FOO...
CRADLE
す...
I HAVEN'T EVEN *BEGUN*...
...TO COLLECT WHAT YOU OWE ME. ♡
SWOOM...
ぐぐ...
UH...
E-EVAN-GELINE-SAN, I...
BR-R-RIIING!

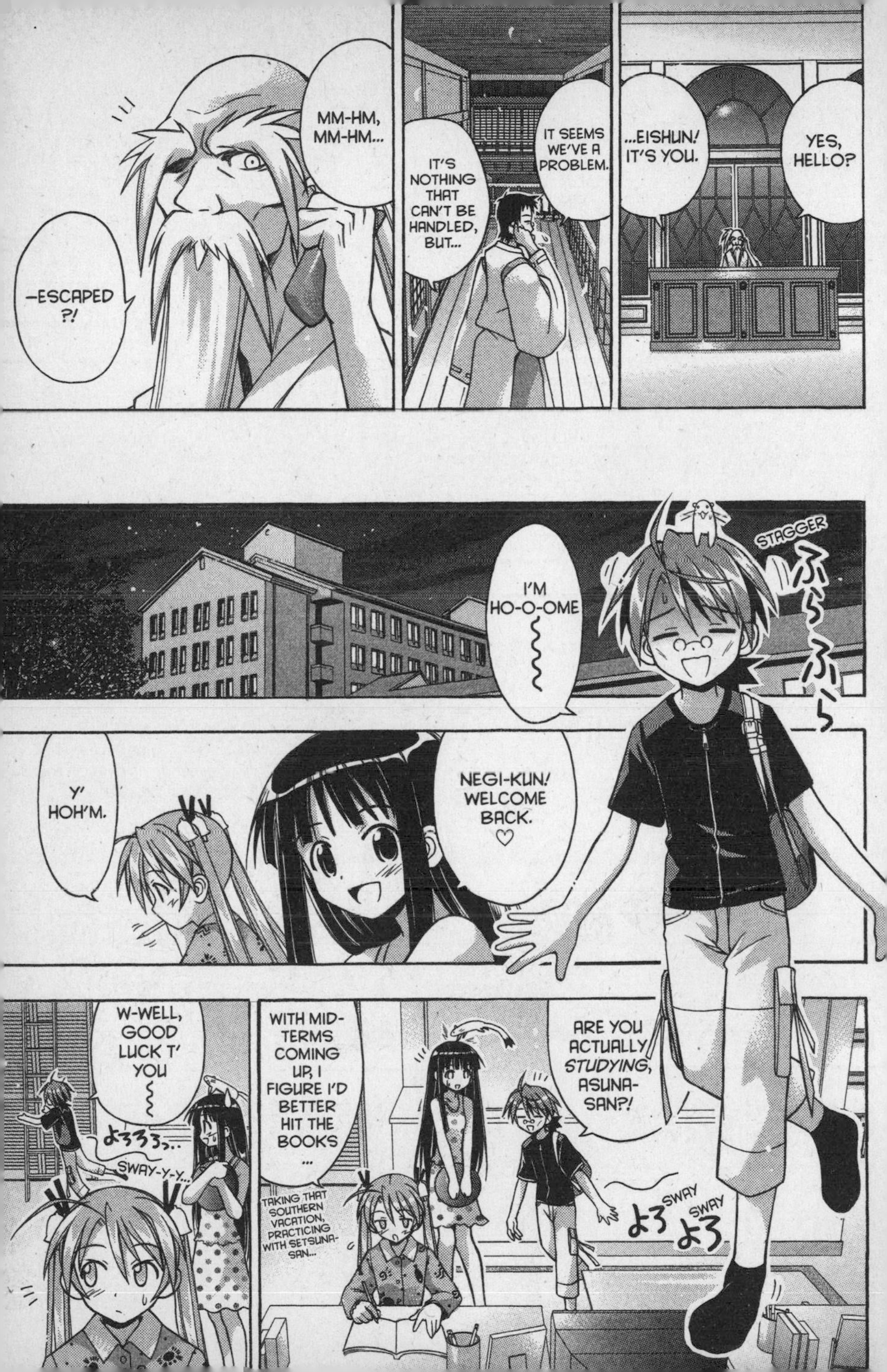
YES, HELLO?
...EISHUN! IT'S YOU.
IT SEEMS WE'VE A PROBLEM.
IT'S NOTHING THAT CAN'T BE HANDLED, BUT...
MM-HM, MM-HM...
—ESCAPED ?!
STAGGER
ふらふら
I'M HO-O-OME
NEGI-KUN! WELCOME BACK. ♡
Y' HOH'M.
ARE YOU ACTUALLY *STUDYING*, ASUNA-SAN?!
よろ SWAY よろ SWAY
WITH MID-TERMS COMING UP, I FIGURE I'D BETTER HIT THE BOOKS ...
TAKING THAT SOUTHERN VACATION, PRACTICING WITH SETSUNA-SAN...
W-WELL, GOOD LUCK T' YOU
よろろろっ..
SWAY-Y-Y...

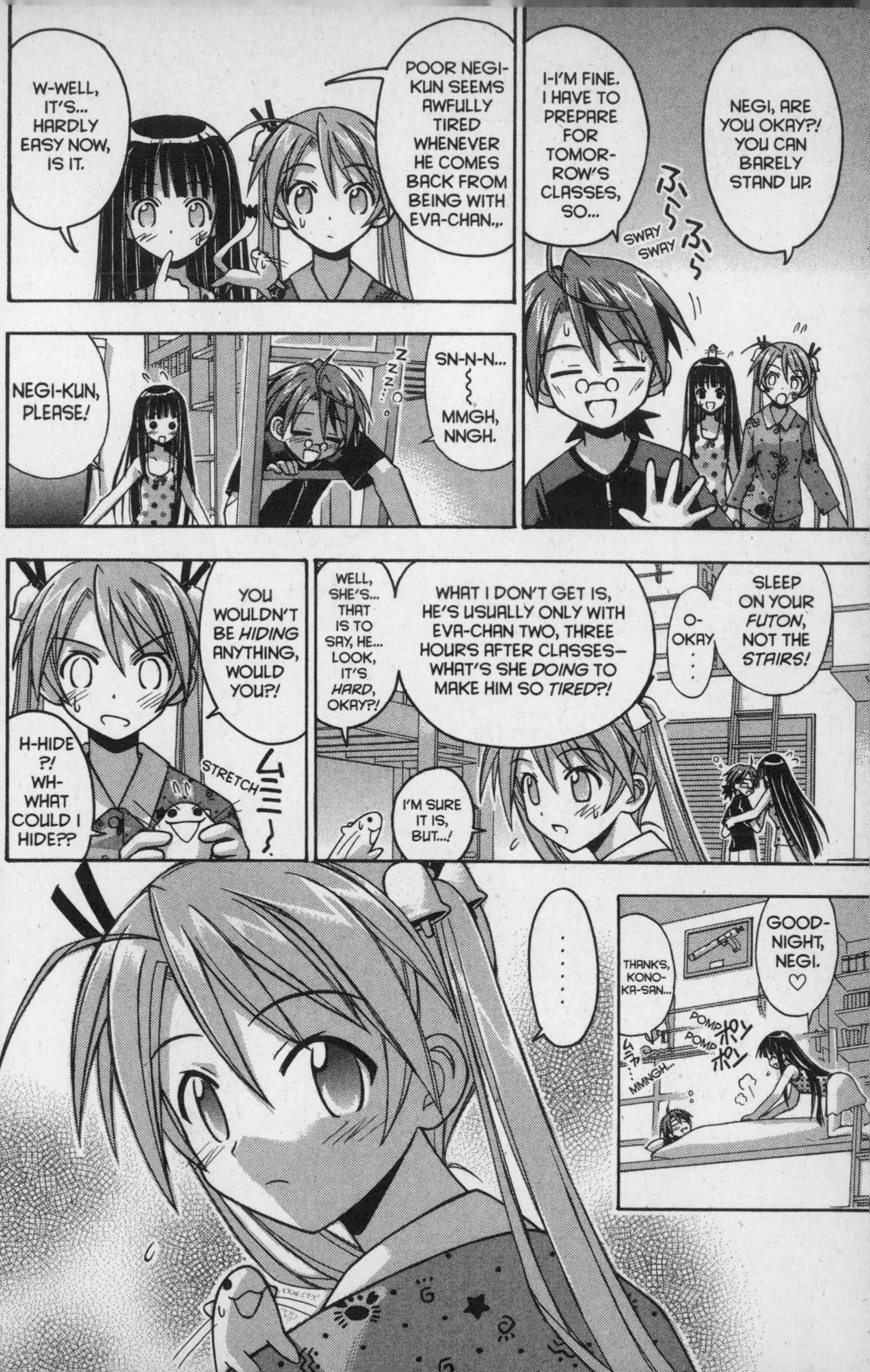

NEGI, ARE YOU OKAY?! YOU CAN BARELY STAND UP.
I-I'M FINE. I HAVE TO PREPARE FOR TOMOR-ROW'S CLASSES, SO...
ふらふら
SWAY SWAY
POOR NEGI-KUN SEEMS AWFULLY TIRED WHENEVER HE COMES BACK FROM BEING WITH EVA-CHAN...
W-WELL, IT'S... HARDLY EASY NOW, IS IT.
SN-N-N... MMGH, NNGH.
NEGI-KUN, PLEASE!
SLEEP ON YOUR FUTON, NOT THE STAIRS!
O-OKAY...
WHAT I DON'T GET IS, HE'S USUALLY ONLY WITH EVA-CHAN TWO, THREE HOURS AFTER CLASSES— WHAT'S SHE DOING TO MAKE HIM SO TIRED?!
WELL, SHE'S... THAT IS TO SAY, HE... LOOK, IT'S HARD, OKAY?!
I'M SURE IT IS, BUT...!
YOU WOULDN'T BE HIDING ANYTHING, WOULD YOU?!
H-HIDE?! WH-WHAT COULD I HIDE??
STRETCH
GOOD-NIGHT, NEGI. ♡
THANKS, KONOKA-SAN...
POMP POMP
ポンポン
MMNGH...
......

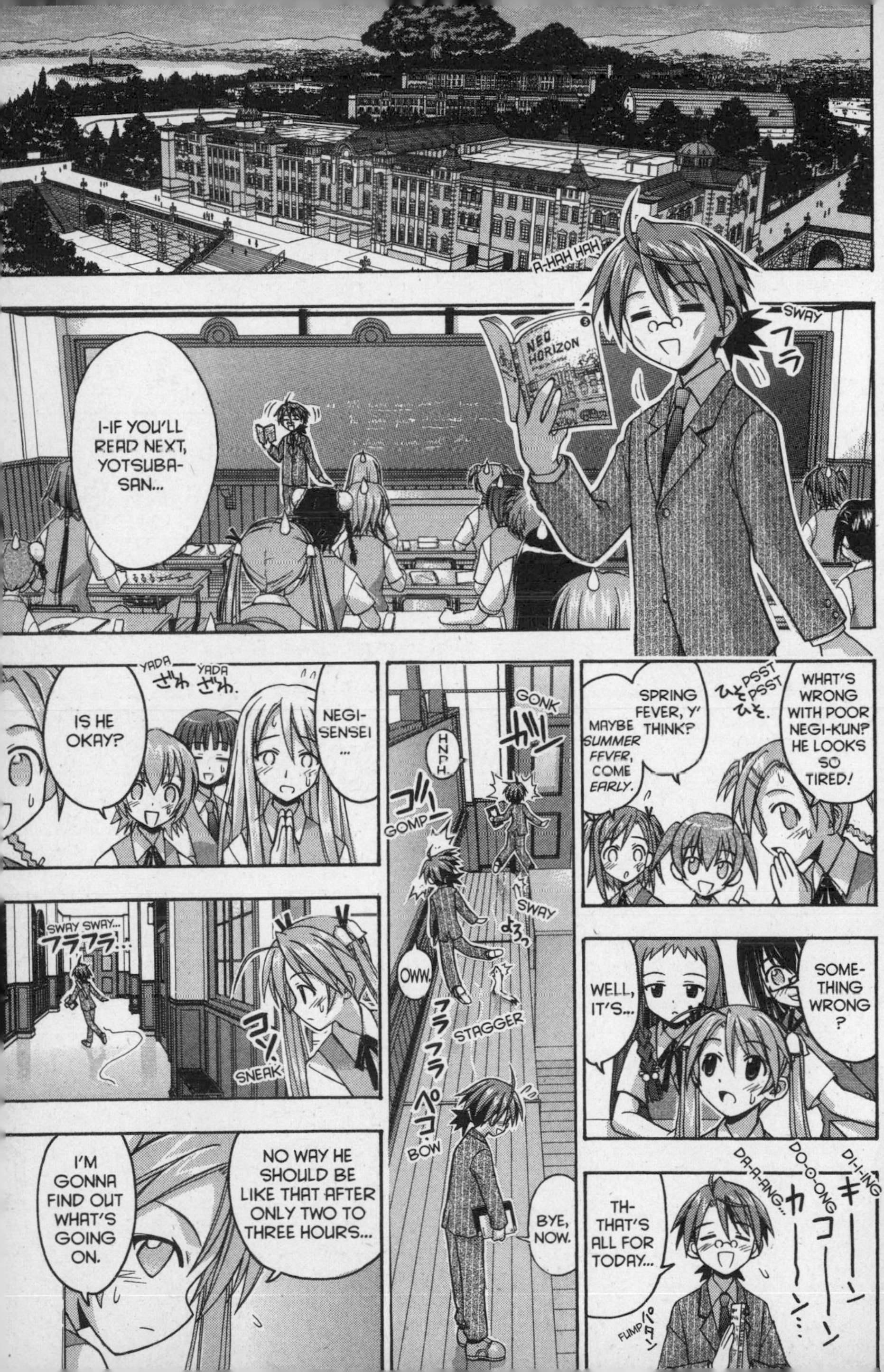
A-HAH HAH
SWAY
フラ
NEO HORIZON
I-IF YOU'LL READ NEXT, YOTSUBA-SAN...
WHAT'S WRONG WITH POOR NEGI-KUN? HE LOOKS SO TIRED!
ひそ PSST ひそ PSST
SPRING FEVER, Y' THINK?
MAYBE SUMMER FFVFR, COME EARLY.
SOME-THING WRONG?
WELL, IT'S...
DI-I-ING キーン
DO-O-ONG カーン...
DA-A-ANG...
TH-THAT'S ALL FOR TODAY...
FUMP パタン
GONK ガン
HNPH.
ゴン GOMP
SWAY よろっ
OWW.
フラフラ STAGGER
ペコ BOW
BYE, NOW.
NEGI-SENSEI...
IS HE OKAY?
YADA ざわ YADA ざわ.
SWAY SWAY... フラフラ...
コソ SNEAK
NO WAY HE SHOULD BE LIKE THAT AFTER ONLY TWO TO THREE HOURS...
I'M GONNA FIND OUT WHAT'S GOING ON.

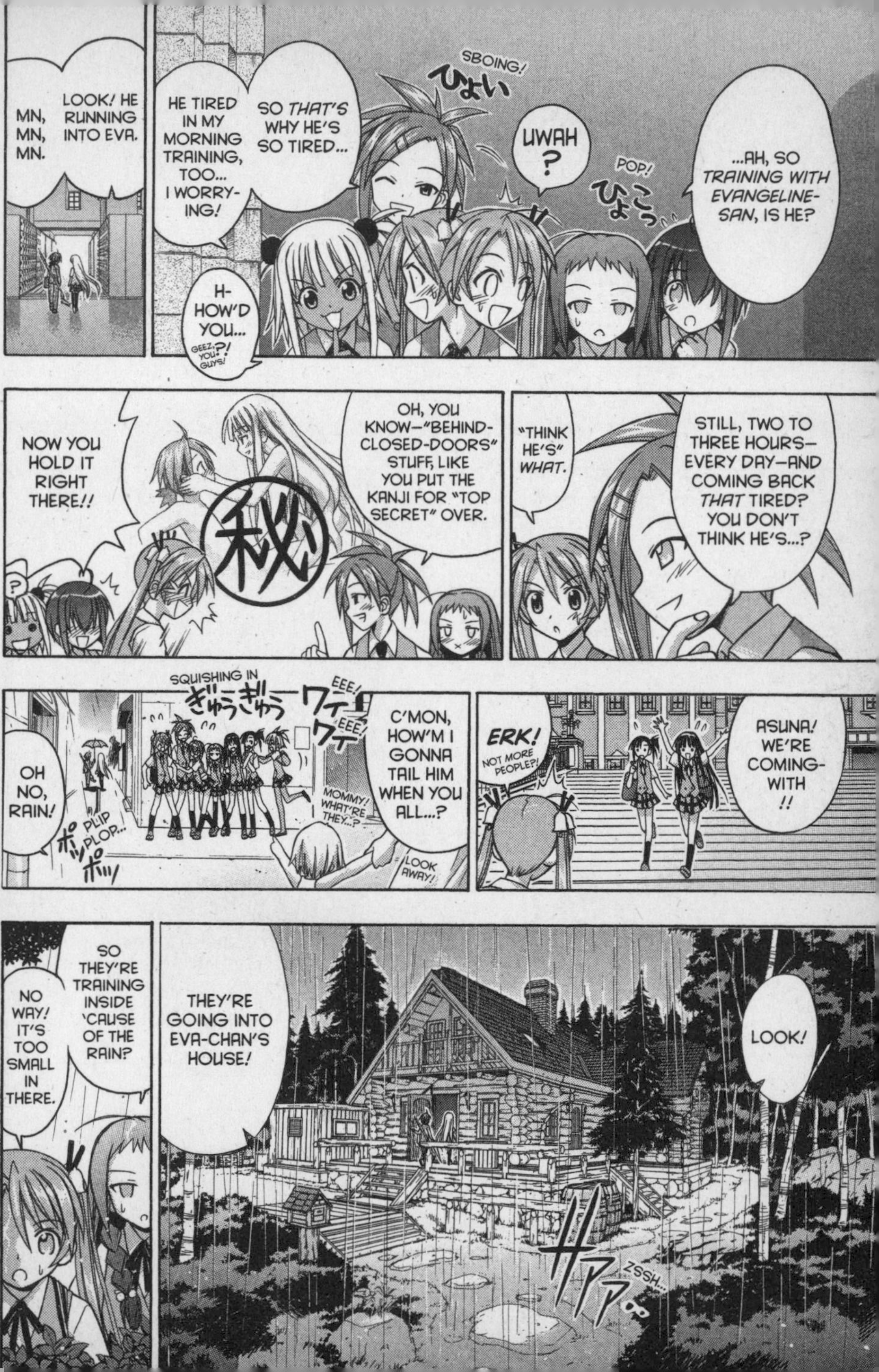
...AH, SO TRAINING WITH EVANGELINE-SAN, IS HE?
POP!
ひょこっ
UWAH ?
SBOING!
ひょい
SO THAT'S WHY HE'S SO TIRED...
HE TIRED IN MY MORNING TRAINING, TOO... I WORRYING!
H-HOW'D YOU...?!
GEEZ, YOU GUYS!
LOOK! HE RUNNING INTO EVA.
MN, MN, MN.
STILL, TWO TO THREE HOURS—EVERY DAY—AND COMING BACK THAT TIRED? YOU DON'T THINK HE'S...?
"THINK HE'S" WHAT.
OH, YOU KNOW—"BEHIND-CLOSED-DOORS" STUFF, LIKE YOU PUT THE KANJI FOR "TOP SECRET" OVER.
秘
NOW YOU HOLD IT RIGHT THERE!!
ASUNA! WE'RE COMING-WITH !!
ERK!
NOT MORE PEOPLE?!
C'MON, HOW'M I GONNA TAIL HIM WHEN YOU ALL...?
EEE! ワイ
EEE! ワイ
SQUISHING IN
ぎゅうぎゅう
MOMMY! WHAT'RE THEY...?
LOOK AWAY!
OH NO, RAIN!
PLIP PLOP...
ポツポツ
LOOK!
ZSSH...
ザァ
THEY'RE GOING INTO EVA-CHAN'S HOUSE!
SO THEY'RE TRAINING INSIDE 'CAUSE OF THE RAIN?
NO WAY! IT'S TOO SMALL IN THERE.

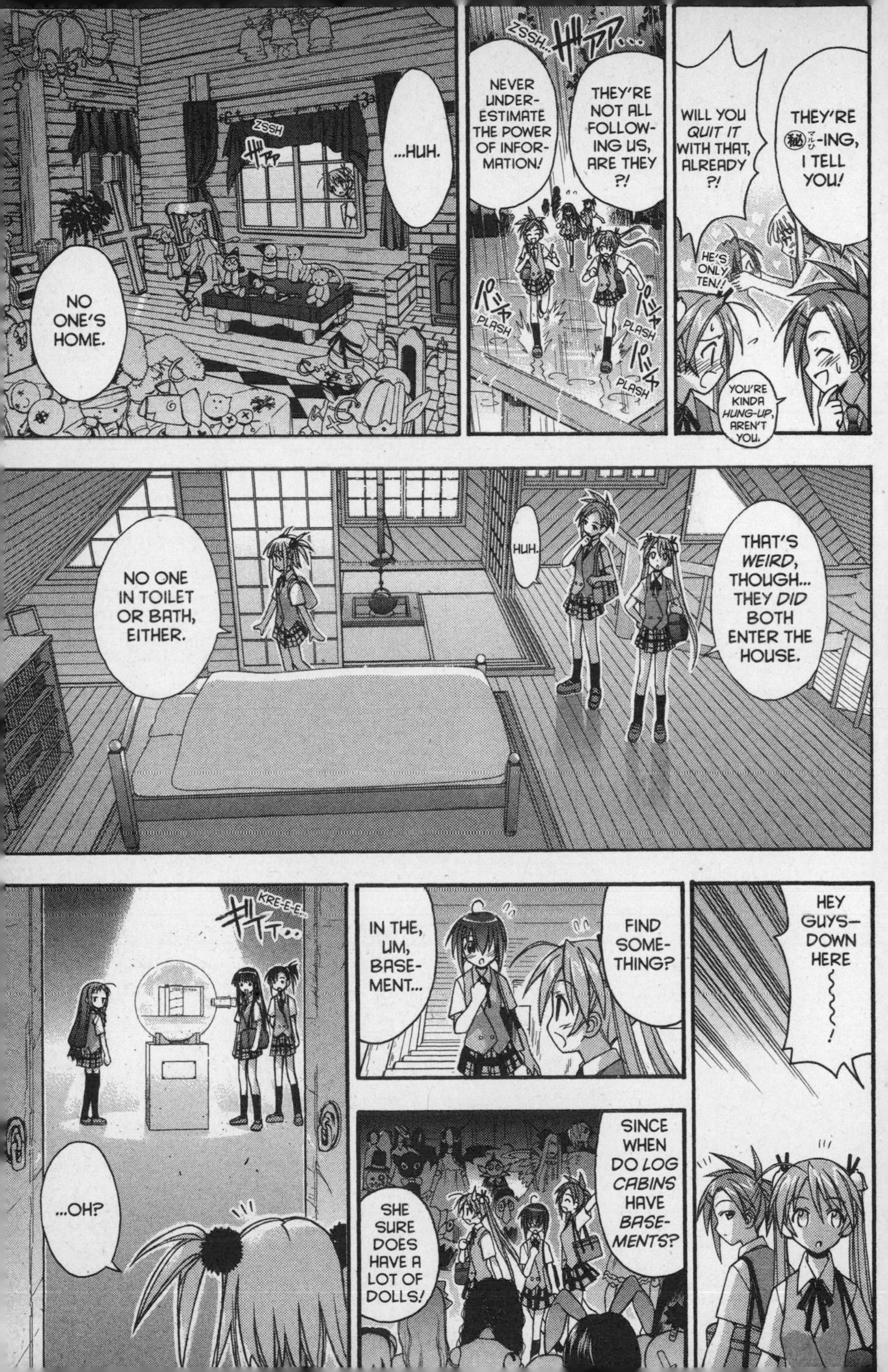
THEY'RE ㊙マルひ-ING, I TELL YOU!
WILL YOU *QUIT IT* WITH THAT, ALREADY ?!
HE'S ONLY TEN!!
YOU'RE KINDA *HUNG-UP*, AREN'T YOU.
ZSSH... ザァア...
THEY'RE NOT ALL FOLLOWING US, ARE THEY ?!
NEVER UNDERESTIMATE THE POWER OF INFORMATION!
パシャ PLASH
パシャ PLASH
パシャ PLASH
ZSSH ザァア
...HUH.
NO ONE'S HOME.
THAT'S *WEIRD*, THOUGH... THEY *DID* BOTH ENTER THE HOUSE.
HUH.
NO ONE IN TOILET OR BATH, EITHER.
HEY GUYS— DOWN HERE ~~~~!
FIND SOMETHING?
IN THE, UM, BASEMENT...
SINCE WHEN DO *LOG CABINS* HAVE *BASEMENTS*?
SHE SURE DOES HAVE A LOT OF DOLLS!
KRE-E-E... ギイイ..
...OH?

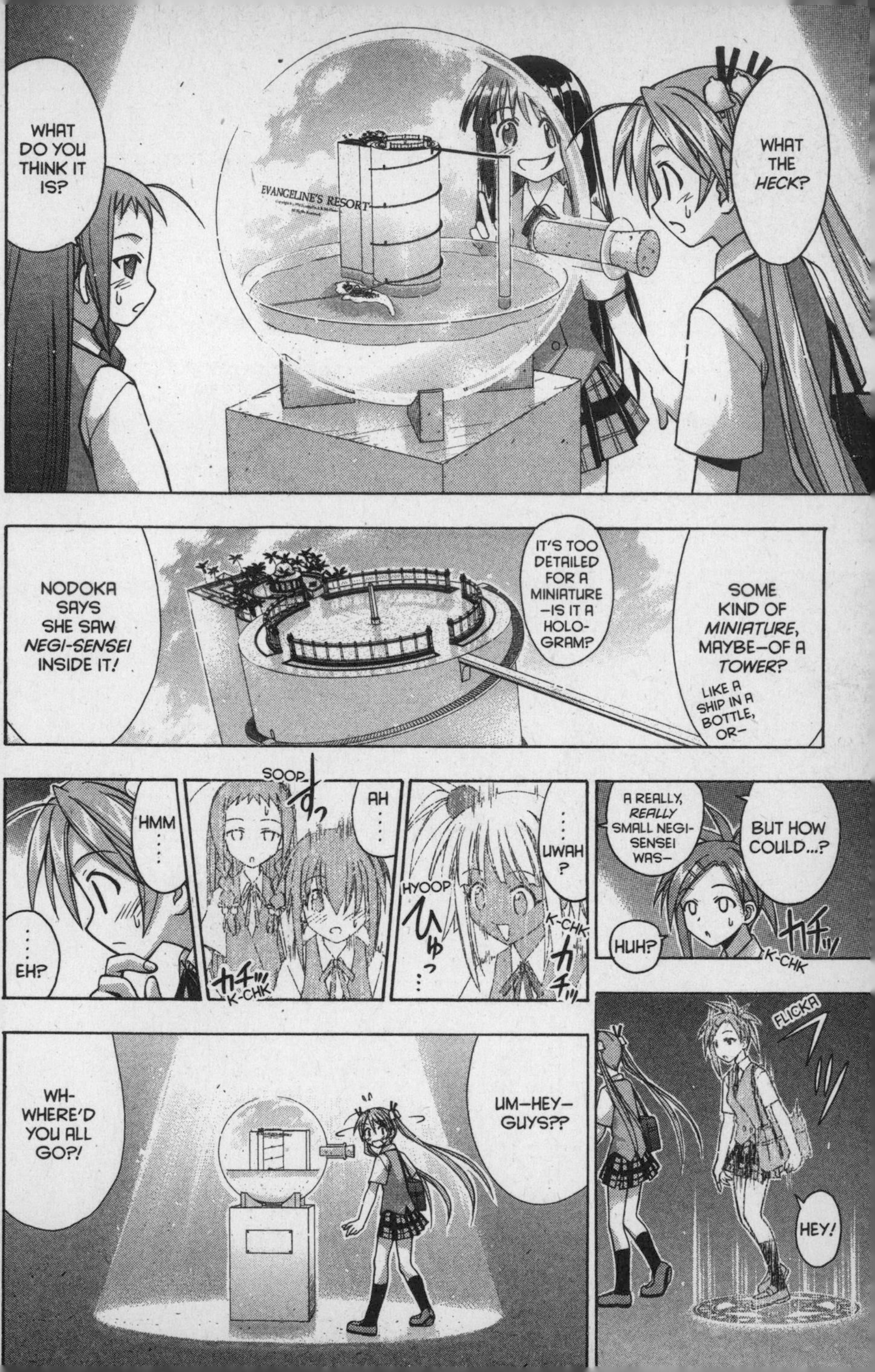

WHAT THE HECK?
WHAT DO YOU THINK IT IS?
EVANGELINE'S RESORT
SOME KIND OF MINIATURE, MAYBE—OF A TOWER?
LIKE A SHIP IN A BOTTLE, OR—
IT'S TOO DETAILED FOR A MINIATURE—IS IT A HOLOGRAM?
NODOKA SAYS SHE SAW NEGI-SENSEI INSIDE IT!
BUT HOW COULD...?
A REALLY, REALLY SMALL NEGI-SENSEI WAS—
HUH?
カチッ
K-CHK
...UWAH?
HYOOP
ひゅっ…
カチッ
K-CHK
AH....
SOOP
すっ
カチッ
K-CHK
HMM....
...EH?
FLICKA
HEY!
UM—HEY—GUYS??
WH-WHERE'D YOU ALL GO?!

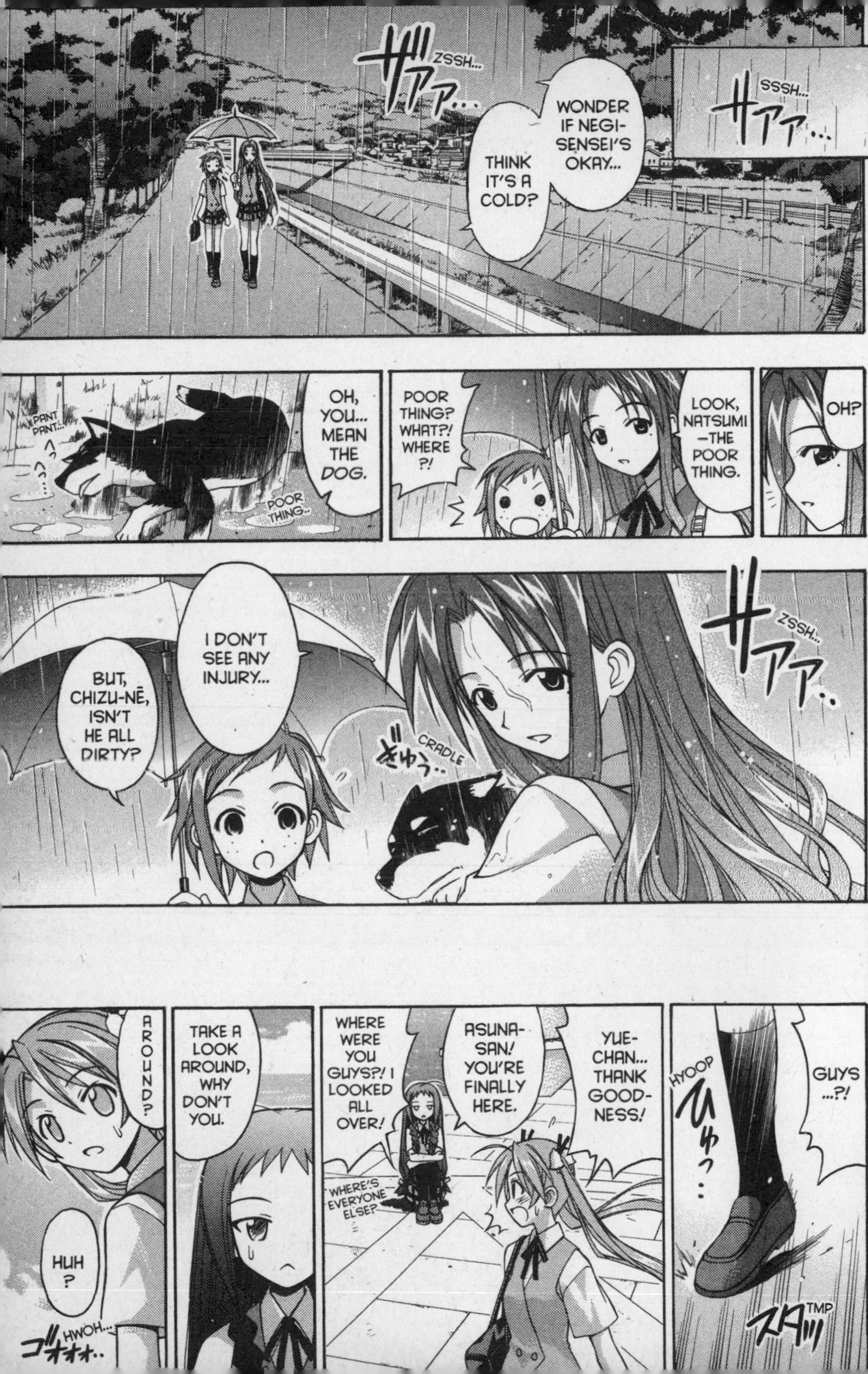

SSSH...
ZSSH...
WONDER IF NEGI-SENSEI'S OKAY...
THINK IT'S A COLD?
OH?
LOOK, NATSUMI—THE POOR THING.
POOR THING? WHAT?! WHERE ?!
OH, YOU... MEAN THE DOG.
PANT PANT...
POOR THING..
ZSSH...
I DON'T SEE ANY INJURY...
BUT, CHIZU-NĒ, ISN'T HE ALL DIRTY?
CRADLE
GUYS ...?!
HYOOP
TMP
YUE-CHAN... THANK GOODNESS!
ASUNA-SAN! YOU'RE FINALLY HERE.
WHERE WERE YOU GUYS?! I LOOKED ALL OVER!
WHERE'S EVERYONE ELSE?
TAKE A LOOK AROUND, WHY DON'T YOU.
AROUND?
HUH ?
HWOH...

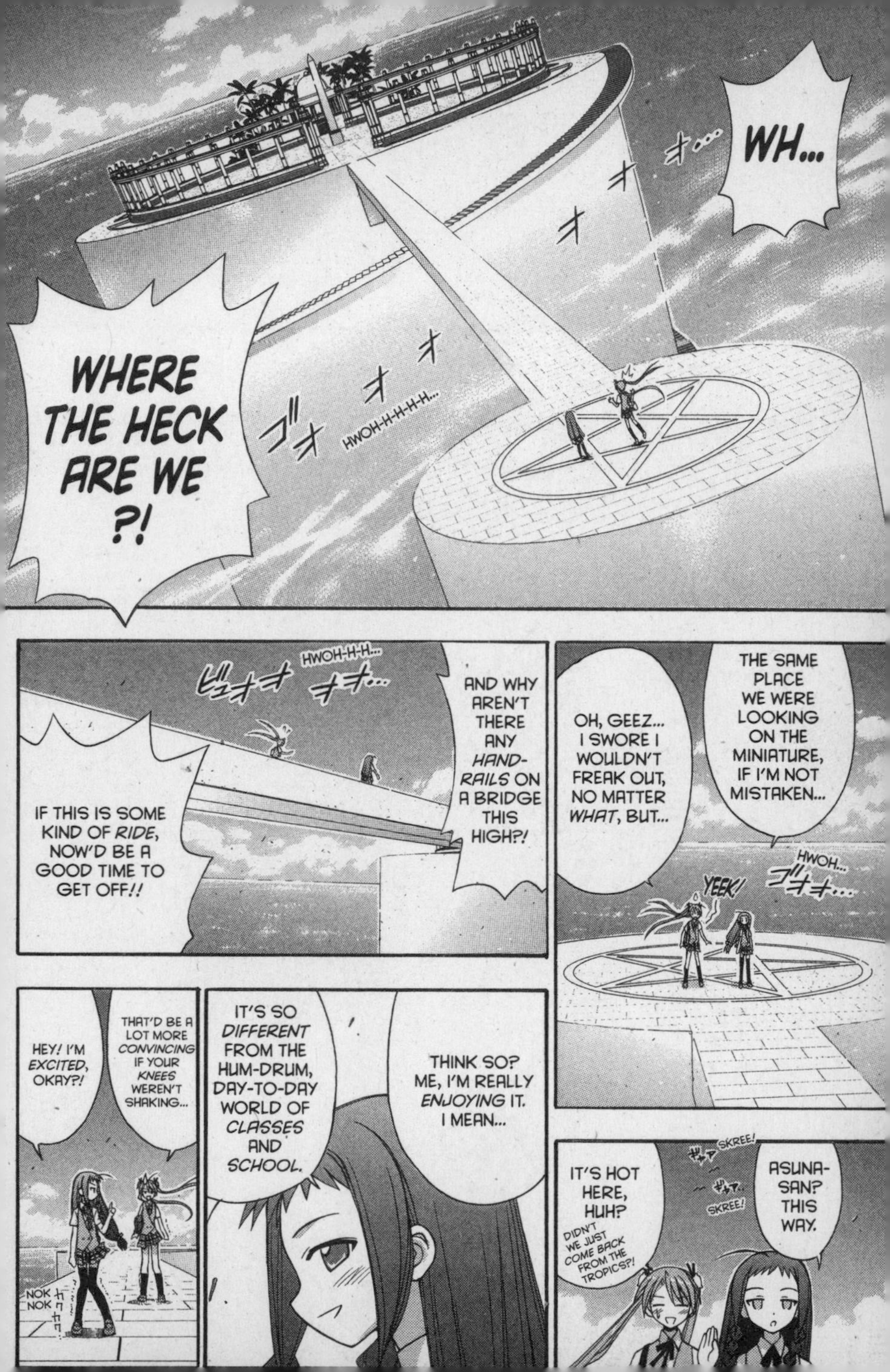
WH...
HWOH-H-H-H-H...
WHERE THE HECK ARE WE ?!
THE SAME PLACE WE WERE LOOKING ON THE MINIATURE, IF I'M NOT MISTAKEN...
OH, GEEZ... I SWORE I WOULDN'T FREAK OUT, NO MATTER *WHAT*, BUT...
HWOH...
YEEK!
HWOH-H-H...
AND WHY AREN'T THERE ANY *HAND-RAILS* ON A BRIDGE THIS HIGH?!
IF THIS IS SOME KIND OF *RIDE*, NOW'D BE A GOOD TIME TO GET OFF!!
THINK SO? ME, I'M REALLY *ENJOYING* IT. I MEAN...
IT'S SO *DIFFERENT* FROM THE HUM-DRUM, DAY-TO-DAY WORLD OF *CLASSES* AND *SCHOOL*.
THAT'D BE A LOT MORE *CONVINCING* IF YOUR *KNEES* WEREN'T SHAKING...
HEY! I'M *EXCITED*, OKAY?!
NOK NOK
SKREE!
SKREE!
ASUNA-SAN? THIS WAY.
IT'S HOT HERE, HUH?
DIDN'T WE JUST COME BACK FROM THE TROPICS?!

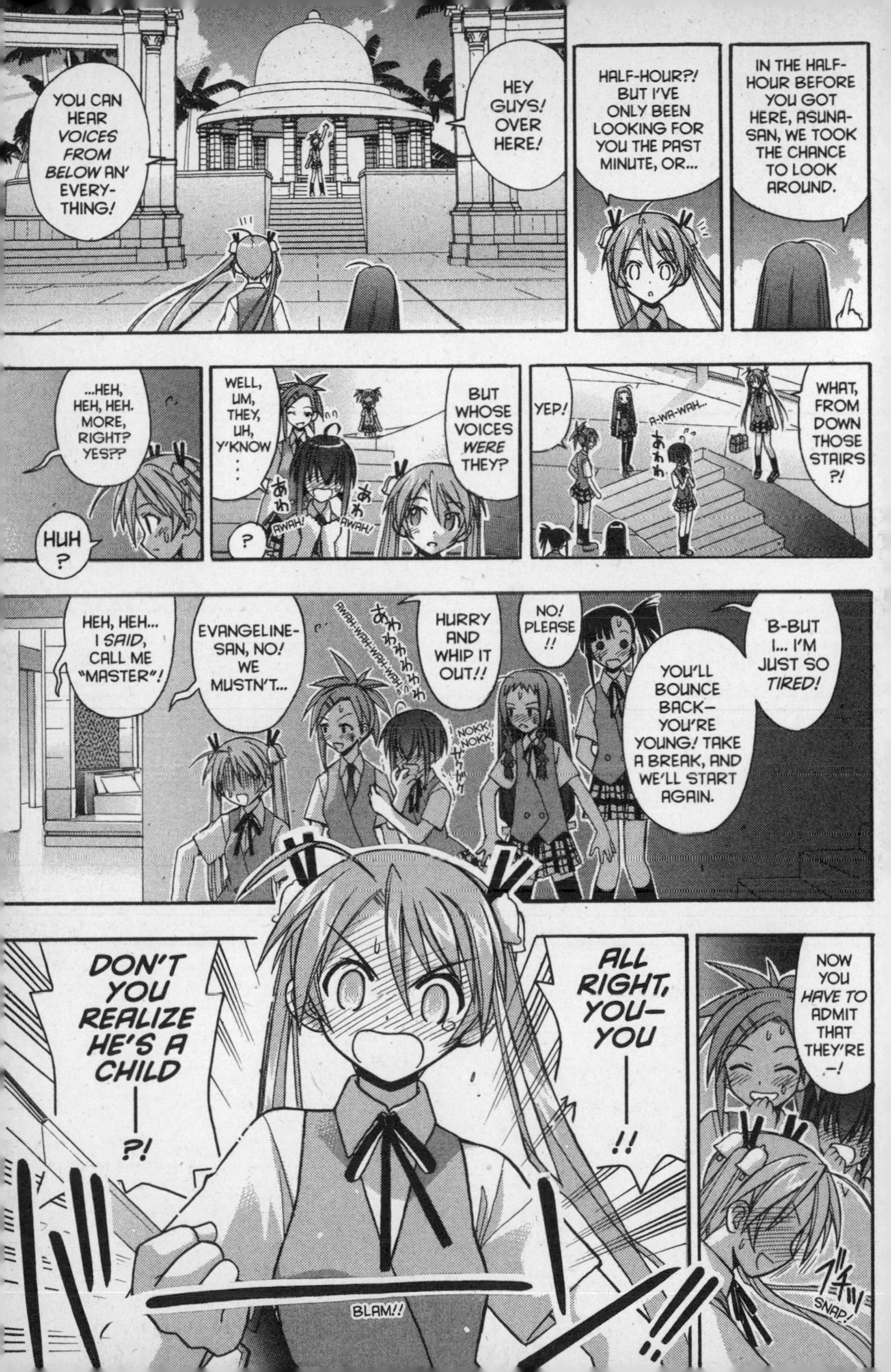
IN THE HALF-HOUR BEFORE YOU GOT HERE, ASUNA-SAN, WE TOOK THE CHANCE TO LOOK AROUND.
HALF-HOUR?! BUT I'VE ONLY BEEN LOOKING FOR YOU THE PAST MINUTE, OR...
HEY GUYS! OVER HERE!
YOU CAN HEAR *VOICES FROM BELOW* AN' EVERY-THING!
WHAT, FROM DOWN THOSE STAIRS?!
YEP!
A-WA-WAH...
あわわ
BUT WHOSE VOICES *WERE* THEY?
WELL, UM, THEY, UH, Y'KNOW . . .
あわ
AWAH!
あわ
AWAH!
?
...HEH, HEH, HEH. MORE, RIGHT? YES??
HUH?
B-BUT I... I'M JUST SO *TIRED!*
YOU'LL BOUNCE BACK— YOU'RE YOUNG! TAKE A BREAK, AND WE'LL START AGAIN.
NO! PLEASE!!
HURRY AND WHIP IT OUT!!
あわわわわわ
AWAH-WAH-WAH-WAH!
NOKK NOKK
EVANGELINE-SAN, NO! WE MUSTN'T...
HEH, HEH... I *SAID,* CALL ME "MASTER"!
NOW YOU *HAVE TO* ADMIT THAT THEY'RE—!
SNAP!
ALL RIGHT, YOU—YOU——!!
DON'T YOU REALIZE HE'S A CHILD——?!
BLAM!!

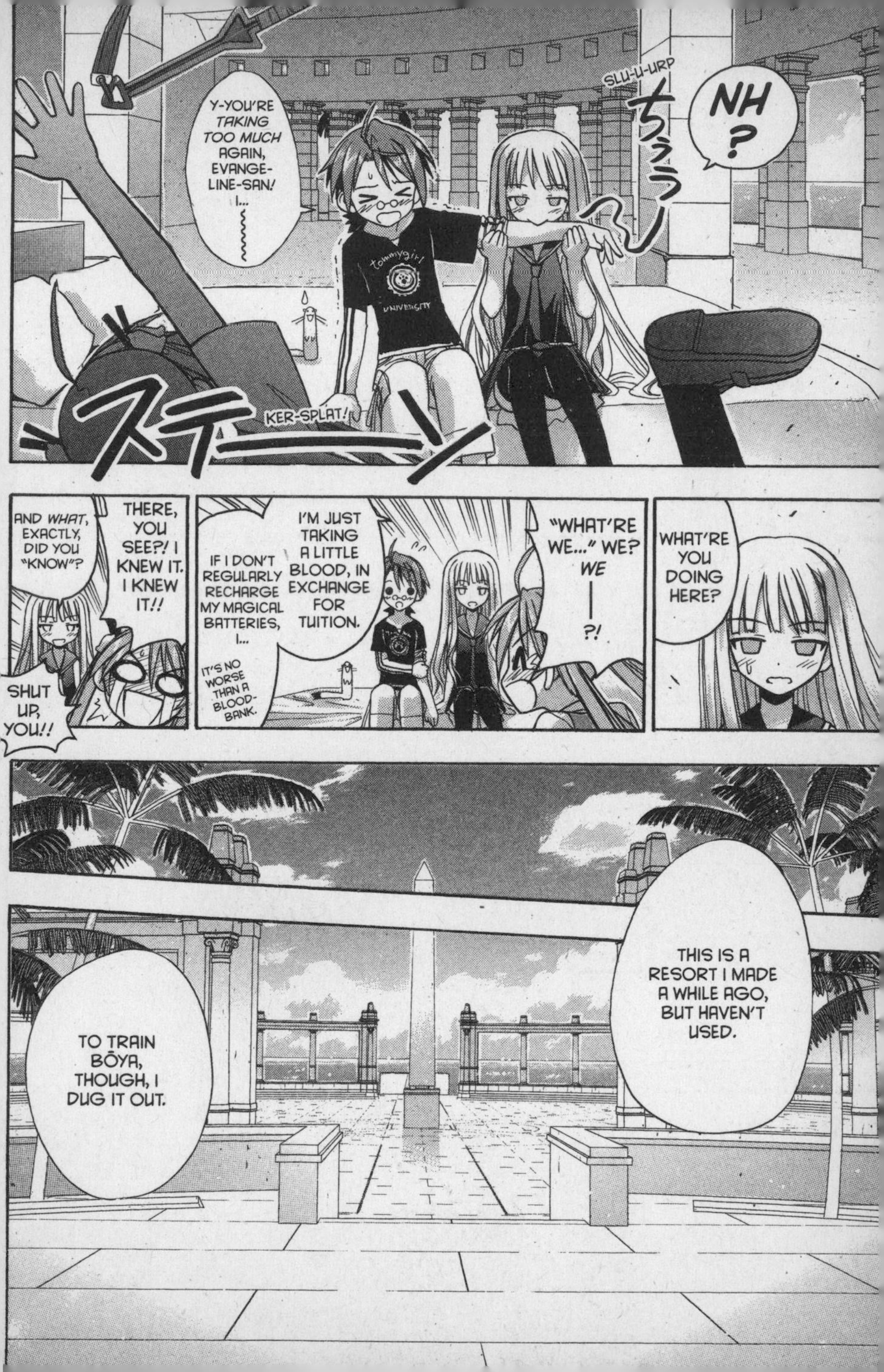
NH ?
SLU-U-URP
Y-YOU'RE TAKING TOO MUCH AGAIN, EVANGE-LINE-SAN! I...
KER-SPLAT!
ステーン
WHAT'RE YOU DOING HERE?
"WHAT'RE WE..." WE? WE —?!
I'M JUST TAKING A LITTLE BLOOD, IN EXCHANGE FOR TUITION.
IF I DON'T REGULARLY RECHARGE MY MAGICAL BATTERIES, I...
IT'S NO WORSE THAN A BLOOD-BANK.
THERE, YOU SEE?! I KNEW IT. I KNEW IT!!
AND WHAT, EXACTLY, DID YOU "KNOW"?
SHUT UP, YOU!!
THIS IS A RESORT I MADE A WHILE AGO, BUT HAVEN'T USED.
TO TRAIN BŌYA, THOUGH, I DUG IT OUT.

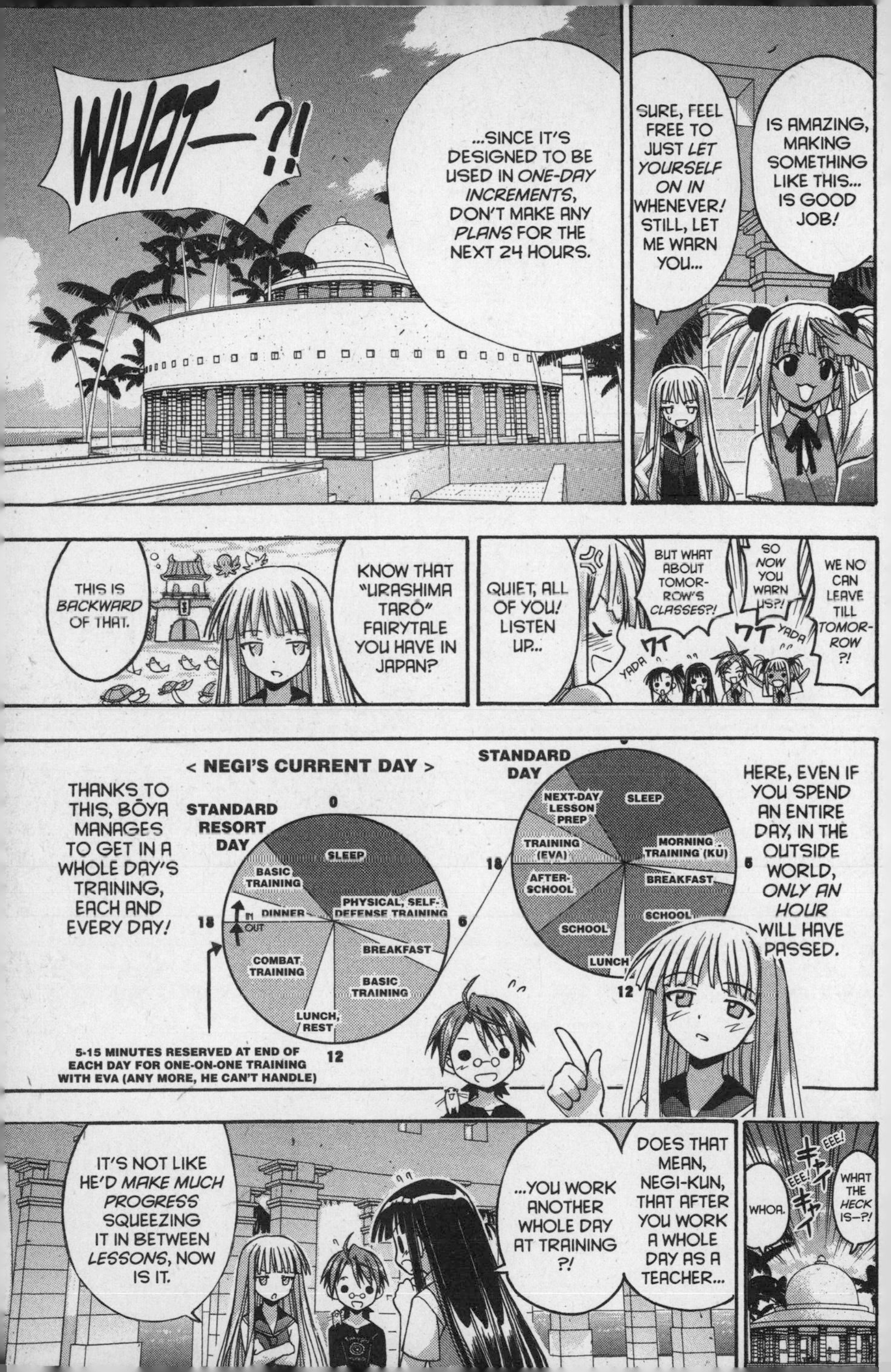

IS AMAZING, MAKING SOMETHING LIKE THIS... IS GOOD JOB!
SURE, FEEL FREE TO JUST *LET YOURSELF ON IN* WHENEVER! STILL, LET ME WARN YOU...
...SINCE IT'S DESIGNED TO BE USED IN *ONE-DAY INCREMENTS*, DON'T MAKE ANY *PLANS* FOR THE NEXT 24 HOURS.
WHAT—?!
WE NO CAN LEAVE TILL *TOMORROW*?!
SO *NOW* YOU WARN US?!
BUT WHAT ABOUT TOMORROW'S *CLASSES*?!
ワイ
ワイ
YADA
YADA
QUIET, ALL OF YOU! LISTEN UP...
KNOW THAT "URASHIMA TARO" FAIRYTALE YOU HAVE IN JAPAN?
THIS IS *BACKWARD* OF THAT.
HERE, EVEN IF YOU SPEND AN ENTIRE DAY, IN THE OUTSIDE WORLD, *ONLY AN HOUR* WILL HAVE PASSED.
< NEGI'S CURRENT DAY >
STANDARD DAY
SLEEP
NEXT-DAY LESSON PREP
TRAINING (EVA)
MORNING TRAINING (KŪ)
AFTER-SCHOOL
BREAKFAST
SCHOOL
SCHOOL
LUNCH
18
6
12
STANDARD RESORT DAY
0
SLEEP
BASIC TRAINING
PHYSICAL, SELF-DEFENSE TRAINING
IN
DINNER
OUT
BREAKFAST
COMBAT TRAINING
BASIC TRAINING
LUNCH, REST
18
6
12
THANKS TO THIS, BŌYA MANAGES TO GET IN A WHOLE DAY'S TRAINING, EACH AND EVERY DAY!
5-15 MINUTES RESERVED AT END OF EACH DAY FOR ONE-ON-ONE TRAINING WITH EVA (ANY MORE, HE CAN'T HANDLE)
EEE!
キャイ
EEE!
キャイ
WHAT THE *HECK* IS—?!
WHOA.
DOES THAT MEAN, NEGI-KUN, THAT AFTER YOU WORK A WHOLE DAY AS A TEACHER...
...YOU WORK ANOTHER WHOLE DAY AT TRAINING?!
IT'S NOT LIKE HE'D *MAKE MUCH PROGRESS* SQUEEZING IT IN BETWEEN *LESSONS*, NOW IS IT.

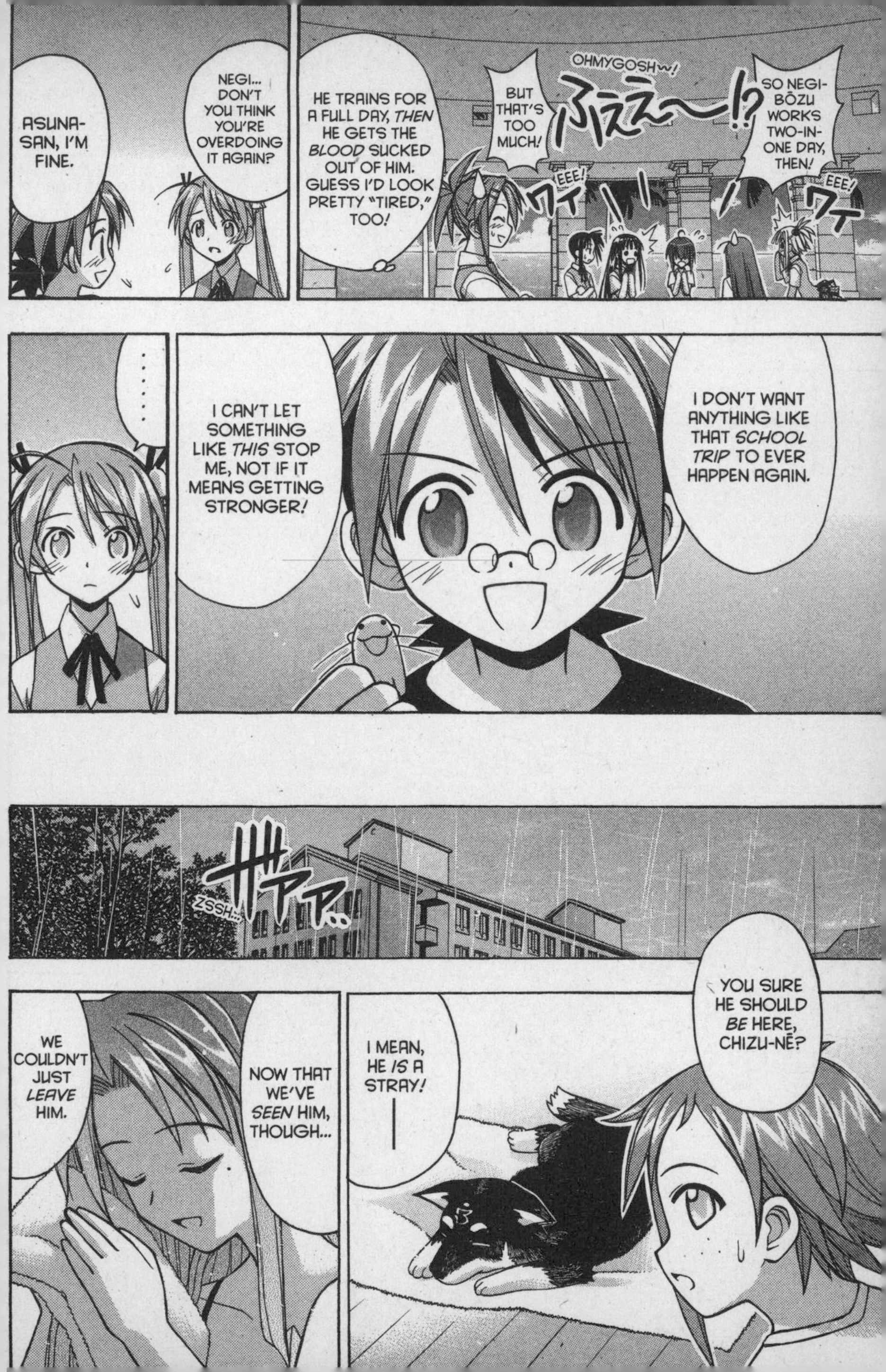
SO NEGI-BŌZU WORKS TWO-IN-ONE DAY, THEN!
EEE!
ふえぇ〜!?
OHMYGOSH~!
EEE!
BUT THAT'S TOO MUCH!
HE TRAINS FOR A FULL DAY, *THEN* HE GETS THE *BLOOD* SUCKED OUT OF HIM. GUESS I'D LOOK PRETTY "TIRED," TOO!
NEGI... DON'T YOU THINK YOU'RE OVERDOING IT AGAIN?
ASUNA-SAN, I'M FINE.
I DON'T WANT ANYTHING LIKE THAT *SCHOOL TRIP* TO EVER HAPPEN AGAIN.
I CAN'T LET SOMETHING LIKE *THIS* STOP ME, NOT IF IT MEANS GETTING STRONGER!
......
ザァァ..
ZSSH...
YOU SURE HE SHOULD *BE* HERE, CHIZU-NĒ?
I MEAN, HE *IS* A STRAY!
NOW THAT WE'VE *SEEN* HIM, THOUGH...
WE COULDN'T JUST *LEAVE* HIM.

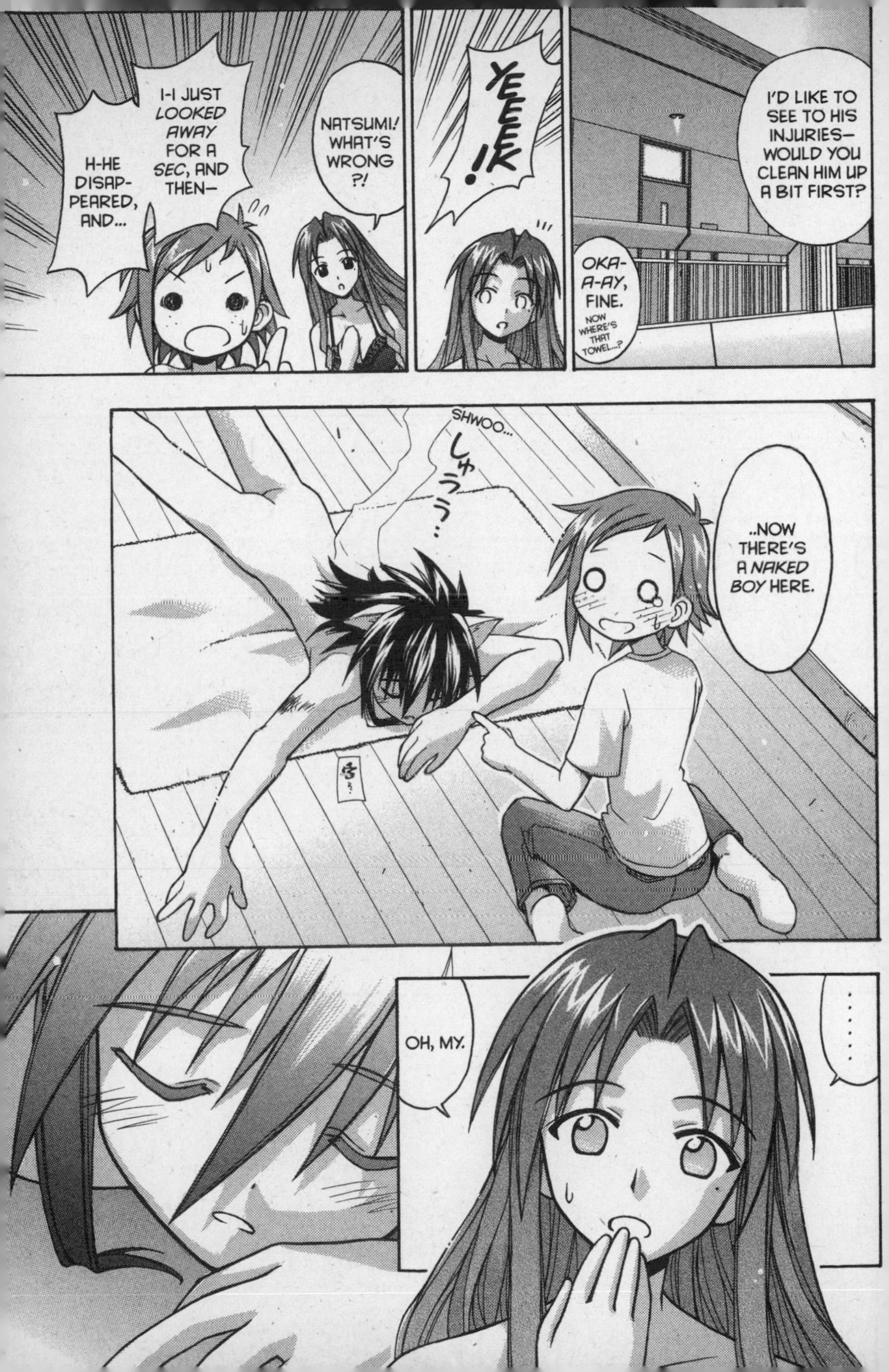

I'D LIKE TO SEE TO HIS INJURIES— WOULD YOU CLEAN HIM UP A BIT FIRST?
OKA-A-AY, FINE.
NOW WHERE'S THAT TOWEL...?
YEEEK!
NATSUMI! WHAT'S WRONG?!
I-I JUST LOOKED AWAY FOR A SEC, AND THEN—
H-HE DISAPPEARED, AND...
SHWOO...
しゅうう…
..NOW THERE'S A NAKED BOY HERE.
......
OH, MY.

NEGIMA!
MAGISTER NEGI MAGI

SIXTY-THIRD PERIOD: "MAGIC WORD" LEXICON

■「来たれ、虚空の雷、薙ぎ払え。『雷の斧』」

(κενότητος ἀστράπσατω δὲ τεμέτω. ΔΙΟΣ ΤΥΚΟΣ)

"COME FORTH, O LIGHTNING FROM THE VOID, AND CUT DOWN MINE ENEMIES. AXE OF LIGHTNING!"

As stated by early Greek philosopher Hesiod, "And again, she bare the Cyclopes, overbearing in spirit, Brontes, and Steropes and stubborn-hearted Arges, who gave Zeus the thunder and made the thunderbolt..." (ll. 139-141). Thunder and lightning were the weapons of the Greek god Zeus; etymologically speaking, ΔΙΟΣ ΤΥΚΟΣ may then also be thought to mean "Axe of Zeus."

Although the area of effect for this spell is relatively small, its incantation is so short and the formation of electrical discharge so quick, on short- to medium-range targets, it is extremely effective.

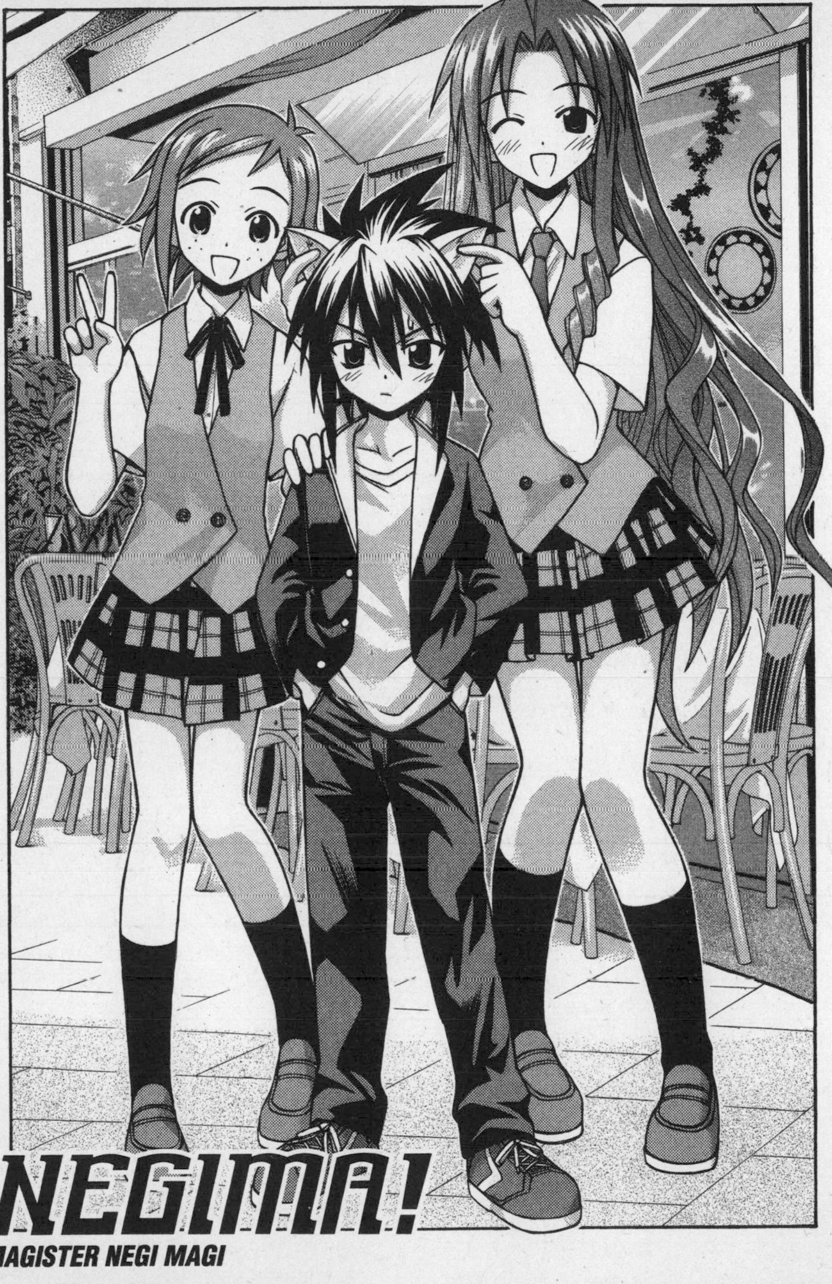
NEGIMA!
MAGISTER NEGI MAGI

SIXTY-FOURTH PERIOD: AFTER THAT MAGIC-TEACHER!

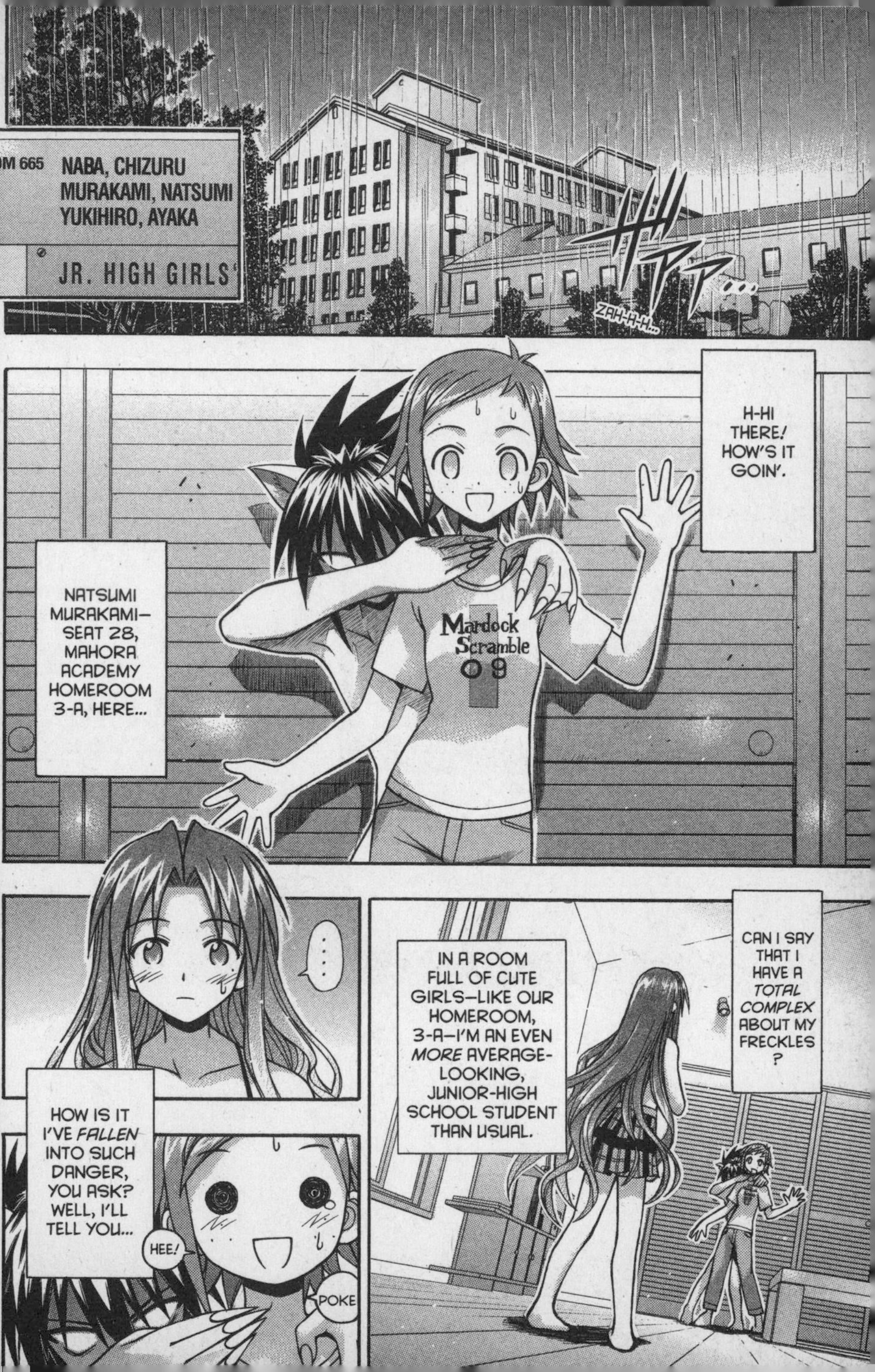
OM 665
NABA, CHIZURU
MURAKAMI, NATSUMI
YUKIHIRO, AYAKA
JR. HIGH GIRLS'
ZAH-A-A-A...
H-HI THERE! HOW'S IT GOIN'.
Mardock Scramble 09
NATSUMI MURAKAMI—SEAT 28, MAHORA ACADEMY HOMEROOM 3-A, HERE...
CAN I SAY THAT I HAVE A *TOTAL COMPLEX* ABOUT MY FRECKLES?
IN A ROOM FULL OF CUTE GIRLS—LIKE OUR HOMEROOM, 3-A—I'M AN EVEN *MORE* AVERAGE-LOOKING, JUNIOR-HIGH SCHOOL STUDENT THAN USUAL.
....
HOW IS IT I'VE *FALLEN* INTO SUCH DANGER, YOU ASK? WELL, I'LL TELL YOU...
HEE!
POKE

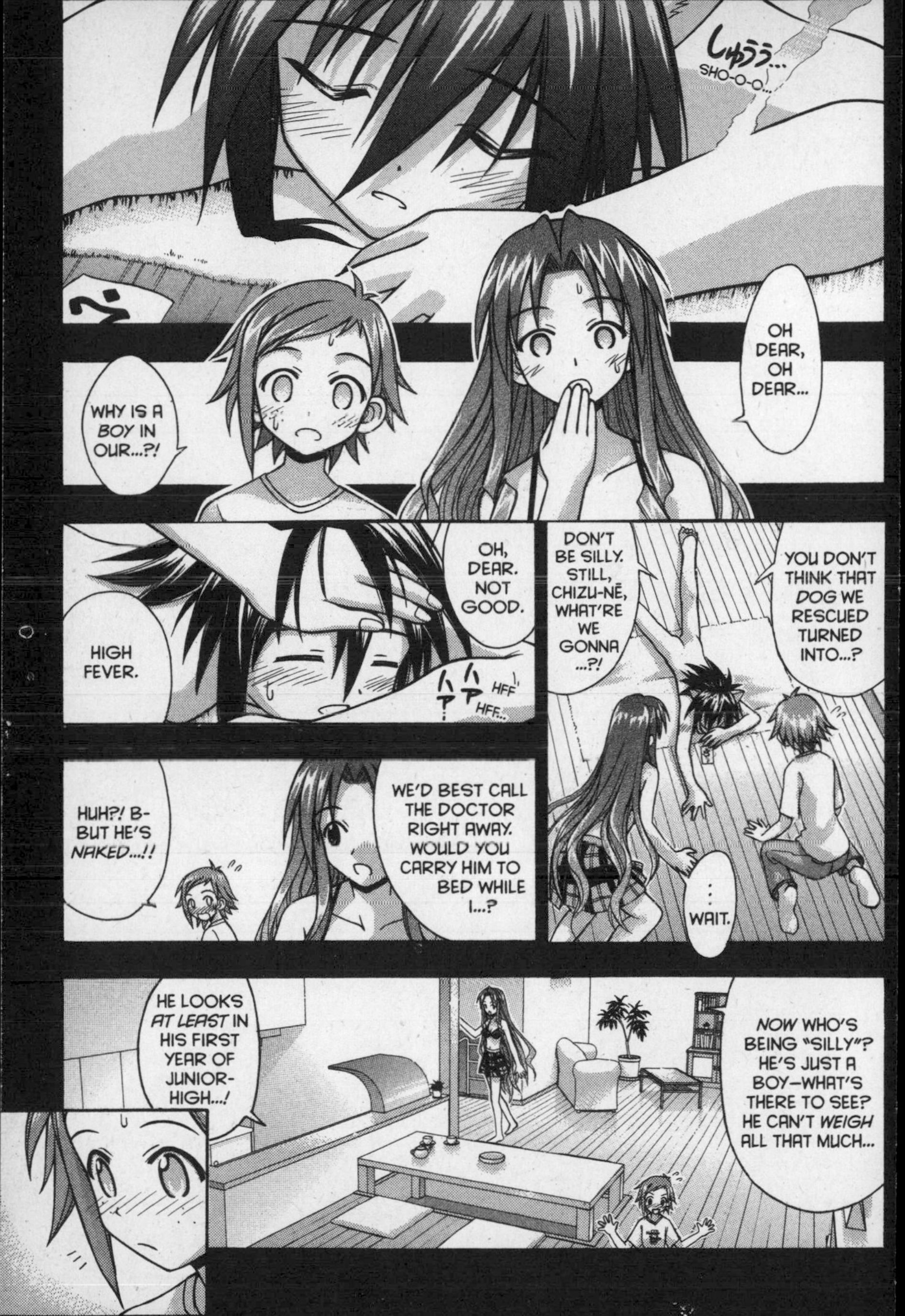
しゅううう...
SHO-O-O...
OH DEAR, OH DEAR...
WHY IS A *BOY* IN OUR...?!
YOU DON'T THINK THAT *DOG* WE RESCUED TURNED INTO...?
DON'T BE SILLY. STILL, CHIZU-NĒ, WHAT'RE WE GONNA ...?!
... WAIT.
OH, DEAR. NOT GOOD.
HIGH FEVER.
ハァ HFF
ハァ HFF...
WE'D BEST CALL THE DOCTOR RIGHT AWAY. WOULD YOU CARRY HIM TO BED WHILE I...?
HUH?! B-BUT HE'S *NAKED*...!!
NOW WHO'S BEING "SILLY"? HE'S JUST A BOY—WHAT'S THERE TO SEE? HE CAN'T *WEIGH* ALL THAT MUCH...
HE LOOKS *AT LEAST* IN HIS FIRST YEAR OF JUNIOR-HIGH...!

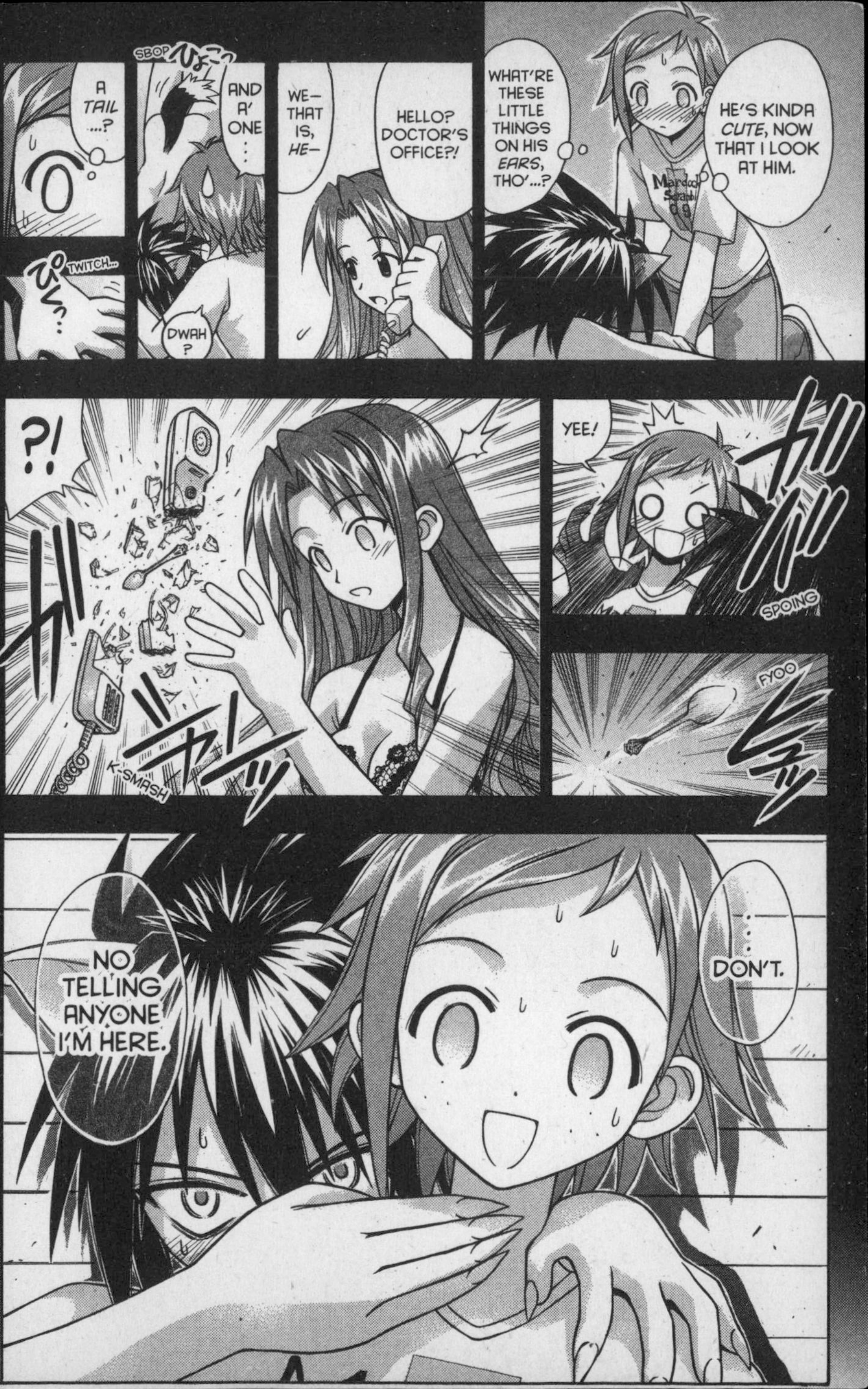
HE'S KINDA CUTE, NOW THAT I LOOK AT HIM.
WHAT'RE THESE LITTLE THINGS ON HIS EARS, THO'...?
HELLO? DOCTOR'S OFFICE?!
WE— THAT IS, HE—
SBOP
AND A' ONE . . .
DWAH ?
A TAIL ...?
TWITCH...
YEE!
SPOING
FYOO
?!
K-SMASH
...DON'T.
NO TELLING ANYONE I'M HERE.

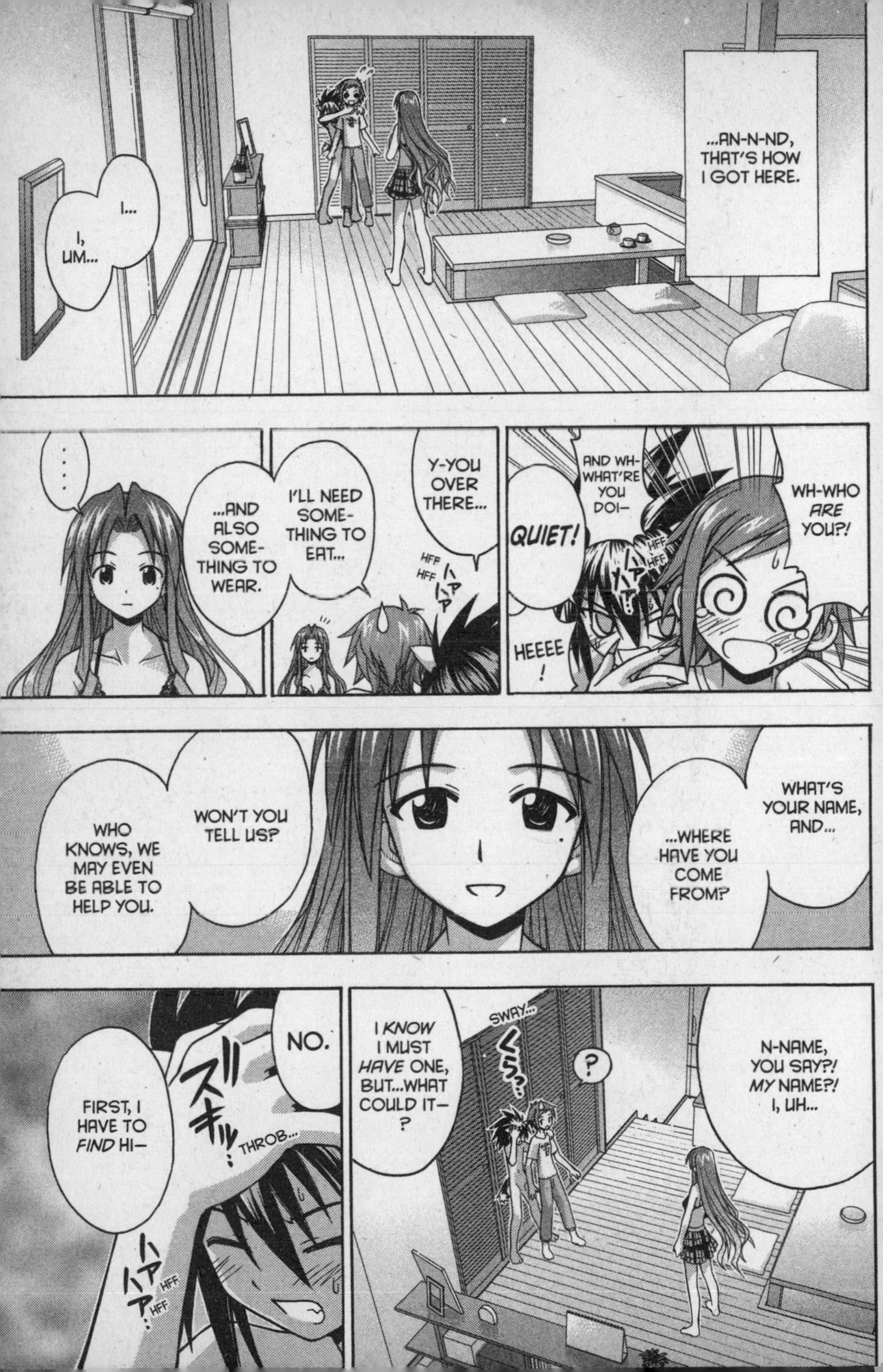
...AN-N-ND, THAT'S HOW I GOT HERE.
I... I, UM...
WH-WHO *ARE* YOU?!
AND WH-WHAT'RE YOU DOI—
QUIET!
HFF HFF
HEEEE!
Y-YOU OVER THERE...
I'LL NEED SOMETHING TO EAT...
...AND ALSO SOMETHING TO WEAR.
HFF HFF ハァハァ
....
WHAT'S YOUR NAME, AND...
...WHERE HAVE YOU COME FROM?
WON'T YOU TELL US?
WHO KNOWS, WE MAY EVEN BE ABLE TO HELP YOU.
N-NAME, YOU SAY?! *MY* NAME?! I, UH...
?
SWAY... くらっ
I *KNOW* I MUST *HAVE* ONE, BUT...WHAT COULD IT— ?
NO.
ズキッ THROB...
FIRST, I HAVE TO *FIND* HI—
ハァハァ HFF HFF

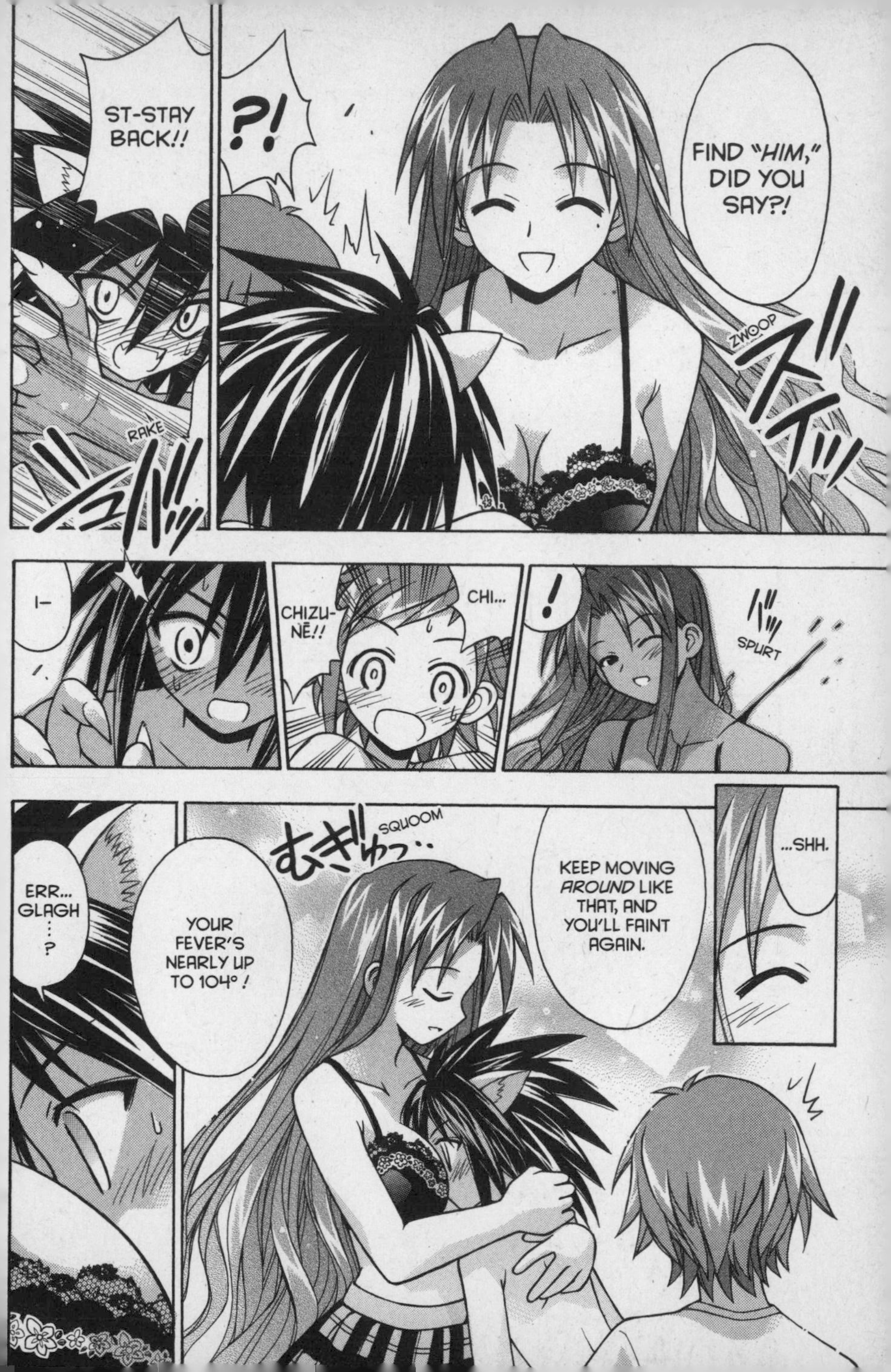
FIND "HIM," DID YOU SAY?!
ZWOOP
?!
ST-STAY BACK!!
RAKE
!
SPURT
CHI...
CHIZU-NĒ!!
I-
...SHH.
KEEP MOVING AROUND LIKE THAT, AND YOU'LL FAINT AGAIN.
SQUOOM
YOUR FEVER'S NEARLY UP TO 104°!
ERR... GLAGH ...?

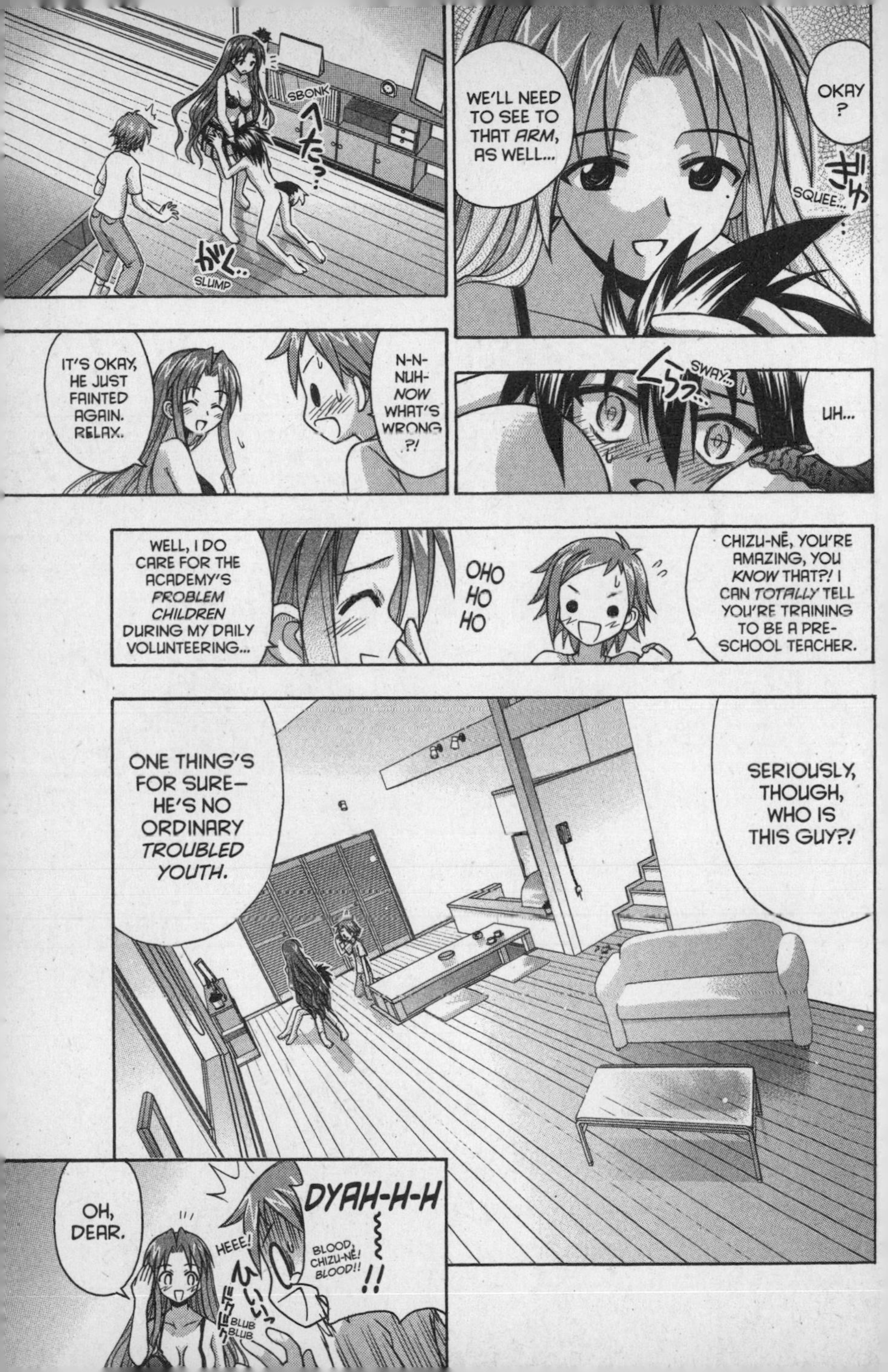
WE'LL NEED TO SEE TO THAT *ARM*, AS WELL...
OKAY?
SQUEE...
SBONK
SLUMP
SWAY...
UH...
N-N-NUH-*NOW* WHAT'S WRONG?!
IT'S OKAY, HE JUST FAINTED AGAIN. RELAX.
CHIZU-NĒ, YOU'RE AMAZING, YOU *KNOW* THAT?! I CAN *TOTALLY* TELL YOU'RE TRAINING TO BE A PRE-SCHOOL TEACHER.
OHO HO HO
WELL, I DO CARE FOR THE ACADEMY'S *PROBLEM CHILDREN* DURING MY DAILY VOLUNTEERING...
SERIOUSLY, THOUGH, WHO IS THIS GUY?!
ONE THING'S FOR SURE— HE'S NO ORDINARY *TROUBLED YOUTH*.
DYAH-H-H!!
BLOOD, CHIZU-NĒ! BLOOD!!
HEEE!
BLUB BLUB
OH, DEAR.

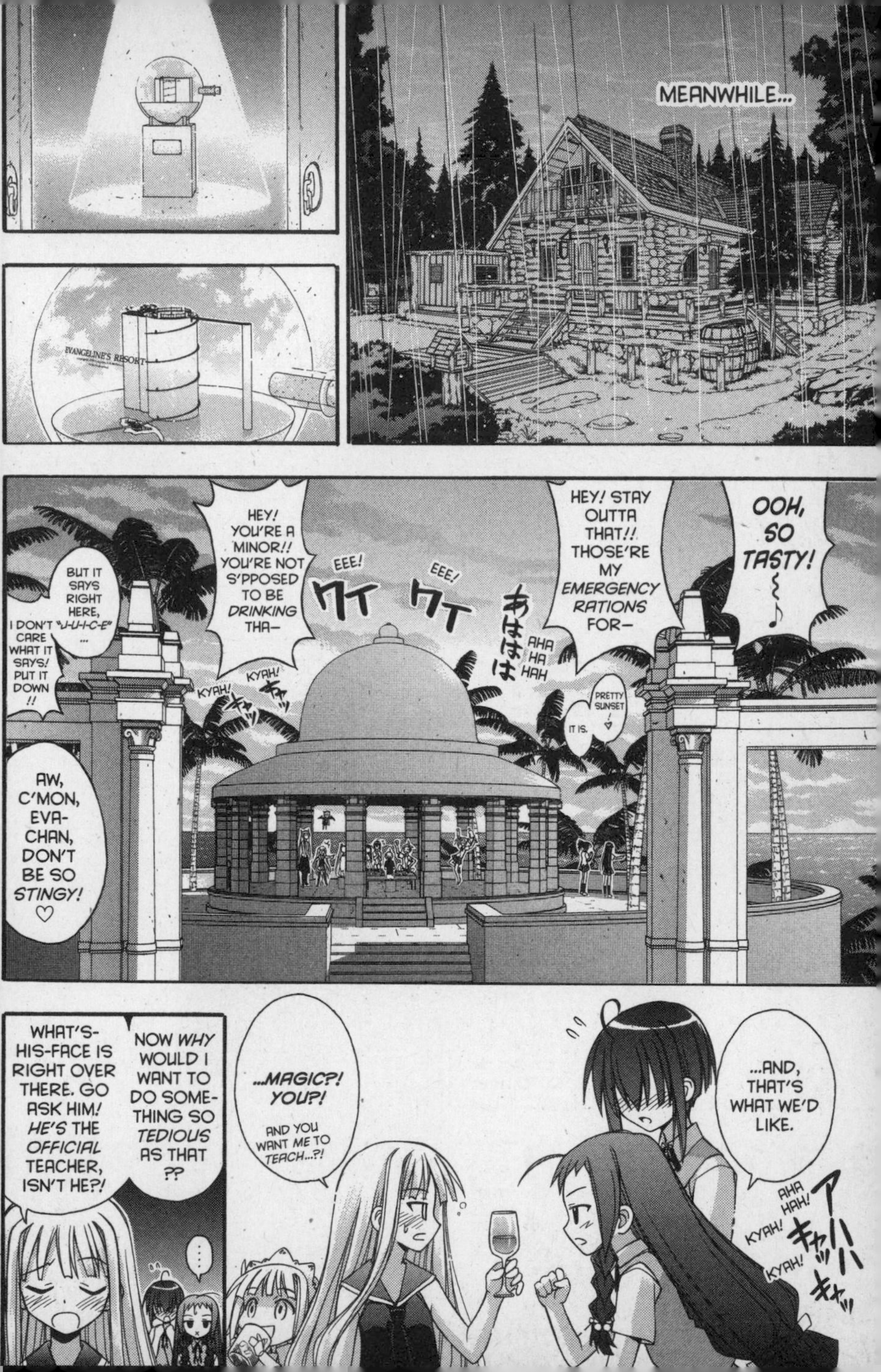

MEANWHILE...
EVANGELINE'S RESORT
OOH, SO TASTY! ~♪
HEY! STAY OUTTA THAT!! THOSE'RE MY EMERGENCY RATIONS FOR–
あははは
AHA HA HAH
EEE! ワイ
EEE! ワイ
HEY! YOU'RE A MINOR!! YOU'RE NOT S'PPOSED TO BE DRINKING THA–
BUT IT SAYS RIGHT HERE, "J-U-I-C-E"...
I DON'T CARE WHAT IT SAYS! PUT IT DOWN!!
KYAH! キャッ
KYAH! キャッ
PRETTY SUNSET ♡
IT IS.
AW, C'MON, EVA-CHAN, DON'T BE SO STINGY! ♡
...AND, THAT'S WHAT WE'D LIKE.
アハハ
AHA HAH!
KYAH! キャッ
KYAH! キャッ
...MAGIC?! YOU?!
AND YOU WANT ME TO TEACH...?!
NOW WHY WOULD I WANT TO DO SOMETHING SO TEDIOUS AS THAT??
WHAT'S-HIS-FACE IS RIGHT OVER THERE. GO ASK HIM! HE'S THE OFFICIAL TEACHER, ISN'T HE?!
...

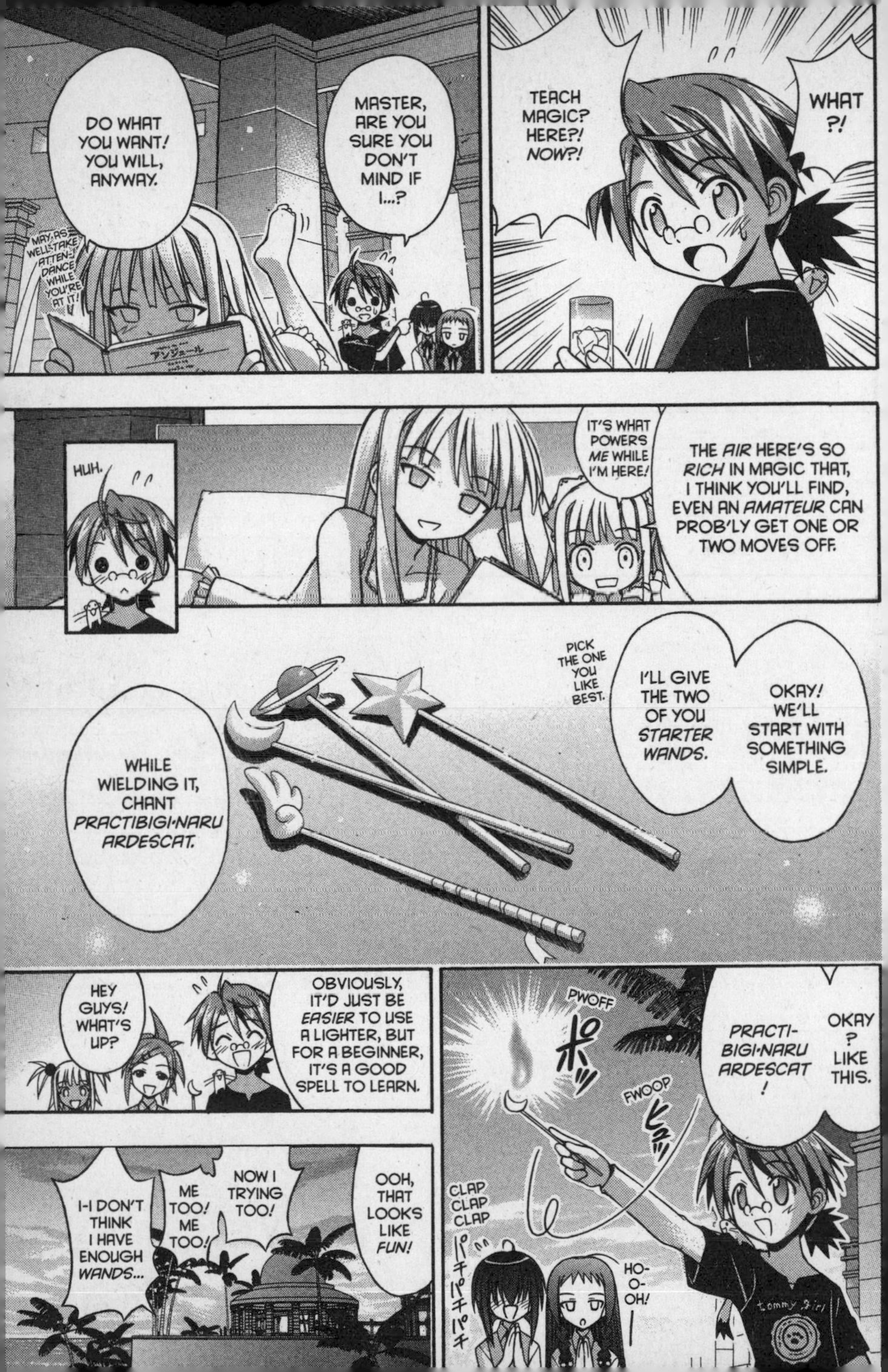
WHAT ?!
TEACH MAGIC? HERE?! *NOW?!*
MASTER, ARE YOU SURE YOU DON'T MIND IF I...?
DO WHAT YOU WANT! YOU WILL, ANYWAY.
MAY AS WELL TAKE ATTEN-DANCE WHILE YOU'RE AT IT!
THE *AIR* HERE'S SO *RICH* IN MAGIC THAT, I THINK YOU'LL FIND, EVEN AN *AMATEUR* CAN PROB'LY GET ONE OR TWO MOVES OFF.
IT'S WHAT POWERS *ME* WHILE I'M HERE!
HUH.
OKAY! WE'LL START WITH SOMETHING SIMPLE.
I'LL GIVE THE TWO OF YOU *STARTER WANDS.*
PICK THE ONE YOU LIKE BEST.
WHILE WIELDING IT, CHANT *PRACTIBIGI·NARU ARDESCAT.*
OKAY? LIKE THIS.
PRACTI-BIGI·NARU ARDESCAT!
PWOFF
ポッ
FWOOP
CLAP CLAP CLAP
パチパチ
HO-O-OH!
OBVIOUSLY, IT'D JUST BE *EASIER* TO USE A LIGHTER, BUT FOR A BEGINNER, IT'S A GOOD SPELL TO LEARN.
HEY GUYS! WHAT'S UP?
OOH, THAT LOOKS LIKE *FUN!*
NOW I TRYING TOO!
ME TOO! ME TOO!
I-I DON'T THINK I HAVE ENOUGH *WANDS...*

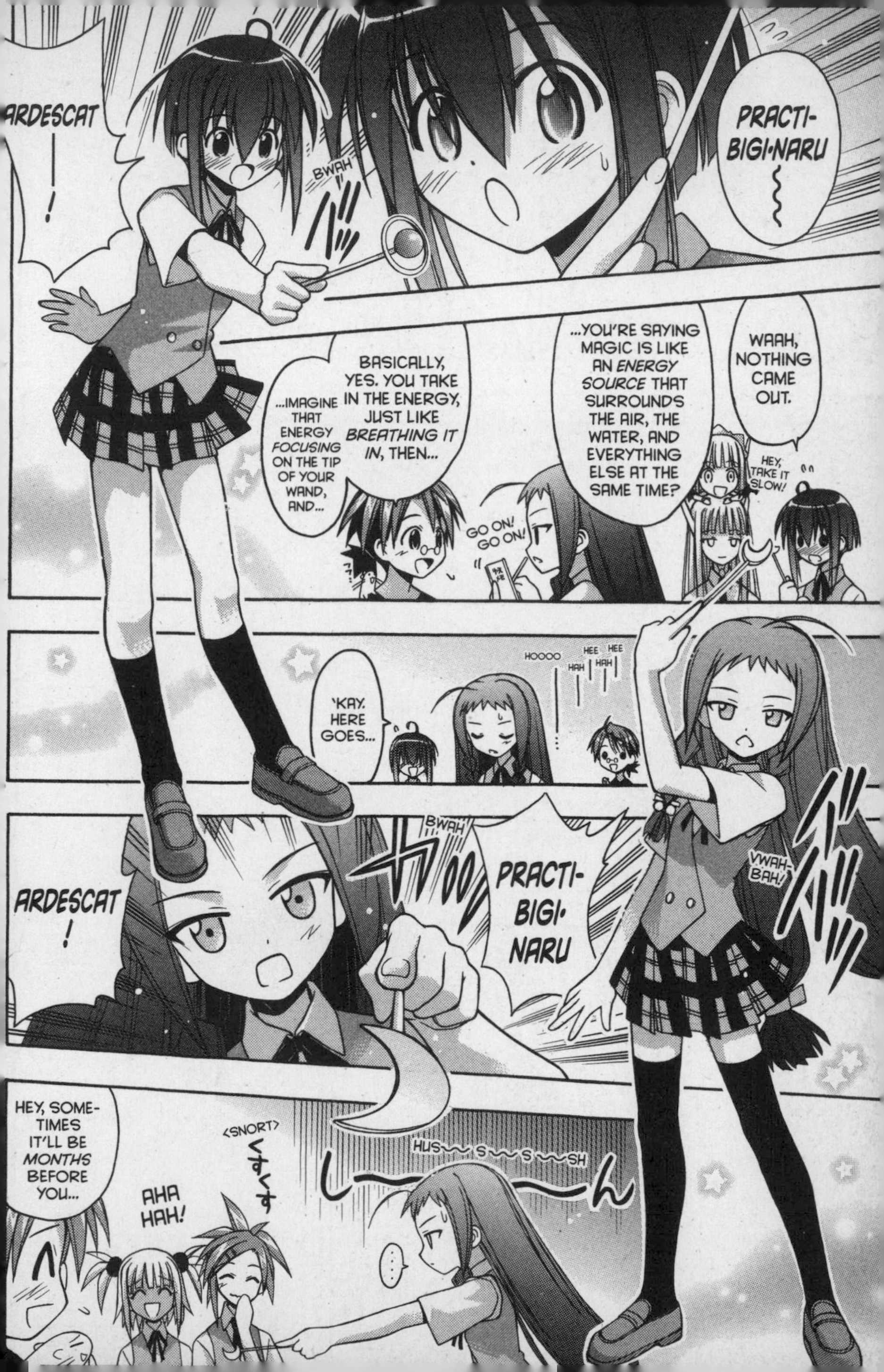
PRACTI-BIGI-NARU ~
BWAH
ARDESCAT —!
WAAH, NOTHING CAME OUT.
HEY, TAKE IT SLOW!
...YOU'RE SAYING MAGIC IS LIKE AN *ENERGY SOURCE* THAT SURROUNDS THE AIR, THE WATER, AND EVERYTHING ELSE AT THE SAME TIME?
GO ON! GO ON!
BASICALLY, YES. YOU TAKE IN THE ENERGY, JUST LIKE *BREATHING IT IN*, THEN...
...IMAGINE THAT ENERGY *FOCUSING* ON THE TIP OF YOUR WAND, AND...
HOOOO
HEE HAH
HEE HAH
'KAY. HERE GOES...
VWAH-BAH!
PRACTI-BIGI-NARU
BWAH
ARDESCAT!
HUS~ S~S~SH
しーーーん
...
<SNORT> くすくす
AHA HAH!
HEY, SOME-TIMES IT'LL BE *MONTHS* BEFORE YOU...

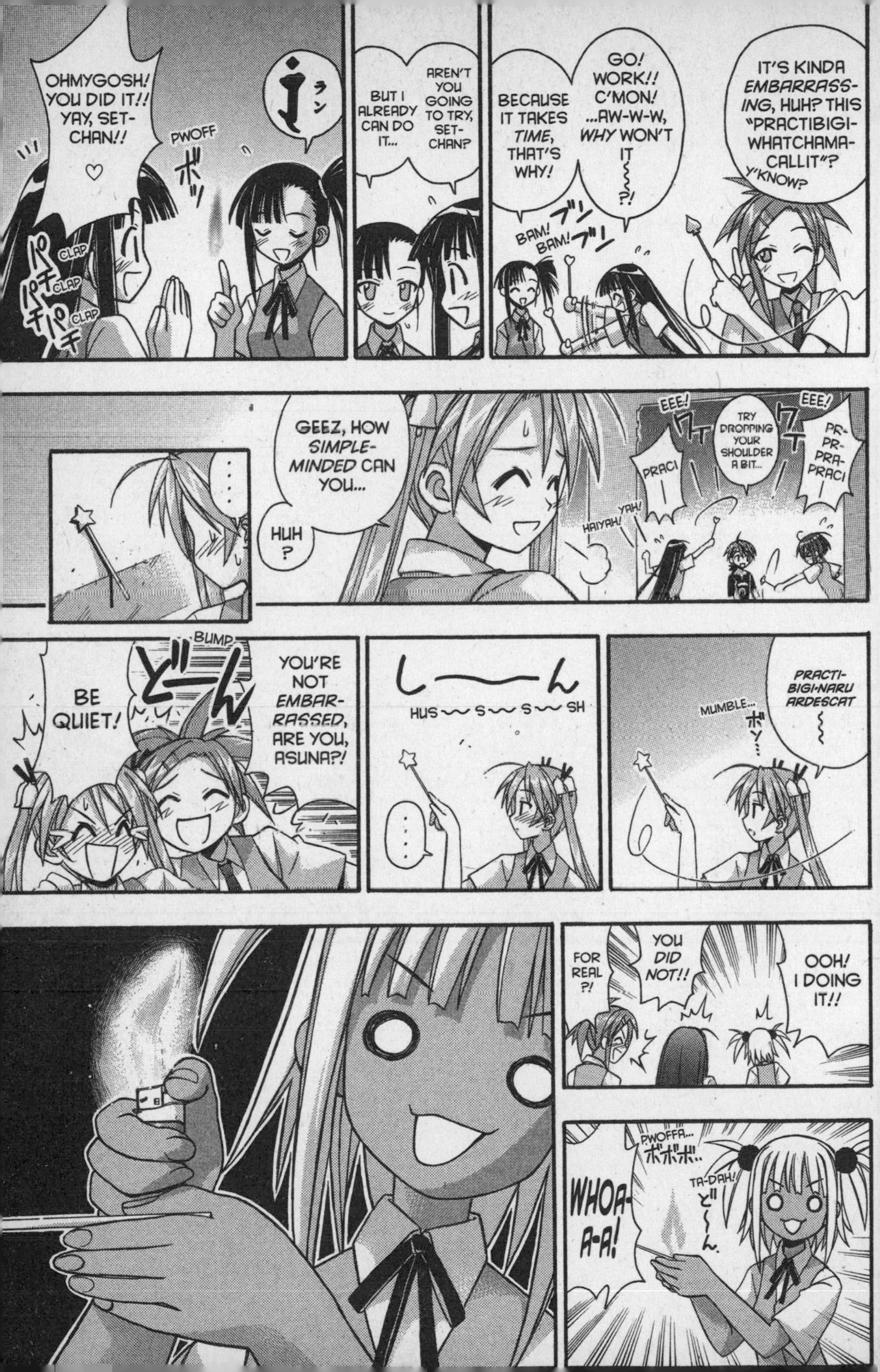
IT'S KINDA EMBARRASSING, HUH? THIS "PRACTIBIGI-WHATCHAMACALLIT"? Y'KNOW?
GO! WORK!! C'MON! ...AW-W-W, WHY WON'T IT~~?!
BECAUSE IT TAKES TIME, THAT'S WHY!
BAM! BAM! ブン ブン
AREN'T YOU GOING TO TRY, SET-CHAN?
BUT I ALREADY CAN DO IT...
¡ ラン
PWOFF ボッ
OHMYGOSH! YOU DID IT!! YAY, SET-CHAN!! ♡
パチ CLAP パチ CLAP パチ CLAP
EEE! ワァ
EEE! ワァ
PR-PR-PRA-PRACI
TRY DROPPING YOUR SHOULDER A BIT...
PRACI
YAH!
HAIYAH!
GEEZ, HOW SIMPLE-MINDED CAN YOU...
HUH?
...
PRACTI-BIGI-NARU ARDESCAT~~
MUMBLE... ボソ...
しーーん
HUS~S~S~SH
...
YOU'RE NOT EMBARRASSED, ARE YOU, ASUNA?!
BUMP どーん
BE QUIET!
OOH! I DOING IT!!
YOU DID NOT!!
FOR REAL?!
PWOFFA... ボボボ...
TA-DAH! どーん.
WHOA-A-A!

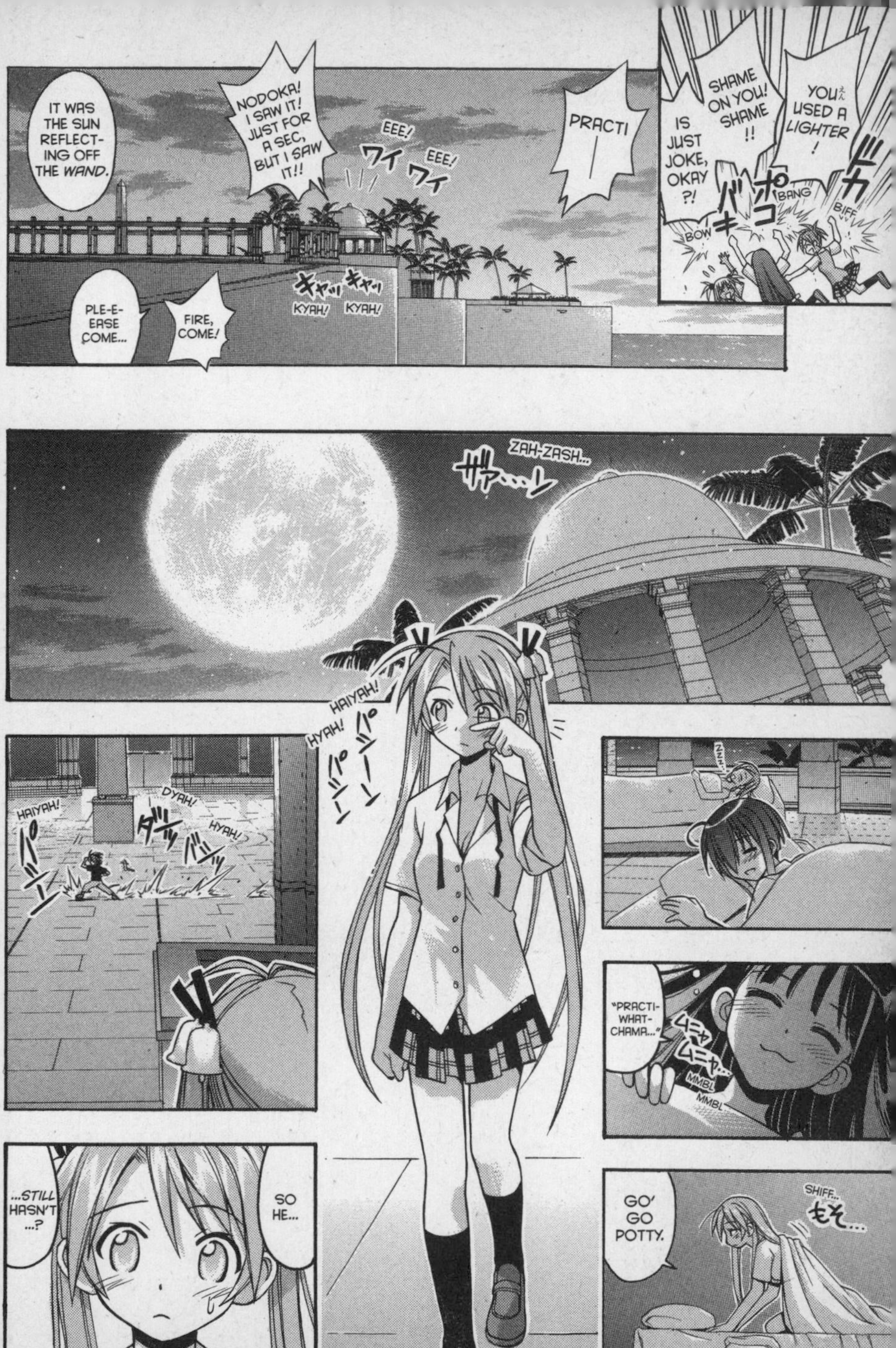
YOU USED A LIGHTER!
SHAME ON YOU! SHAME!!
IS JUST JOKE, OKAY?!
ドカ
BIFF
ポコ
BANG
バキ
BOW
PRACTI—
EEE! ワイ
EEE! ワイ
NODOKA! I SAW IT! JUST FOR A SEC, BUT I SAW IT!!
IT WAS THE SUN REFLECTING OFF THE WAND.
キャッ KYAH!
キャッ KYAH!
FIRE, COME!
PLE-E-EASE COME...
ザァ…ン
ZAH-ZASH...
"PRACTI-WHAT-CHAMA..."
ムニャ ムニャ…
MMBL MMBL
SHIFF...
もそ…
GO' GO POTTY.
HAIYAH!
HYAH!
パシーン
パシーン
HAIYAH!
パーン
DYAH!
ダッ
HYAH!
バシッ
SO HE...
...STILL HASN'T...?

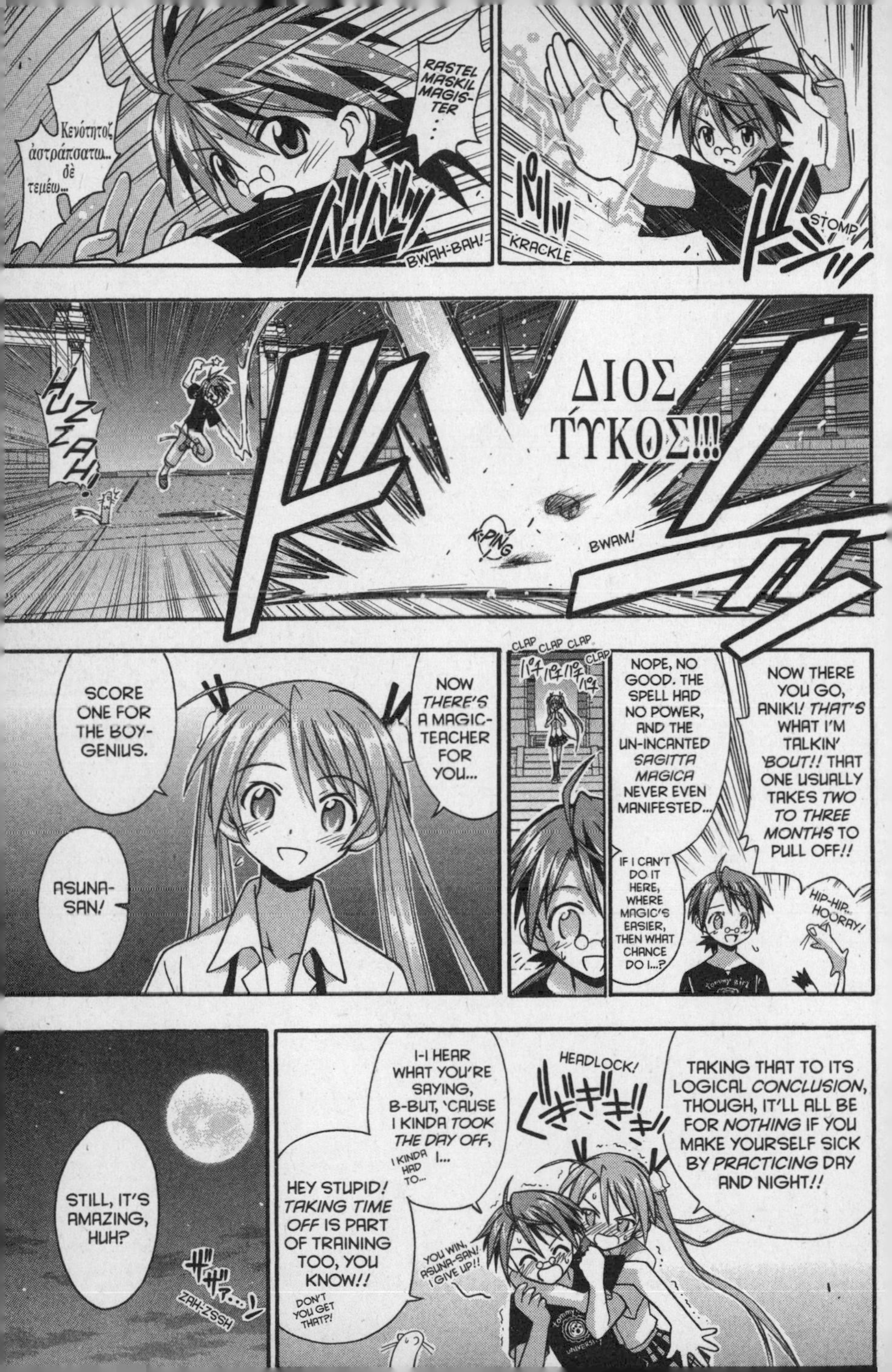
KRACKLE
STOMP
RASTEL MASKIL MAGISTER...
Κενότητος ἀστράπσατω... δὲ τεμέω...
BWAH-BAH!
ΔΙΟΣ ΤΎΚΟΣ!!!
HUZZAH!
BWAM!
K-PING
NOW THERE YOU GO, ANIKI! THAT'S WHAT I'M TALKIN' 'BOUT!! THAT ONE USUALLY TAKES TWO TO THREE MONTHS TO PULL OFF!!
NOPE, NO GOOD. THE SPELL HAD NO POWER, AND THE UN-INCANTED SAGITTA MAGICA NEVER EVEN MANIFESTED...
IF I CAN'T DO IT HERE, WHERE MAGIC'S EASIER, THEN WHAT CHANCE DO I...?
HIP-HIP... HOORAY!
CLAP CLAP CLAP CLAP
NOW THERE'S A MAGIC-TEACHER FOR YOU...
SCORE ONE FOR THE BOY-GENIUS.
ASUNA-SAN!
TAKING THAT TO ITS LOGICAL CONCLUSION, THOUGH, IT'LL ALL BE FOR NOTHING IF YOU MAKE YOURSELF SICK BY PRACTICING DAY AND NIGHT!!
HEADLOCK!
I-I HEAR WHAT YOU'RE SAYING, B-BUT, 'CAUSE I KINDA TOOK THE DAY OFF, I...
I KINDA HAD TO...
HEY STUPID! TAKING TIME OFF IS PART OF TRAINING TOO, YOU KNOW!!
DON'T YOU GET THAT?!
YOU WIN, ASUNA-SAN! I GIVE UP!!
STILL, IT'S AMAZING, HUH?
ZAH-ZSSH

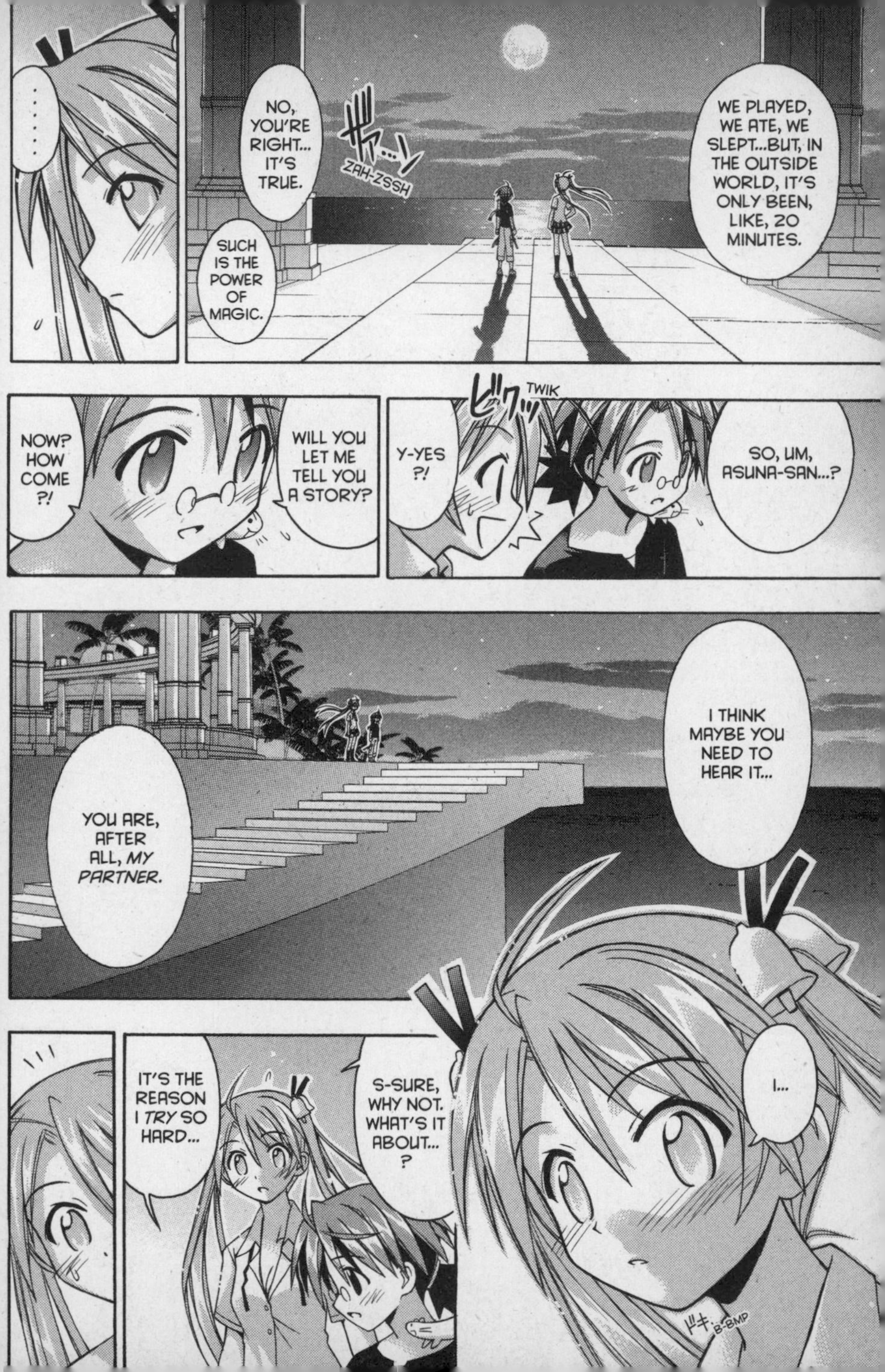

WE PLAYED, WE ATE, WE SLEPT...BUT, IN THE OUTSIDE WORLD, IT'S ONLY BEEN, LIKE, 20 MINUTES.
NO, YOU'RE RIGHT... IT'S TRUE.
ZAH-ZSSH
SUCH IS THE POWER OF MAGIC.
......
SO, UM, ASUNA-SAN...?
TWIK
Y-YES?!
WILL YOU LET ME TELL YOU A STORY?
NOW? HOW COME?!
I THINK MAYBE YOU NEED TO HEAR IT...
YOU ARE, AFTER ALL, *MY PARTNER*.
I...
B-BMP
S-SURE, WHY NOT. WHAT'S IT ABOUT...?
IT'S THE REASON I *TRY* SO HARD...

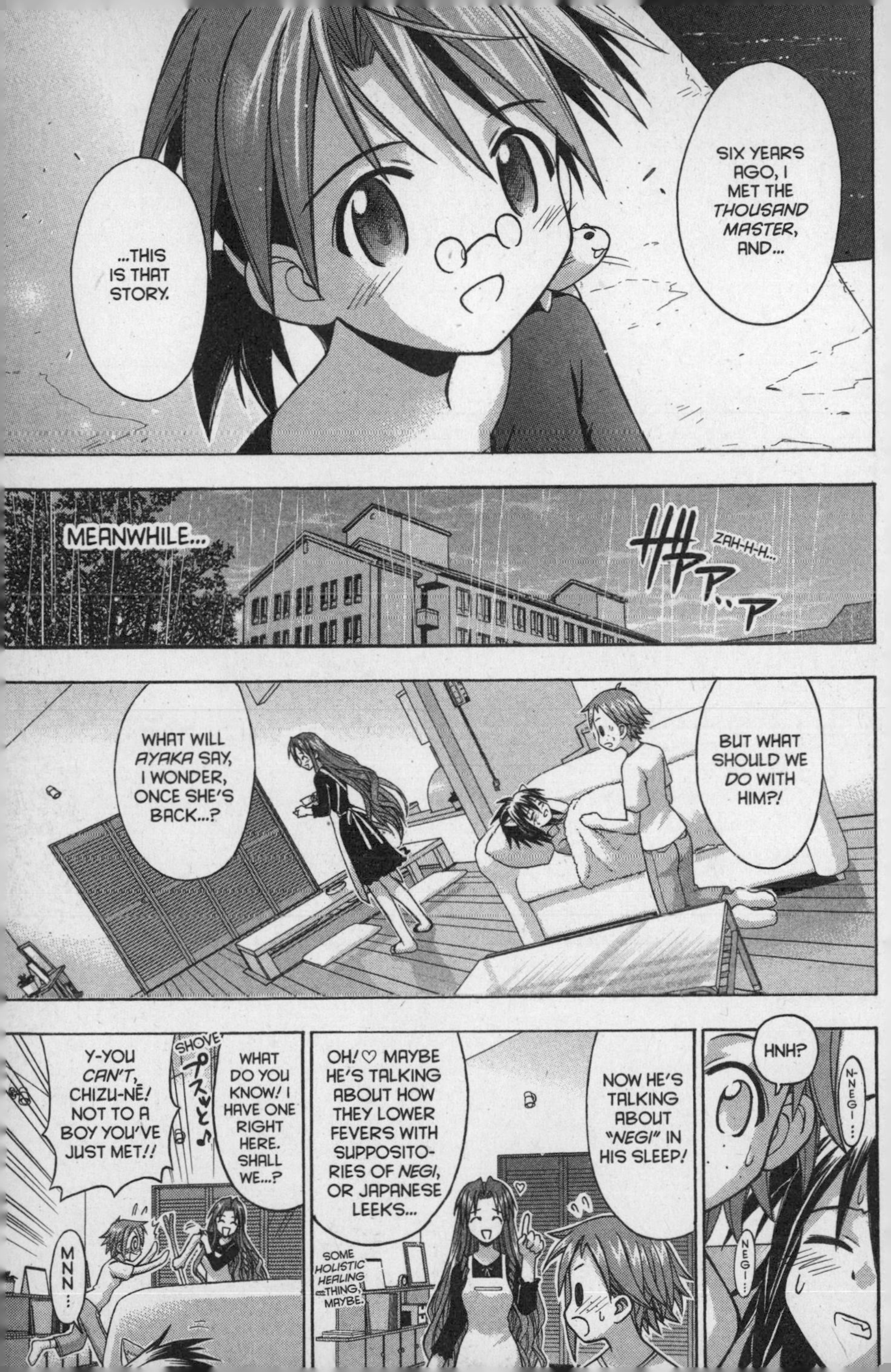
SIX YEARS AGO, I MET THE THOUSAND MASTER, AND...
...THIS IS THAT STORY.
ZAH-H-H...
MEANWHILE...
BUT WHAT SHOULD WE DO WITH HIM?!
WHAT WILL AYAKA SAY, I WONDER, ONCE SHE'S BACK...?
HNH?
N-NEGI...
NEGI...
NOW HE'S TALKING ABOUT "NEGI" IN HIS SLEEP!
OH! ♡ MAYBE HE'S TALKING ABOUT HOW THEY LOWER FEVERS WITH SUPPOSITORIES OF NEGI, OR JAPANESE LEEKS...
SOME HOLISTIC HEALING THING, MAYBE.
WHAT DO YOU KNOW! I HAVE ONE RIGHT HERE. SHALL WE...?
SHOVE
Y-YOU CAN'T, CHIZU-NÉ! NOT TO A BOY YOU'VE JUST MET!!
MNN...

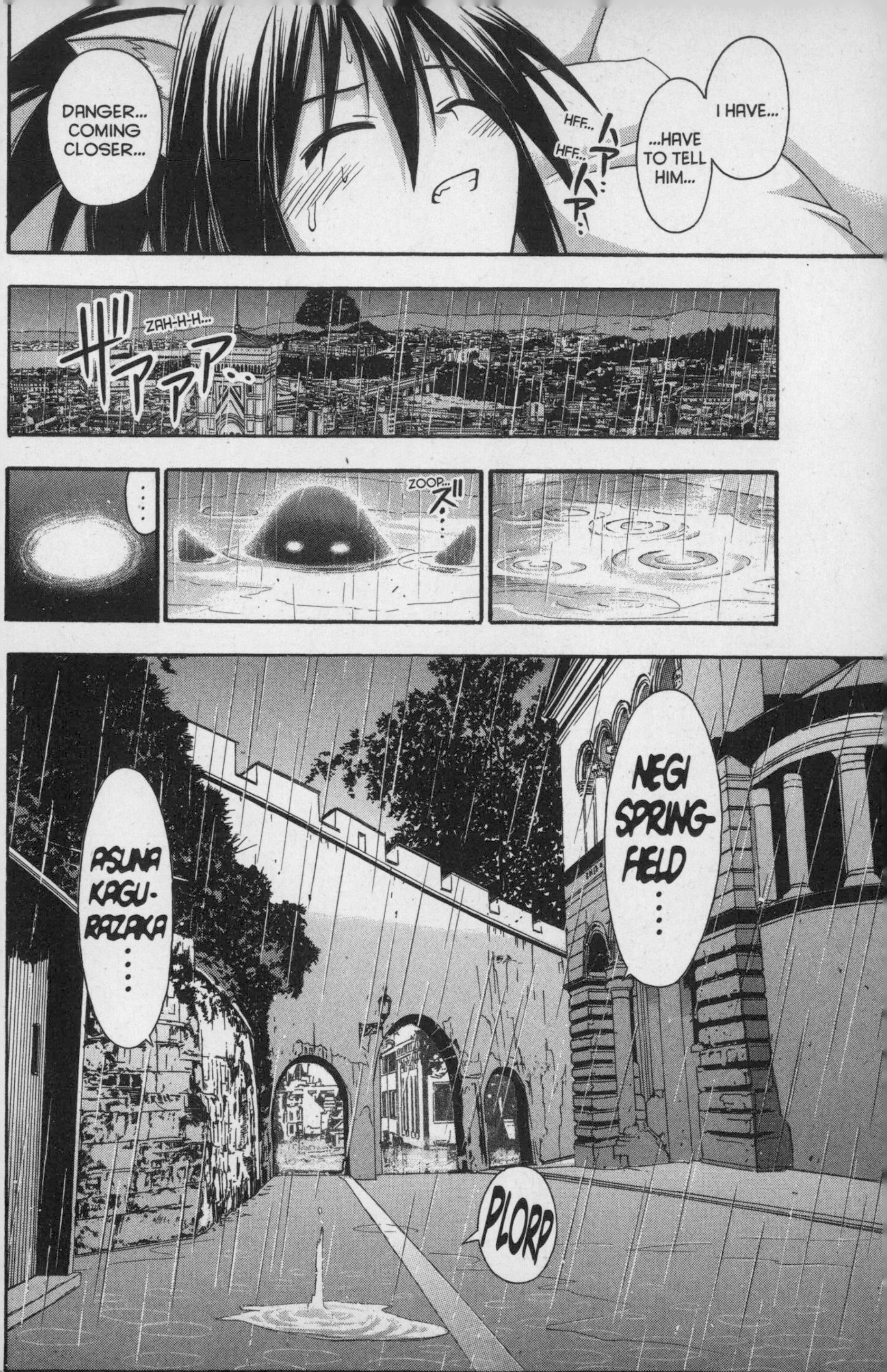
I HAVE...
...HAVE TO TELL HIM...
HFF... HFF...
ハァ… ハァ…
DANGER... COMING CLOSER...
ZAH-H-H...
ザァァ…
ZOOP...
ズ…
....
NEGI SPRING-FIELD....
ASUNA KAGU-RAZAKA....
PLORD

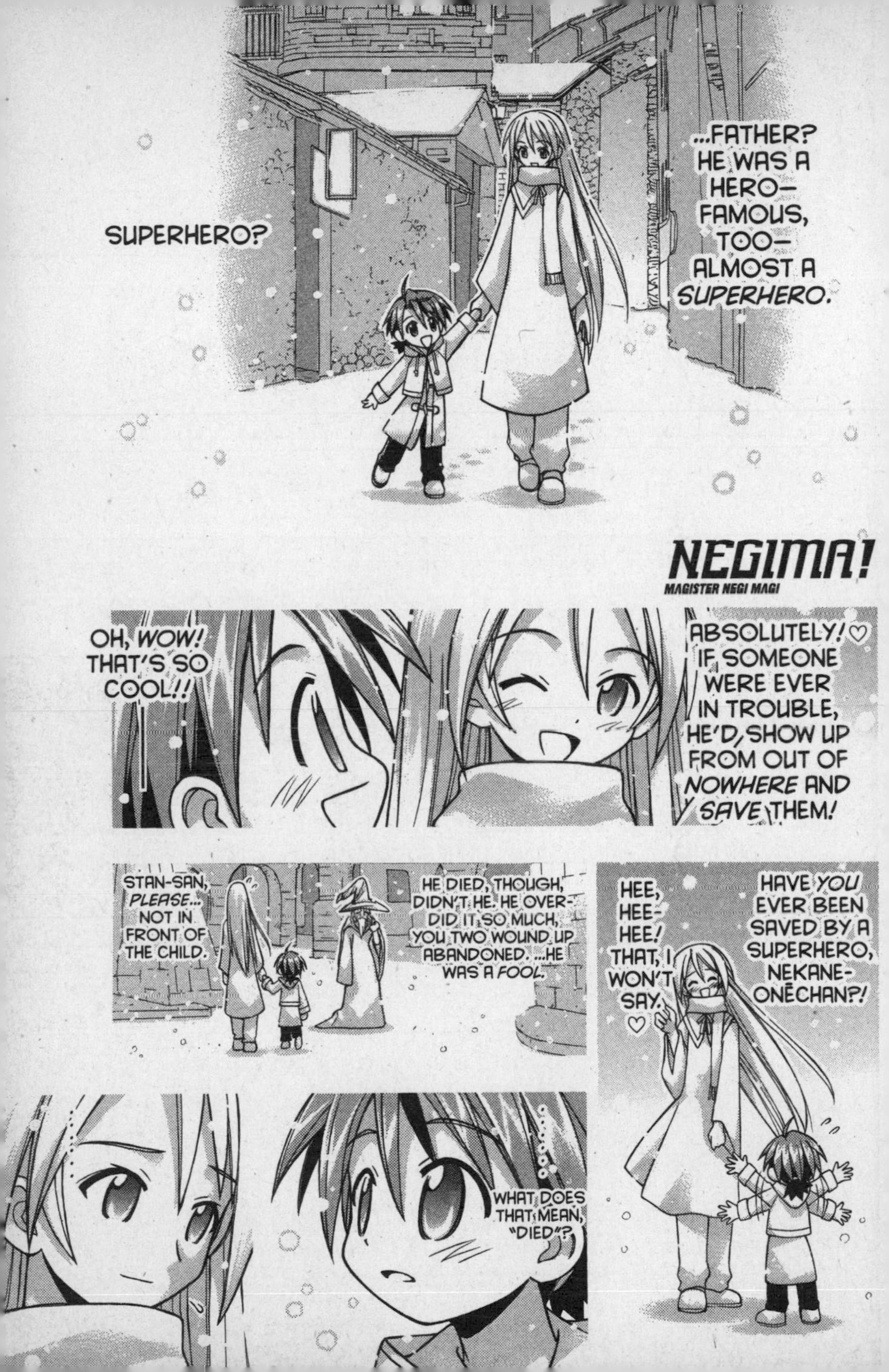
...FATHER? HE WAS A HERO—FAMOUS, TOO—ALMOST A SUPERHERO.
SUPERHERO?
NEGIMA!
MAGISTER NEGI MAGI
ABSOLUTELY! ♡ IF SOMEONE WERE EVER IN TROUBLE, HE'D SHOW UP FROM OUT OF NOWHERE AND SAVE THEM!
OH, WOW! THAT'S SO COOL!!
HAVE YOU EVER BEEN SAVED BY A SUPERHERO, NEKANE-ONĒCHAN?!
HEE, HEE-HEE! THAT, I WON'T SAY. ♡
HE DIED, THOUGH, DIDN'T HE. HE OVER-DID IT SO MUCH, YOU TWO WOUND UP ABANDONED. ...HE WAS A FOOL.
STAN-SAN, PLEASE... NOT IN FRONT OF THE CHILD.
WHAT DOES THAT MEAN, "DIED"?

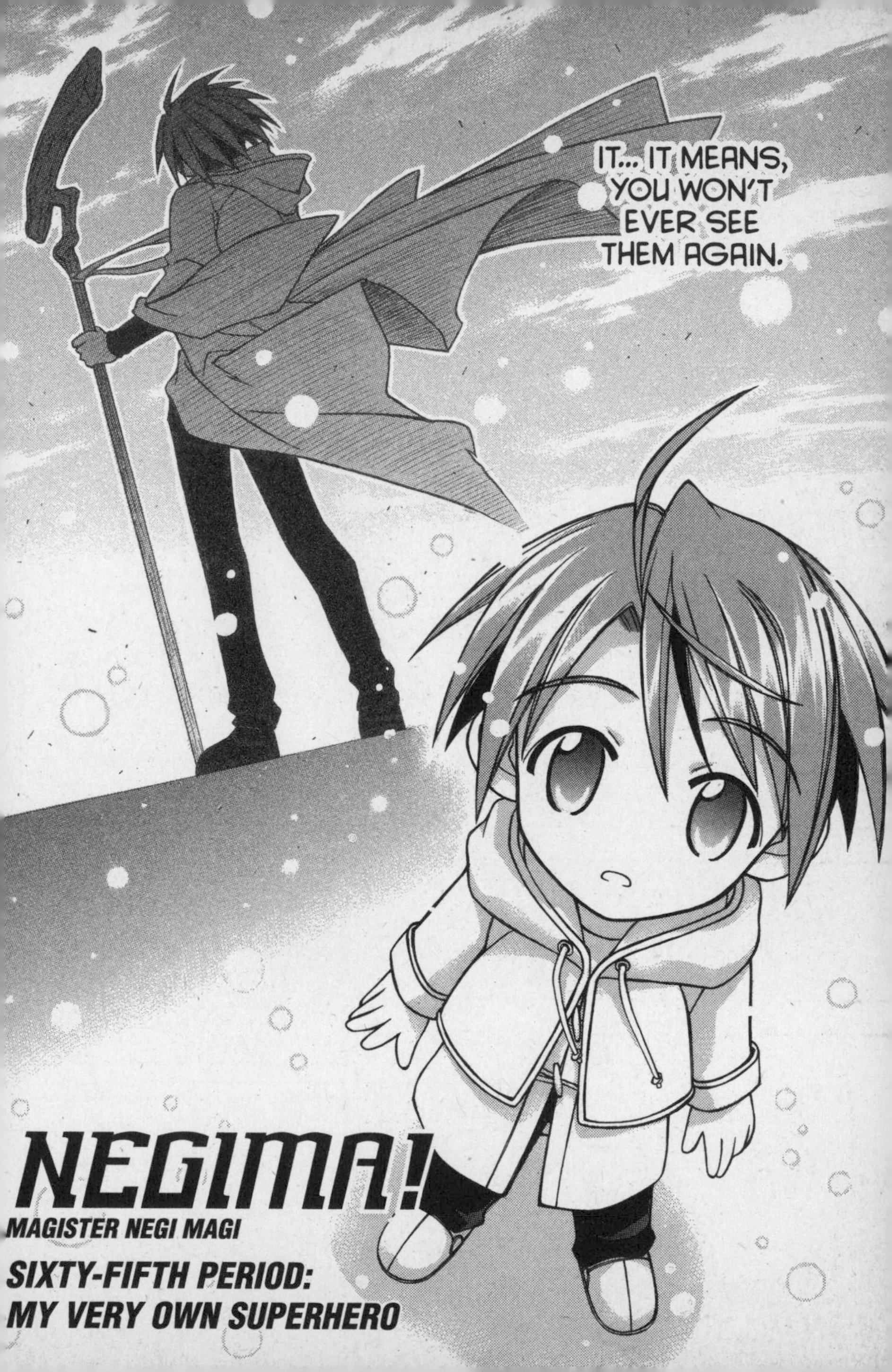
IT... IT MEANS, YOU WON'T EVER SEE THEM AGAIN.

NEGIMA!
MAGISTER NEGI MAGI

SIXTY-FIFTH PERIOD: MY VERY OWN SUPERHERO

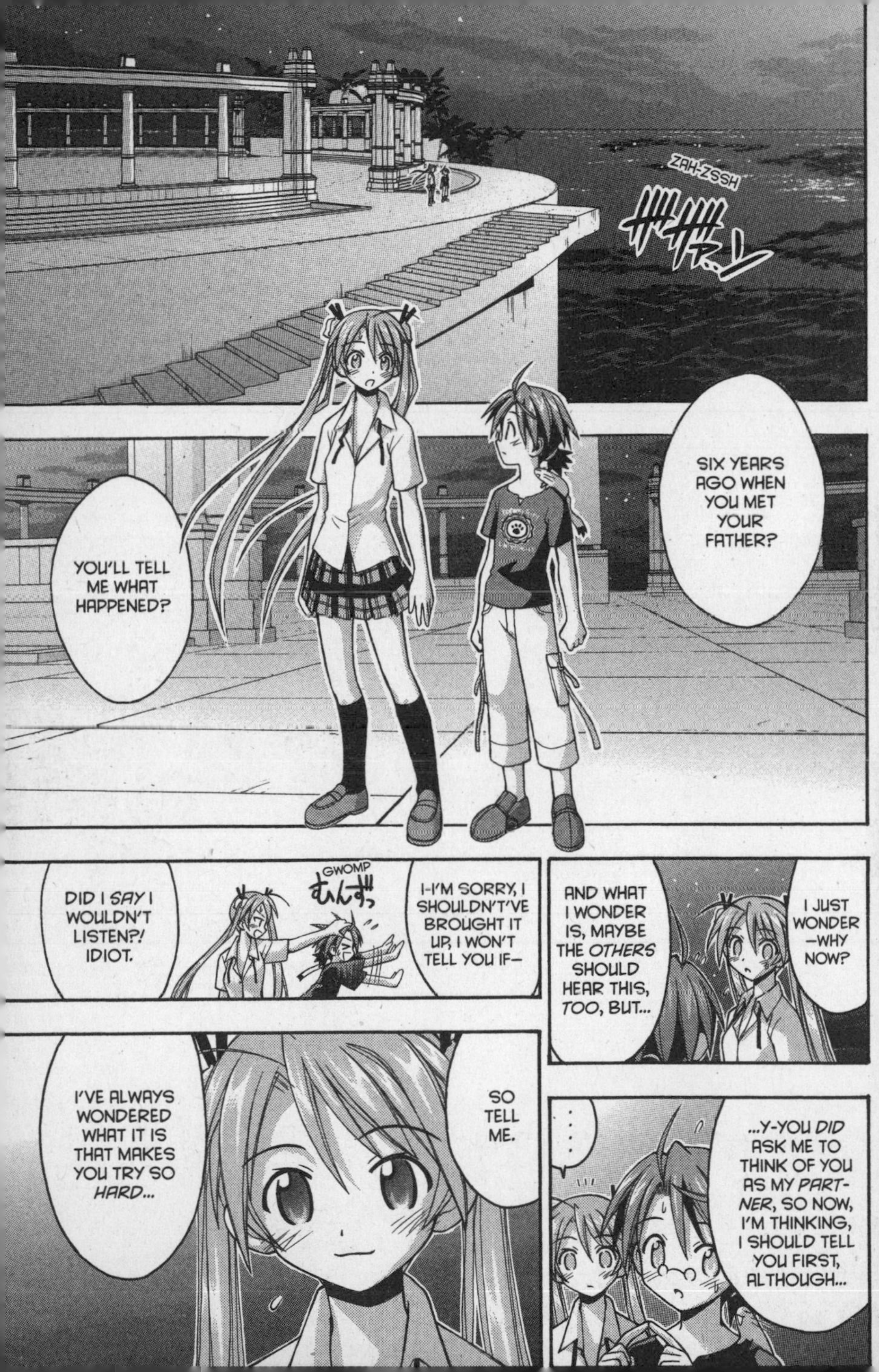
ZAH-ZSSH
SIX YEARS AGO WHEN YOU MET YOUR FATHER?
YOU'LL TELL ME WHAT HAPPENED?
I JUST WONDER —WHY NOW?
AND WHAT I WONDER IS, MAYBE THE *OTHERS* SHOULD HEAR THIS, *TOO*, BUT...
I-I'M SORRY, I SHOULDN'T'VE BROUGHT IT UP, I WON'T TELL YOU IF—
GWOMP
むんずっ
DID I *SAY* I WOULDN'T LISTEN?! IDIOT.
...Y-YOU *DID* ASK ME TO THINK OF YOU AS MY *PARTNER*, SO NOW, I'M THINKING, I SHOULD TELL YOU FIRST, ALTHOUGH...
....
SO TELL ME.
I'VE ALWAYS WONDERED WHAT IT IS THAT MAKES YOU TRY SO *HARD*...

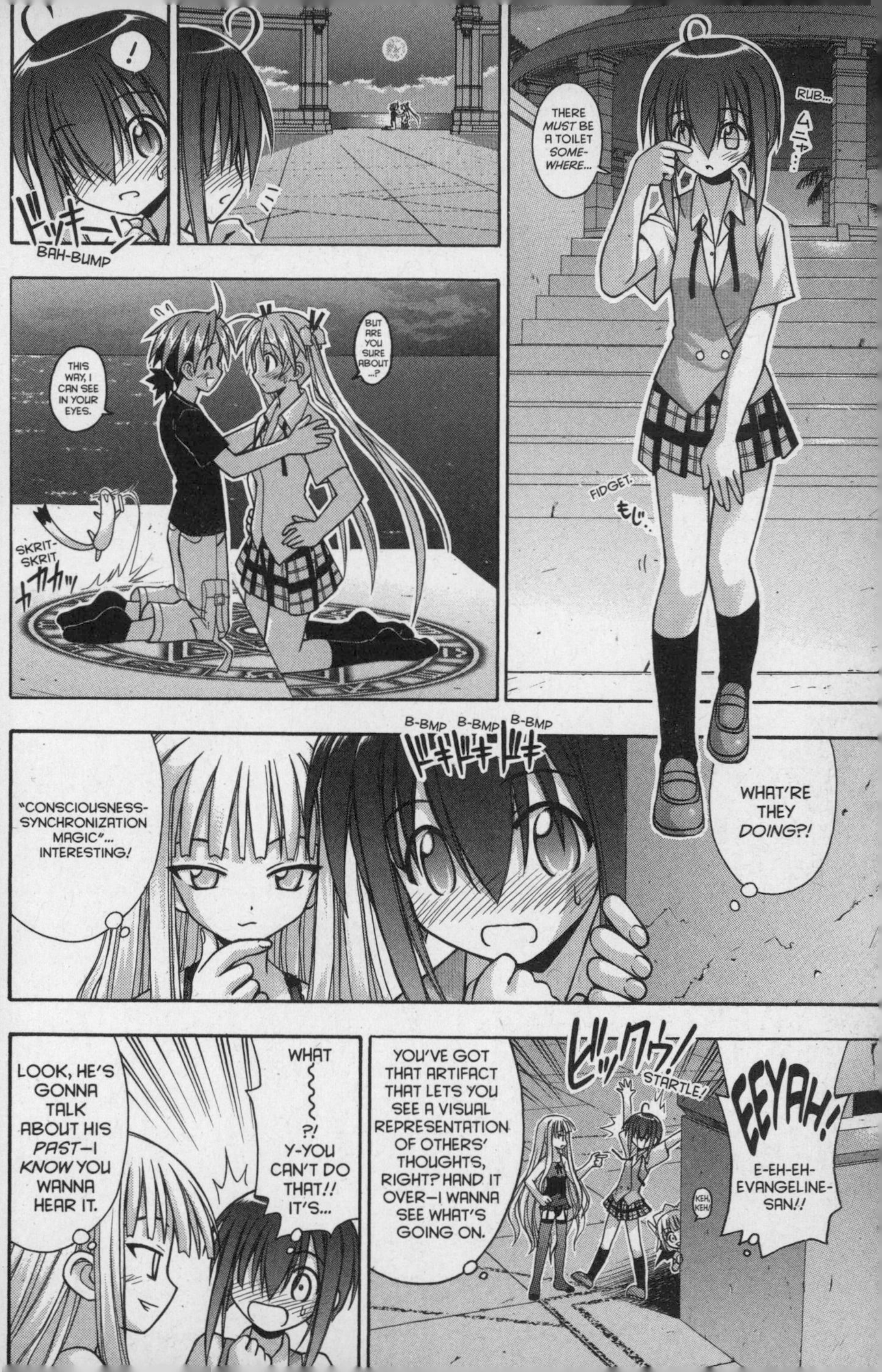

THERE MUST BE A TOILET SOMEWHERE...
RUB...
ムニャ...
FIDGET.
もじ..
!
ドッキーン
BAH-BUMP
BUT ARE YOU SURE ABOUT ...?
THIS WAY, I CAN SEE IN YOUR EYES.
SKRIT-SKRIT
カカカッ
B-BMP B-BMP B-BMP
ドキドキドキ
WHAT'RE THEY DOING?!
"CONSCIOUSNESS-SYNCHRONIZATION MAGIC"... INTERESTING!
EEYAH!
E-EH-EH-EVANGELINE-SAN!!
ビックゥ!
STARTLE!
KEH, KEH,
YOU'VE GOT THAT ARTIFACT THAT LETS YOU SEE A VISUAL REPRESENTATION OF OTHERS' THOUGHTS, RIGHT? HAND IT OVER—I WANNA SEE WHAT'S GOING ON.
WHAT ~ ?! Y-YOU CAN'T DO THAT!! IT'S...
LOOK, HE'S GONNA TALK ABOUT HIS PAST—I KNOW YOU WANNA HEAR IT.

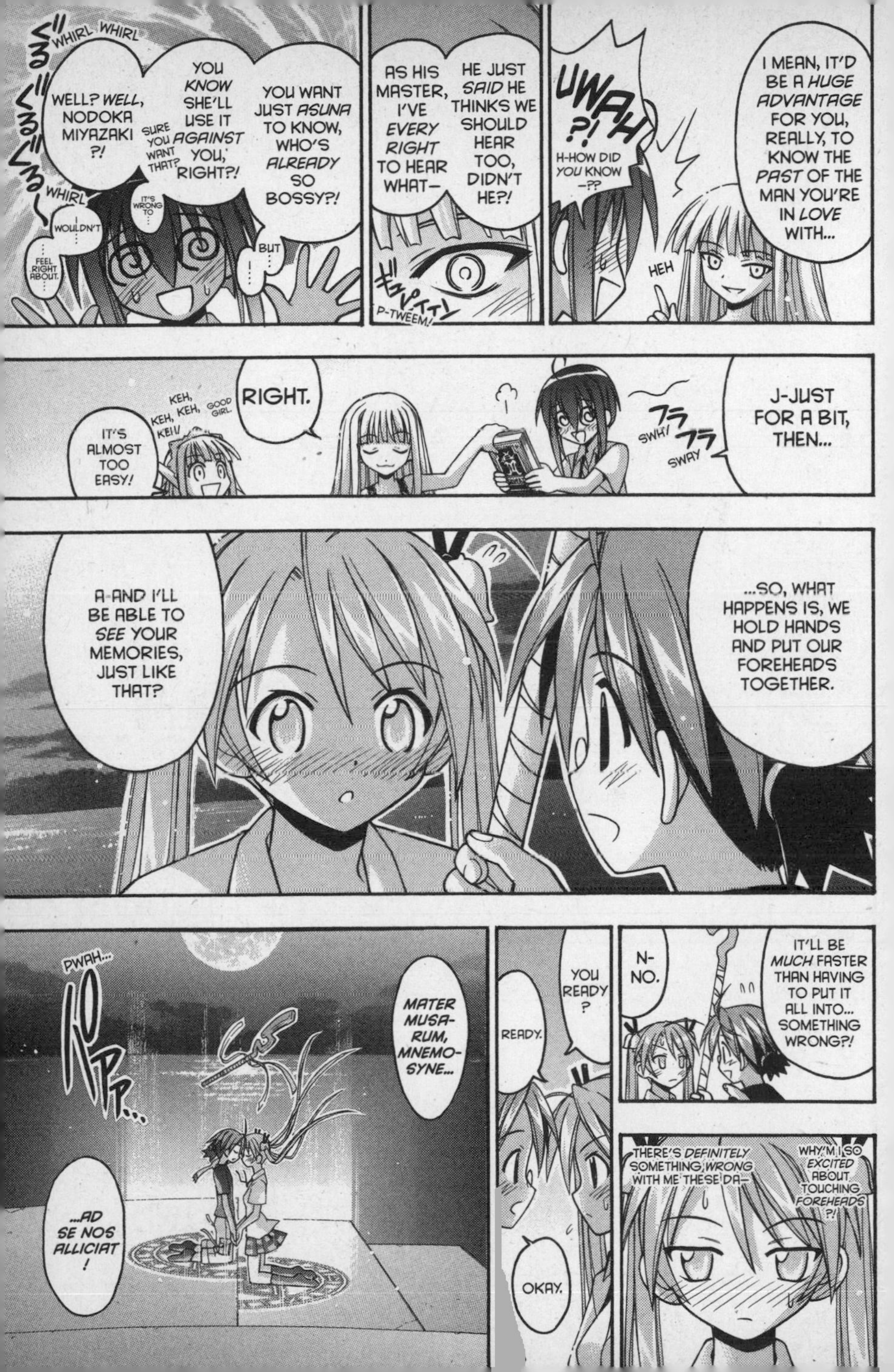
I MEAN, IT'D BE A HUGE ADVANTAGE FOR YOU, REALLY, TO KNOW THE PAST OF THE MAN YOU'RE IN LOVE WITH...
HEH
UWAH ?!
H-HOW DID YOU KNOW —??
HE JUST SAID HE THINKS WE SHOULD HEAR TOO, DIDN'T HE?!
AS HIS MASTER, I'VE EVERY RIGHT TO HEAR WHAT—
P-TWEEM!
YOU WANT JUST ASUNA TO KNOW, WHO'S ALREADY SO BOSSY?!
YOU KNOW SHE'LL USE IT AGAINST YOU, RIGHT?!
SURE YOU WANT THAT?
WELL? WELL, NODOKA MIYAZAKI ?!
WHIRL WHIRL
BUT ...
IT'S WRONG TO...
WHIRL
I WOULDN'T...
FEEL RIGHT ABOUT...
J-JUST FOR A BIT, THEN...
SWAY
SWAY
RIGHT.
GOOD GIRL.
KEH, KEH, KEH, KEH!
IT'S ALMOST TOO EASY!
...SO, WHAT HAPPENS IS, WE HOLD HANDS AND PUT OUR FOREHEADS TOGETHER.
A-AND I'LL BE ABLE TO SEE YOUR MEMORIES, JUST LIKE THAT?
IT'LL BE MUCH FASTER THAN HAVING TO PUT IT ALL INTO... SOMETHING WRONG?!
N-NO.
WHY'M I SO EXCITED ABOUT TOUCHING FOREHEADS?!
THERE'S DEFINITELY SOMETHING WRONG WITH ME THESE DA—
YOU READY?
READY.
OKAY.
MATER MUSARUM, MNEMOSYNE...
...AD SE NOS ALLICIAT!
PWAH...
POPP...

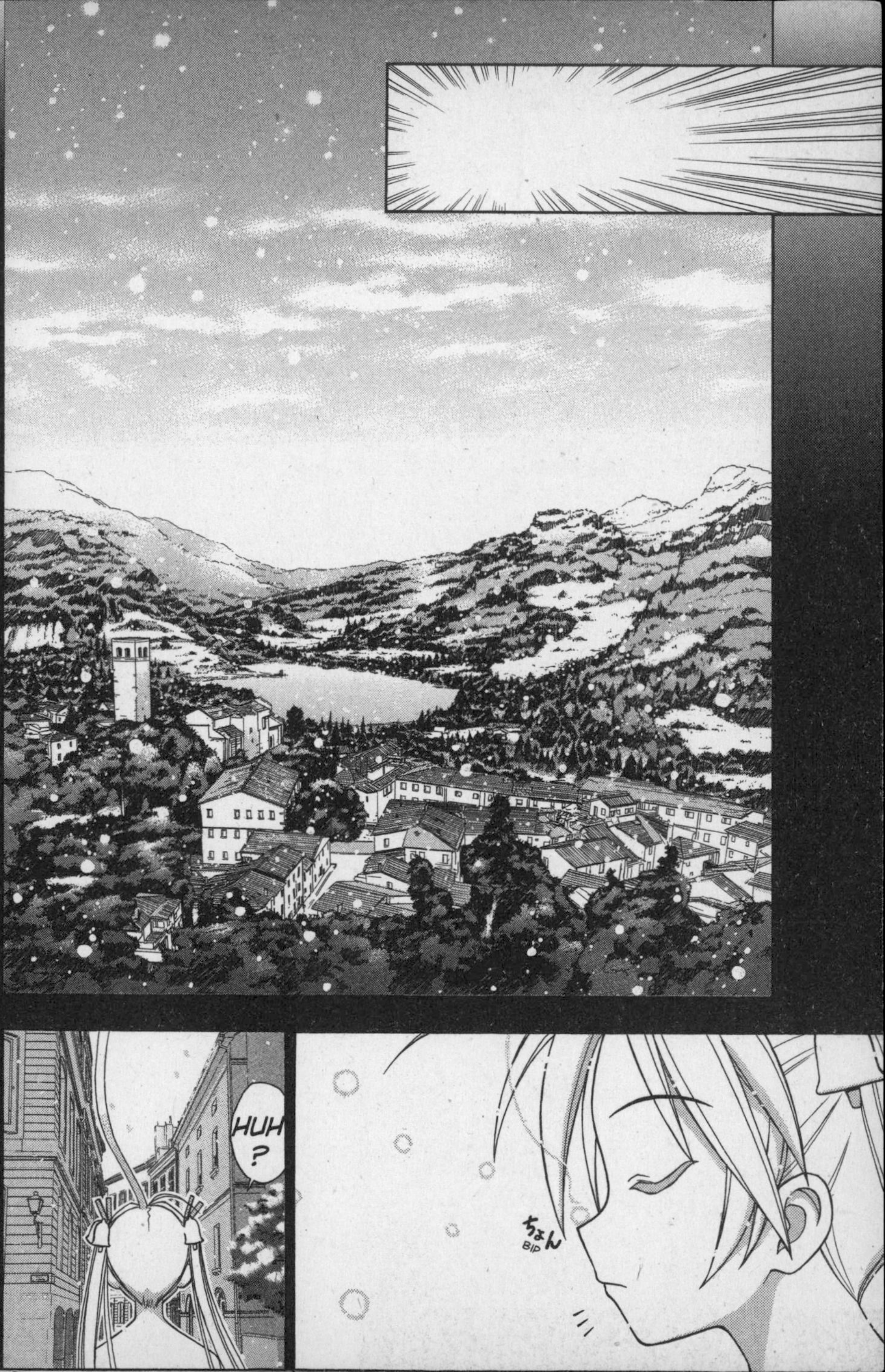
ちょん
BIP
HUH?

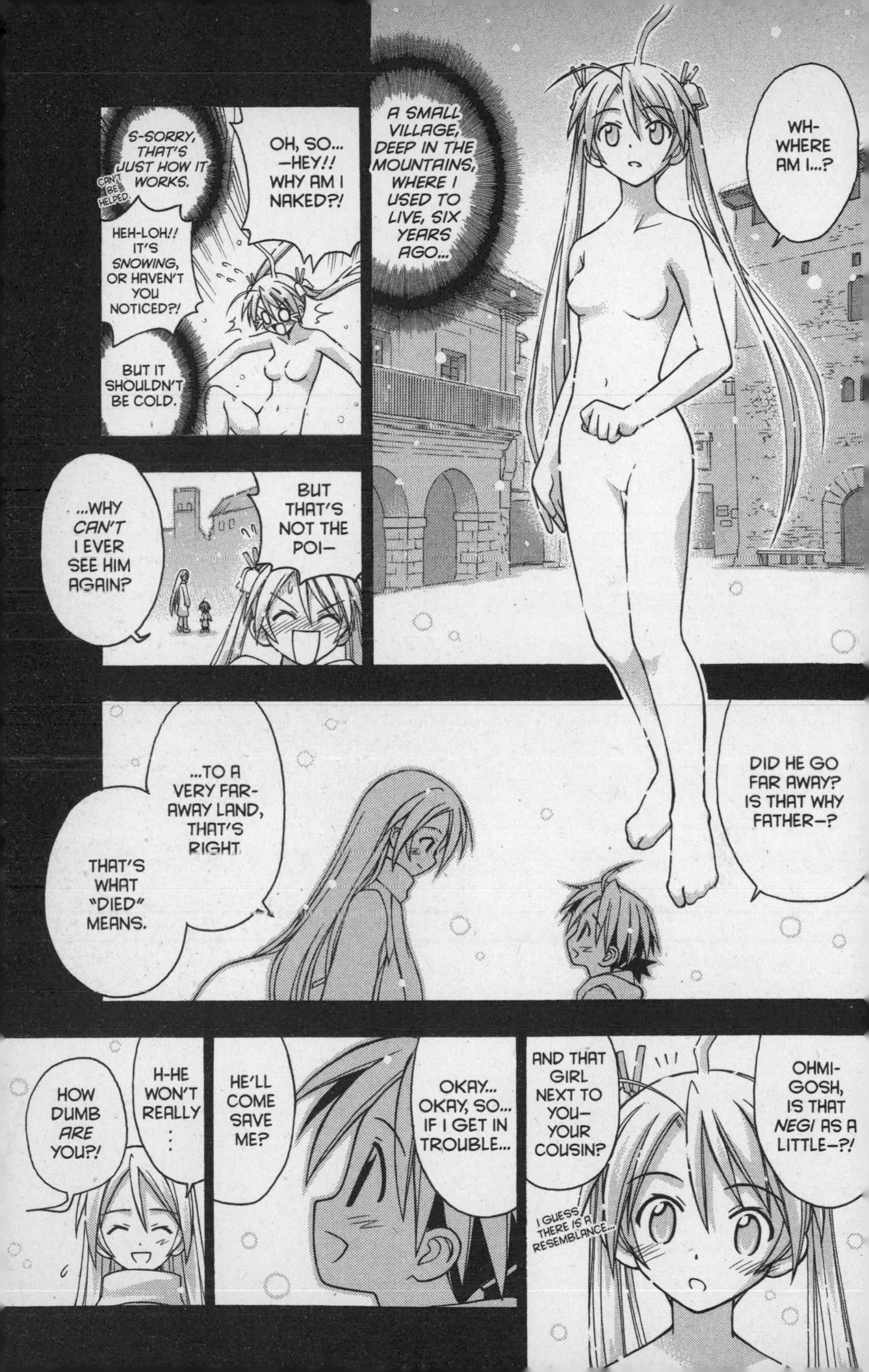
WH- WHERE AM I...?
A SMALL VILLAGE, DEEP IN THE MOUNTAINS, WHERE I USED TO LIVE, SIX YEARS AGO...
OH, SO... —HEY!! WHY AM I NAKED?!
S-SORRY, THAT'S JUST HOW IT WORKS.
CAN'T BE HELPED.
HEH-LOH!! IT'S *SNOWING*, OR HAVEN'T YOU NOTICED?!
BUT IT SHOULDN'T BE COLD.
BUT THAT'S NOT THE POI—
...WHY *CAN'T* I EVER SEE HIM AGAIN?
DID HE GO FAR AWAY? IS THAT WHY FATHER—?
...TO A VERY FAR-AWAY LAND, THAT'S RIGHT.
THAT'S WHAT "DIED" MEANS.
OHMI-GOSH, IS THAT *NEGI* AS A LITTLE—?!
AND THAT GIRL NEXT TO YOU—YOUR COUSIN?
I GUESS THERE IS A RESEMBLANCE...
OKAY... OKAY, SO... IF I GET IN TROUBLE...
HE'LL COME SAVE ME?
H-HE WON'T REALLY . . .
HOW DUMB *ARE* YOU?!

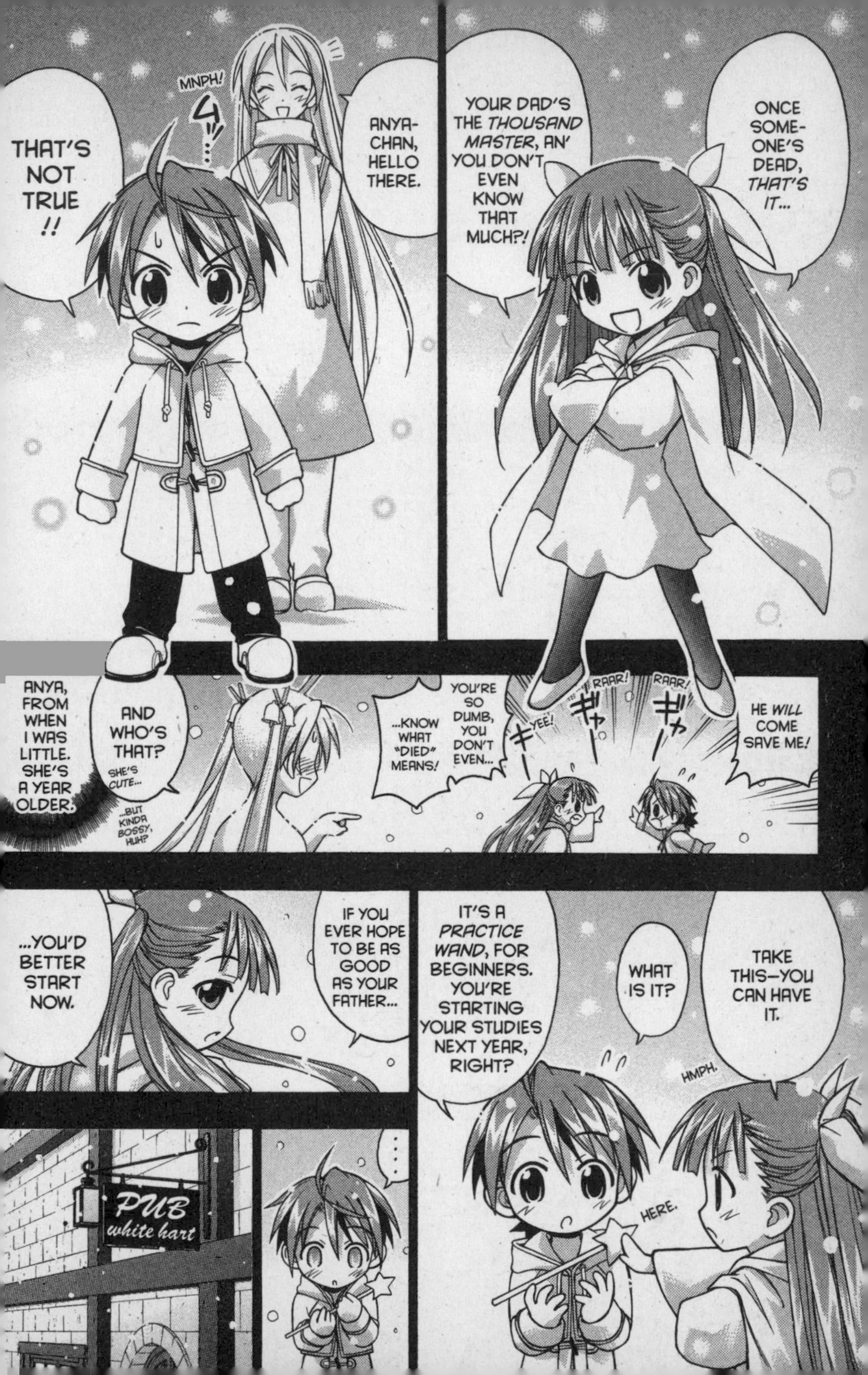
ONCE SOME-ONE'S DEAD, *THAT'S* IT...
YOUR DAD'S THE *THOUSAND MASTER*, AN' YOU DON'T EVEN KNOW THAT MUCH?!
ANYA-CHAN, HELLO THERE.
MNPH!
THAT'S NOT TRUE !!
HE *WILL* COME SAVE ME!
RAAR!
RAAR!
YEE!
YOU'RE SO DUMB, YOU DON'T EVEN...
...KNOW WHAT "DIED" MEANS!
AND WHO'S THAT?
SHE'S *CUTE*...
...BUT KINDA BOSSY, HUH?
ANYA, FROM WHEN I WAS LITTLE. SHE'S A YEAR OLDER.
TAKE THIS—YOU CAN HAVE IT.
WHAT IS IT?
IT'S A *PRACTICE WAND*, FOR BEGINNERS. YOU'RE STARTING YOUR STUDIES NEXT YEAR, RIGHT?
HMPH.
HERE.
IF YOU EVER HOPE TO BE AS GOOD AS YOUR FATHER...
...YOU'D BETTER START NOW.
.....
PUB
white hart

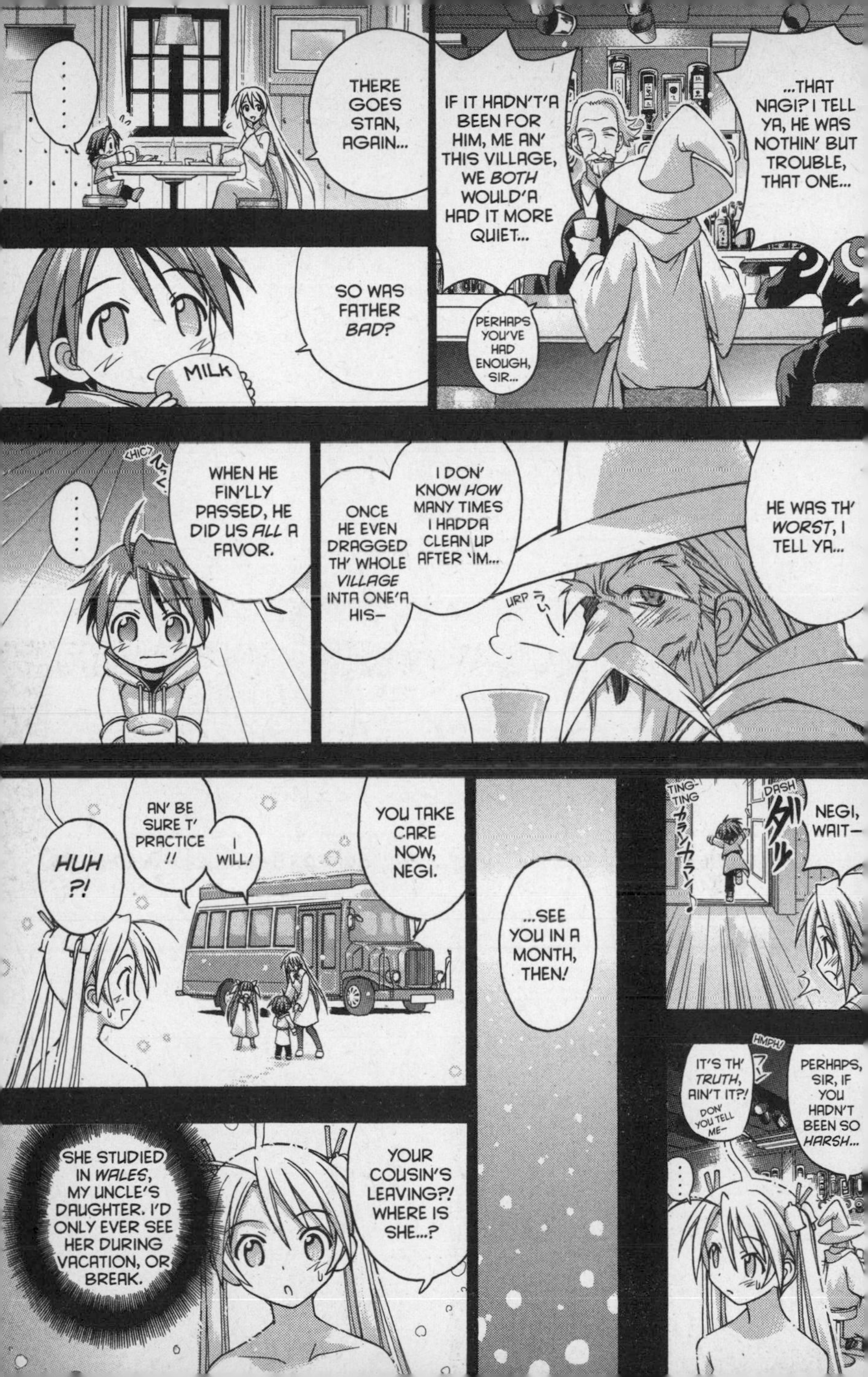
...THAT NAGI? I TELL YA, HE WAS NOTHIN' BUT TROUBLE, THAT ONE...
IF IT HADN'T'A BEEN FOR HIM, ME AN' THIS VILLAGE, WE *BOTH* WOULD'A HAD IT MORE QUIET...
PERHAPS YOU'VE HAD ENOUGH, SIR...
THERE GOES STAN, AGAIN...
......
SO WAS FATHER *BAD*?
MILK
HE WAS TH' *WORST*, I TELL YA...
I DON' KNOW *HOW* MANY TIMES I HADDA CLEAN UP AFTER 'IM...
ONCE HE EVEN DRAGGED TH' WHOLE *VILLAGE* INTA ONE'A HIS—
URP
WHEN HE FIN'LLY PASSED, HE DID US *ALL* A FAVOR.
<HIC>
......
NEGI, WAIT—
DASH
TING-TING
PERHAPS, SIR, IF YOU HADN'T BEEN SO *HARSH*...
HMPH!
IT'S TH' *TRUTH*, AIN'T IT?!
DON' YOU TELL ME—
......
...SEE YOU IN A MONTH, THEN!
YOU TAKE CARE NOW, NEGI.
AN' BE SURE T' PRACTICE!!
I WILL!
HUH?!
YOUR COUSIN'S LEAVING?! WHERE IS SHE...?
SHE STUDIED IN *WALES*, MY UNCLE'S DAUGHTER. I'D ONLY EVER SEE HER DURING VACATION, OR BREAK.

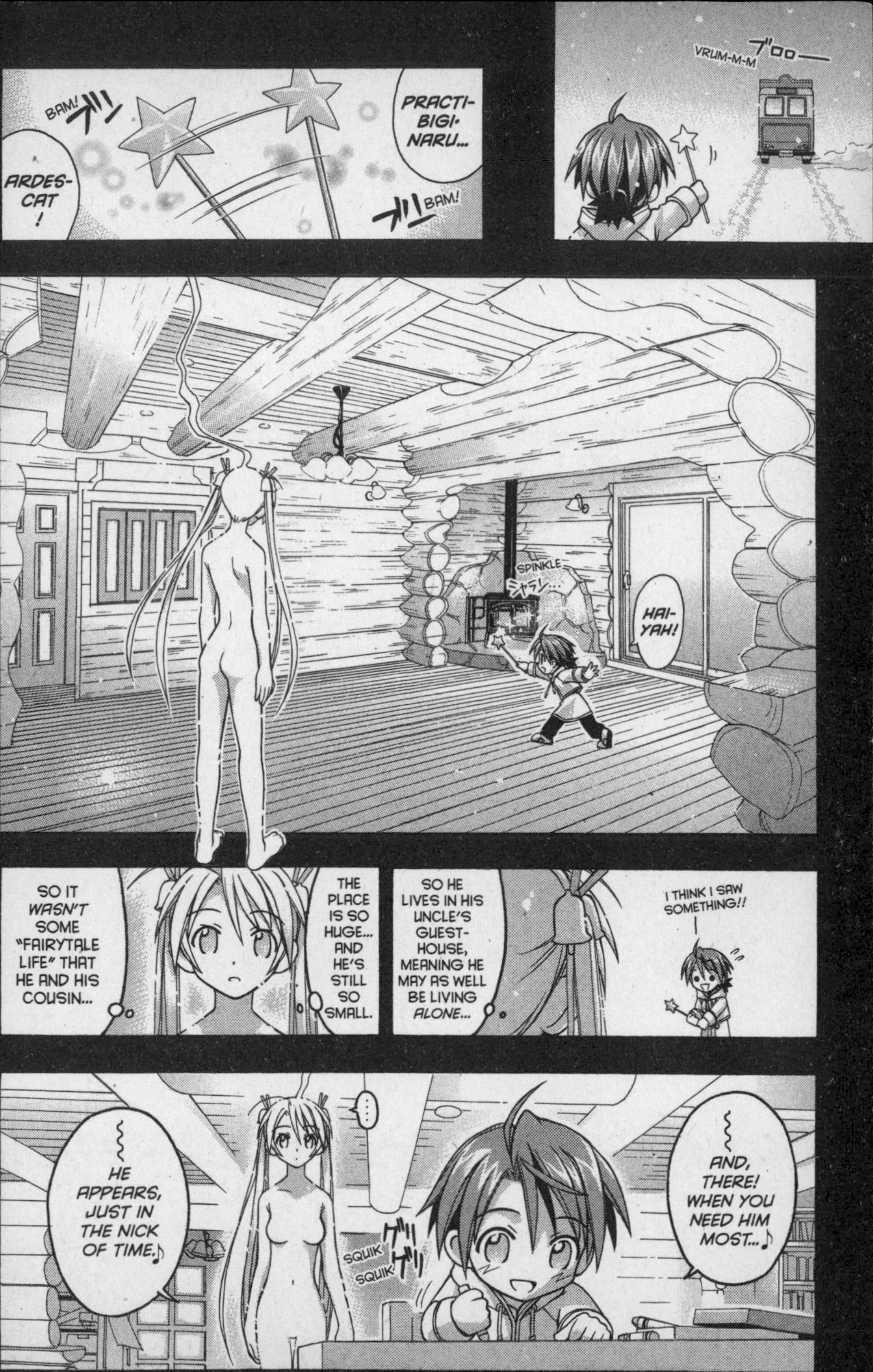
VRUM-M-M ブロロー
PRACTI-BIGI-NARU...
BAM! ブン
ARDES-CAT!
ブン BAM!
HAI-YAH!
SPINKLE シャラン...
I THINK I SAW SOMETHING!!
SO HE LIVES IN HIS UNCLE'S GUEST-HOUSE, MEANING HE MAY AS WELL BE LIVING ALONE...
THE PLACE IS SO HUGE... AND HE'S STILL SO SMALL.
SO IT WASN'T SOME "FAIRYTALE LIFE" THAT HE AND HIS COUSIN...
AND, THERE! WHEN YOU NEED HIM MOST...♪
....
SQUIK SQUIK ギリギリ
HE APPEARS, JUST IN THE NICK OF TIME.♪

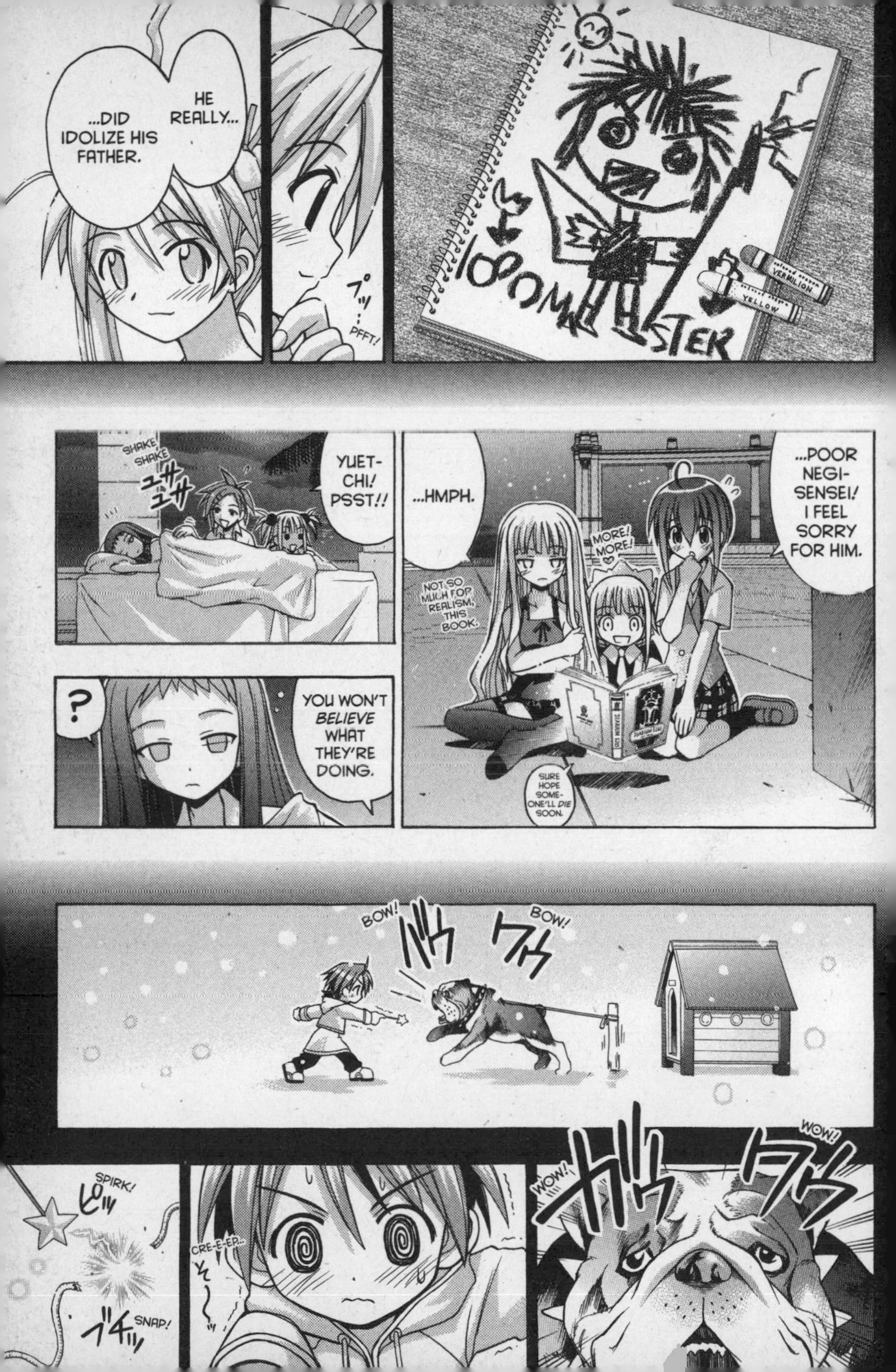
VERMILION
YELLOW
プッ
PFFT!
HE REALLY...
...DID IDOLIZE HIS FATHER.
...POOR NEGI-SENSEI! I FEEL SORRY FOR HIM.
MORE! MORE!
...HMPH.
NOT SO MUCH FOR REALISM, THIS BOOK.
SURE HOPE SOME-ONE'LL DIE SOON.
YUET-CHI! PSST!!
SHAKE SHAKE
ユサユサ
YOU WON'T BELIEVE WHAT THEY'RE DOING.
?
BOW!
バウ
BOW!
ワウ
WOW!
ガウ
WOW!
ウウ
CRE-E-EP...
SPIRK!
ピッ
SNAP!
ブチッ

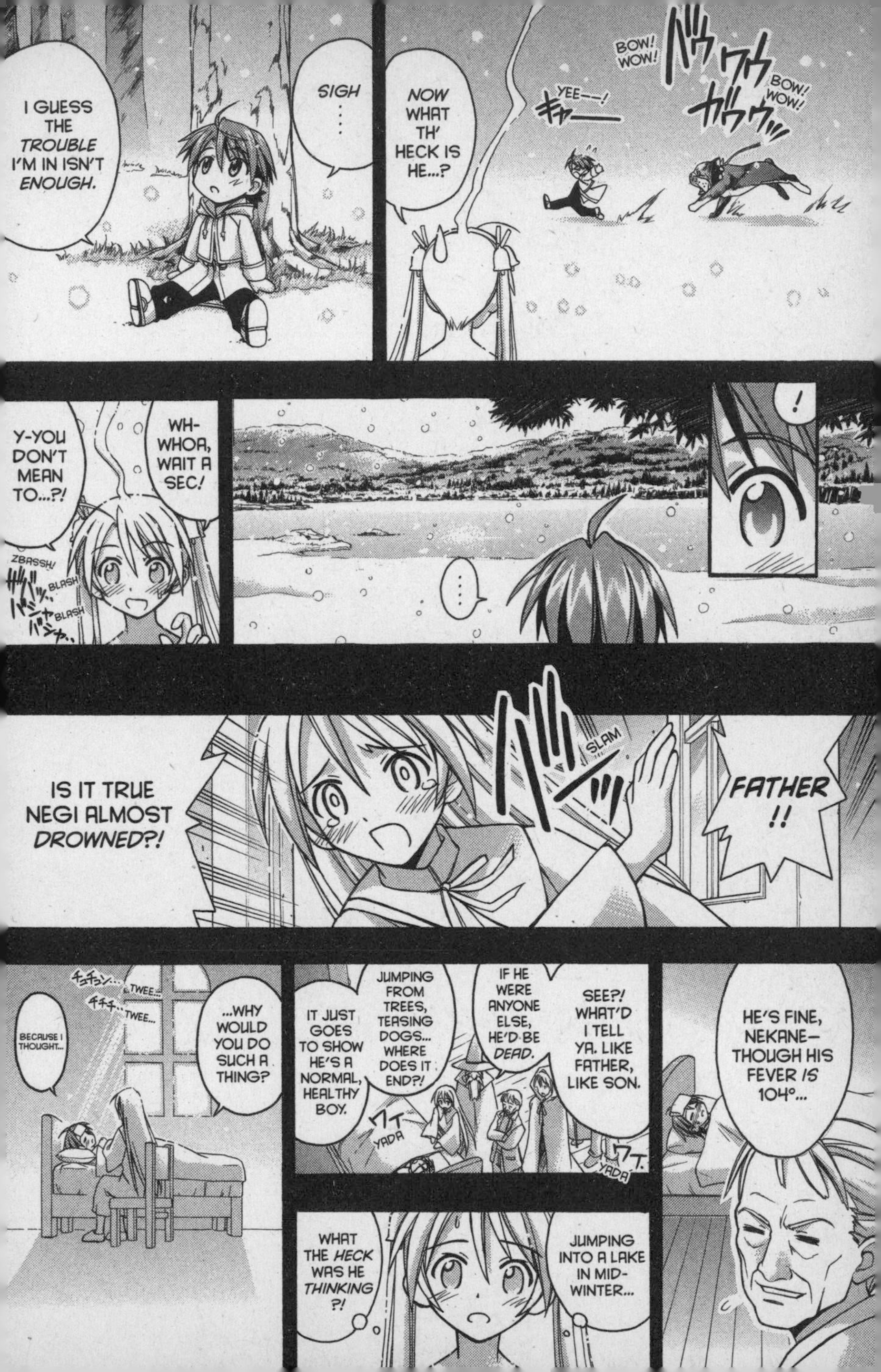
BOW! WOW!
BOW! WOW!
YEE—!
NOW WHAT TH' HECK IS HE...?
SIGH ...
I GUESS THE TROUBLE I'M IN ISN'T ENOUGH.
!
...
WH-WHOA, WAIT A SEC!
Y-YOU DON'T MEAN TO...?!
ZBASSH!
BLASH
BLASH
FATHER!!
SLAM
IS IT TRUE NEGI ALMOST DROWNED?!
HE'S FINE, NEKANE—THOUGH HIS FEVER IS 104°...
SEE?! WHAT'D I TELL YA. LIKE FATHER, LIKE SON.
IF HE WERE ANYONE ELSE, HE'D BE DEAD.
JUMPING FROM TREES, TEASING DOGS... WHERE DOES IT END?!
IT JUST GOES TO SHOW HE'S A NORMAL, HEALTHY BOY.
YADA
YADA
JUMPING INTO A LAKE IN MID-WINTER...
WHAT THE HECK WAS HE THINKING?!
...WHY WOULD YOU DO SUCH A THING?
TWEE...
TWEE...
BECAUSE I THOUGHT...

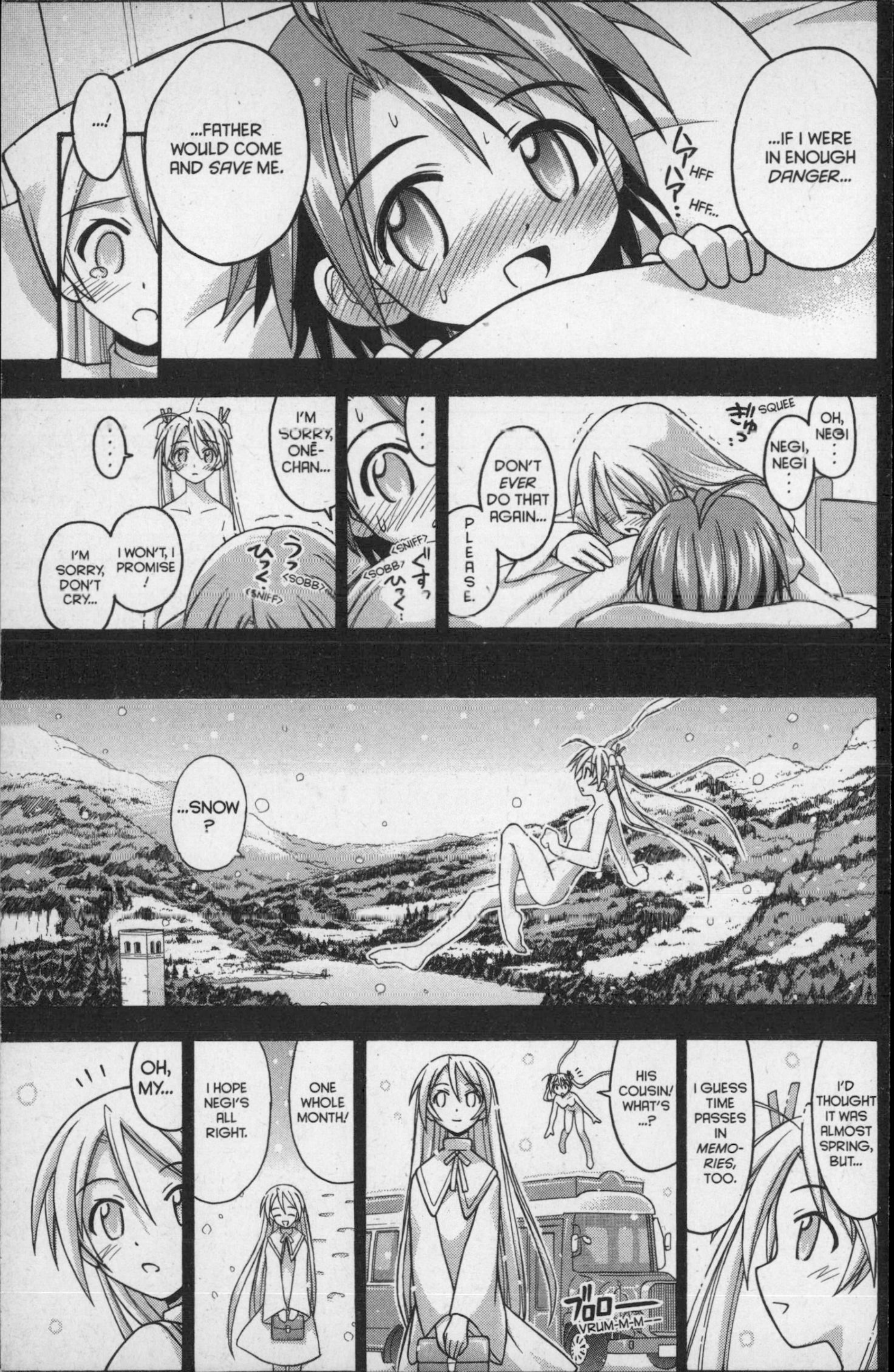
...IF I WERE IN ENOUGH DANGER...
ハァハァ… HFF HFF...
...FATHER WOULD COME AND SAVE ME.
...!
きゅっ SQUEE
OH, NEGI...
NEGI, NEGI...
DON'T EVER DO THAT AGAIN...
PLEASE.
...
ぐすっ <SNIFF>
ひっく… <SOBB>
I'M SORRY, ONĒ-CHAN...
...
うっ <SOBB>
ひっく <SNIFF>
I WON'T, I PROMISE!
I'M SORRY, DON'T CRY...
...SNOW?
I'D THOUGHT IT WAS ALMOST SPRING, BUT...
I GUESS TIME PASSES IN MEMORIES, TOO.
HIS COUSIN! WHAT'S ...?
ブロロー VRUM-M-M
ONE WHOLE MONTH!
I HOPE NEGI'S ALL RIGHT.
OH, MY...

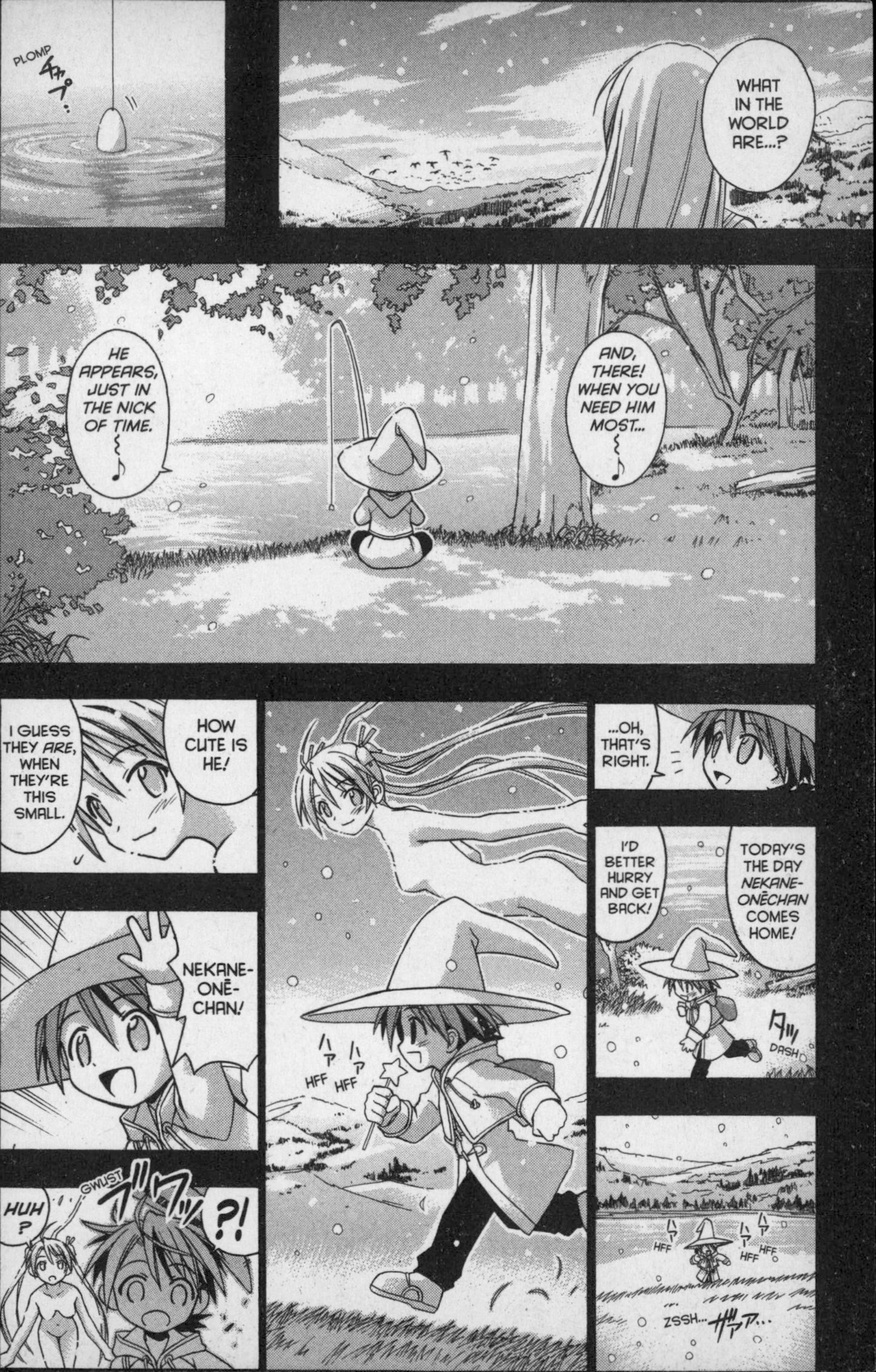
WHAT IN THE WORLD ARE...?
PLOMP
チャプ..
AND, THERE! WHEN YOU NEED HIM MOST...~♪
HE APPEARS, JUST IN THE NICK OF TIME.~♪
...OH, THAT'S RIGHT.
TODAY'S THE DAY NEKANE-ONĒCHAN COMES HOME!
I'D BETTER HURRY AND GET BACK!
タッ DASH
ハァ HFF
ハァ HFF
ZSSH... ザァ...
ハァ HFF
ハァ HFF
HOW CUTE IS HE!
I GUESS THEY ARE, WHEN THEY'RE THIS SMALL.
NEKANE-ONĒ-CHAN!
?!
GWUST ブワッ
HUH?

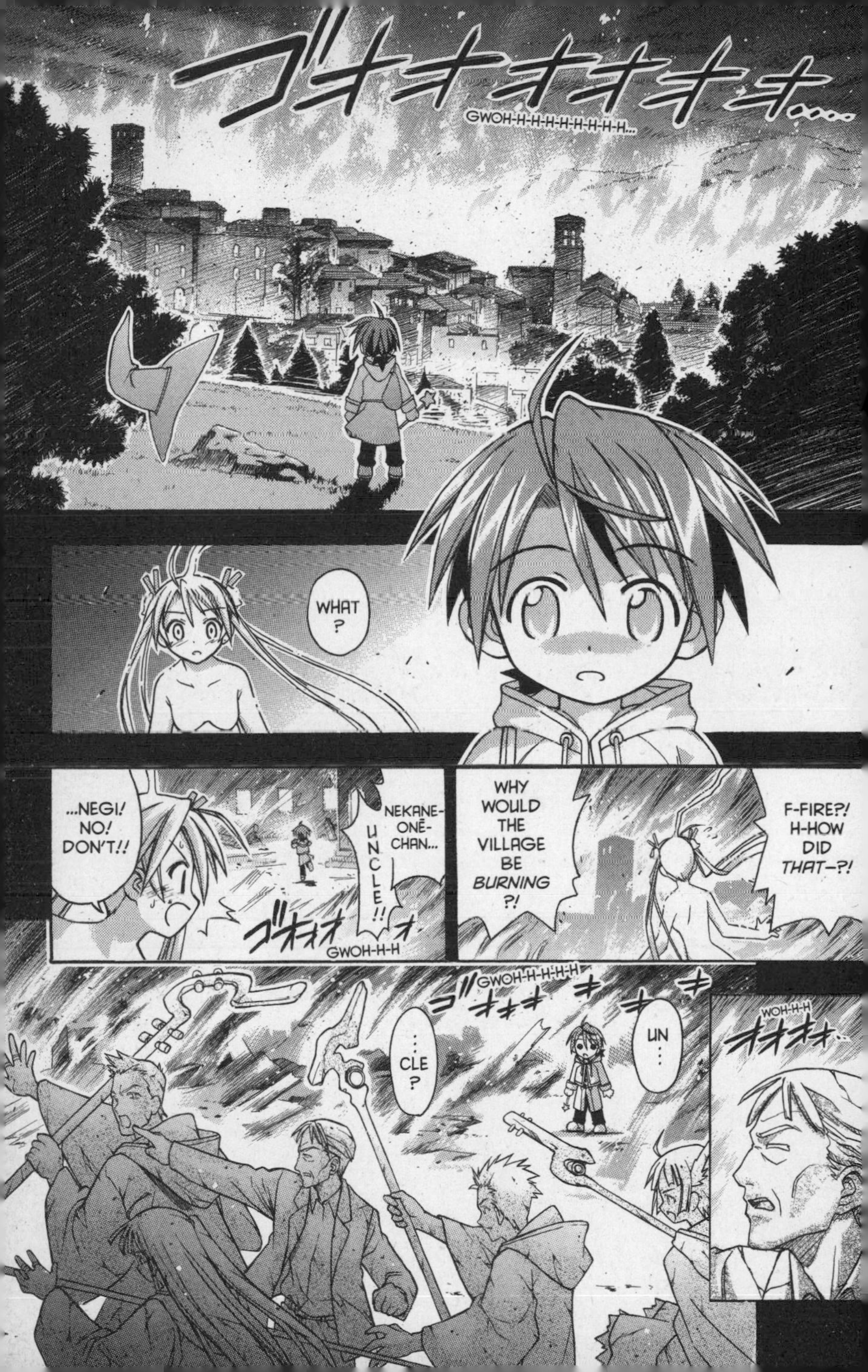
ゴオオオオオオオオ...
GWOH-H-H-H-H-H-H-H-H...
WHAT?
F-FIRE?! H-HOW DID THAT—?!
WHY WOULD THE VILLAGE BE BURNING?!
NEKANE-ONĒ-CHAN...
UNCLE!!
GWOH-H-H
...NEGI! NO! DON'T!!
WOH-H-H
GWOH-H-H-H-H
UN...
...CLE?

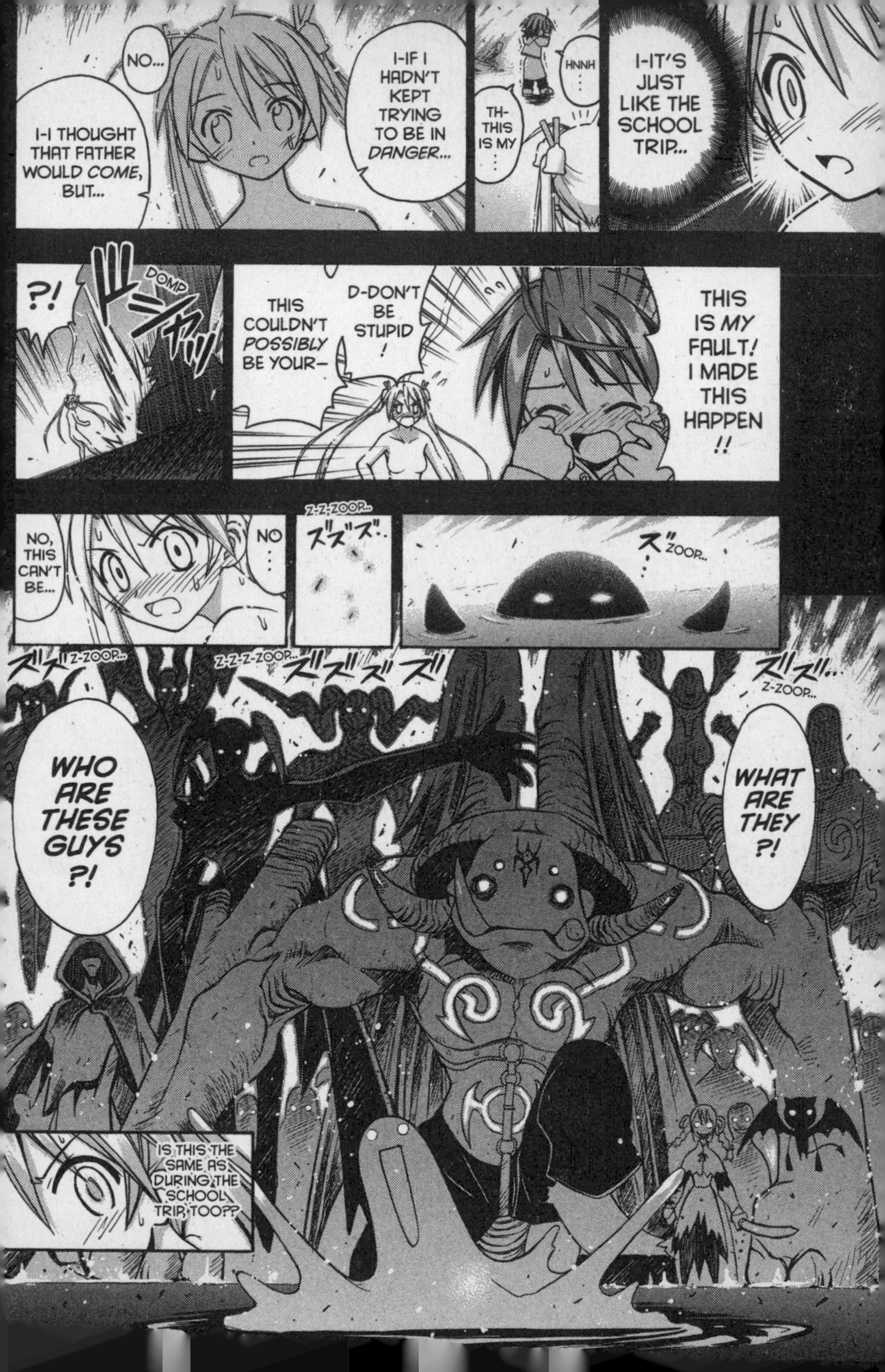
I-IT'S JUST LIKE THE SCHOOL TRIP...
HNNH...
TH-THIS IS MY...
I-IF I HADN'T KEPT TRYING TO BE IN *DANGER*...
NO...
I-I THOUGHT THAT FATHER WOULD *COME*, BUT...
THIS IS *MY* FAULT! I MADE THIS HAPPEN!!
D-DON'T BE STUPID!
THIS COULDN'T *POSSIBLY* BE YOUR–
DOMP
?!
ズ ZOOP...
ズズズ Z-Z-ZOOP...
NO...
NO, THIS CAN'T BE...
ズズ Z-ZOOP...
WHAT ARE THEY?!
ズズズズ Z-Z-Z-ZOOP...
ズズ Z-ZOOP...
WHO ARE THESE GUYS?!
IS THIS THE SAME AS DURING THE SCHOOL TRIP, TOO??

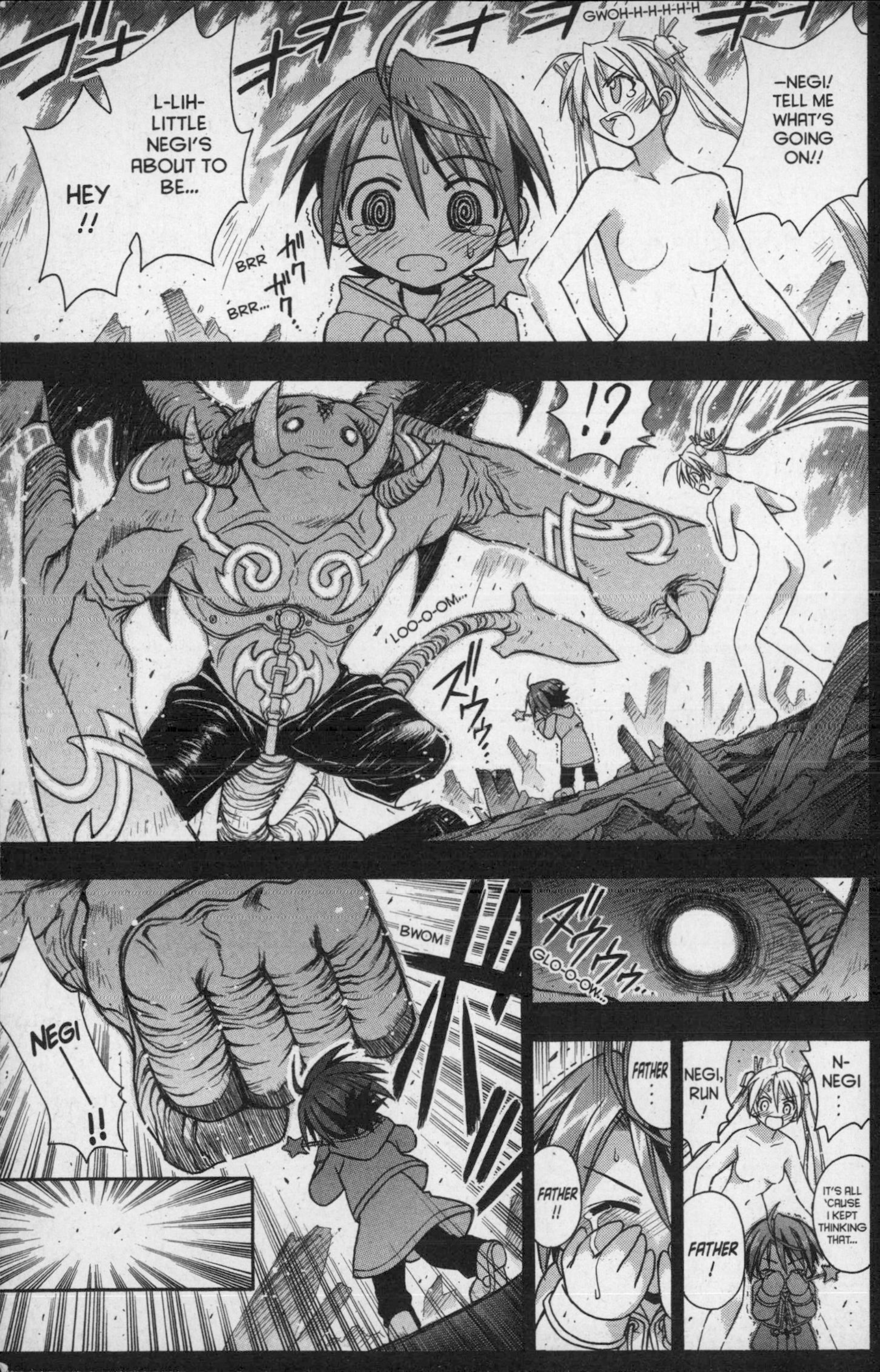
GWOH-H-H-H-H-H
—NEGI! TELL ME WHAT'S GOING ON!!
L-LIH-LITTLE NEGI'S ABOUT TO BE...
HEY !!
BRR
BRR...
!?
LOO-O-OM...
GLO-O-OW...
N-NEGI...
NEGI, RUN!
FATHER...
IT'S ALL 'CAUSE I KEPT THINKING THAT...
FATHER!
FATHER!!
BWOM
NEGI—!!

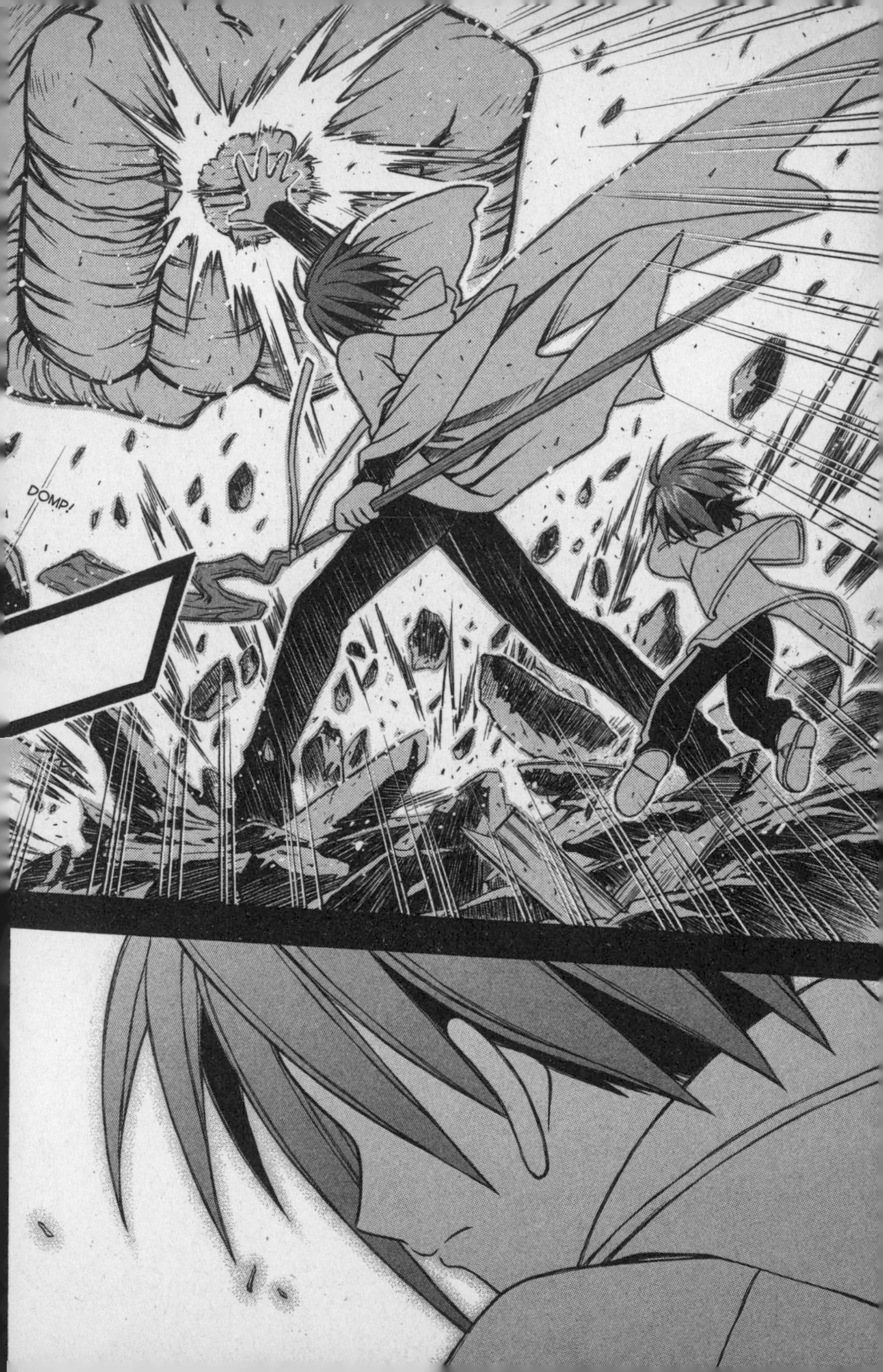
DOMP!

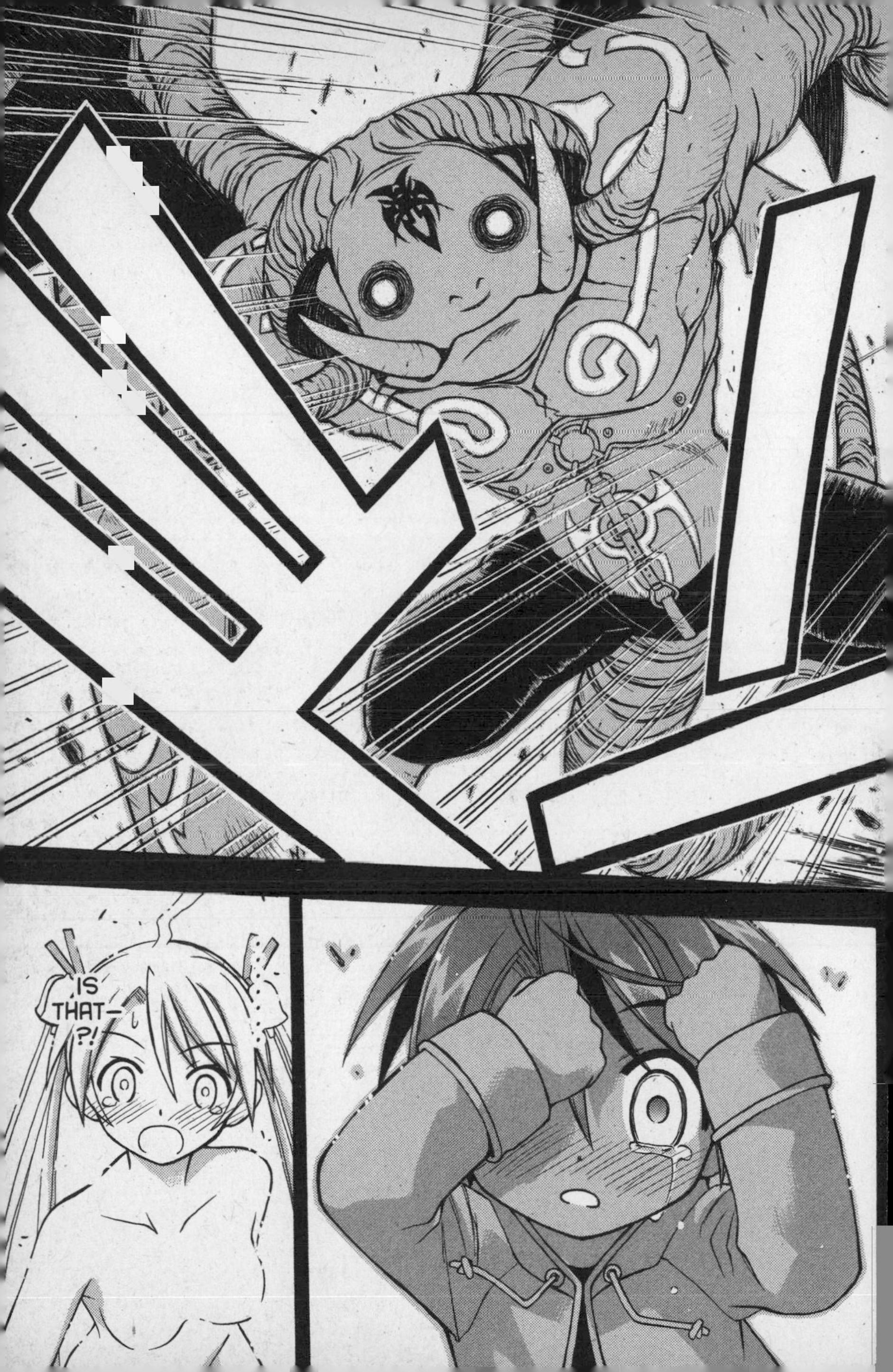
IS THAT—?!

NEGIMA!
MAGISTER NEGI MAGI

SIXTY-FOURTH to SIXTY-FIFTH PERIOD: "MAGIC WORD" LEXICON

■「火よ、灯れ。」

ARDESCAT

In producing upon invocation only the smallest of flame upon the tip of the caster's wand, this spell may at first seem insignificant, but because it can create flame even in vacuum, its usefulness should not be underestimated. Unlike a "natural" flame, then, the nature of a flame produced by the "Ardescat" spell may be considered to be magical.

True as Negi's joke that it'd be "easier to use a lighter" may be, there is of course deeper meaning for novice mages to begin their study of the magical arts with the summoning of fire. As Plato writes in *Protagoras,*

> "Once upon a time there were gods only, and no mortal creatures. But when the time came that these also should be created, the gods fashioned them out of earth and fire and various mixtures of both elements in the interior of the earth; and when they were about to bring them into the light of day, they ordered Prometheus and Epimetheus to equip them, and to distribute to them severally their proper qualities. Epimetheus said to Prometheus: 'Let me distribute, and do you inspect'.... The appointed hour was approaching when man in his turn was to go forth into the light of day; and Prometheus, not knowing how he could devise his salvation, stole the mechanical arts of Hephaestus and Athene, and fire with them (they could neither have been acquired nor used without fire), and gave them to man. Thus man had the wisdom necessary to the support of life..." (320c–321d).

As this passage from Greek mythology about their cultural heroes shows, fire is integral in the development of the learned technologies. Therefore, as mastering fire was the first step in the development of man, so should it be the first step in the development of a mage—to create something (fire) from nothing. Because of its mythological background, even Negi himself started with this spell....

■ ï

RAN

According to the Japanese religious reference *Shugēn Hashira Moto Shinpo,* the five root words of the word 阿尾羅吽欠 are detailed in the *Taizokaī Mandara,* a collection of mantras credited to Buddha Dainichi Nyorai ("Mahavairocana" in Sanskrit). Of those five roots— 阿 ("A"), 尾 ("VA"), 羅 ("RA"), 吽 ("KA"), and 欠 ("KYA")—each can be attributed to the elements earth, water, fire, wind, and air (void). Add a "dot" accent mark above it, and 羅 ("RA") becomes ï or *ran,* or "fire of knowledge."

■「ムーサ達の母、ムネーモシュネーよ。おのがもとへと我らを誘え。」

MATER MUSARUM, MNEMOSYNE, AD SE NOS ALLICIAT

The spell that allows the target to experience or share the memories of the caster. Mnemosyne is the personification of memory and its goddess; she is also the mother of the Nine Muses (cf. Hesiod's *Theogony,* ll. 51-54, 914-197). Normally, it would be impossible even for the caster to re-experience the actual visual and auditory stimuli of the past; such moments are of the present (*praesentia*) and, once they have passed into the past, may no longer be accessed. As Aristotle once said, "Without the existence of the soul, time cannot exist...."

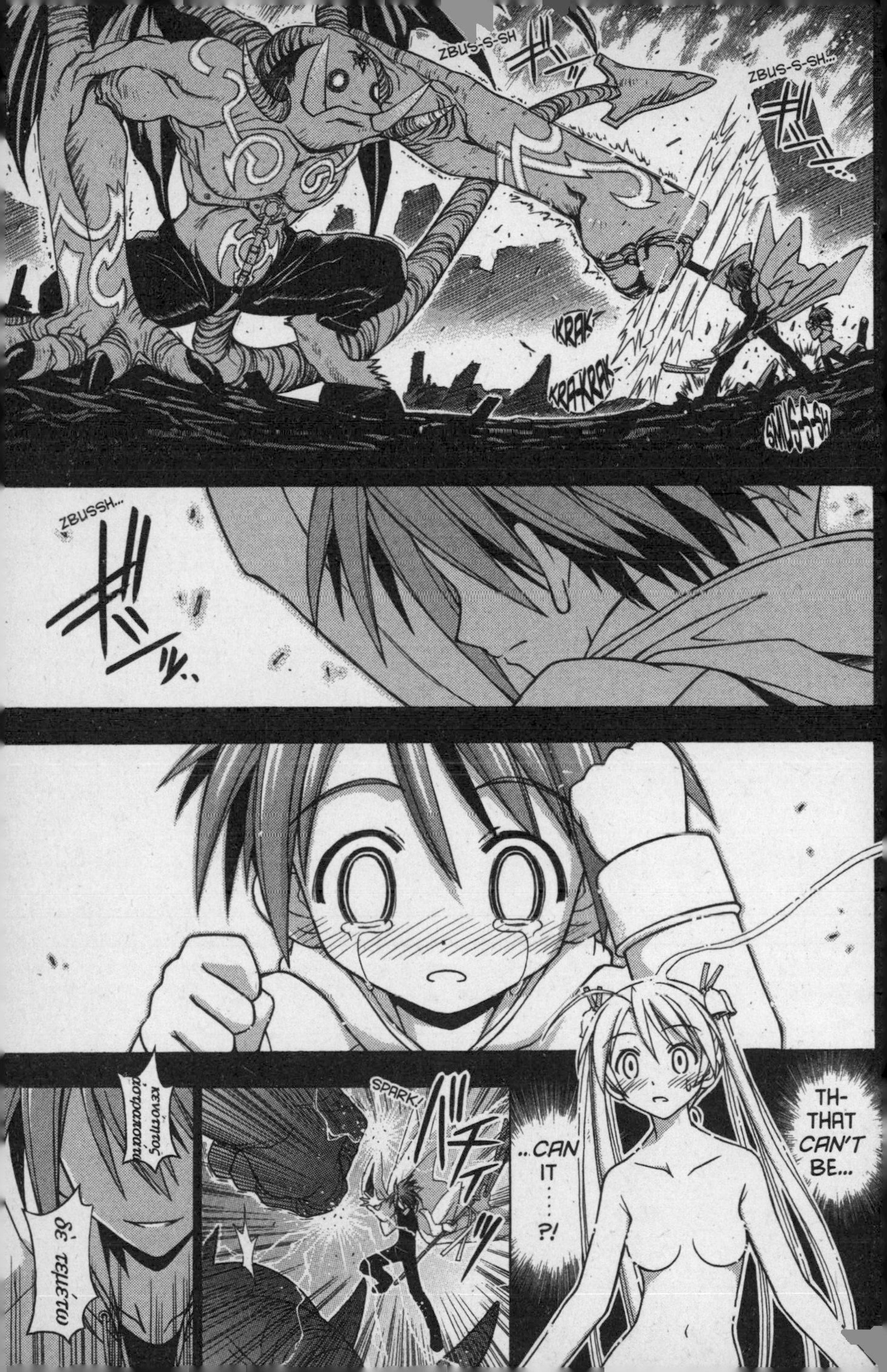
ZBUS-S-SH
ZBUS-S-SH...
KRAK
KRA-KRAK
SHUS-S-SH
ZBUSSH...
TH-THAT CAN'T BE...
...CAN IT.....?!
SPARK!

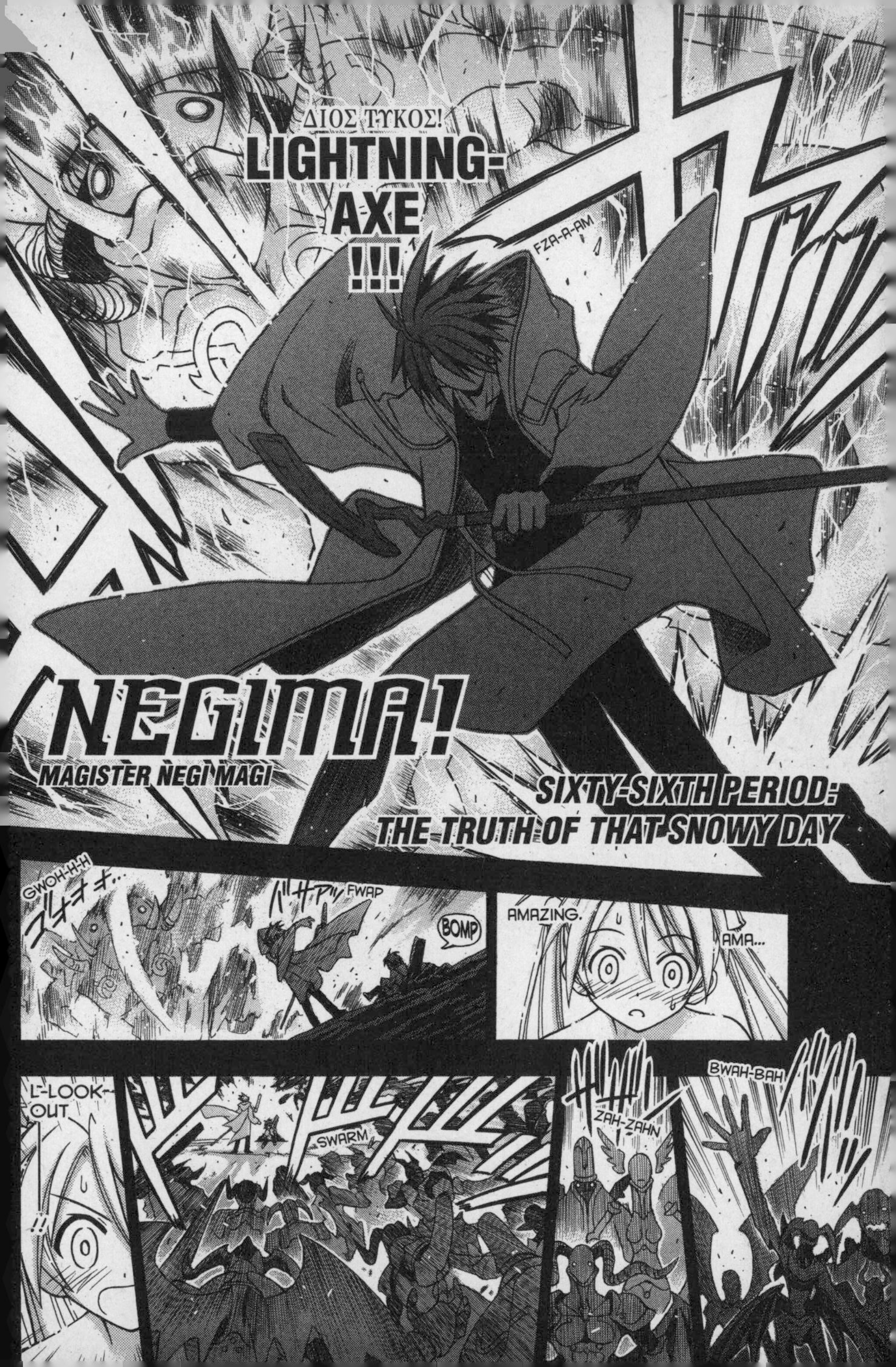
ΔΙΟΣ ΤΥΚΟΣ!
LIGHTNING-AXE!!!
FZA-A-AM
NEGIMA!
MAGISTER NEGI MAGI
SIXTY-SIXTH PERIOD: THE TRUTH OF THAT SNOWY DAY
AMAZING.
AMA...
FWAP
BOMP
GWOH-H-H
BWAH-BAH
ZAH-ZAHN
SWARM
L-LOOK-OUT
!!

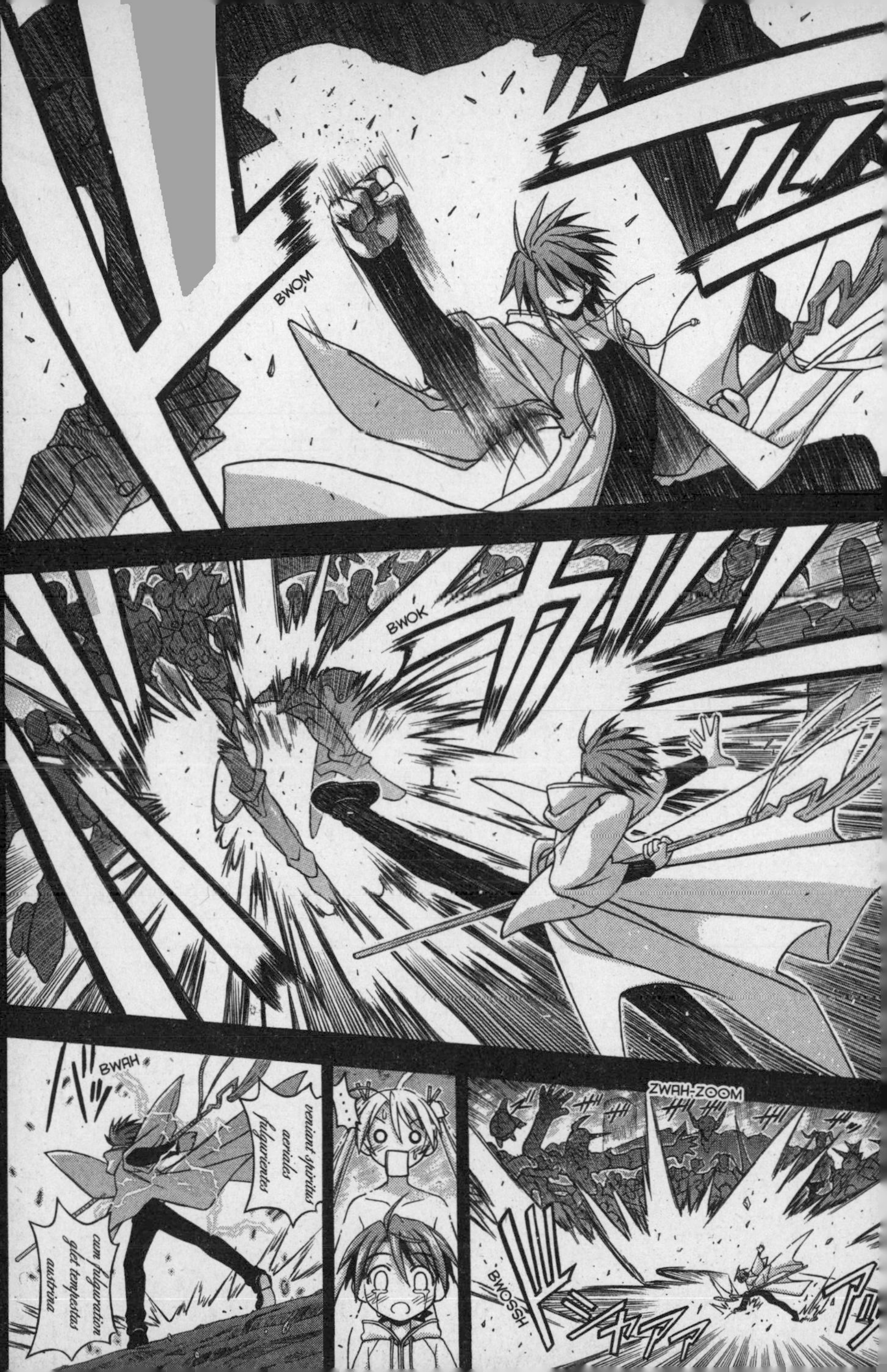
BWOM
BWOK
ZWAH-ZOOM
BWOSSH
BWAH
veniant spiritus aeriales fulgurientes
cum fulguration flet tempestas austrina

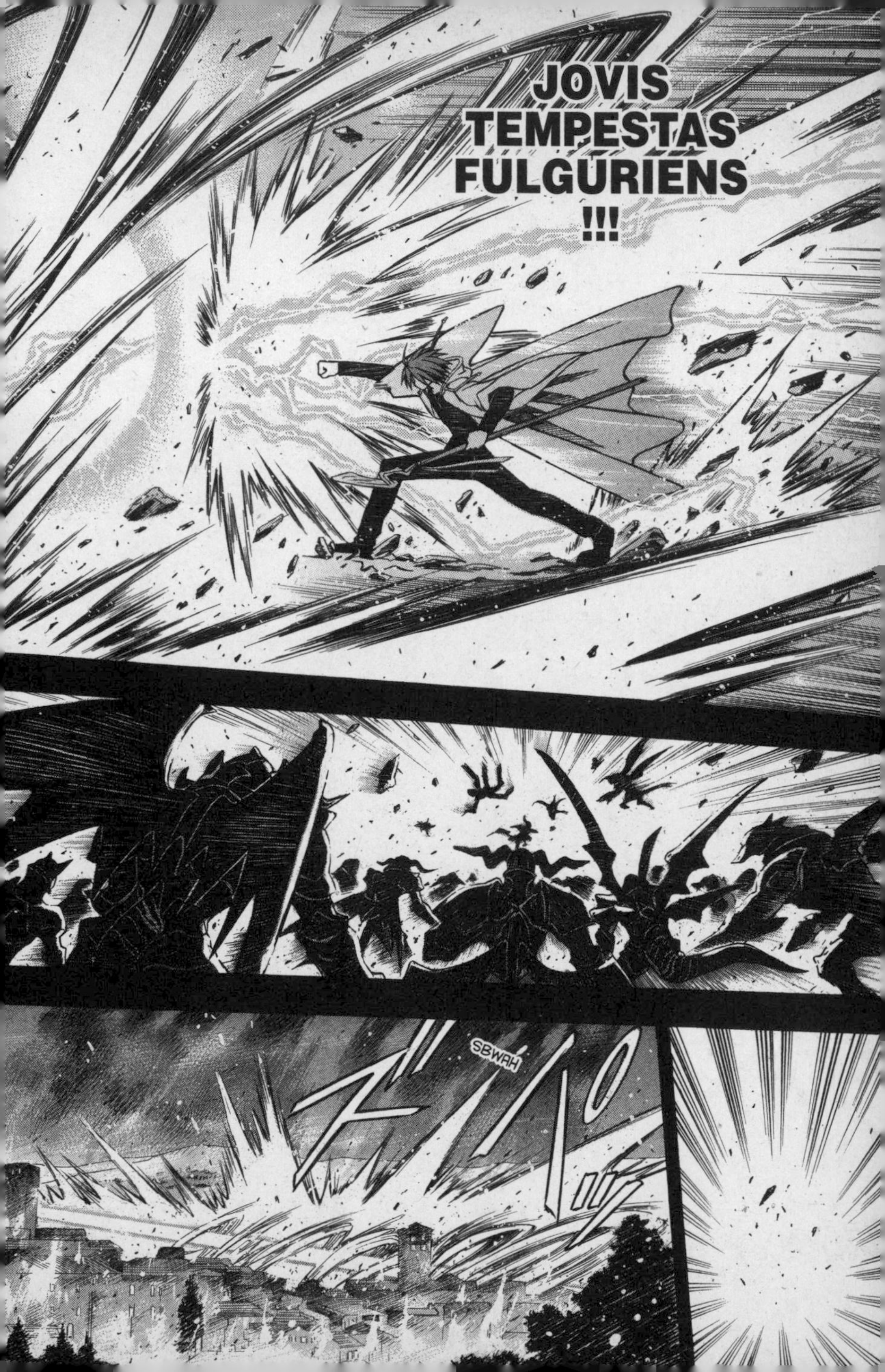
JOVIS TEMPESTAS FULGURIENS !!!
SBWAH

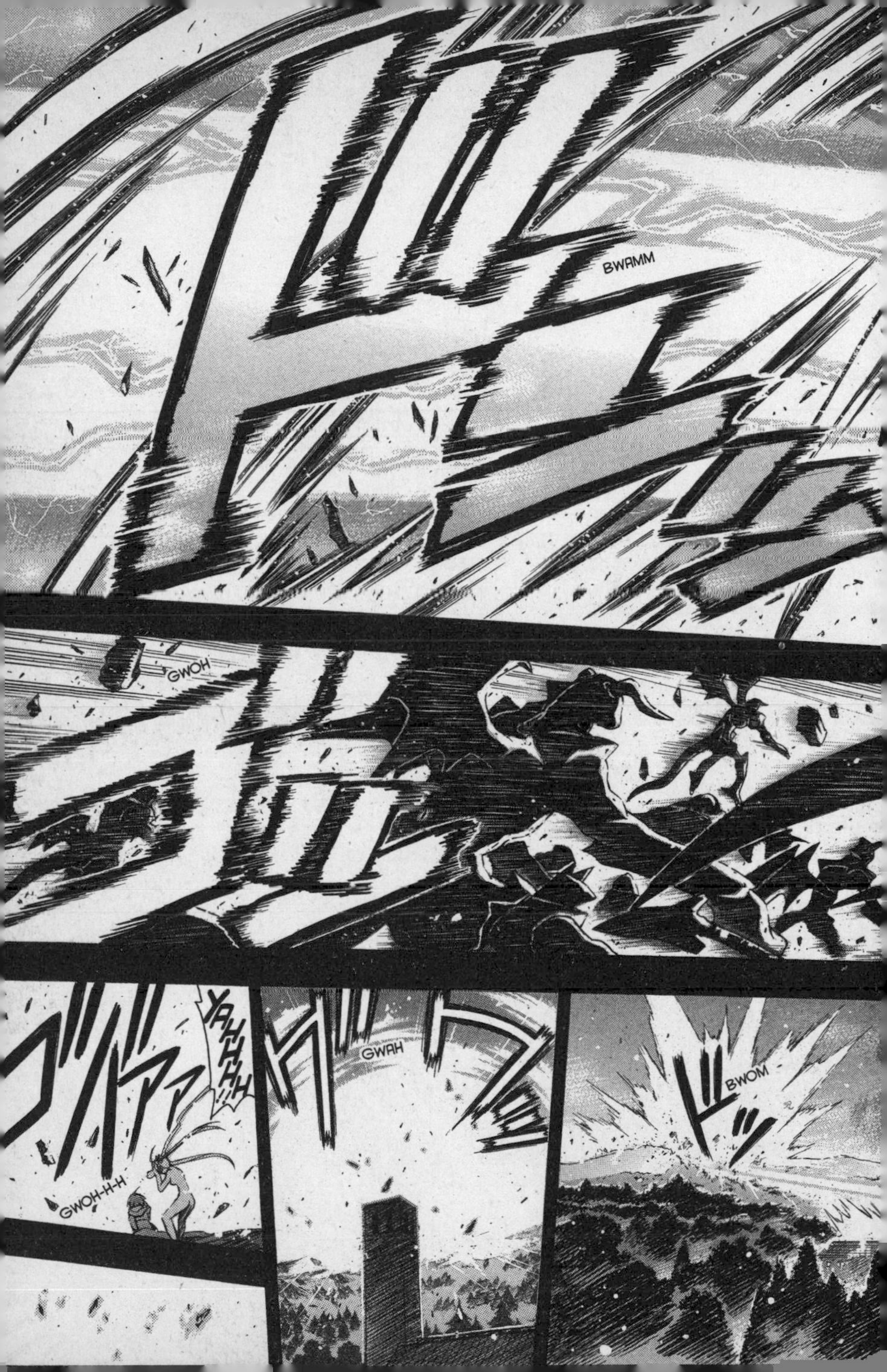
BWAMM
GWOH
BWOM
GWAH
YAHHHH!!!
GWOH-H-H

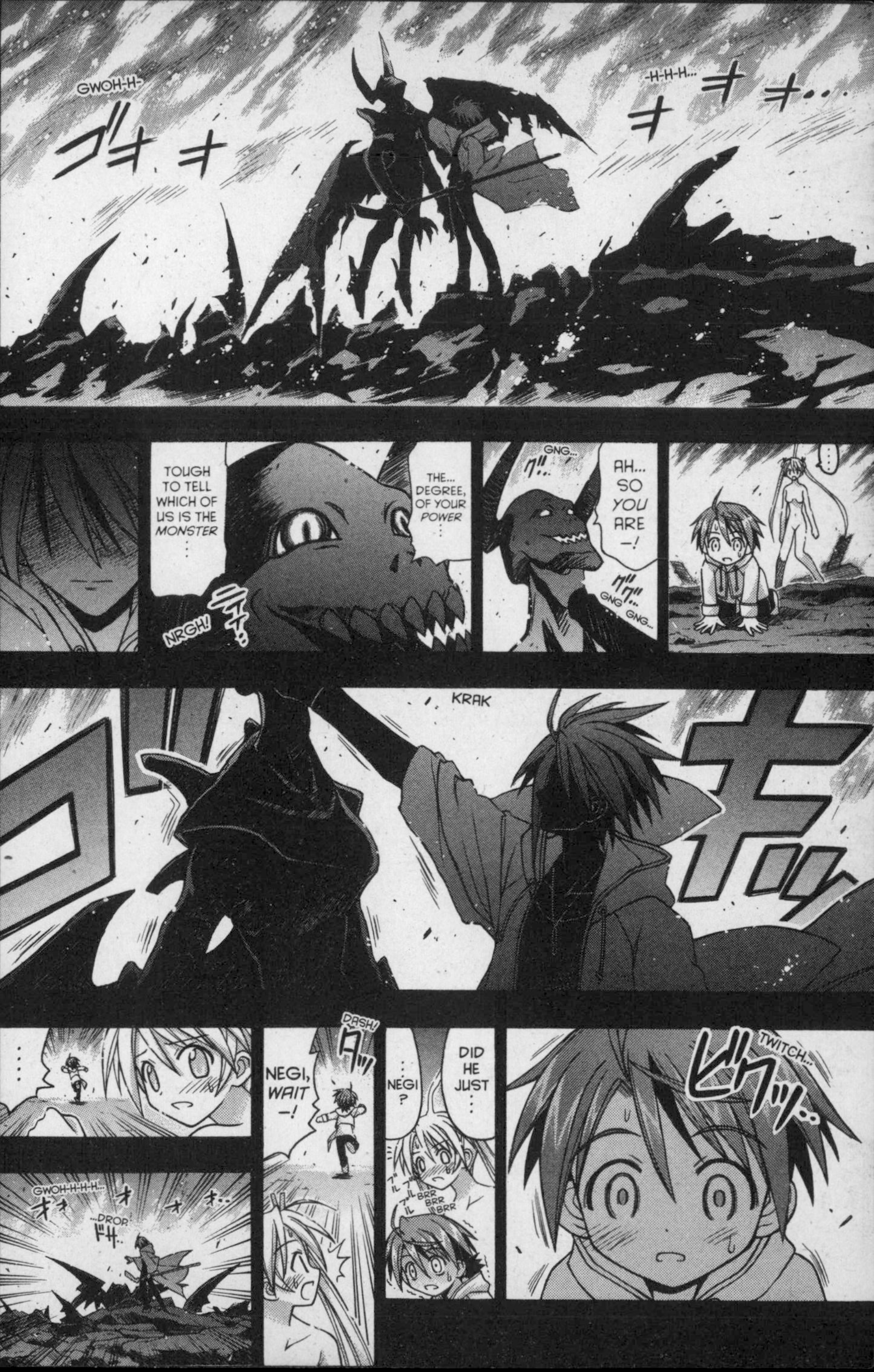
GWOH-H-
-H-H-H...
…
GNG GNG...
AH... SO *YOU* ARE —!
GNG...
THE... DEGREE, OF YOUR *POWER* ...
TOUGH TO TELL WHICH OF US IS THE *MONSTER* ...
NRGH!
KRAK
TWITCH...
DID HE JUST ...
...NEGI?
BRR BRR
DASH!
NEGI, WAIT —!
...
GWOH-H-H-H...
...DROP

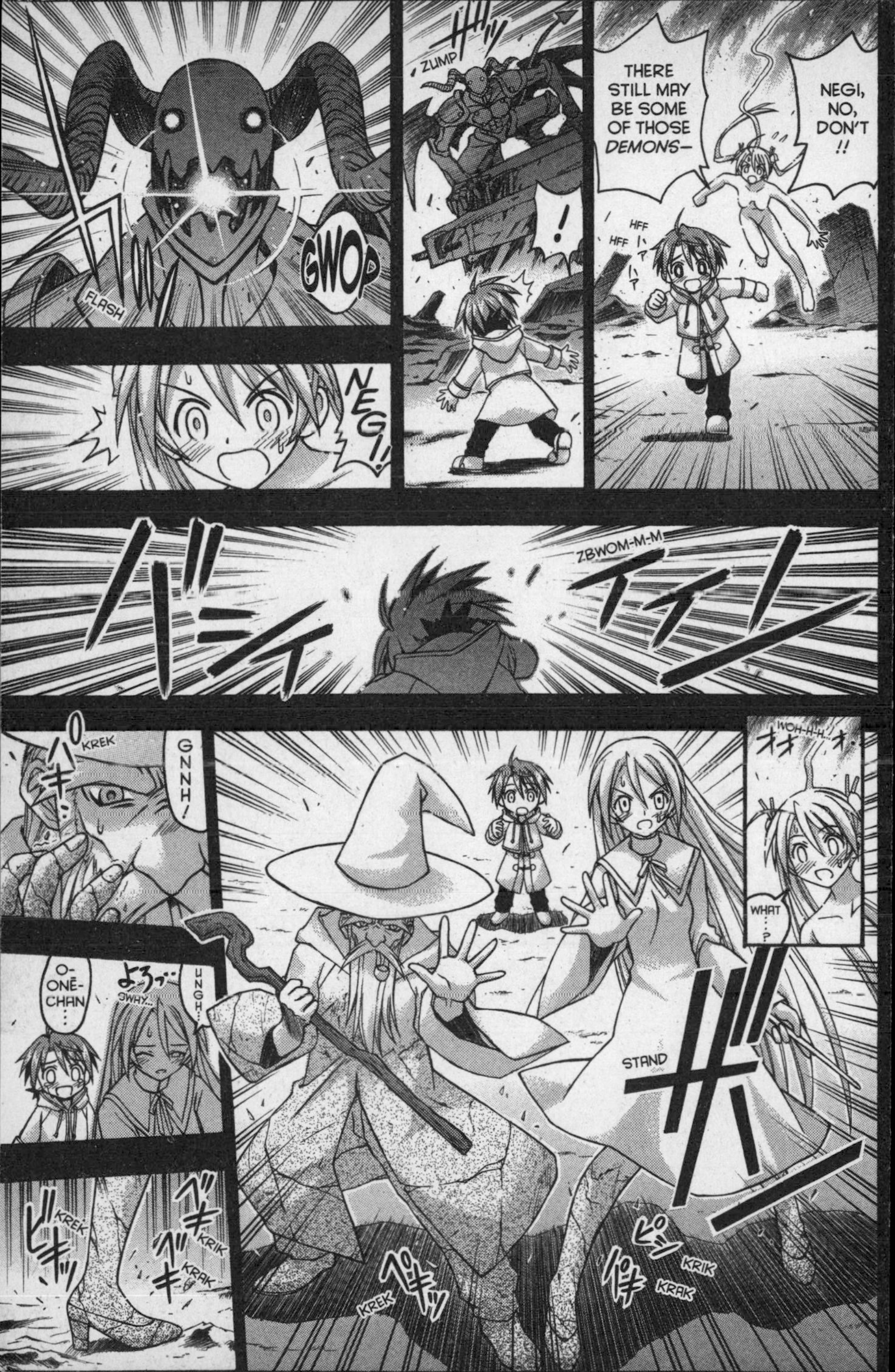
NEGI, NO, DON'T !!
THERE STILL MAY BE SOME OF THOSE *DEMONS*—
HFF HFF
ZUMP
!
GWOP
FLASH
NEGI!!
ZBWOM-M-M
WOH-H-H...
WHAT ...?
STAND
KRIK KRAK
KREK
KREK
GNNH!
UNGH...
SWAY...
O-ONĒ-CHAN ...
KREK
KRIK
KRAK

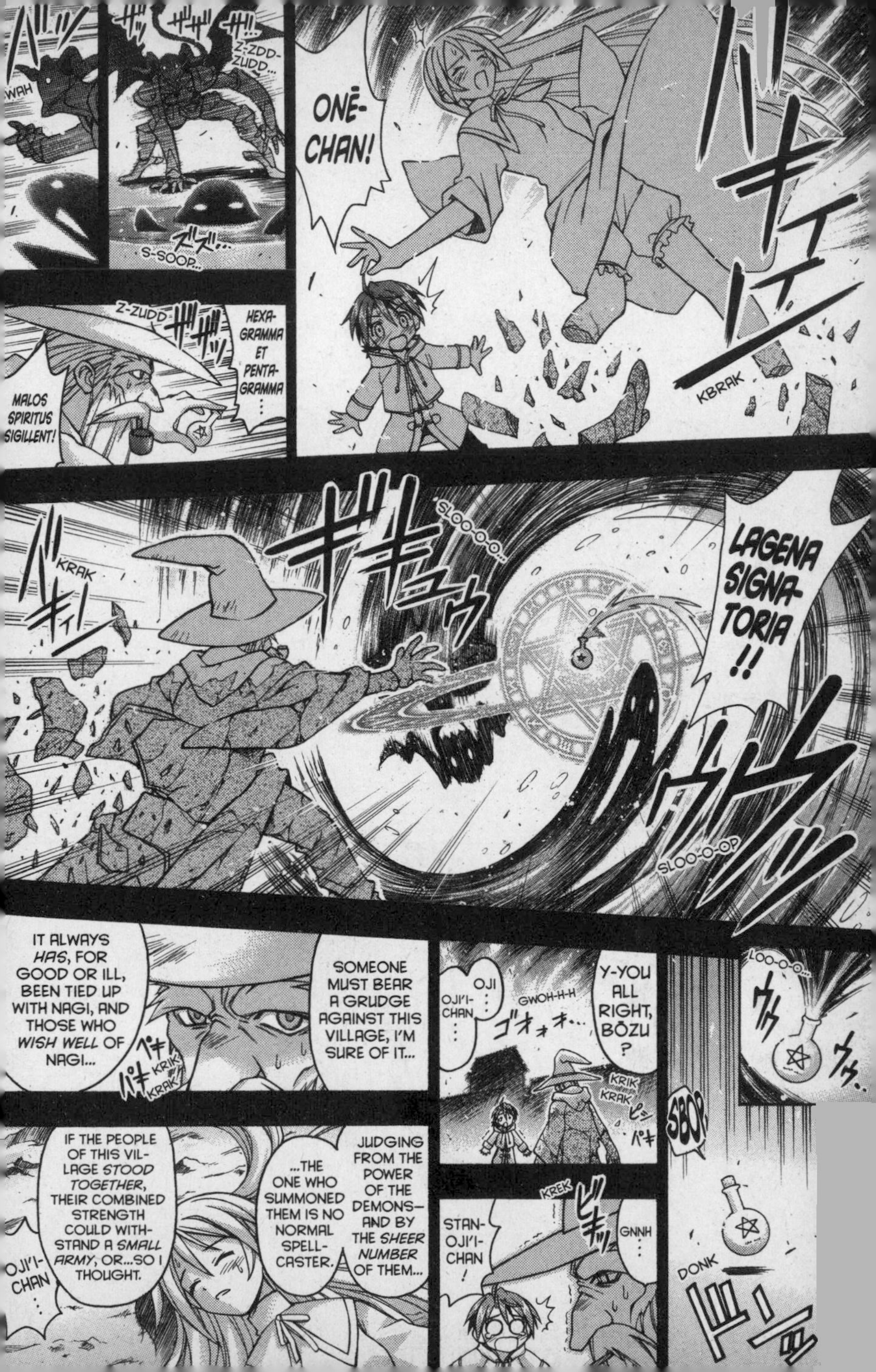
ONĒ-CHAN!
KBRAK
Z-ZDD-ZUDD...
S-SOOP...
WAH
HEXA-GRAMMA ET PENTA-GRAMMA...
Z-ZUDD
MALOS SPIRITUS SIGILLENT!
LAGENA SIGNA-TORIA!!
SLOO-O-O...
KRAK
SLOO-O-OP
LOO-O-O...
SBOP
DONK
Y-YOU ALL RIGHT, BŌZU?
OJI...
OJI'I-CHAN...
GWOH-H-H
KRIK KRAK
STAN-OJI'I-CHAN!
GNNH
KREK
SOMEONE MUST BEAR A GRUDGE AGAINST THIS VILLAGE, I'M SURE OF IT...
IT ALWAYS HAS, FOR GOOD OR ILL, BEEN TIED UP WITH NAGI, AND THOSE WHO WISH WELL OF NAGI...
KRIK KRAK
JUDGING FROM THE POWER OF THE DEMONS—AND BY THE SHEER NUMBER OF THEM...
...THE ONE WHO SUMMONED THEM IS NO NORMAL SPELL-CASTER.
IF THE PEOPLE OF THIS VIL-LAGE STOOD TOGETHER, THEIR COMBINED STRENGTH COULD WITH-STAND A SMALL ARMY, OR...SO I THOUGHT.
OJI'I-CHAN...

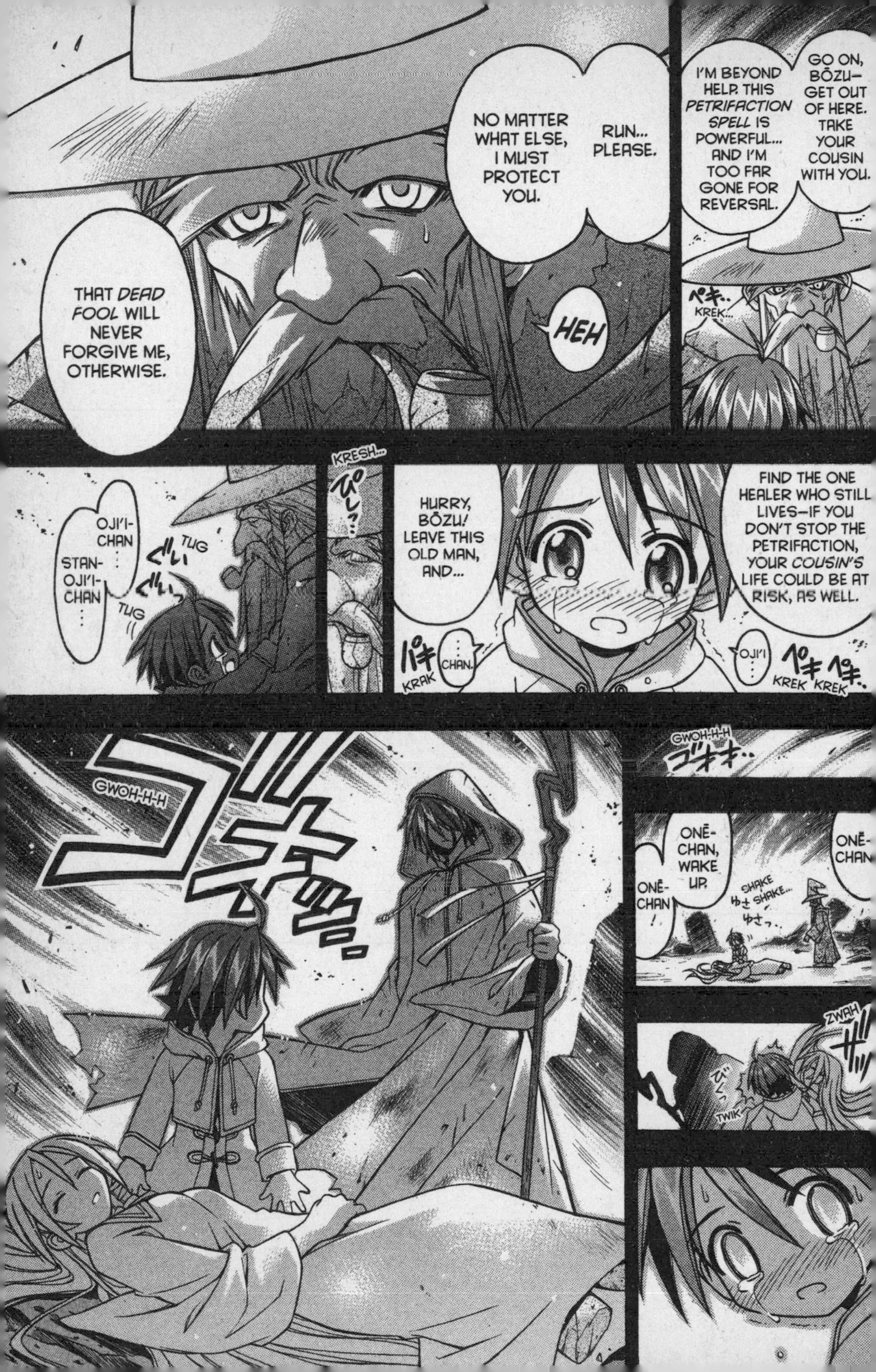
GO ON, BŌZU—GET OUT OF HERE. TAKE YOUR COUSIN WITH YOU.
I'M BEYOND HELP. THIS *PETRIFACTION SPELL* IS POWERFUL... AND I'M TOO FAR GONE FOR REVERSAL.
ペキ… KREK...
RUN... PLEASE.
NO MATTER WHAT ELSE, I MUST PROTECT YOU.
HEH
THAT *DEAD FOOL* WILL NEVER FORGIVE ME, OTHERWISE.
FIND THE ONE HEALER WHO STILL LIVES—IF YOU DON'T STOP THE PETRIFACTION, YOUR *COUSIN'S* LIFE COULD BE AT RISK, AS WELL.
HURRY, BŌZU! LEAVE THIS OLD MAN, AND...
OJI'I...
...CHAN.
ペキ ペキ.. KREK KREK
パキ KRAK
ぴし… KRESH...
OJI'I-CHAN...
STAN-OJI'I-CHAN...
ぐい ぐい TUG TUG
ゴオオ.. GWOH-H-H
ONĒ-CHAN
ONĒ-CHAN, WAKE UP.
ONĒ-CHAN!
ゆさ ゆさっ SHAKE SHAKE...
ザッ ZWAH
びくっ TWIK
ゴオオッ GWOH-H-H

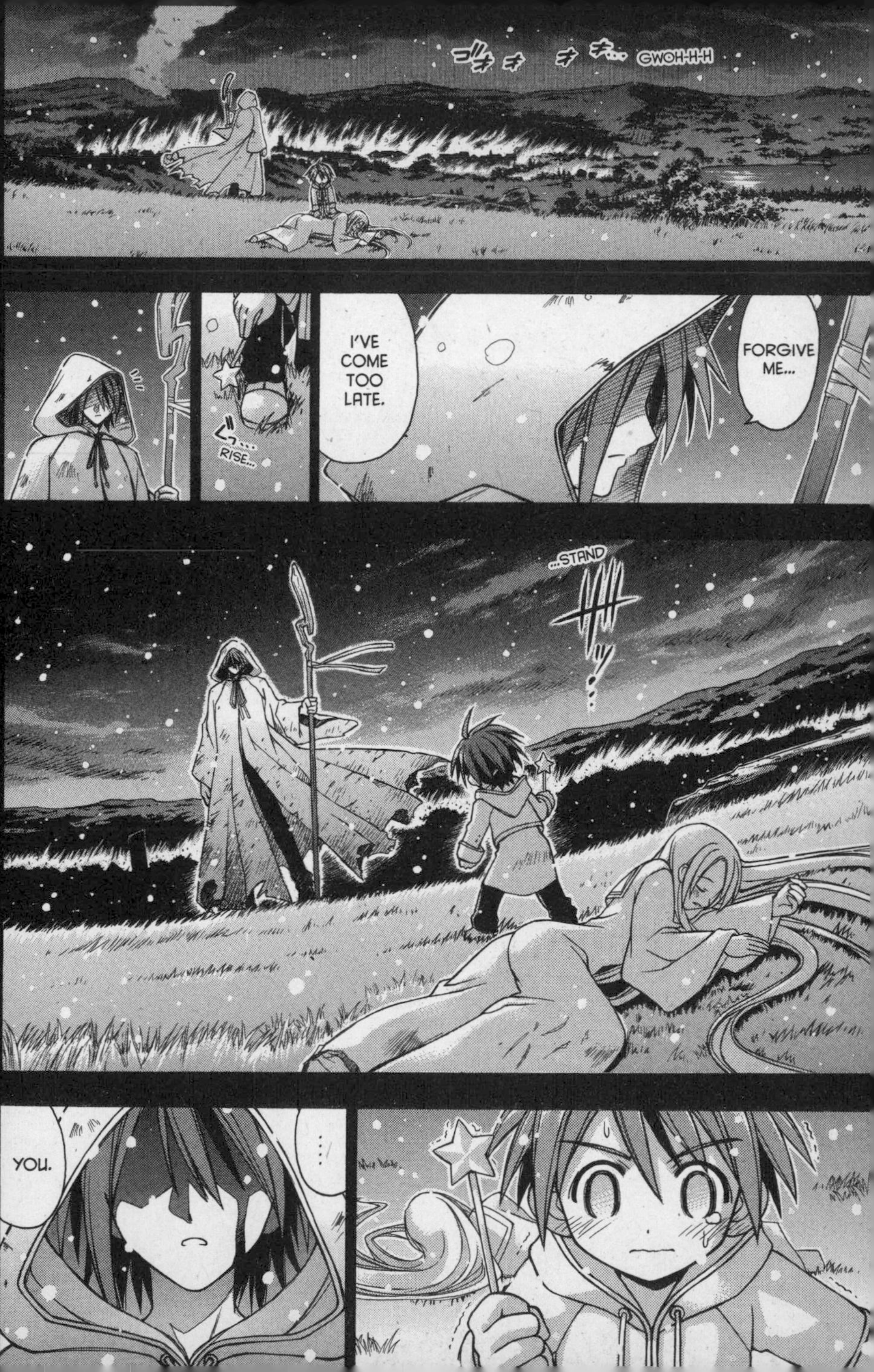
GWOH-H-H
FORGIVE ME...
I'VE COME TOO LATE.
RISE...
...STAND
...
YOU.

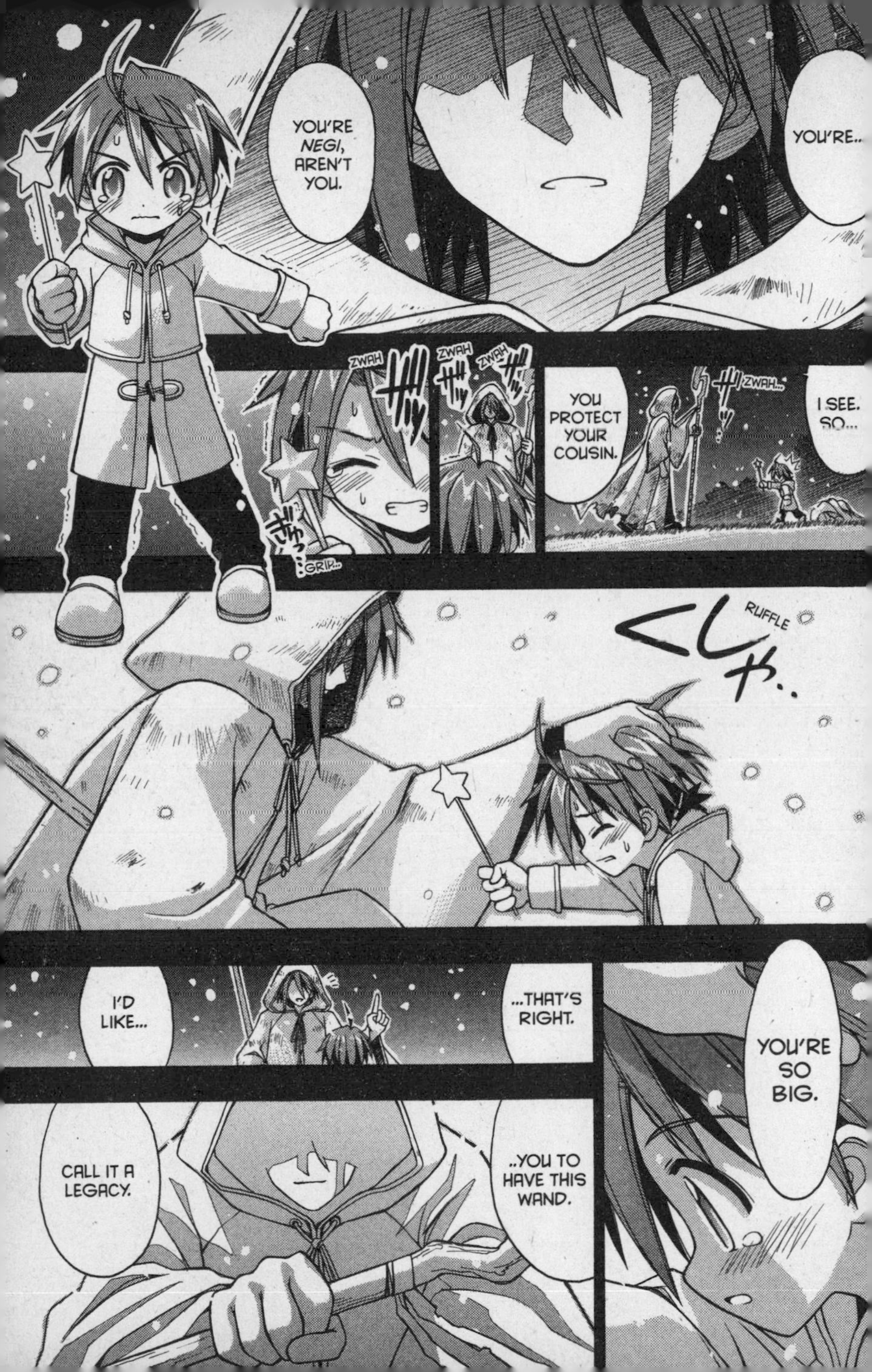
YOU'RE..
YOU'RE NEGI, AREN'T YOU.
I SEE. SO...
YOU PROTECT YOUR COUSIN.
ZWAH...
ZWAH
ZWAH
ZWAH
GRIP...
RUFFLE
YOU'RE SO BIG.
...THAT'S RIGHT.
I'D LIKE...
..YOU TO HAVE THIS WAND.
CALL IT A LEGACY.

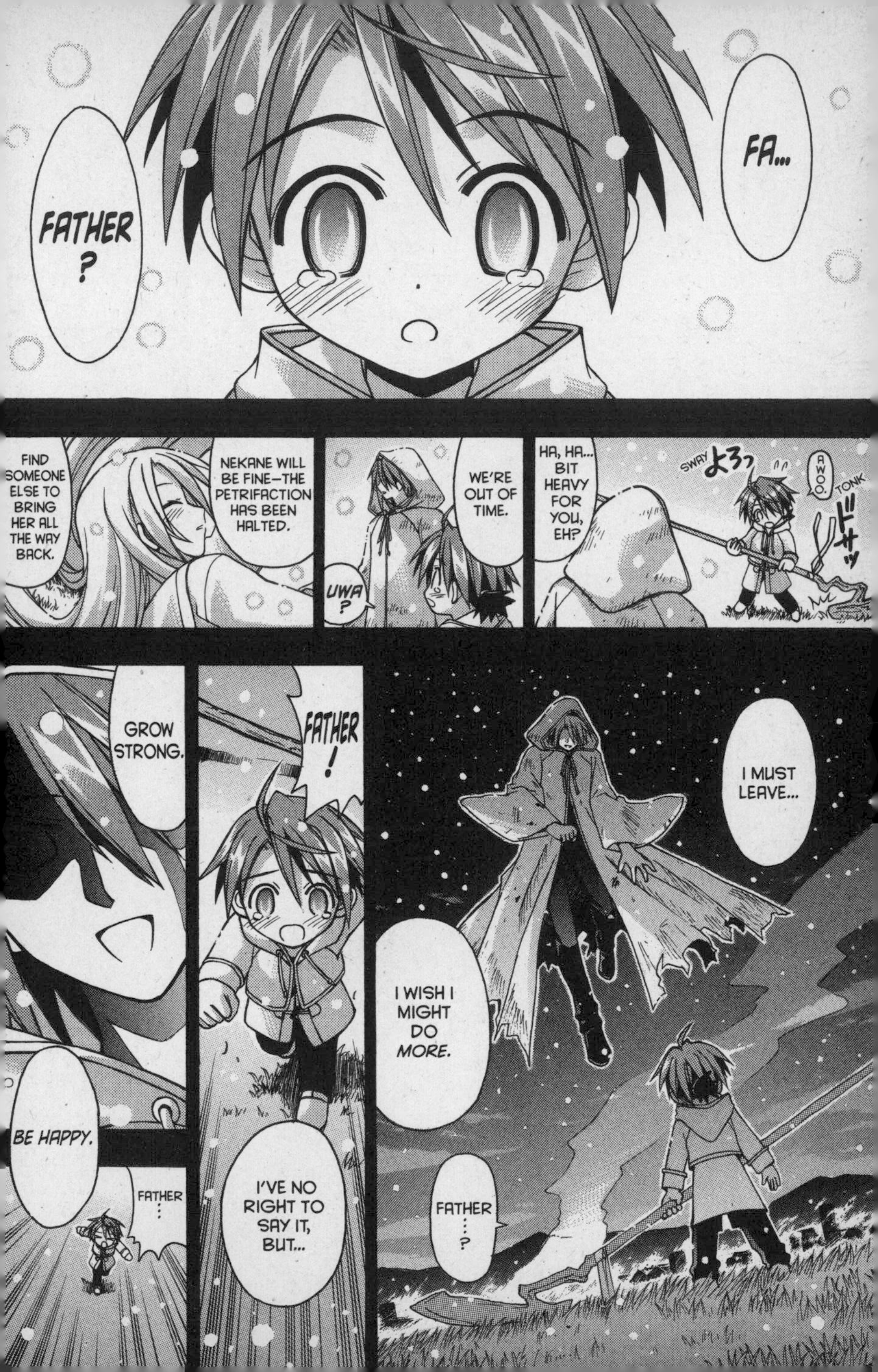
FA...
FATHER ?
SWAY よろっ
AWOO.
TONK ドサッ
HA, HA... BIT HEAVY FOR YOU, EH?
WE'RE OUT OF TIME.
UWA ?
NEKANE WILL BE FINE—THE PETRIFACTION HAS BEEN HALTED.
FIND SOMEONE ELSE TO BRING HER ALL THE WAY BACK.
I MUST LEAVE...
I WISH I MIGHT DO MORE.
FATHER ...?
FATHER !
I'VE NO RIGHT TO SAY IT, BUT...
GROW STRONG.
BE HAPPY.
FATHER ...

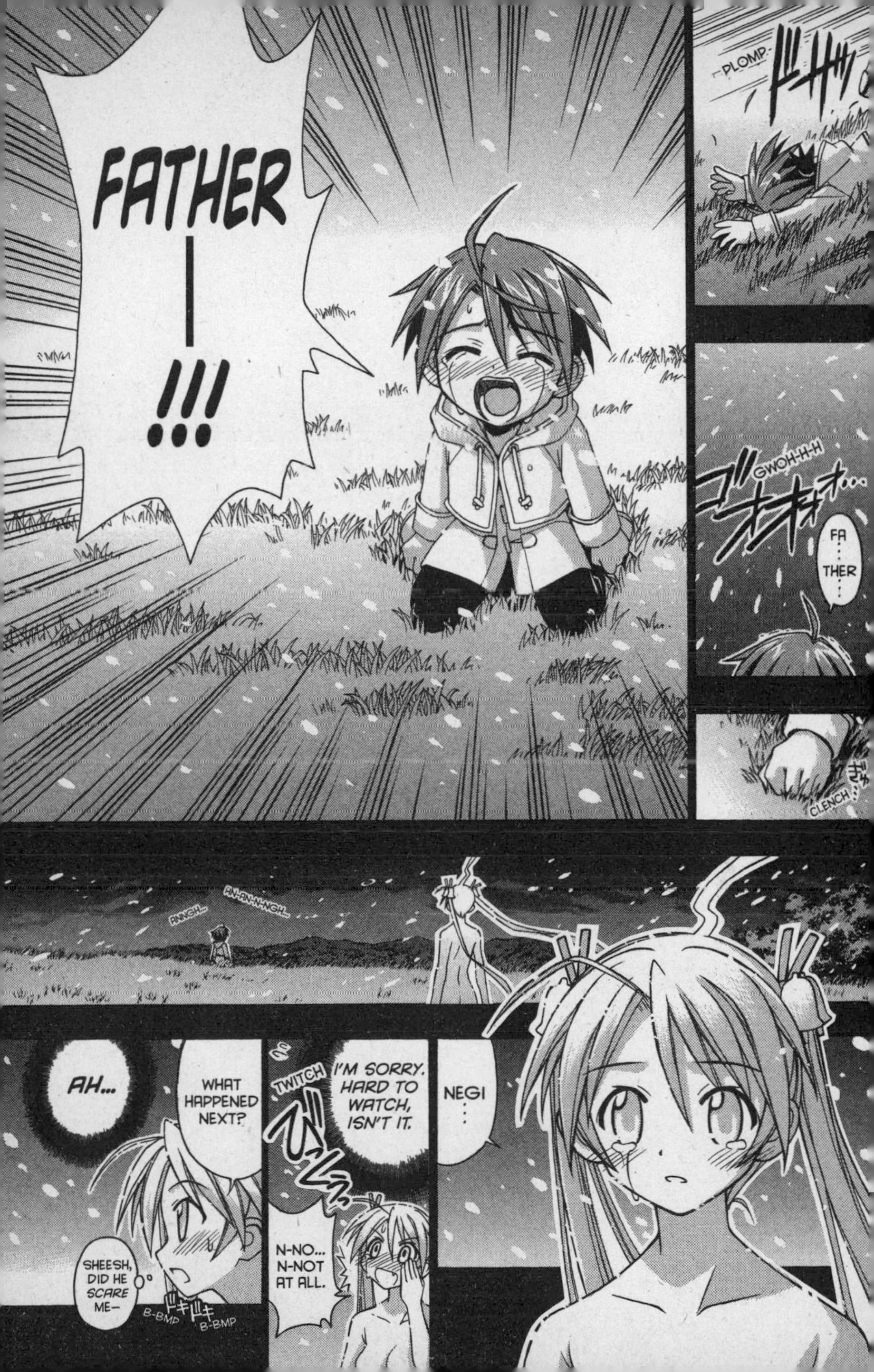

PLOMP
GWOH-H-H
FA... THER...
CLENCH
FATHER
—!!!
AN-AN-N-NGH...
ANNGH...
NEGI...
I'M SORRY. HARD TO WATCH, ISN'T IT.
TWITCH
N-NO... N-NOT AT ALL.
WHAT HAPPENED NEXT?
AH...
SHEESH, DID HE SCARE ME—
B-BMP B-BMP

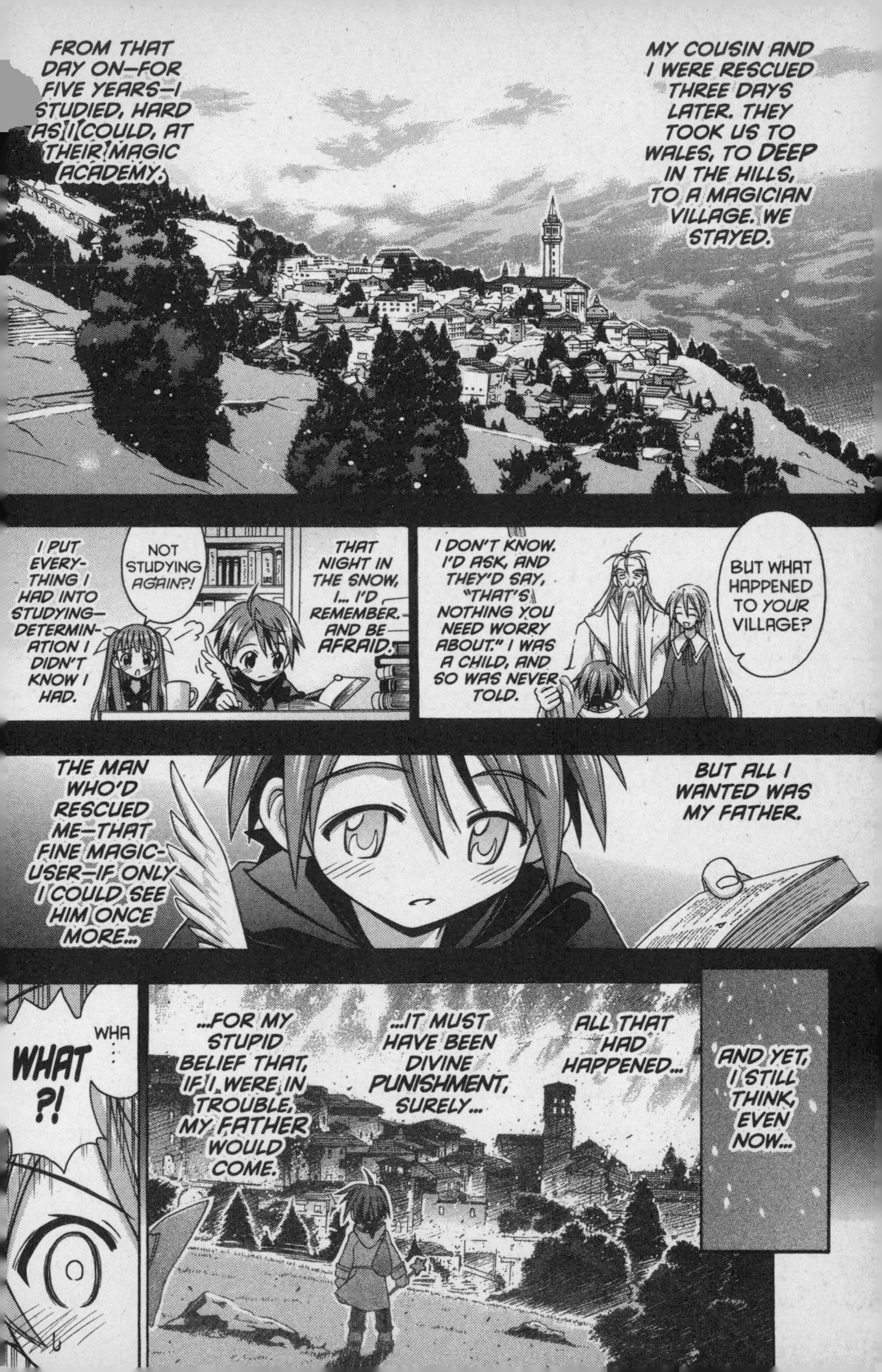
MY COUSIN AND I WERE RESCUED THREE DAYS LATER. THEY TOOK US TO WALES, TO DEEP IN THE HILLS, TO A MAGICIAN VILLAGE. WE STAYED.
FROM THAT DAY ON—FOR FIVE YEARS—I STUDIED, HARD AS I COULD, AT THEIR MAGIC ACADEMY.
BUT WHAT HAPPENED TO YOUR VILLAGE?
I DON'T KNOW. I'D ASK, AND THEY'D SAY, "THAT'S NOTHING YOU NEED WORRY ABOUT." I WAS A CHILD, AND SO WAS NEVER TOLD.
THAT NIGHT IN THE SNOW, I... I'D REMEMBER. AND BE AFRAID.
NOT STUDYING AGAIN?!
I PUT EVERYTHING I HAD INTO STUDYING—DETERMINATION I DIDN'T KNOW I HAD.
BUT ALL I WANTED WAS MY FATHER.
THE MAN WHO'D RESCUED ME—THAT FINE MAGIC-USER—IF ONLY I COULD SEE HIM ONCE MORE...
AND YET, I STILL THINK, EVEN NOW...
ALL THAT HAD HAPPENED...
...IT MUST HAVE BEEN DIVINE PUNISHMENT, SURELY...
...FOR MY STUPID BELIEF THAT, IF I WERE IN TROUBLE, MY FATHER WOULD COME.
WHA...
WHAT ?!

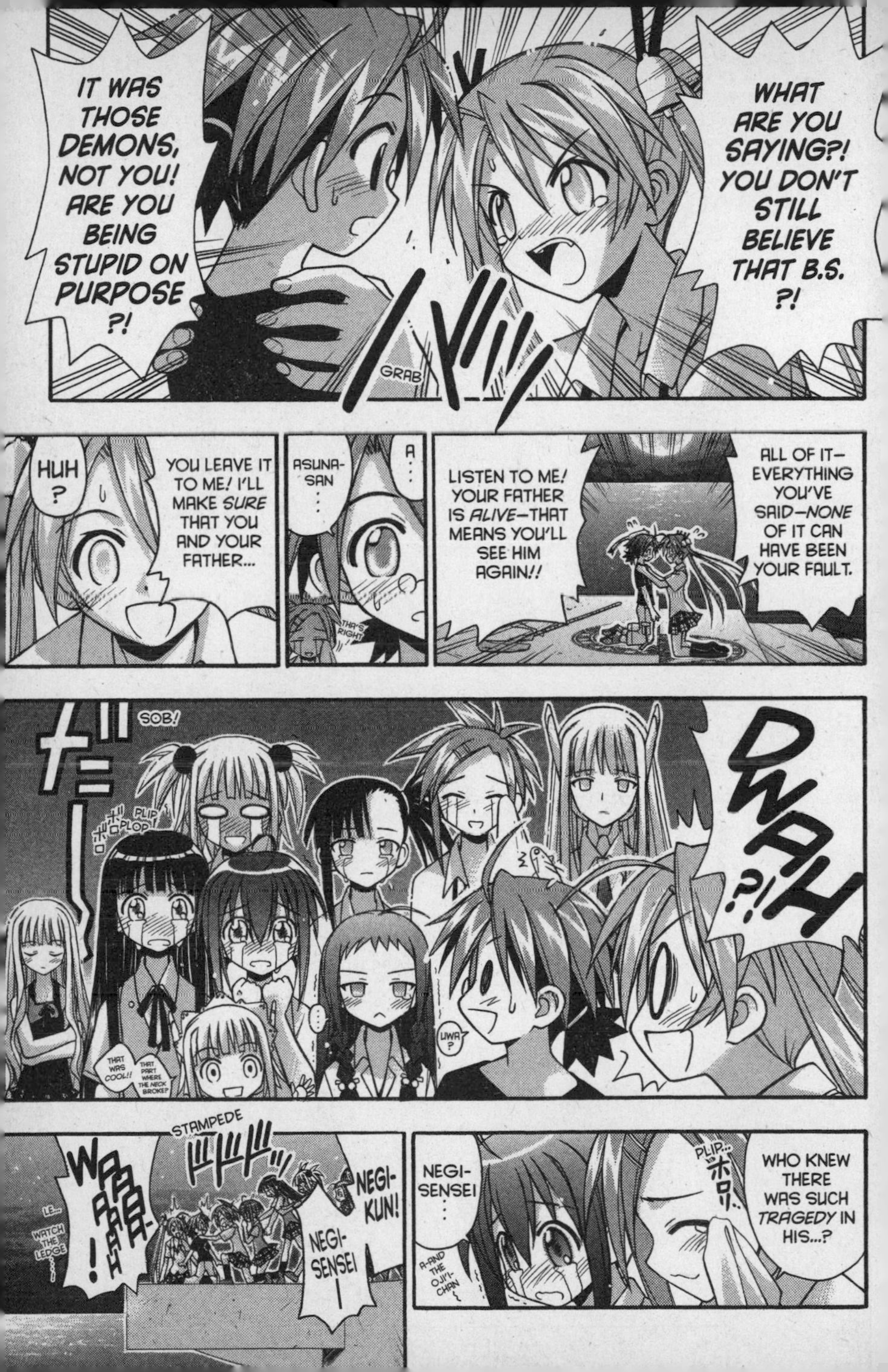
WHAT ARE YOU SAYING?! YOU DON'T STILL BELIEVE THAT B.S. ?!
IT WAS THOSE DEMONS, NOT YOU! ARE YOU BEING STUPID ON PURPOSE ?!
GRAB
ALL OF IT—EVERYTHING YOU'VE SAID—NONE OF IT CAN HAVE BEEN YOUR FAULT.
LISTEN TO ME! YOUR FATHER IS ALIVE—THAT MEANS YOU'LL SEE HIM AGAIN!!
A...
ASUNA-SAN...
THA'S RIGHT!
YOU LEAVE IT TO ME! I'LL MAKE SURE THAT YOU AND YOUR FATHER...
HUH?
DWAH?!
SOB!
PLIP PLOP
UWA?
THAT WAS COOL!!
THAT PART WHERE THE NECK BROKE!
WHO KNEW THERE WAS SUCH TRAGEDY IN HIS...?
PLIP...
NEGI-SENSEI...
A-AND THE OJI'I-CHAN
NEGI-KUN!
NEGI-SENSEI!
STAMPEDE
WAAAAAH!
LE... WATCH THE LEDGE...

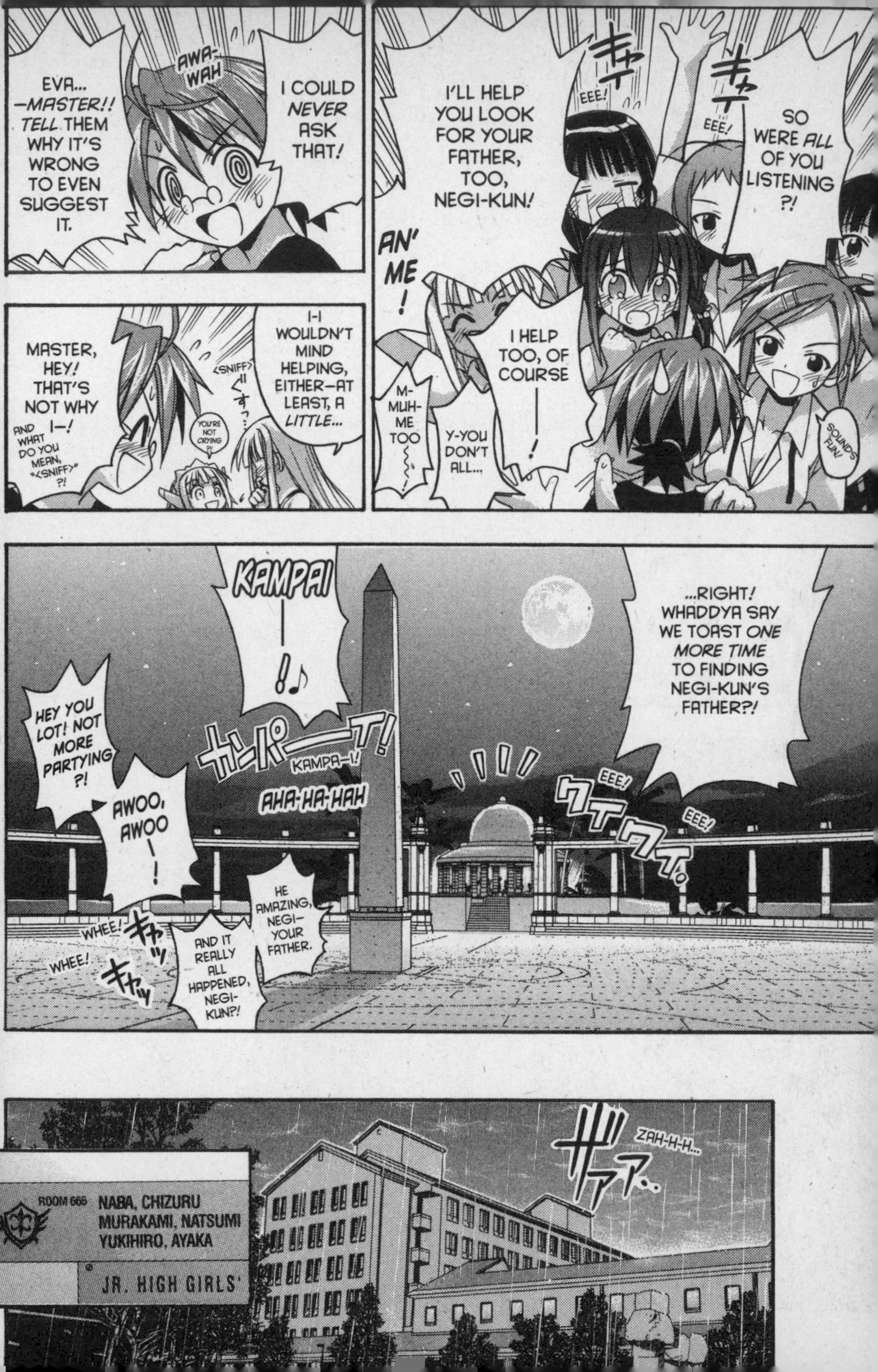
SO WERE ALL OF YOU LISTENING?!
キャ
EEE!
キャ
EEE!
I'LL HELP YOU LOOK FOR YOUR FATHER, TOO, NEGI-KUN!
AN' ME!
I HELP TOO, OF COURSE—!
SOUNDS FUN!
Y-YOU DON'T ALL...
M-MUH-ME TOO~~!
I COULD NEVER ASK THAT!
AWA-WAH
EVA... —MASTER!! TELL THEM WHY IT'S WRONG TO EVEN SUGGEST IT.
I-I WOULDN'T MIND HELPING, EITHER—AT LEAST, A LITTLE...
<SNIFF> ぐすっ...
YOU'RE NOT CRYING?!
MASTER, HEY! THAT'S NOT WHY I—!
AND WHAT DO YOU MEAN, "<SNIFF>"?!
...RIGHT! WHADDYA SAY WE TOAST ONE MORE TIME TO FINDING NEGI-KUN'S FATHER?!
KAMPAI—!♪
EEE! ワイ EEE! ワイ
カンパーイ! KAMPA—I!
AHA-HA-HAH
HEY YOU LOT! NOT MORE PARTYING?!
AWOO, AWOO—!
HE AMAZING, NEGI—YOUR FATHER.
AND IT REALLY ALL HAPPENED, NEGI-KUN?!
WHEE! キャッ
WHEE! キャッ
ザァア.. ZAH-H-H...
ROOM 665
NABA, CHIZURU
MURAKAMI, NATSUMI
YUKIHIRO, AYAKA
JR. HIGH GIRLS'

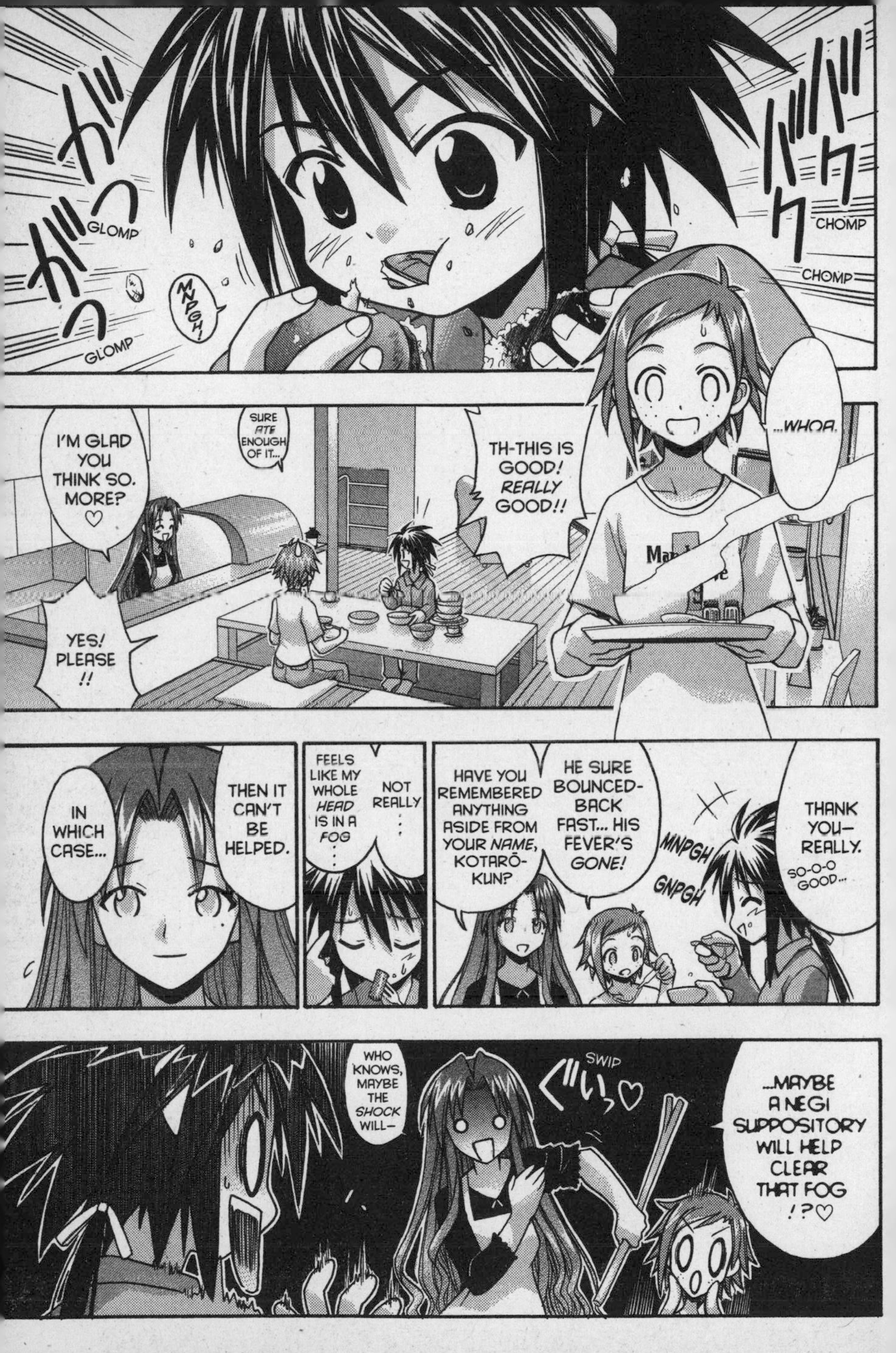
CHOMP
CHOMP
GLOMP
MNPGH!
GLOMP
...WHOA.
TH-THIS IS GOOD! REALLY GOOD!!
SURE ATE ENOUGH OF IT...
I'M GLAD YOU THINK SO. MORE? ♡
YES! PLEASE !!
THANK YOU— REALLY.
SO-O-O GOOD...
MNPGH
GNPGH
HE SURE BOUNCED-BACK FAST... HIS FEVER'S GONE!
HAVE YOU REMEMBERED ANYTHING ASIDE FROM YOUR NAME, KOTARŌ-KUN?
NOT REALLY...
FEELS LIKE MY WHOLE HEAD IS IN A FOG...
THEN IT CAN'T BE HELPED.
IN WHICH CASE...
...MAYBE A NEGI SUPPOSITORY WILL HELP CLEAR THAT FOG !?♡
SWIP
WHO KNOWS, MAYBE THE SHOCK WILL—
PLEASE

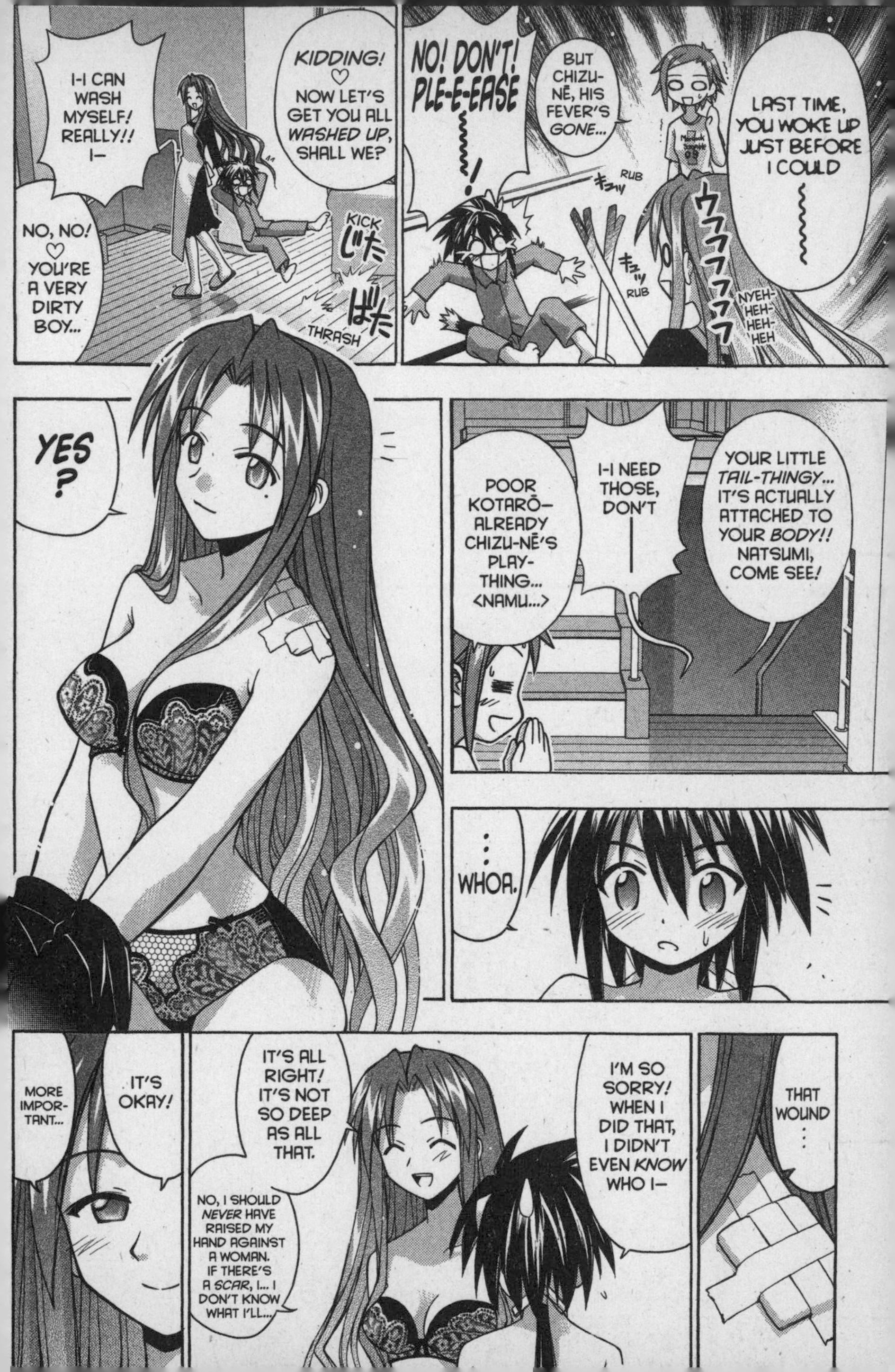
LAST TIME, YOU WOKE UP JUST BEFORE I COULD ~~~~~
NYEH-HEH-HEH-HEH
BUT CHIZU-NĒ, HIS FEVER'S GONE...
RUB
RUB
NO! DON'T! PLE-E-EASE ~~~~~!
KIDDING! ♡ NOW LET'S GET YOU ALL *WASHED UP*, SHALL WE?
I-I CAN WASH MYSELF! REALLY!! I—
NO, NO! ♡ YOU'RE A VERY DIRTY BOY...
KICK
THRASH
YOUR LITTLE *TAIL-THINGY*... IT'S ACTUALLY ATTACHED TO YOUR *BODY*!! NATSUMI, COME SEE!
I-I NEED THOSE, DON'T I—
POOR KOTARŌ— ALREADY CHIZU-NĒ'S PLAYTHING... <NAMU...>
...WHOA.
YES?
THAT WOUND...
I'M SO SORRY! WHEN I DID THAT, I DIDN'T EVEN *KNOW* WHO I—
IT'S ALL RIGHT! IT'S NOT SO DEEP AS ALL THAT.
NO, I SHOULD *NEVER* HAVE RAISED MY HAND AGAINST A WOMAN. IF THERE'S A *SCAR*, I... I DON'T KNOW WHAT I'LL...
IT'S OKAY!
MORE IMPORTANT...

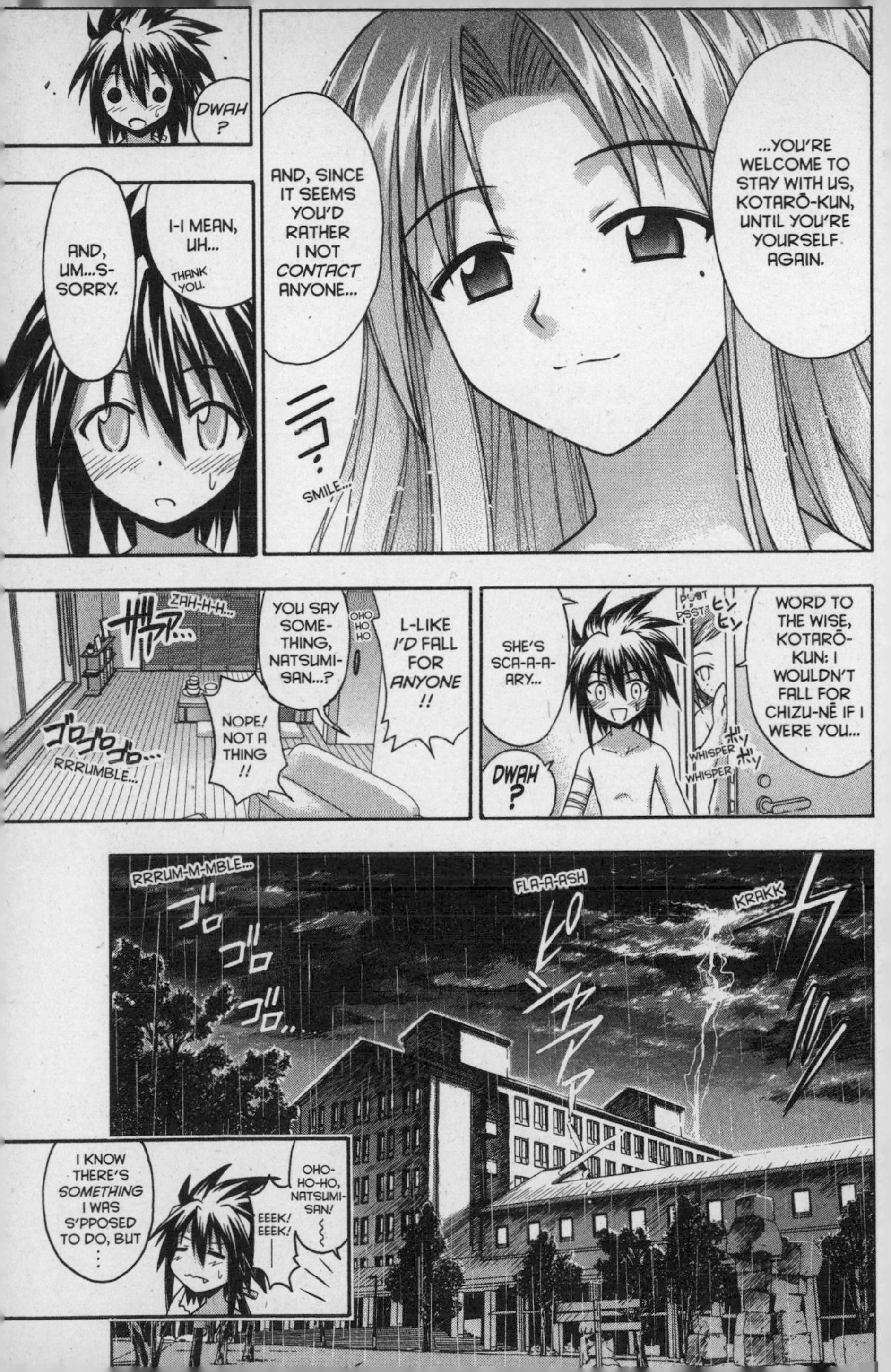
...YOU'RE WELCOME TO STAY WITH US, KOTARŌ-KUN, UNTIL YOU'RE YOURSELF AGAIN.
AND, SINCE IT SEEMS YOU'D RATHER I NOT *CONTACT* ANYONE...
SMILE...
DWAH?
I-I MEAN, UH...
THANK YOU.
AND, UM...S-SORRY.
WORD TO THE WISE, KOTARŌ-KUN: I WOULDN'T FALL FOR CHIZU-NĒ IF I WERE YOU...
PSST PSST
WHISPER WHISPER
SHE'S SCA-A-A-ARY...
DWAH?
L-LIKE *I'D* FALL FOR *ANYONE*!!
OHO HO HO
YOU SAY SOME-THING, NATSUMI-SAN...?
NOPE! NOT A THING!!
ZAH-H-H...
RRRUMBLE...
KRAKK
FLA-A-ASH
RRRUM-M-MBLE...
OHO-HO-HO, NATSUMI-SAN!
EEEK! EEEK!
I KNOW THERE'S *SOMETHING* I WAS S'PPOSED TO DO, BUT...

NEGIMA!
MAGISTER NEGI MAGI

SIXTY-SIXTH PERIOD: "MAGIC WORD" LEXICON

■「六芒の星と五芒の星よ、悪しき霊に封印を。『封魔の瓶』」

HEXAGRAMMA ET PENTAGRAMMA, MALOS SPIRITUS SIGILLENT · LAGENA SIGNATORIA

Spell that combines the use of a magical item to seal away and/or render powerless an opponent with spiritual or magical powers of an extremely high or puissant nature. In that a being with truly developed spiritual powers can continue to exist even after its corporeal form (*caro*) is destroyed—the *Ryomen Sukuna no Kami*, for example, had its body shattered by extreme cold, and yet still needed to be sealed away (see 53rd Period for details)—the "Lagena Signatoria," while not ideal for all situations, may, for some opponents, be the only truly effective counter.

When, during 66th Period, Stan referred to the target as a "demon," it may not in fact have been the most pertinent translation of the Japanese *akuma*. "Demon" in English, "dämon" in German, "daemon" or "daemonium" in Latin, and "δαίμων, δαιμόνιον" in Ancient Greek.... It is in ancient Greek, actually, that "δαίμων, δαιμόνιον" is defined as a "god-like, spiritual being." As noted by Plato in his *Apology of Socrates*,

> Socrates: How obliging you are in having hardly answered, though compelled by these judges! You assert, then, that I do believe and teach things relating to demons, whether they be new or old; therefore, according to your admission, I do believe in things relating to demons, and this you have sworn in the bill of indictment. If, then, I believe in things relating to demons, there is surely an absolute necessity that I should believe that there are demons. Is it not so? It is. For I suppose you to assent, since you do not answer. But with respect to demons, do we not allow that they are gods, or the children of gods? Do you admit this or not?
>
> Melitus: Certainly.

As defined here, to be a "demon" is to have an existence as powerful as that of the gods, and to be possessed of equally vaulted spiritual powers. Thus, only "δαίμων, δαιμόνιον" of high rank may hope to prove equal opponents to the gods. This belief may have sprung from the clash of various multi-god religions and the belief of the "one God." Consider these famous verses from the New Testament:

> "But when the Pharisees heard it, they said, 'This fellow doth cast out devils, but by Beelzebub the prince of the devils.'" (Matthew 12:24)
>
> "And the scribes which came down from Jerusalem said, 'He hath Beelzebub, and by the prince of the devils casteth he out devils.'" (Mark 3:22)
>
> "But some of them said, 'He casteth out devils through Beelzebub, chief of the devils. And others, tempting him, sought of him a sign from heaven.'" (Luke 11:15-16)

Therefore, "δαίμων, δαιμόνιον" as the perfect representation of a god-opposing force—or that of good and evil—notwithstanding, the demonic existence must be thought of as possessing great spiritual power, and nothing more. The word "demon," then, is not necessarily limited in meaning to current, popular understanding.

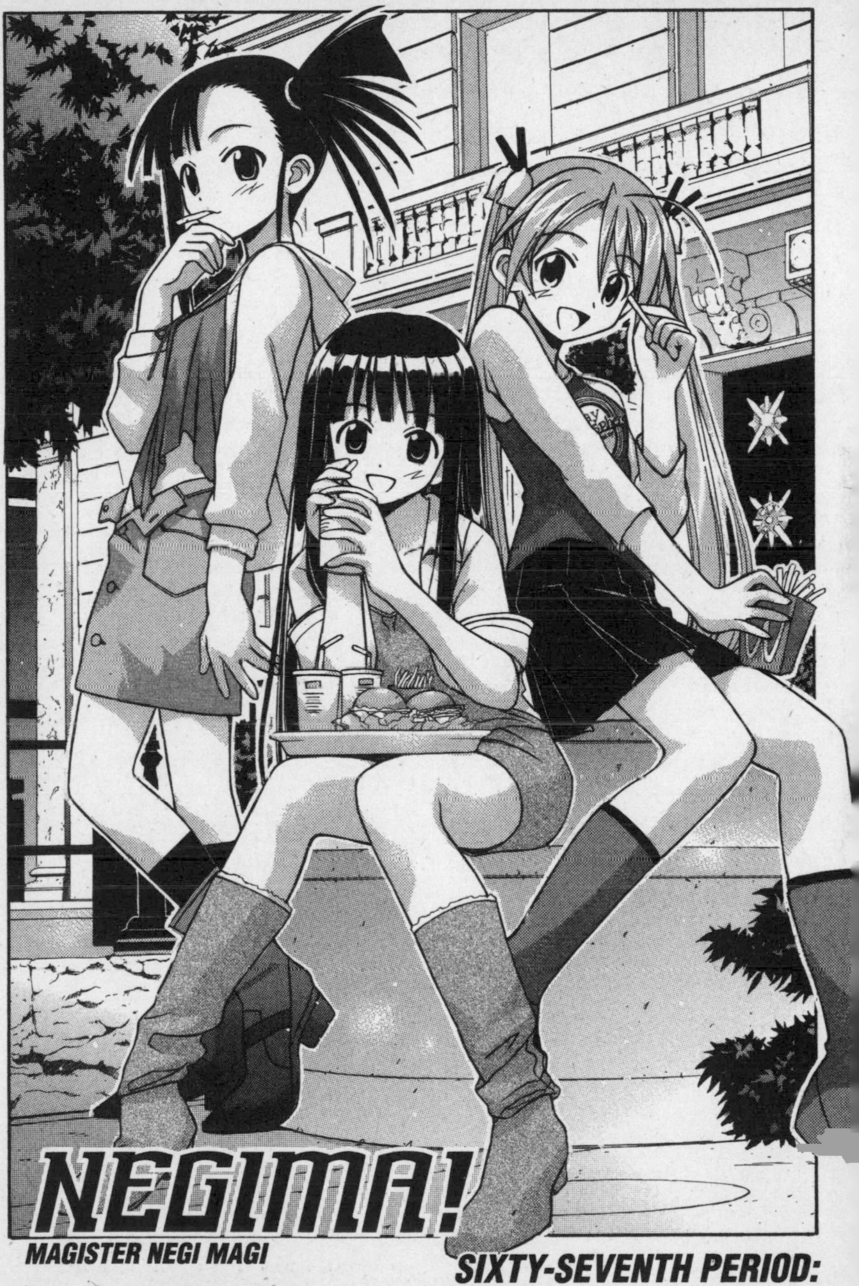
NEGIMA!

MAGISTER NEGI MAGI

SIXTY-SEVENTH PERIOD: RUB-A-DUB-DUB, THERE'S SLIME IN THE TUB

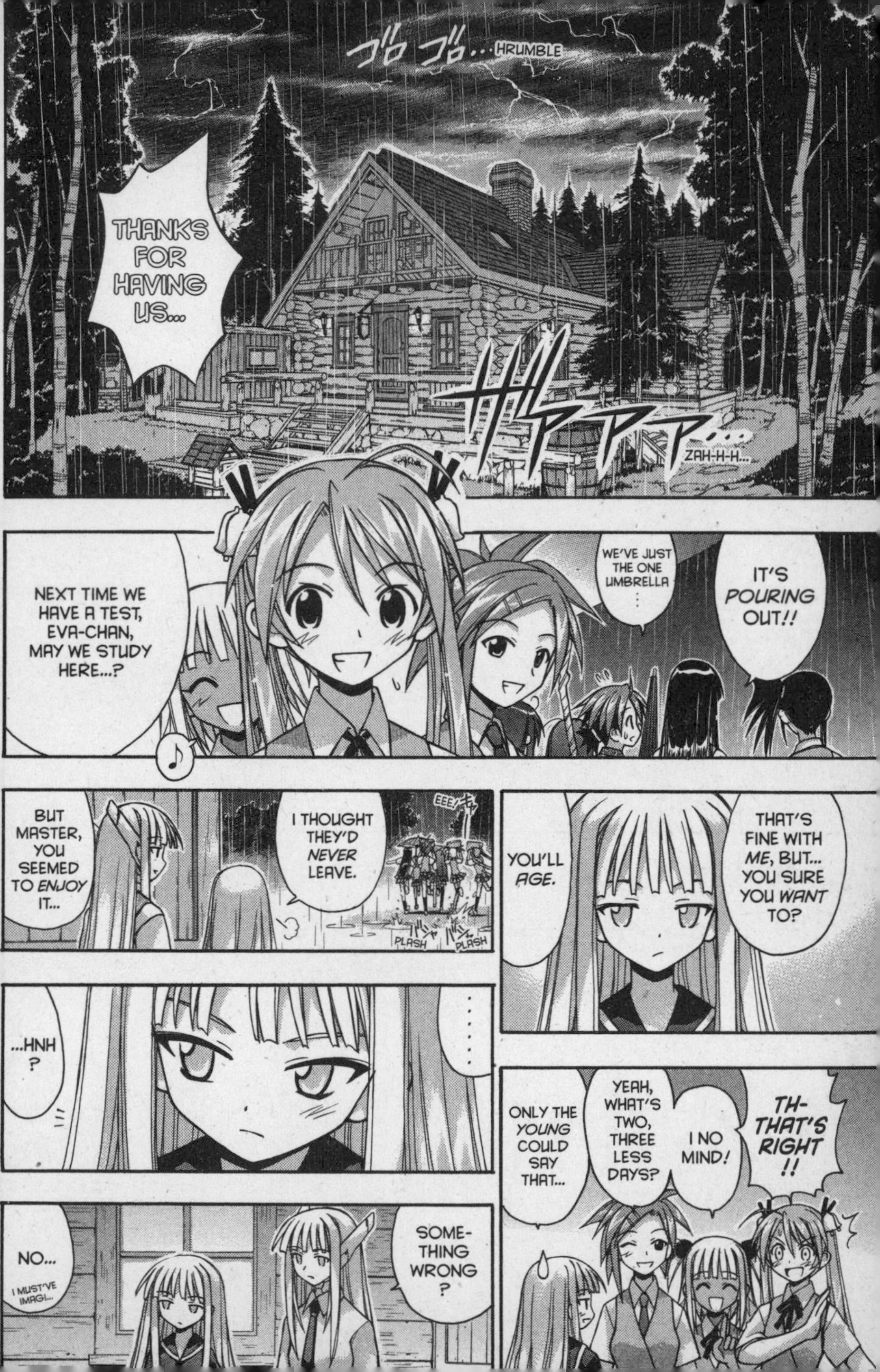
ゴロゴロ... HRUMBLE
THANKS FOR HAVING US...
ZAH-H-H...
IT'S *POURING* OUT!!
WE'VE JUST THE ONE UMBRELLA ...
NEXT TIME WE HAVE A TEST, EVA-CHAN, MAY WE STUDY HERE...?
♪
THAT'S FINE WITH *ME*, BUT... YOU SURE YOU *WANT* TO?
YOU'LL *AGE*.
TH-THAT'S RIGHT!!
I NO MIND!
YEAH, WHAT'S TWO, THREE LESS DAYS?
ONLY THE *YOUNG* COULD SAY THAT...
EEE!
I THOUGHT THEY'D *NEVER* LEAVE.
PLASH
PLASH
BUT MASTER, YOU SEEMED TO *ENJOY* IT...
......
...HNH ?
SOME-THING WRONG ?
NO...
I MUST'VE IMAGI...

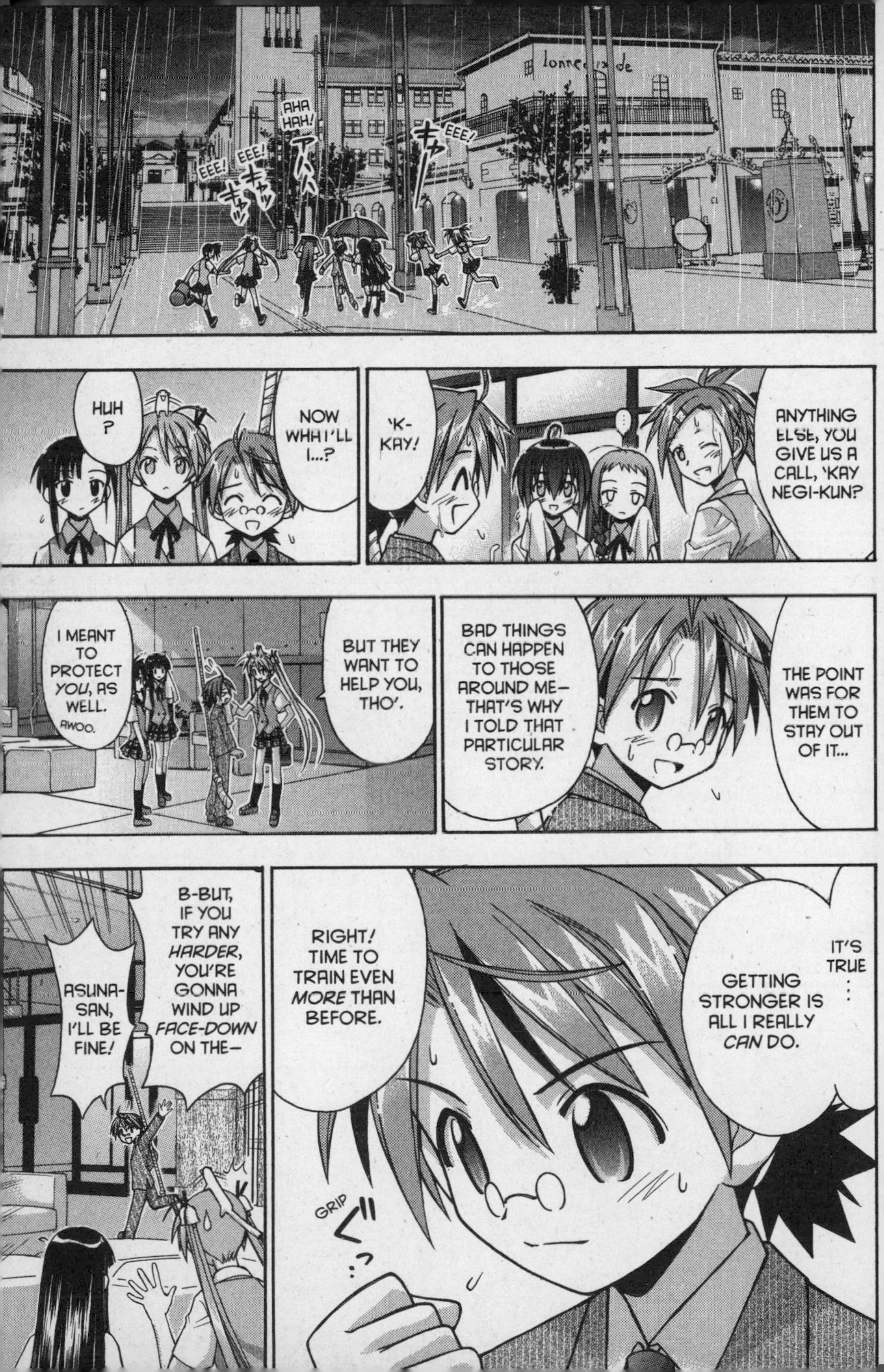
EEE!
AHA HAH!
EEE! EEE!
ANYTHING ELSE, YOU GIVE US A CALL, 'KAY NEGI-KUN?
...
'K-KAY!
NOW WHAT I'LL I...?
HUH ?
THE POINT WAS FOR THEM TO STAY OUT OF IT...
BAD THINGS CAN HAPPEN TO THOSE AROUND ME—THAT'S WHY I TOLD THAT PARTICULAR STORY.
BUT THEY WANT TO HELP YOU, THO'.
I MEANT TO PROTECT *YOU*, AS WELL.
AWOO.
IT'S TRUE ...
GETTING STRONGER IS ALL I REALLY *CAN* DO.
GRIP
RIGHT! TIME TO TRAIN EVEN *MORE* THAN BEFORE.
B-BUT, IF YOU TRY ANY *HARDER*, YOU'RE GONNA WIND UP *FACE-DOWN* ON THE—
ASUNA-SAN, I'LL BE FINE!

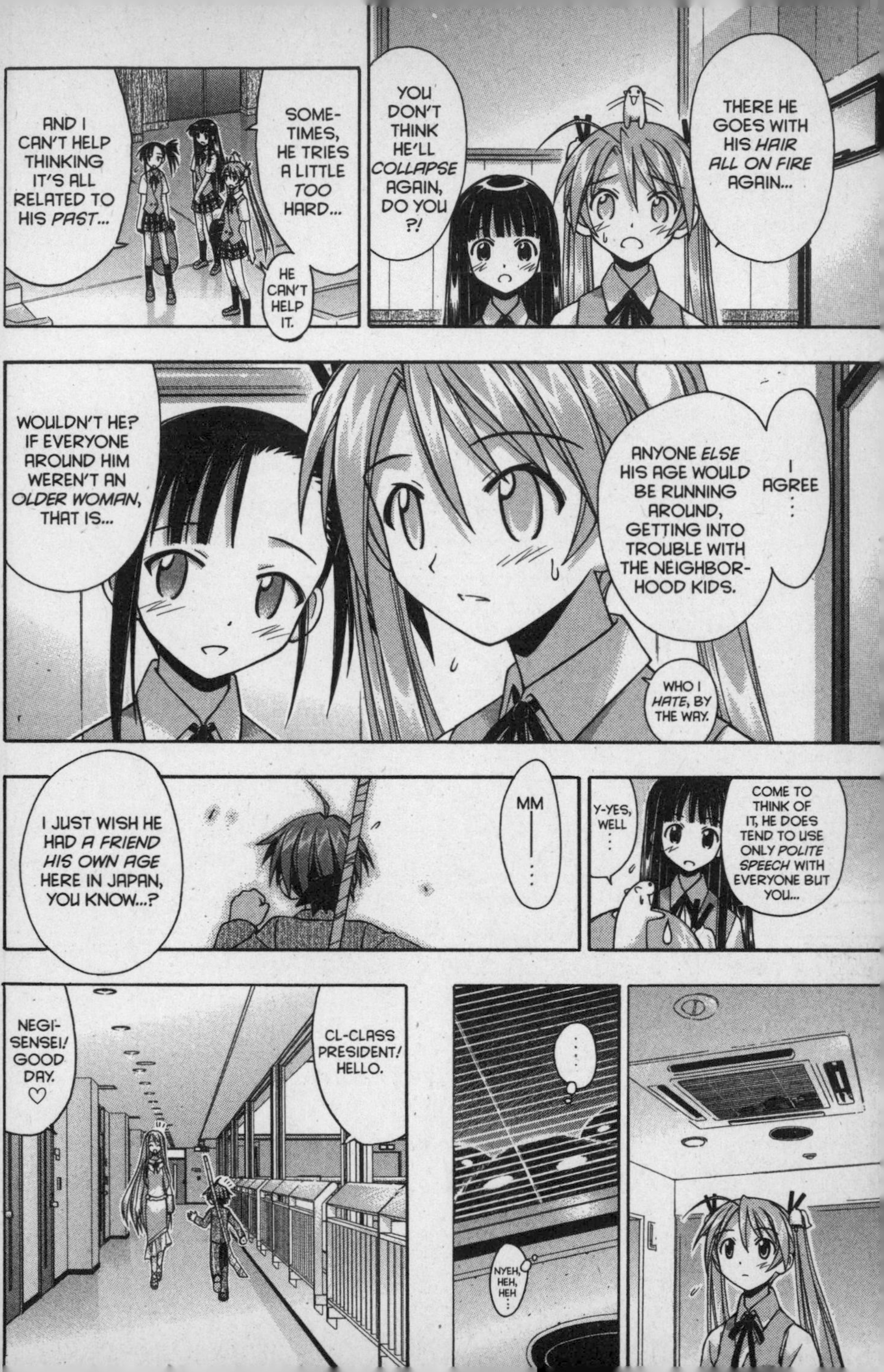
THERE HE GOES WITH HIS HAIR ALL ON FIRE AGAIN...
YOU DON'T THINK HE'LL COLLAPSE AGAIN, DO YOU ?!
SOME-TIMES, HE TRIES A LITTLE TOO HARD...
AND I CAN'T HELP THINKING IT'S ALL RELATED TO HIS PAST...
HE CAN'T HELP IT.
I AGREE...
ANYONE ELSE HIS AGE WOULD BE RUNNING AROUND, GETTING INTO TROUBLE WITH THE NEIGHBOR-HOOD KIDS.
WHO I HATE, BY THE WAY.
WOULDN'T HE? IF EVERYONE AROUND HIM WEREN'T AN OLDER WOMAN, THAT IS...
COME TO THINK OF IT, HE DOES TEND TO USE ONLY POLITE SPEECH WITH EVERYONE BUT YOU...
Y-YES, WELL...
MM—...
I JUST WISH HE HAD A FRIEND HIS OWN AGE HERE IN JAPAN, YOU KNOW...?
......
NYEH, HEH, HEH...
CL-CLASS PRESIDENT! HELLO.
NEGI-SENSEI! GOOD DAY. ♡

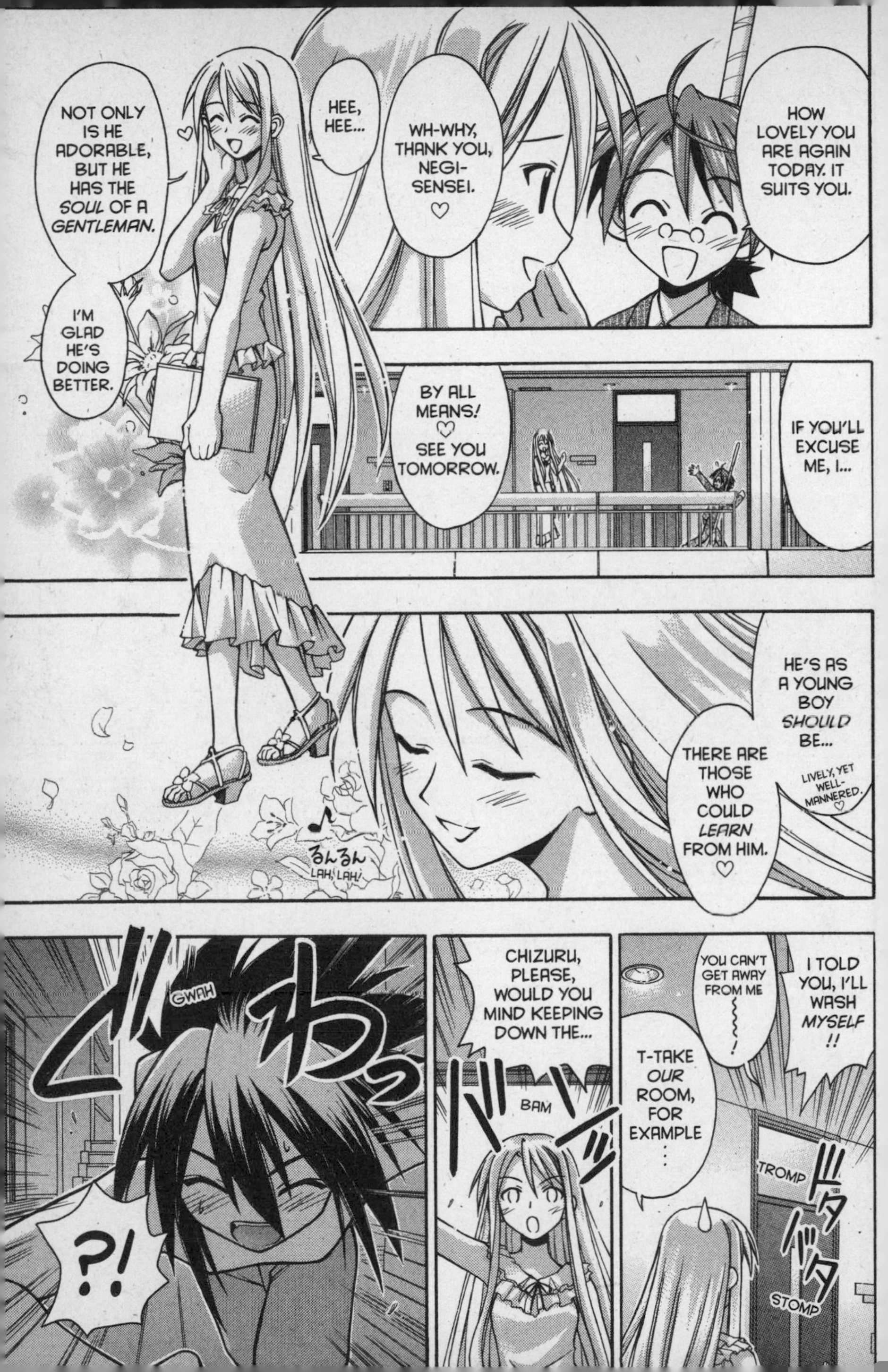
HOW LOVELY YOU ARE AGAIN TODAY. IT SUITS YOU.
WH-WHY, THANK YOU, NEGI-SENSEI. ♡
HEE, HEE...
IF YOU'LL EXCUSE ME, I...
BY ALL MEANS! ♡ SEE YOU TOMORROW.
NOT ONLY IS HE ADORABLE, BUT HE HAS THE *SOUL* OF A *GENTLEMAN*.
I'M GLAD HE'S DOING BETTER.
るんるん
LAH, LAH!
HE'S AS A YOUNG BOY *SHOULD* BE...
LIVELY, YET WELL-MANNERED. ♡
THERE ARE THOSE WHO COULD *LEARN* FROM HIM. ♡
I TOLD YOU, I'LL WASH *MYSELF* !!
YOU CAN'T GET AWAY FROM ME ~~~!
ドタバタ
TROMP
STOMP
CHIZURU, PLEASE, WOULD YOU MIND KEEPING DOWN THE...
T-TAKE *OUR* ROOM, FOR EXAMPLE...
バーン
BAM
ぐわっ
GWAH
?!

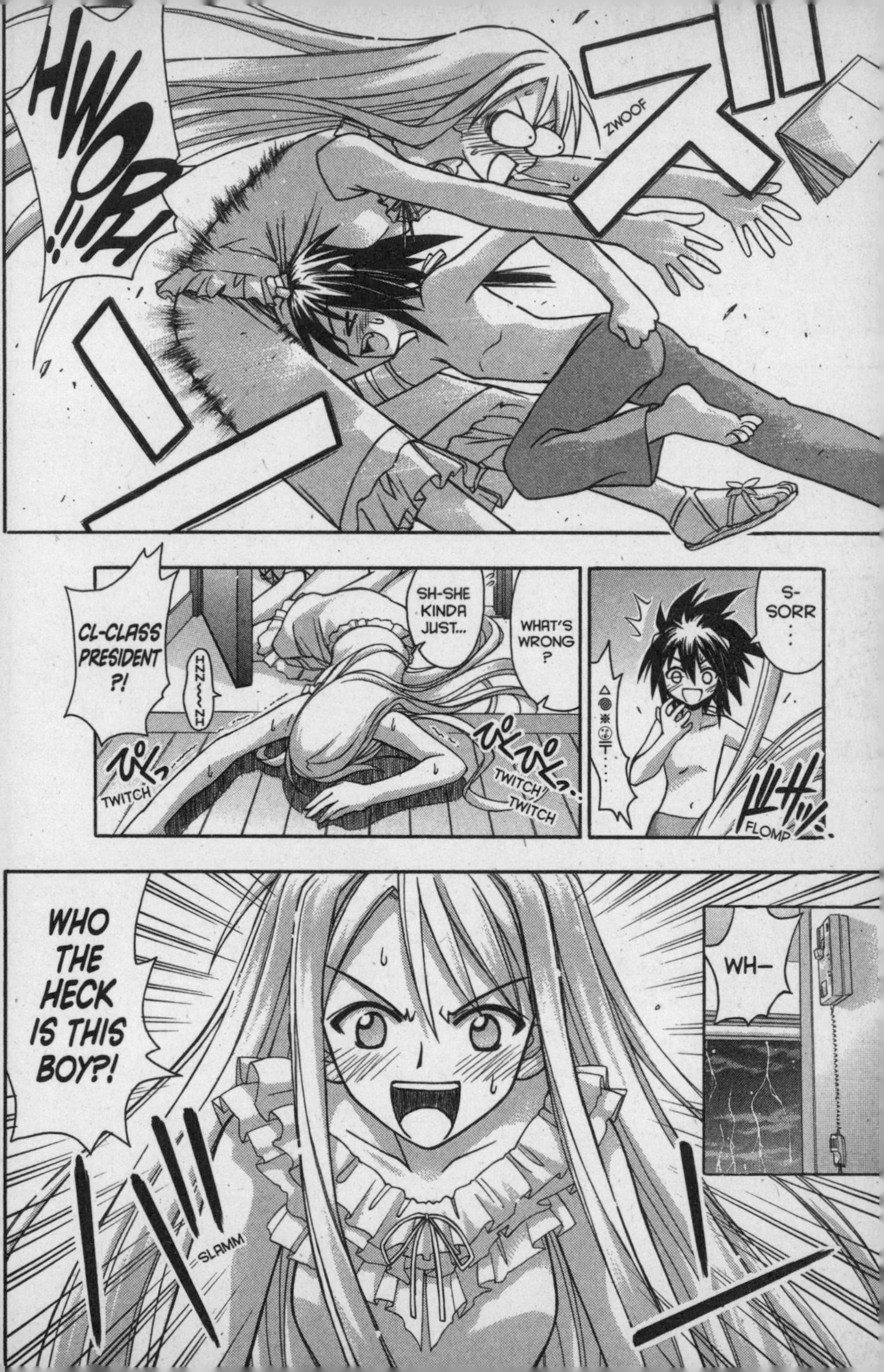
ZWOOF
HWOAH!!
S-SORR...
FLOMP
WHAT'S WRONG?
SH-SHE KINDA JUST...
CL-CLASS PRESIDENT?!
INN~~NH
TWITCH TWITCH
TWITCH
WH—
WHO THE HECK IS THIS BOY?!
SLAMM

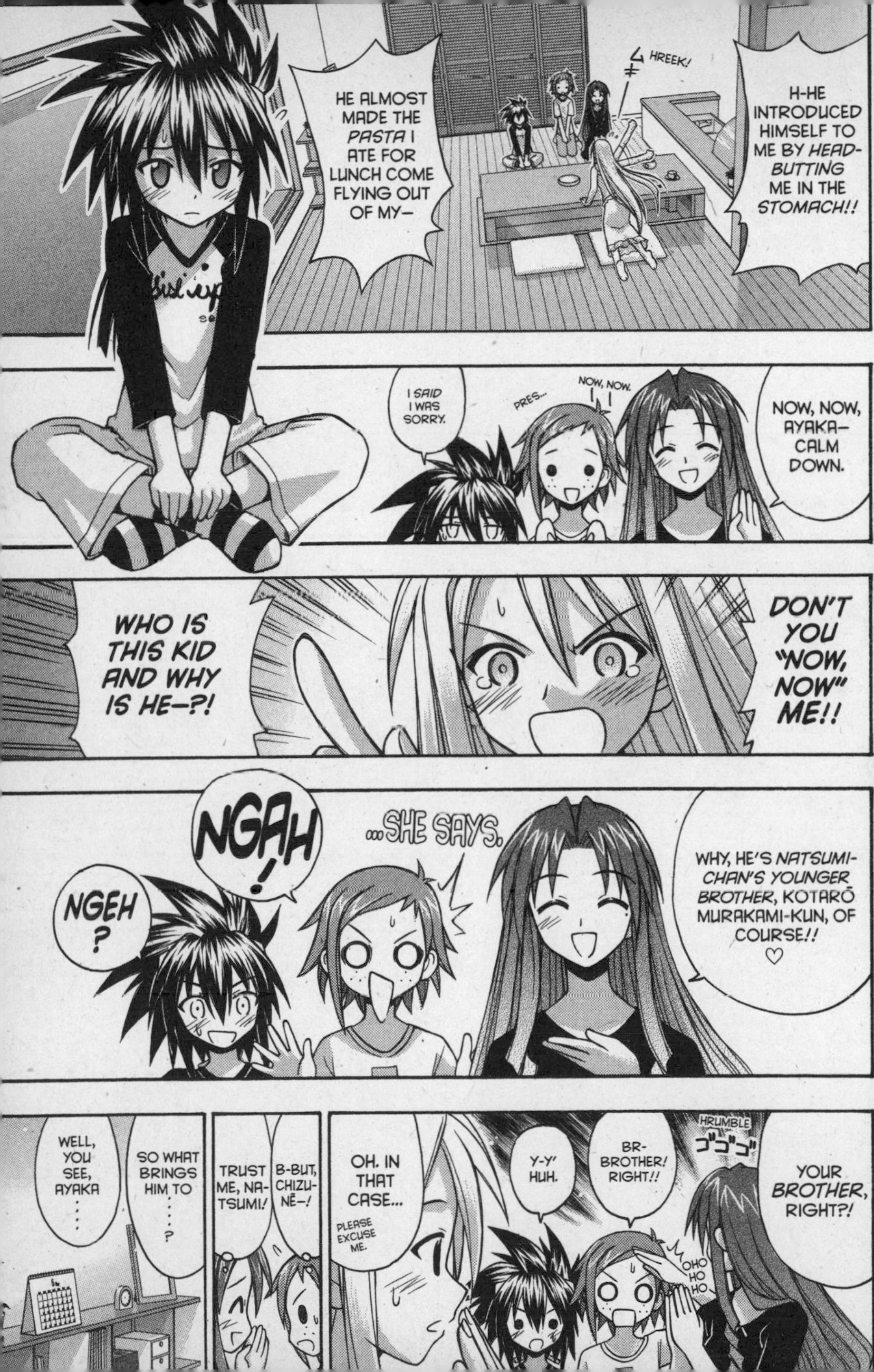
H-HE INTRODUCED HIMSELF TO ME BY HEAD-BUTTING ME IN THE STOMACH!!
HREEK!
HE ALMOST MADE THE PASTA I ATE FOR LUNCH COME FLYING OUT OF MY—
NOW, NOW, AYAKA— CALM DOWN.
NOW, NOW.
PRES...
I SAID I WAS SORRY.
DON'T YOU "NOW, NOW" ME!!
WHO IS THIS KID AND WHY IS HE—?!
WHY, HE'S NATSUMI-CHAN'S YOUNGER BROTHER, KOTARŌ MURAKAMI-KUN, OF COURSE!! ♡
...SHE SAYS.
NGAH!
NGEH?
YOUR BROTHER, RIGHT?!
HRUMBLE
ゴゴゴ
OHO HO HO
BR-BROTHER! RIGHT!!
Y-Y' HUH.
OH. IN THAT CASE...
PLEASE EXCUSE ME.
B-BUT, CHIZU-NĒ—!
TRUST ME, NA-TSUMI!
SO WHAT BRINGS HIM TO .....?
WELL, YOU SEE, AYAKA .....

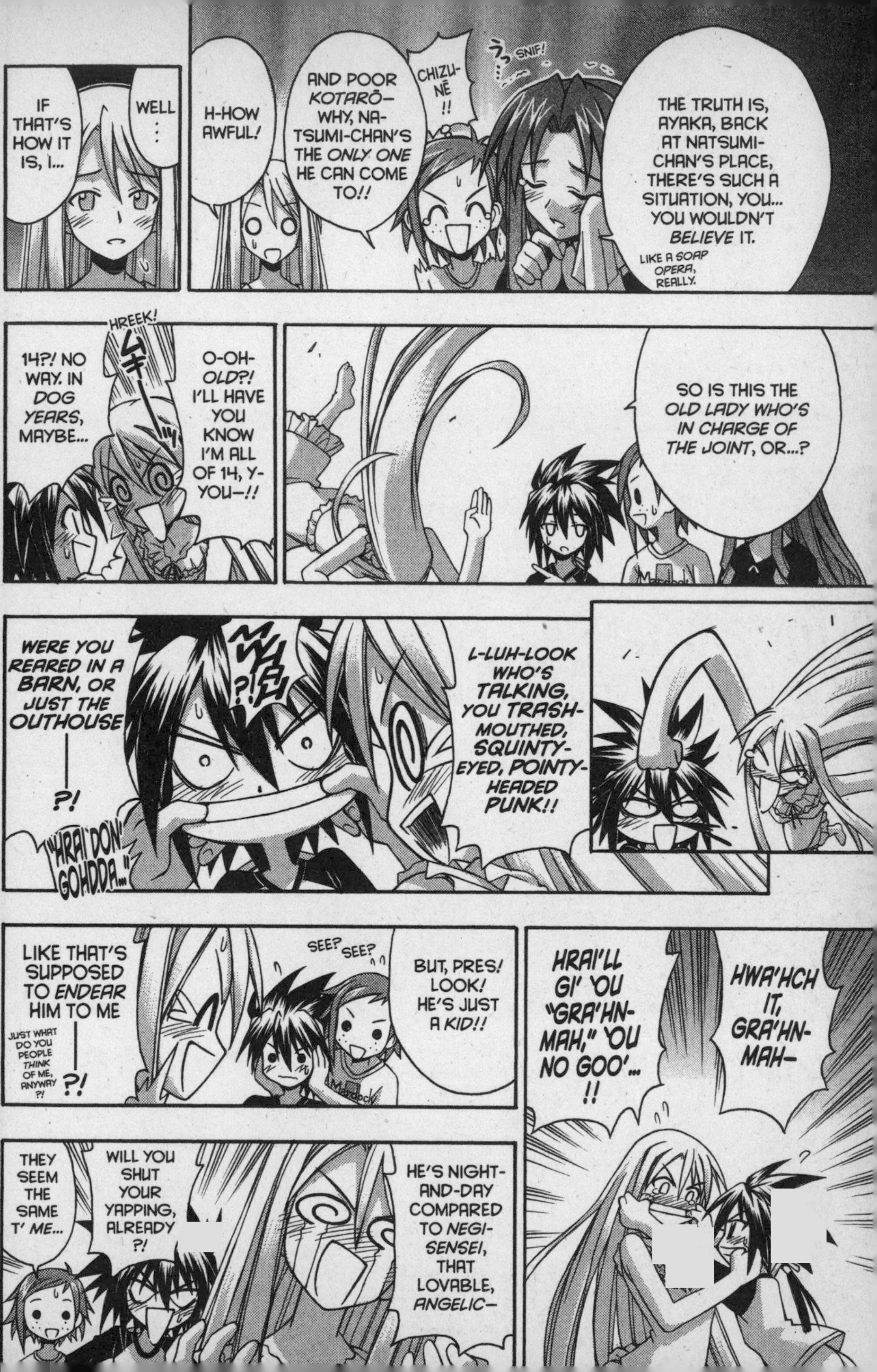
うっ
SNIF!
THE TRUTH IS, AYAKA, BACK AT NATSUMI-CHAN'S PLACE, THERE'S SUCH A SITUATION, YOU... YOU WOULDN'T BELIEVE IT.
LIKE A SOAP OPERA, REALLY.
CHIZU-NĒ!!
AND POOR KOTARŌ—WHY, NATSUMI-CHAN'S THE ONLY ONE HE CAN COME TO!!
H-HOW AWFUL!
WELL...
IF THAT'S HOW IT IS, I...
SO IS THIS THE OLD LADY WHO'S IN CHARGE OF THE JOINT, OR...?
HREEK!
ムキ
O-OH-OLD?! I'LL HAVE YOU KNOW I'M ALL OF 14, Y-YOU—!!
14?! NO WAY. IN DOG YEARS, MAYBE...
L-LUH-LOOK WHO'S TALKING, YOU TRASH-MOUTHED, SQUINTY-EYED, POINTY-HEADED PUNK!!
WERE YOU REARED IN A BARN, OR JUST THE OUTHOUSE—?!
"HRAI DON' GOHDDA..."
HWA'HCH IT, GRA'HN-MAH—
HRAI'LL GI' 'OU "GRA'HN-MAH," 'OU NO GOO'...!!
BUT, PRES! LOOK! HE'S JUST A KID!!
SEE? SEE?
LIKE THAT'S SUPPOSED TO ENDEAR HIM TO ME—?!
JUST WHAT DO YOU PEOPLE THINK OF ME, ANYWAY?!
HE'S NIGHT-AND-DAY COMPARED TO NEGI-SENSEI, THAT LOVABLE, ANGELIC—
WILL YOU SHUT YOUR YAPPING, ALREADY?!
THEY SEEM THE SAME T' ME...

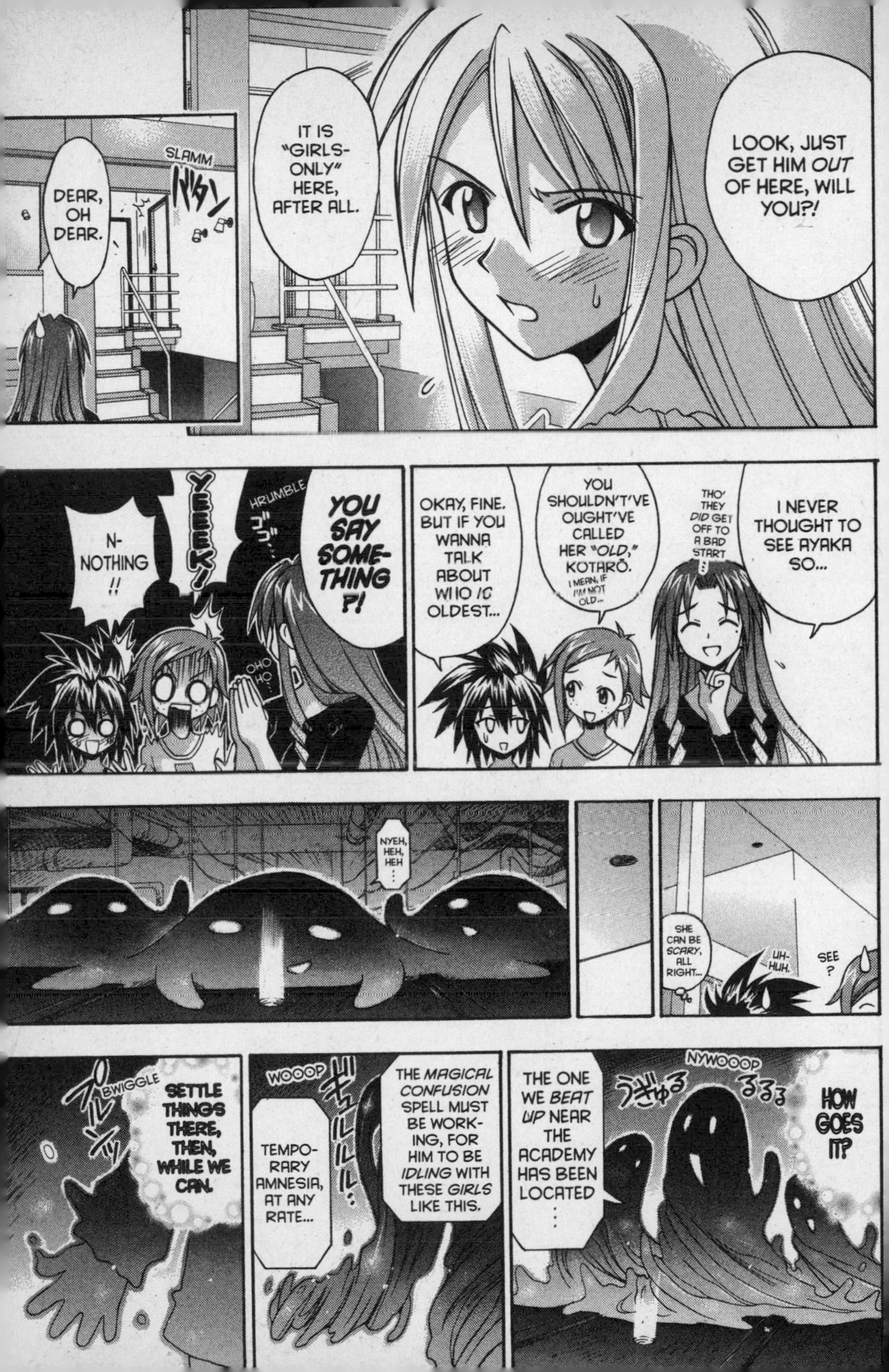
LOOK, JUST GET HIM OUT OF HERE, WILL YOU?!
IT IS "GIRLS-ONLY" HERE, AFTER ALL.
SLAMM
DEAR, OH DEAR.
I NEVER THOUGHT TO SEE AYAKA SO...
THO' THEY DID GET OFF TO A BAD START
YOU SHOULDN'T'VE OUGHT'VE CALLED HER "OLD," KOTARŌ.
I MEAN, IF I'M NOT OLD...
OKAY, FINE. BUT IF YOU WANNA TALK ABOUT WHO IS OLDEST...
YOU SAY SOMETHING?!
HRUMBLE
YEEEK!
N-NOTHING!!
OHO HO
SEE?
UH-HUH.
SHE CAN BE SCARY, ALL RIGHT...
NYEH, HEH, HEH...
HOW GOES IT?
NYWOOOP
THE ONE WE BEAT UP NEAR THE ACADEMY HAS BEEN LOCATED...
THE MAGICAL CONFUSION SPELL MUST BE WORKING, FOR HIM TO BE IDLING WITH THESE GIRLS LIKE THIS.
WOOOP
TEMPORARY AMNESIA, AT ANY RATE...
BWIGGLE
SETTLE THINGS THERE, THEN, WHILE WE CAN.

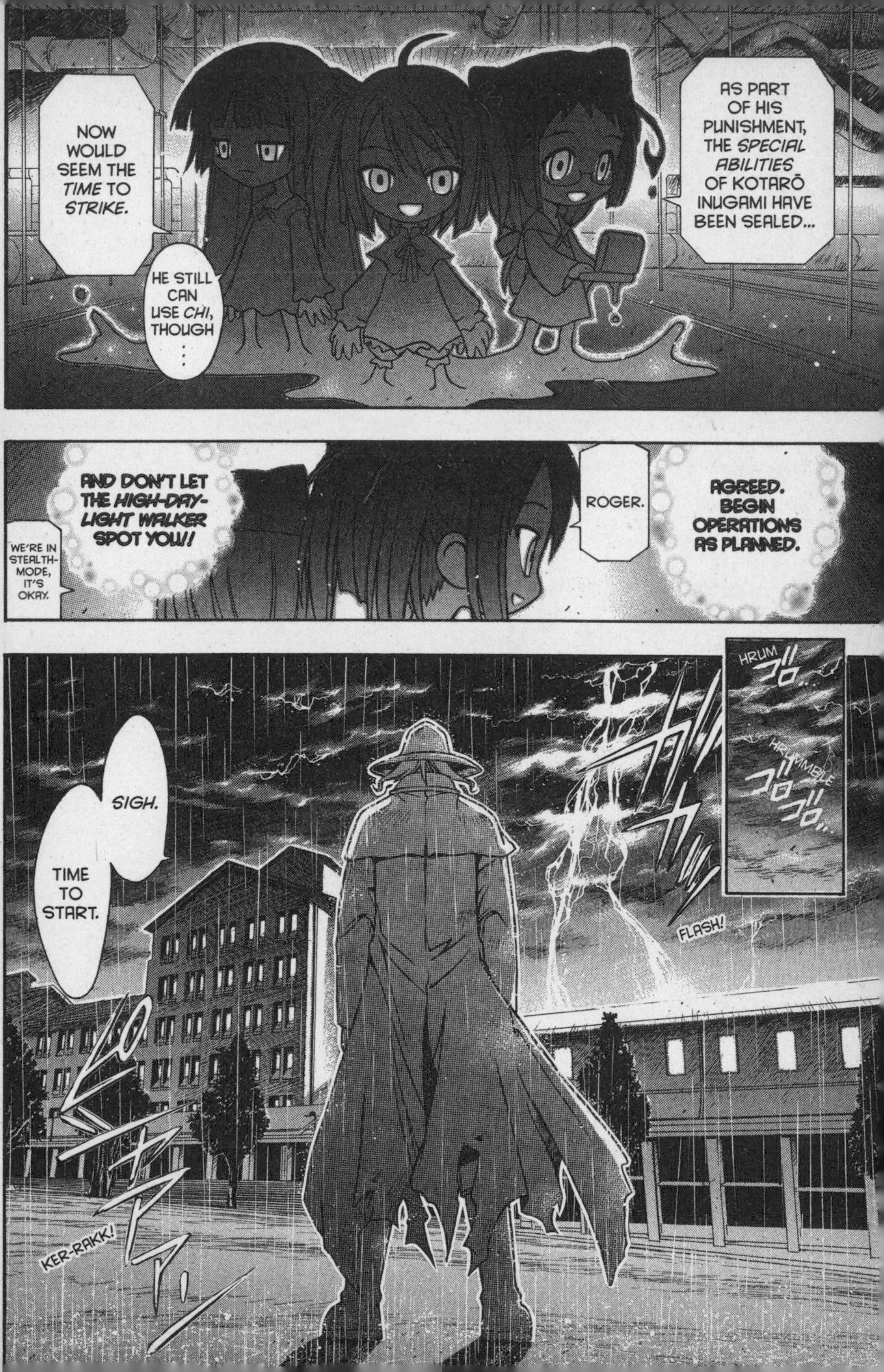
AS PART OF HIS PUNISHMENT, THE SPECIAL ABILITIES OF KOTARŌ INUGAMI HAVE BEEN SEALED...
NOW WOULD SEEM THE TIME TO STRIKE.
HE STILL CAN USE CHI, THOUGH...
AGREED. BEGIN OPERATIONS AS PLANNED.
ROGER.
AND DON'T LET THE HIGH-DAYLIGHT WALKER SPOT YOU!!
WE'RE IN STEALTH-MODE, IT'S OKAY.
HRUM
HRUMMBLE
FLASH!
SIGH.
TIME TO START.
KER-RAKK!

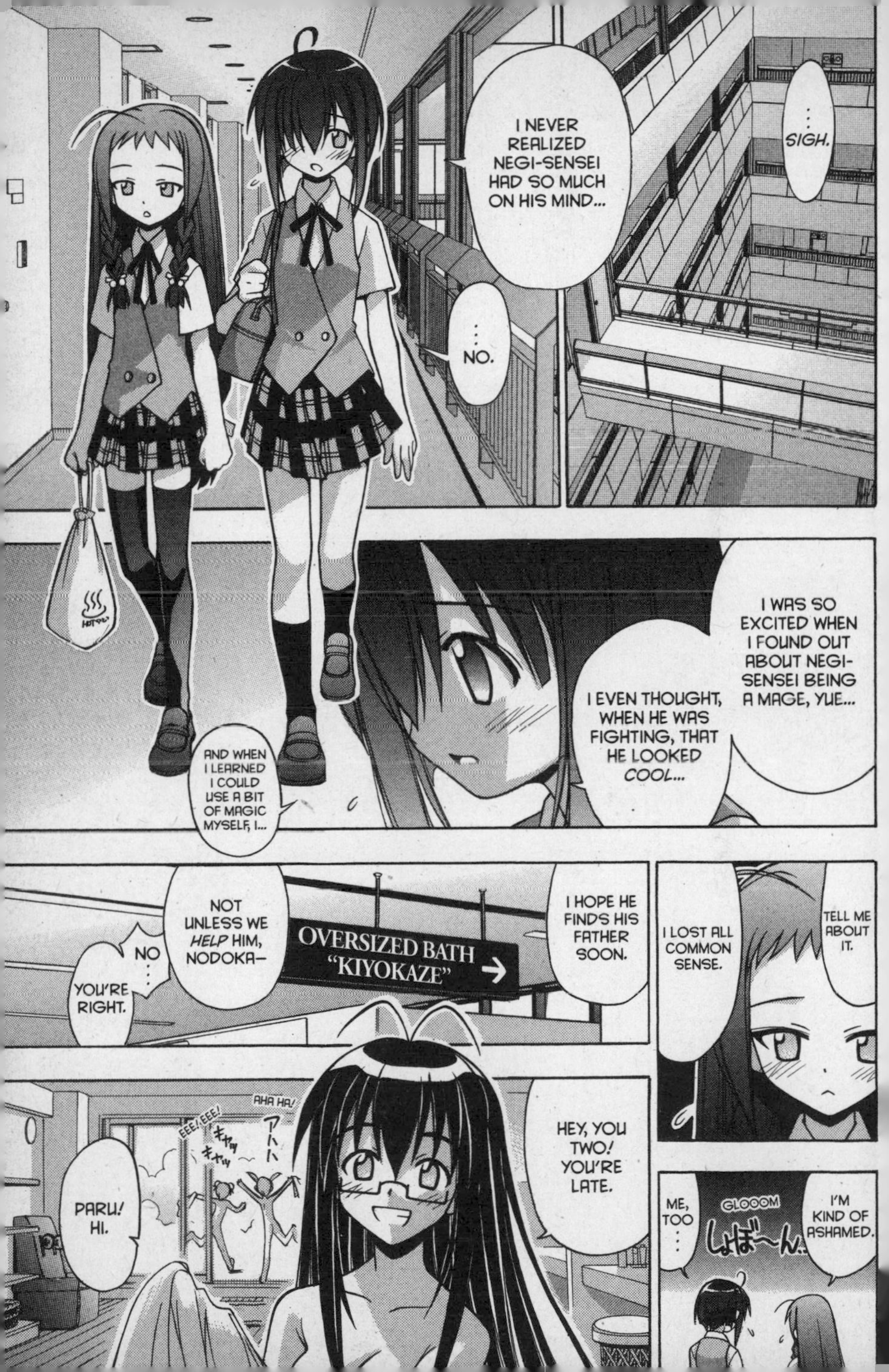
...SIGH.
I NEVER REALIZED NEGI-SENSEI HAD SO MUCH ON HIS MIND...
...NO.
I WAS SO EXCITED WHEN I FOUND OUT ABOUT NEGI-SENSEI BEING A MAGE, YUE...
I EVEN THOUGHT, WHEN HE WAS FIGHTING, THAT HE LOOKED *COOL*...
AND WHEN I LEARNED I COULD USE A BIT OF MAGIC MYSELF, I...
TELL ME ABOUT IT.
I LOST ALL COMMON SENSE.
I HOPE HE FINDS HIS FATHER SOON.
NOT UNLESS WE *HELP* HIM, NODOKA—
OVERSIZED BATH "KIYOKAZE"
NO... YOU'RE RIGHT.
I'M KIND OF ASHAMED.
GLOOOM
しょぼ〜ん...
ME, TOO...
HEY, YOU TWO! YOU'RE LATE.
AHA HA!
アハハ
EEE! EEE!
キャッキャッ
PARU! HI.

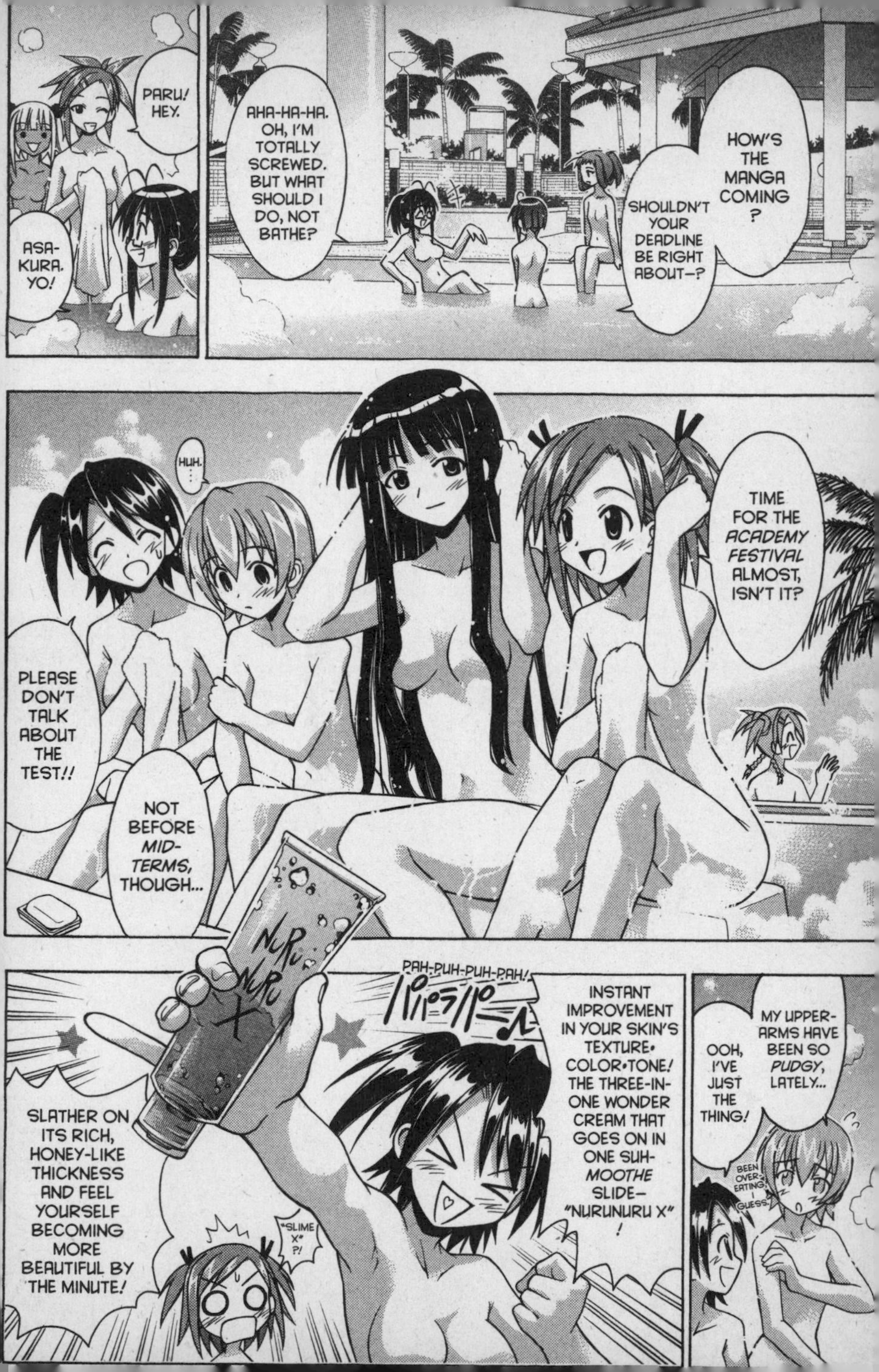
HOW'S THE MANGA COMING?
SHOULDN'T YOUR DEADLINE BE RIGHT ABOUT—?
AHA-HA-HA. OH, I'M TOTALLY SCREWED. BUT WHAT SHOULD I DO, NOT BATHE?
PARU! HEY.
ASA-KURA. YO!
TIME FOR THE *ACADEMY FESTIVAL* ALMOST, ISN'T IT?
HUH...
NOT BEFORE *MID-TERMS*, THOUGH...
PLEASE DON'T TALK ABOUT THE TEST!!
MY UPPER-ARMS HAVE BEEN SO *PUDGY*, LATELY...
OOH, I'VE JUST THE THING!
BEEN OVER-EATING, I GUESS.
PAH-PUH-PUH-PAH!
INSTANT IMPROVEMENT IN YOUR SKIN'S TEXTURE•COLOR•TONE! THE THREE-IN-ONE WONDER CREAM THAT GOES ON IN ONE SUH-*MOOTHE* SLIDE—"NURUNURU X"!
NURU NURU X
SLATHER ON ITS RICH, HONEY-LIKE THICKNESS AND FEEL YOURSELF BECOMING MORE BEAUTIFUL BY THE MINUTE!
"SLIME X"?!

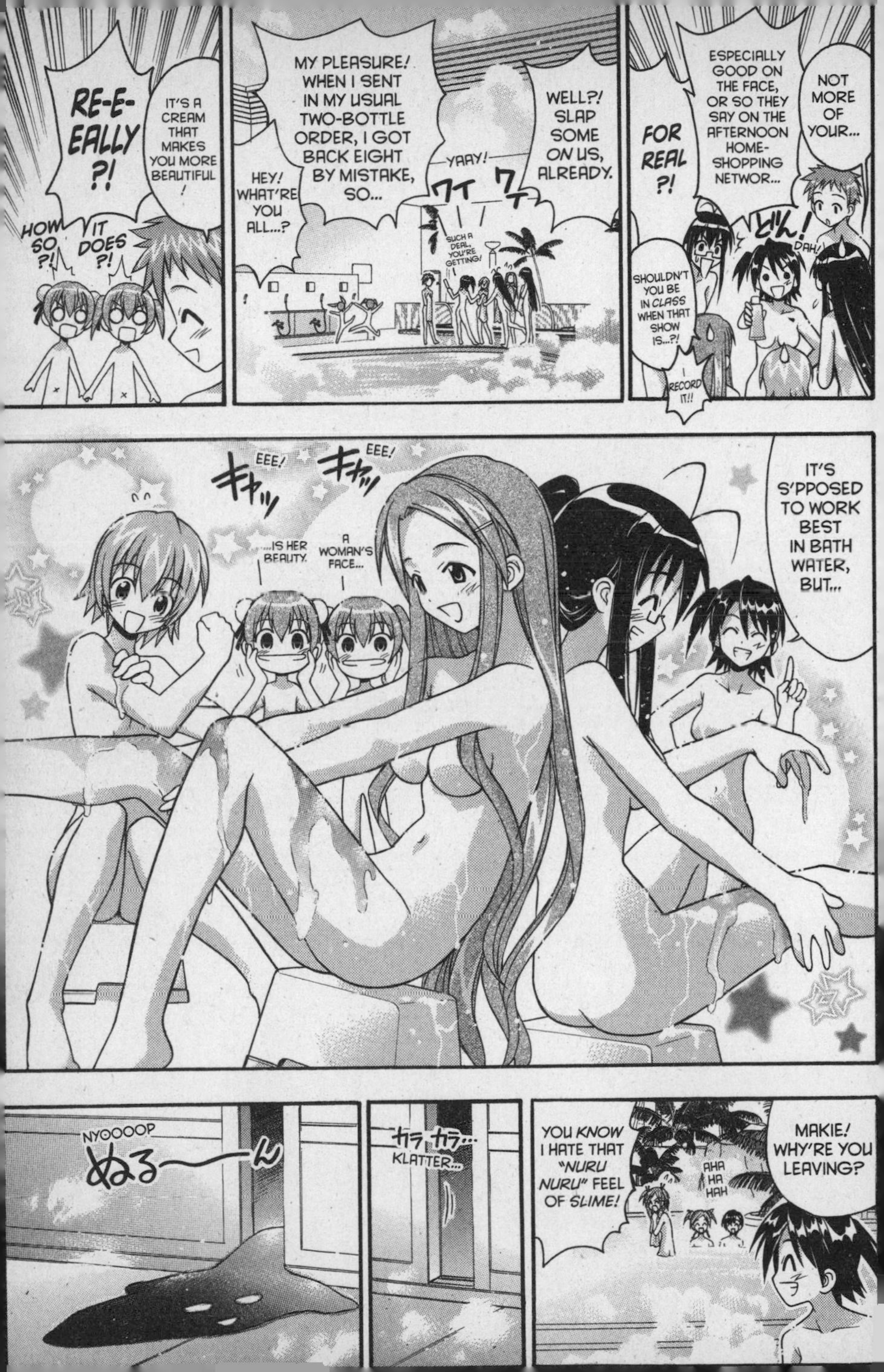
NOT MORE OF YOUR...
ESPECIALLY GOOD ON THE FACE, OR SO THEY SAY ON THE AFTERNOON HOME-SHOPPING NETWOR...
FOR REAL ?!
どん!
DAH!
SHOULDN'T YOU BE IN CLASS WHEN THAT SHOW IS...?!
I RECORD IT!!
WELL?! SLAP SOME ON US, ALREADY.
MY PLEASURE! WHEN I SENT IN MY USUAL TWO-BOTTLE ORDER, I GOT BACK EIGHT BY MISTAKE, SO...
ワイ ワイ
YAAY!
SUCH A DEAL, YOU'RE GETTING!
HEY! WHAT'RE YOU ALL...?
IT'S A CREAM THAT MAKES YOU MORE BEAUTIFUL!
RE-E-EALLY ?!
IT DOES ?!
HOW SO ?!
IT'S S'PPOSED TO WORK BEST IN BATH WATER, BUT...
キャッ
EEE!
キャッ
EEE!
A WOMAN'S FACE...
...IS HER BEAUTY.
MAKIE! WHY'RE YOU LEAVING?
YOU KNOW I HATE THAT "NURU NURU" FEEL OF SLIME!
AHA HA HAH
カラ カラ…
KLATTER...
NYOOOOP
ぬる〜〜ん

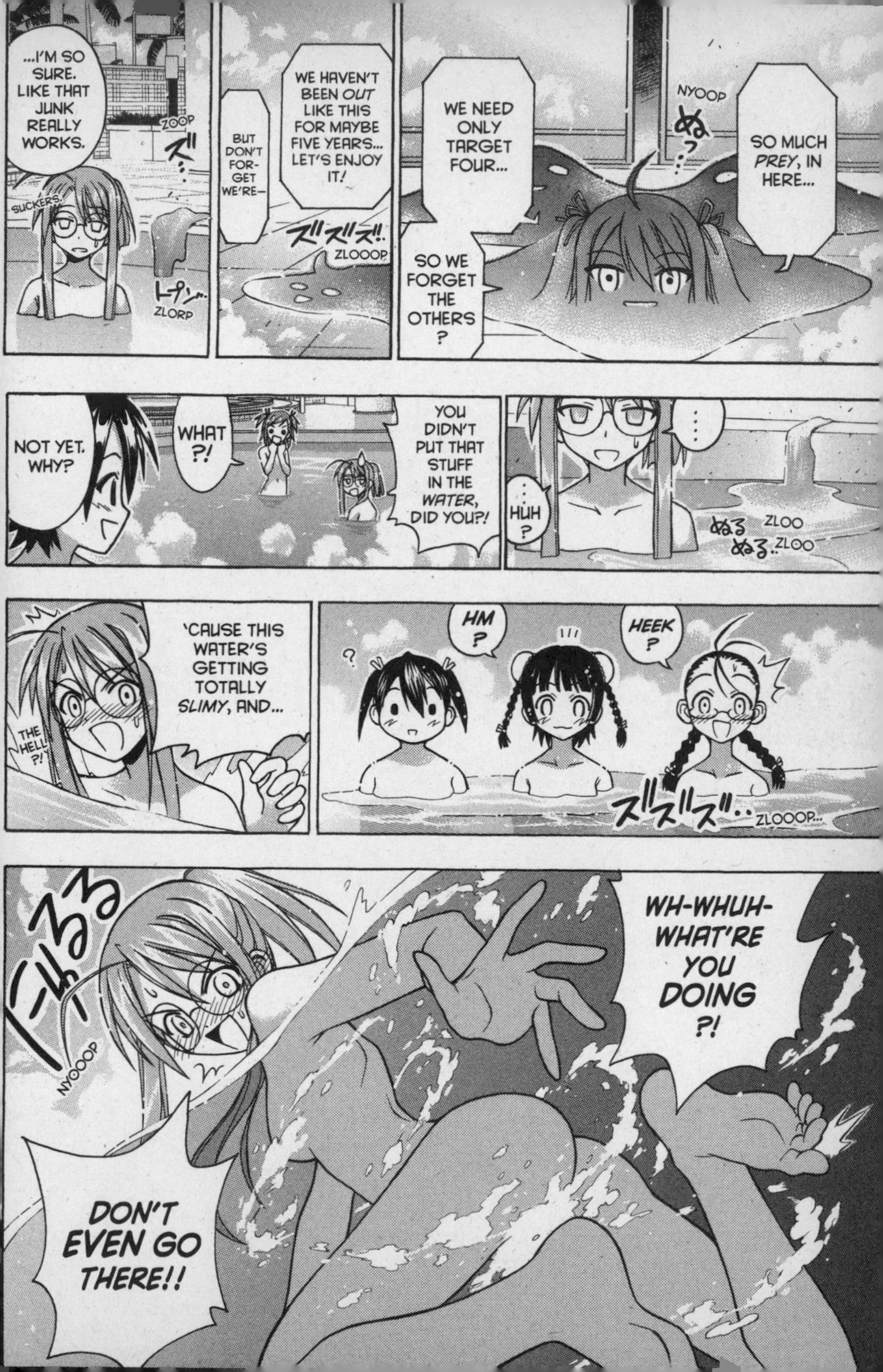
NYOOP
ぬっ
SO MUCH PREY, IN HERE...
WE NEED ONLY TARGET FOUR...
SO WE FORGET THE OTHERS?
WE HAVEN'T BEEN OUT LIKE THIS FOR MAYBE FIVE YEARS... LET'S ENJOY IT!
BUT DON'T FOR-GET WE'RE—
ズズズ!!
ZLOOOP
...I'M SO SURE. LIKE THAT JUNK REALLY WORKS.
ZOOP
ズ
SUCKERS.
トプン
ZLORP
...
...HUH?
ぬるぬる
ZLOO ZLOO
YOU DIDN'T PUT THAT STUFF IN THE WATER, DID YOU?!
WHAT?!
NOT YET. WHY?
HEEK?
HM?
ズズズ..
ZLOOOP...
'CAUSE THIS WATER'S GETTING TOTALLY SLIMY, AND...
THE HELL?!
WH-WHUH-WHAT'RE YOU DOING?!
にゅるる
NYOOOP
DON'T EVEN GO THERE!!

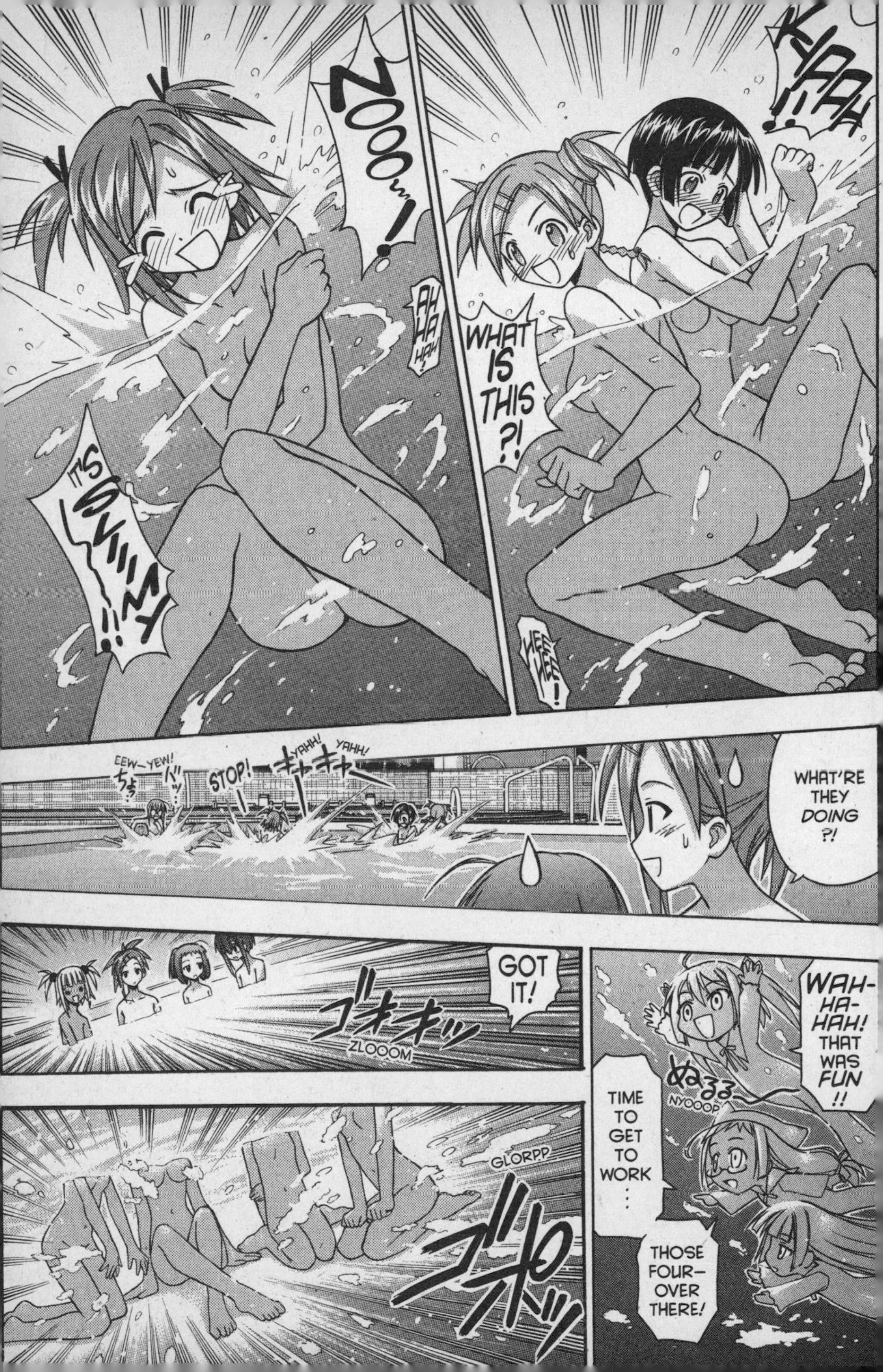
KYAAAH!!
WHAT IS THIS?!
HEE HEE!
NOOOO~!
AH HA HA HAH!
IT'S SLIMY!!
WHAT'RE THEY DOING?!
YAHH! YAHH!
キャーキャー
STOP!
EEW—YEW!
ちょ—バッ
WAH-HA-HAH! THAT WAS FUN!!
ぬるる
NYOOOP
TIME TO GET TO WORK...
THOSE FOUR—OVER THERE!
GOT IT!
ゴオオッ
ZLOOOM
GLORPP
ゴポッ

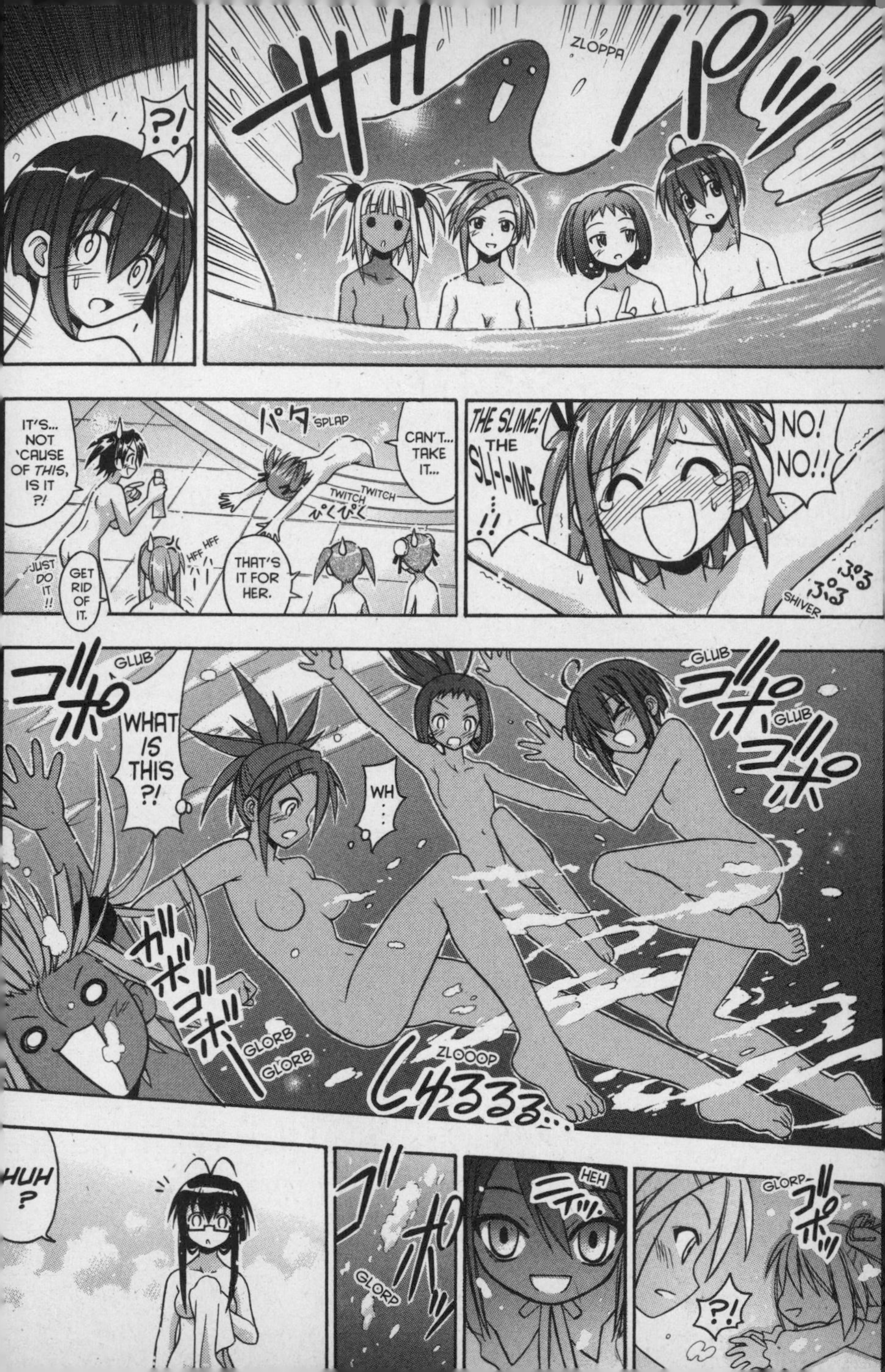

ザッパッ
ZLOPPA
?!
NO! NO!!
THE SLIME! THE SLI-I-IME...!!
ぷるぷる
SHIVER
CAN'T... TAKE IT...
パタ
SPLAP
IT'S... NOT 'CAUSE OF THIS, IS IT ?!
TWITCH TWITCH
ぴくぴく
THAT'S IT FOR HER.
HFF HFF
GET RID OF IT.
JUST DO IT !!
GLUB
ゴポゴポ
GLUB
WH...
WHAT IS THIS ?!
GLUB
ゴポ
ZLOOOP
しゅるるる…
ガボゴボー
GLORB GLORB
GLORP
ゴポッ
?!
HEH
ニィッ
ゴバッ
GLORP
HUH ?

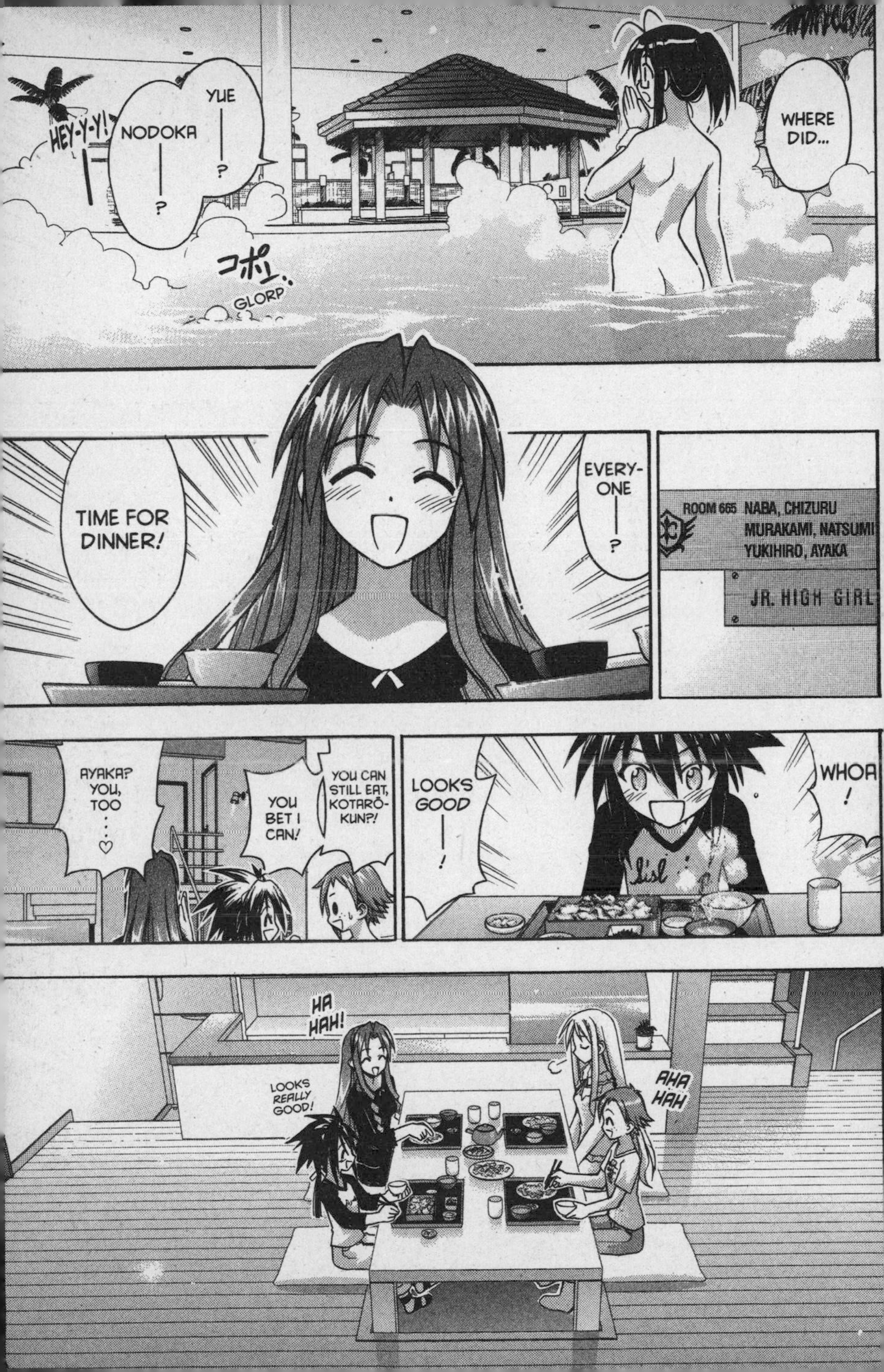
WHERE DID...
YUE ——?
HEY-Y-Y!
NODOKA ——?
コポ…
GLORP
ROOM 665 NABA, CHIZURU MURAKAMI, NATSUMI YUKIHIRO, AYAKA
JR. HIGH GIRL
EVERY-ONE ——?
TIME FOR DINNER!
WHOA!
LOOKS GOOD ——!
YOU CAN STILL EAT, KOTARŌ-KUN?!
YOU BET I CAN!
AYAKA? YOU, TOO...♡
AHA HAH
HA HAH!
LOOKS REALLY GOOD!

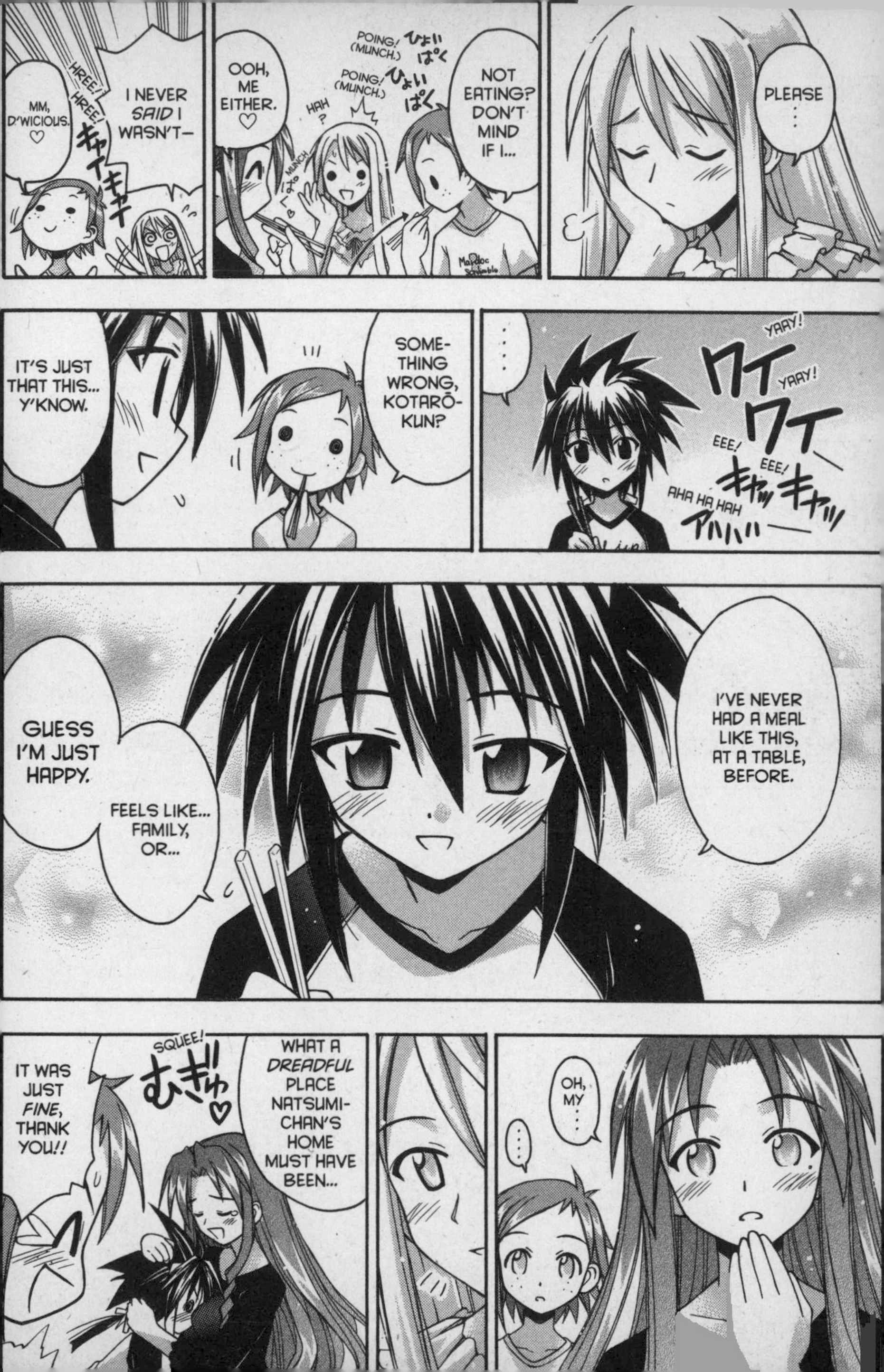
PLEASE . . .
NOT EATING? DON'T MIND IF I...
POING! (MUNCH.) ひょい ぱく
POING! (MUNCH.) ひょい ぱく
HAH?
MUNCH
OOH, ME EITHER. ♡
I NEVER *SAID* I WASN'T—
HREE! HREE! キャイキャイ
MM, D'WICIOUS. ♡
YAAY! ワイ
YAAY! ワイ
EEE! EEE! キャッキャッ
AHA HA HAH アハハー
. . .
SOME-THING WRONG, KOTARŌ-KUN?
IT'S JUST THAT THIS... Y'KNOW.
I'VE NEVER HAD A MEAL LIKE THIS, AT A TABLE, BEFORE.
GUESS I'M JUST HAPPY.
FEELS LIKE... FAMILY, OR...
OH, MY . . .
. . .
WHAT A *DREADFUL* PLACE NATSUMI-CHAN'S HOME MUST HAVE BEEN...
SQUEE! むぎゅ ♡
IT WAS JUST *FINE*, THANK YOU!!

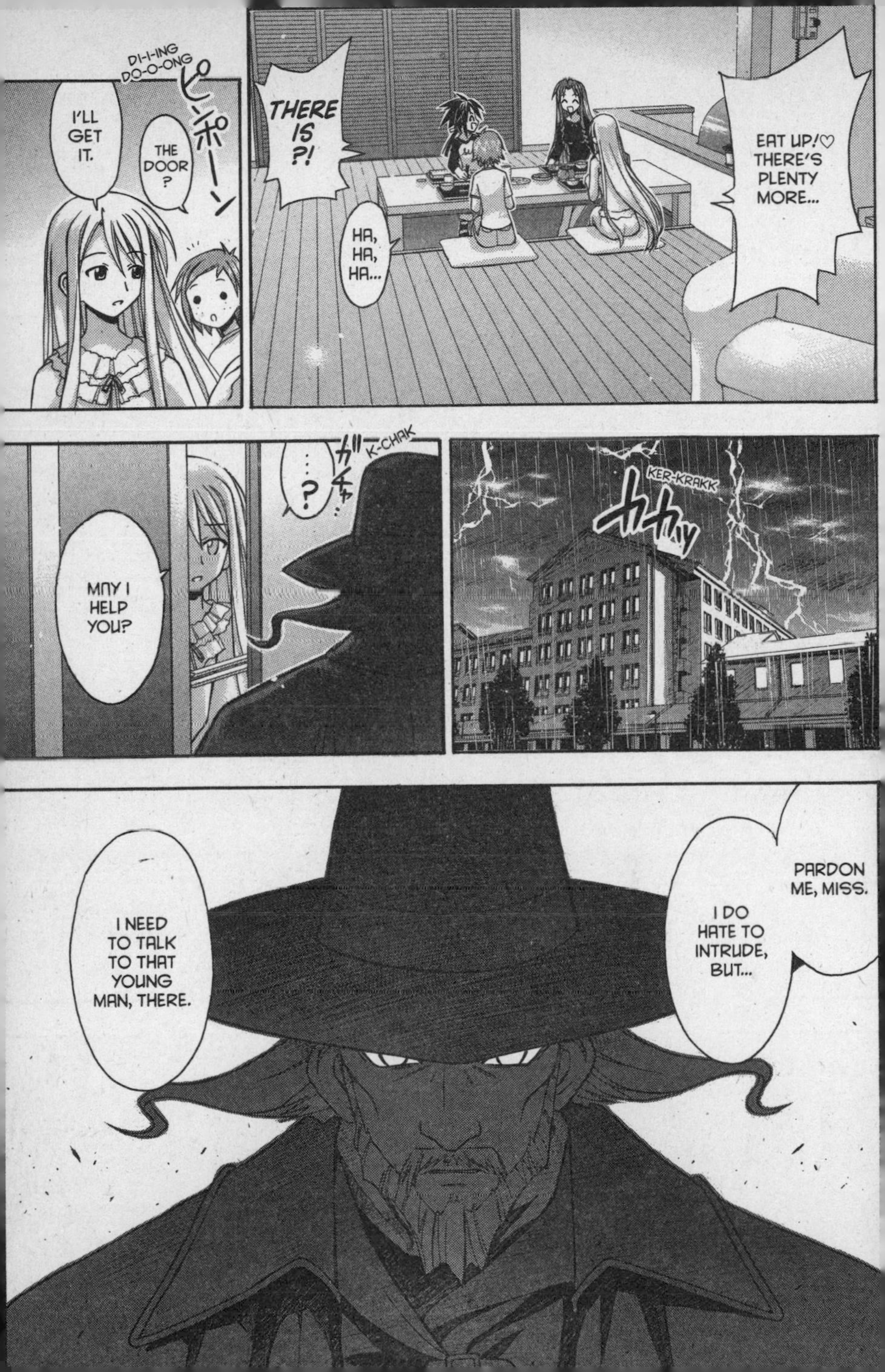
EAT UP!♡ THERE'S PLENTY MORE...
THERE IS ?!
HA, HA, HA...
DI-I-ING DO-O-ONG
ピンポーン
THE DOOR ?
I'LL GET IT.
KER-KRAKK
カカッ
K-CHAK
ガチャ
...?
MAY I HELP YOU?
PARDON ME, MISS.
I DO HATE TO INTRUDE, BUT...
I NEED TO TALK TO THAT YOUNG MAN, THERE.

STUDENT NUMBER 21
NABA, CHIZURU

BORN: JANUARY 29, 1989
BLOOD TYPE: A
LIKES: LIFE WITHOUT INCIDENT,
      CARING FOR OTHERS
DISLIKES: BEING ALONE. PERSONAL
      RELATIONSHIPS OF A DISTANT NATURE
CLUB AFFILIATIONS: ASTRONOMY
REMARKS: VOLUNTEERS AT MAHORA ACADEMY
      DAYCARE CENTER. MOST WELL-ENDOWED.

STUDENT NUMBER 28
MURAKAMI, NATSUMI

BORN: OCTOBER 21, 1988
BLOODTYPE: A
LIKES: ACTING, ESPECIALLY THE MOMENT
      RIGHT BEFORE TAKING THE STAGE
      (FEELING SOMETHING *CHANGE*
      INSIDE)
DISLIKES: MYSELF (MY FRECKLES!). MY
      UNMANAGEABLE RED HAIR.
      MY AD LIBS...
CLUB AFFILIATIONS: THEATER
REMARKS: ALSO A MEMBER OF THE NO. 3
      COLLEGE THEATER CLUB

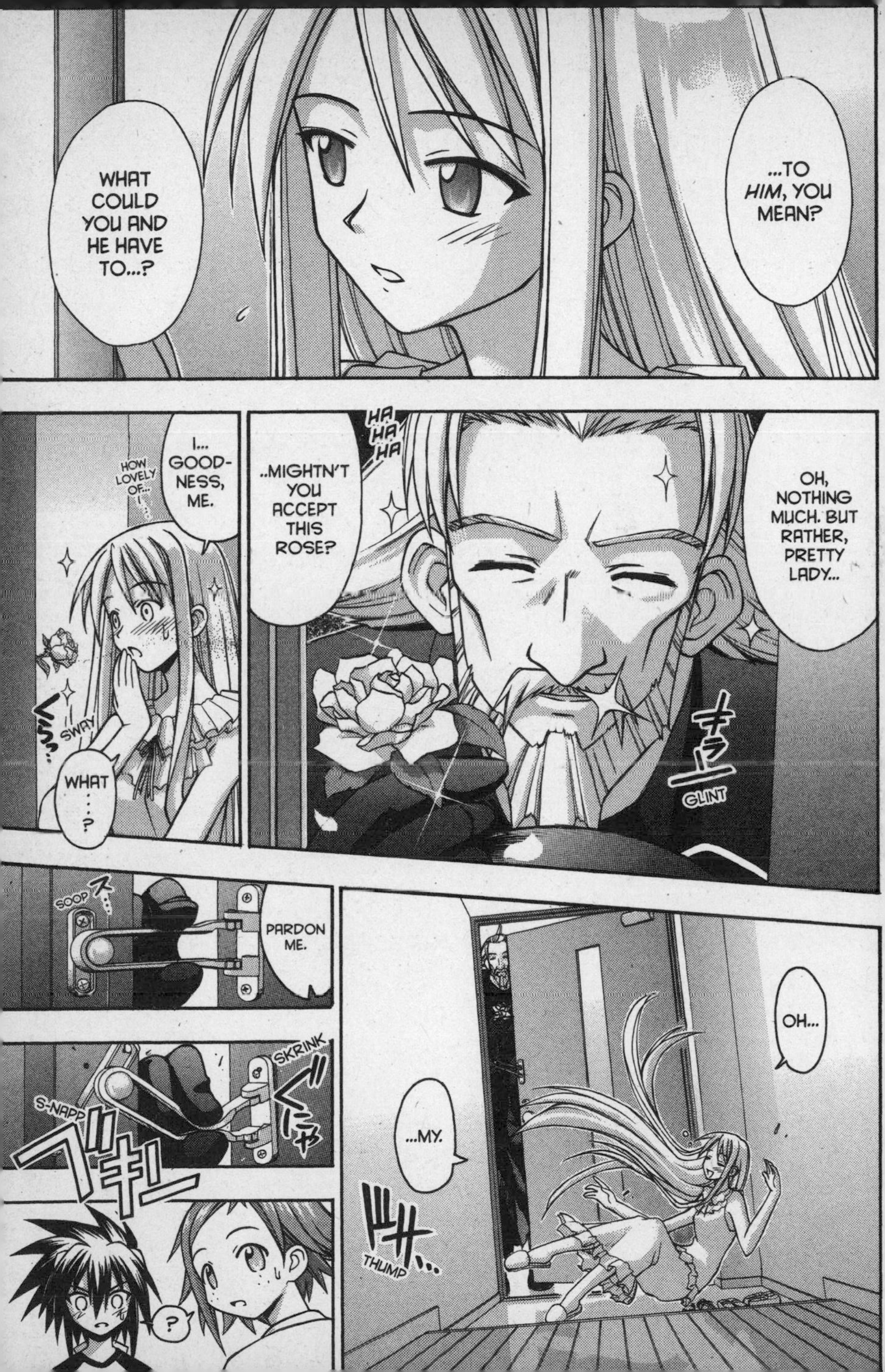
...TO HIM, YOU MEAN?
WHAT COULD YOU AND HE HAVE TO...?
OH, NOTHING MUCH. BUT RATHER, PRETTY LADY...
HA HA HA
GLINT
..MIGHTN'T YOU ACCEPT THIS ROSE?
I... GOODNESS, ME.
HOW LOVELY OF... I...
SWAY
WHAT...?
OH...
...MY.
THUMP
PARDON ME.
SOOP
SKRINK
S-NAPP
?

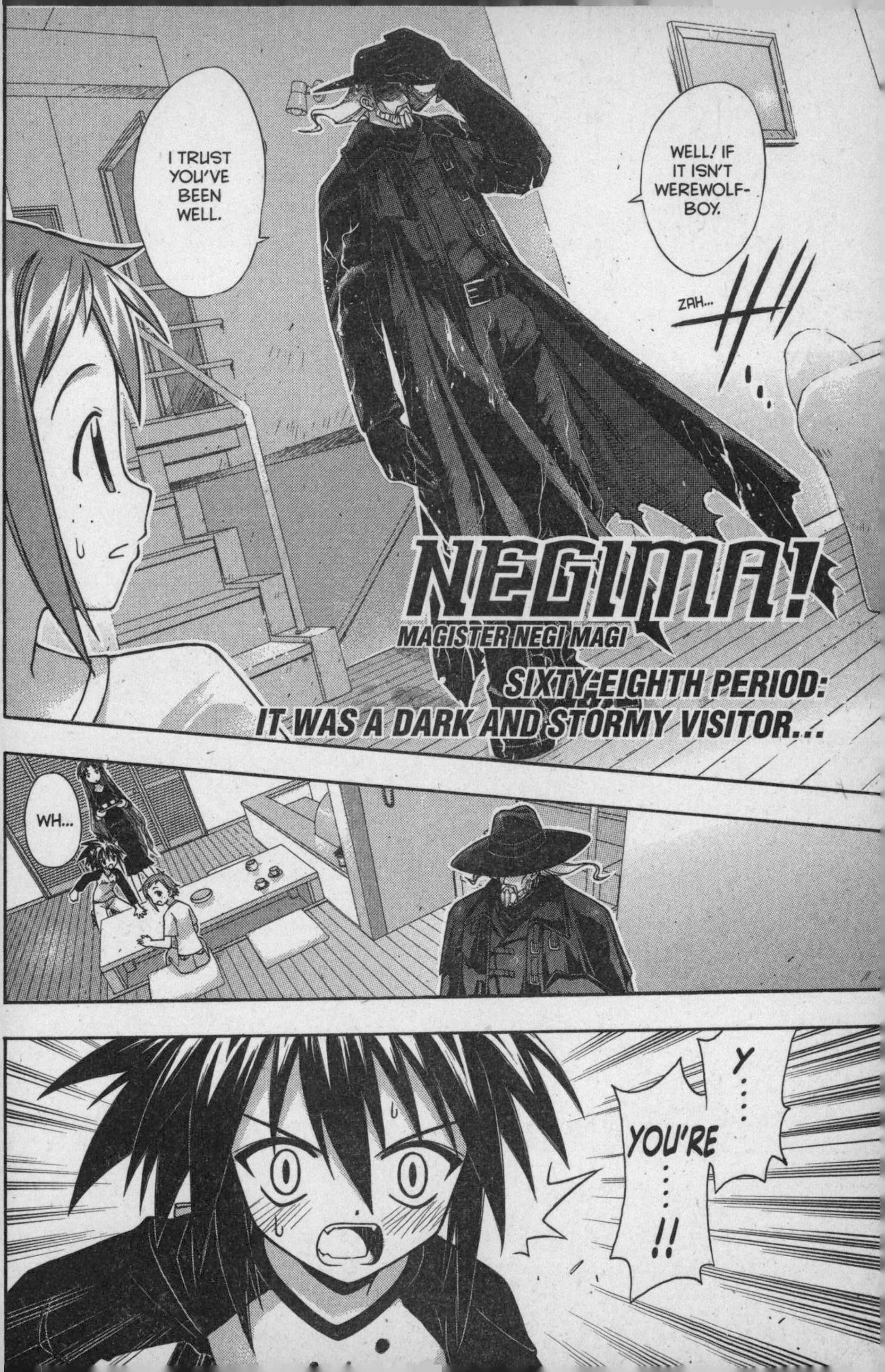
WELL! IF IT ISN'T WEREWOLF-BOY.
ZAH...
I TRUST YOU'VE BEEN WELL.
NEGIMA!
MAGISTER NEGI MAGI
SIXTY-EIGHTH PERIOD:
IT WAS A DARK AND STORMY VISITOR...
WH...
Y... YOU'RE...!!

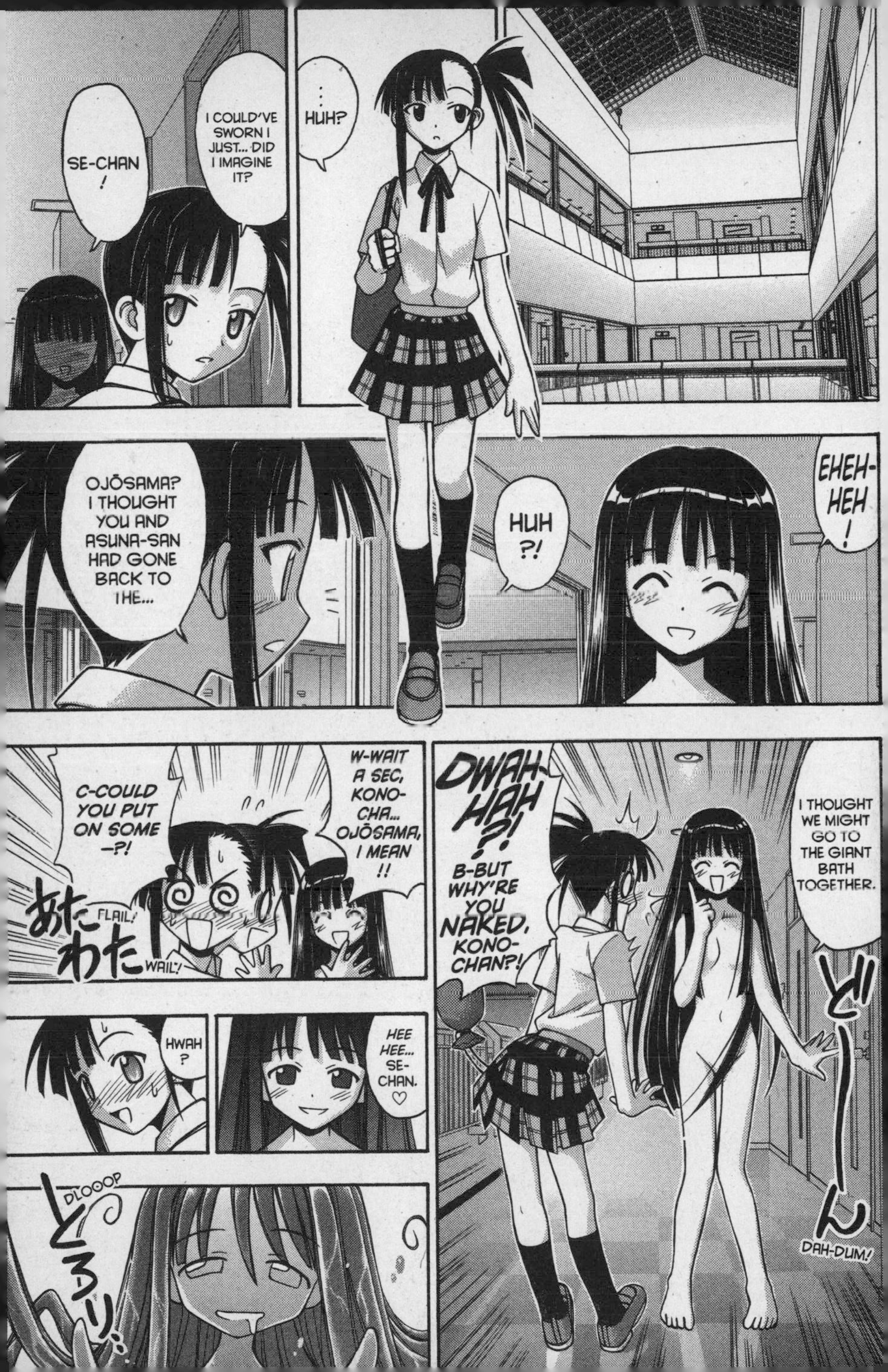

...
HUH?
I COULD'VE SWORN I JUST... DID I IMAGINE IT?
SE-CHAN!
EHEH-HEH!
HUH?!
OJŌSAMA? I THOUGHT YOU AND ASUNA-SAN HAD GONE BACK TO THE...
I THOUGHT WE MIGHT GO TO THE GIANT BATH TOGETHER.
DWAH-HAH?!
B-BUT WHY'RE YOU NAKED, KONO-CHAN?!
どーん
DAH-DUM!
W-WAIT A SEC, KONO-CHA... OJŌSAMA, I MEAN!!
C-COULD YOU PUT ON SOME—?!
あたわた
FLAIL!
WAIL!
HEE HEE... SE-CHAN. ♡
HWAH?
とろ～り
DLOOOP

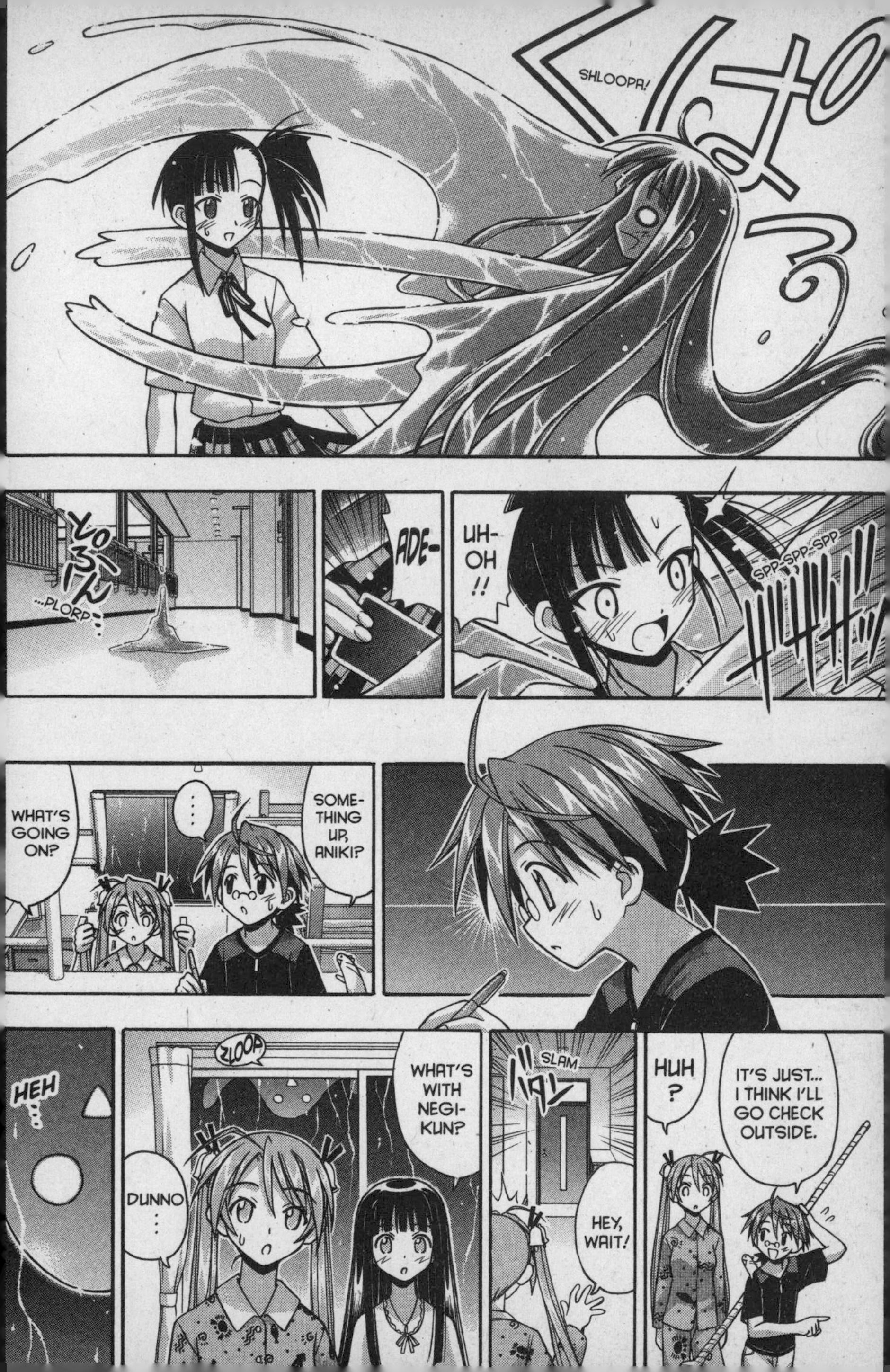
SHLOOPA!
SPP-SPP-SPP
UH-OH !!
ADE-
...PLORP
SOME-THING UP, ANIKI?
....
WHAT'S GOING ON?
IT'S JUST... I THINK I'LL GO CHECK OUTSIDE.
HUH ?
HEY, WAIT!
SLAM
WHAT'S WITH NEGI-KUN?
ZLOOP
DUNNO ...
HEH ...

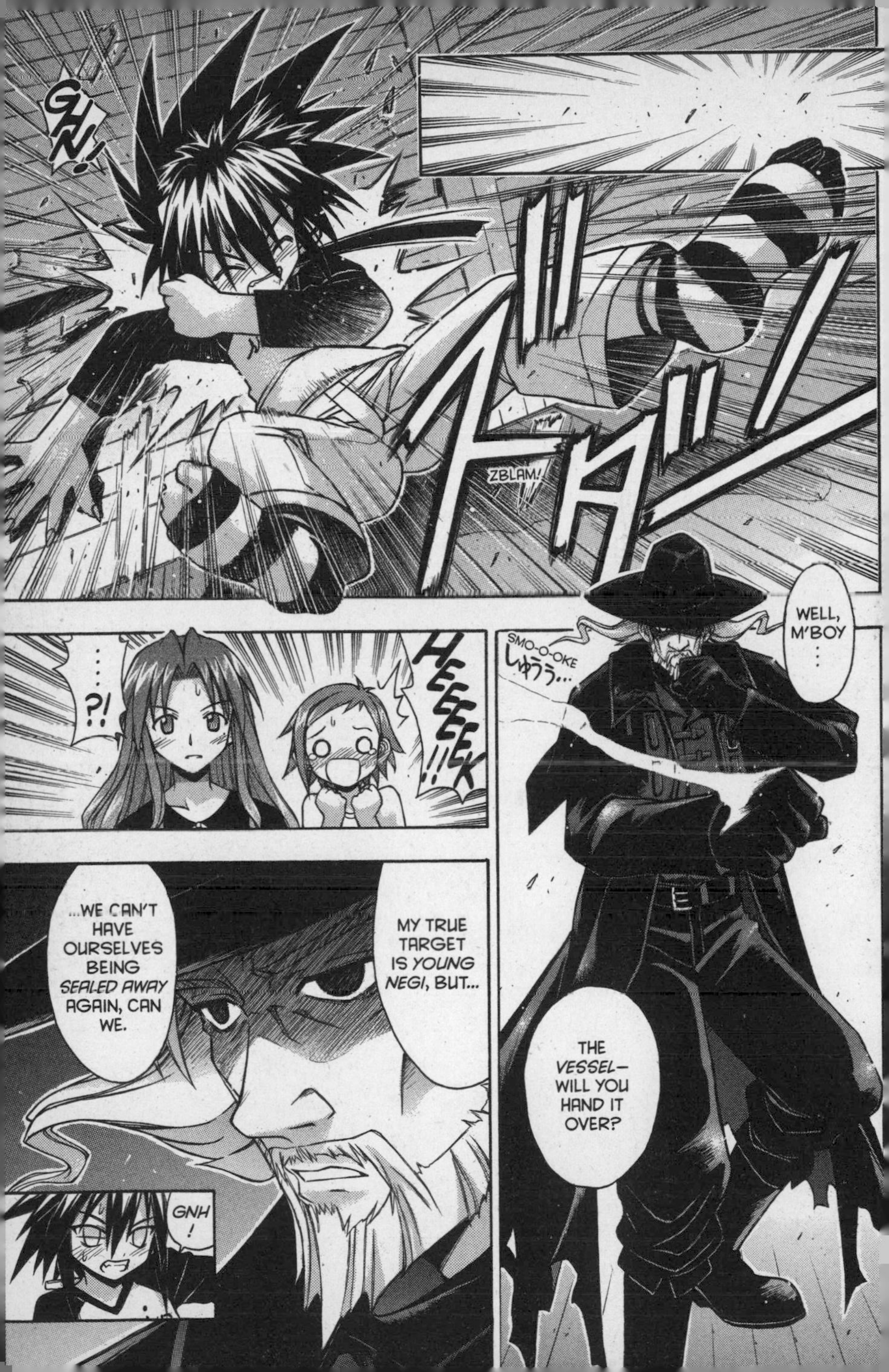
GHN!
ZBLAM!
WELL, M'BOY...
SMO-O-OKE しゅうう...
THE VESSEL— WILL YOU HAND IT OVER?
HEEEEEK!!!
...?!
MY TRUE TARGET IS YOUNG NEGI, BUT...
...WE CAN'T HAVE OURSELVES BEING SEALED AWAY AGAIN, CAN WE.
GNH!

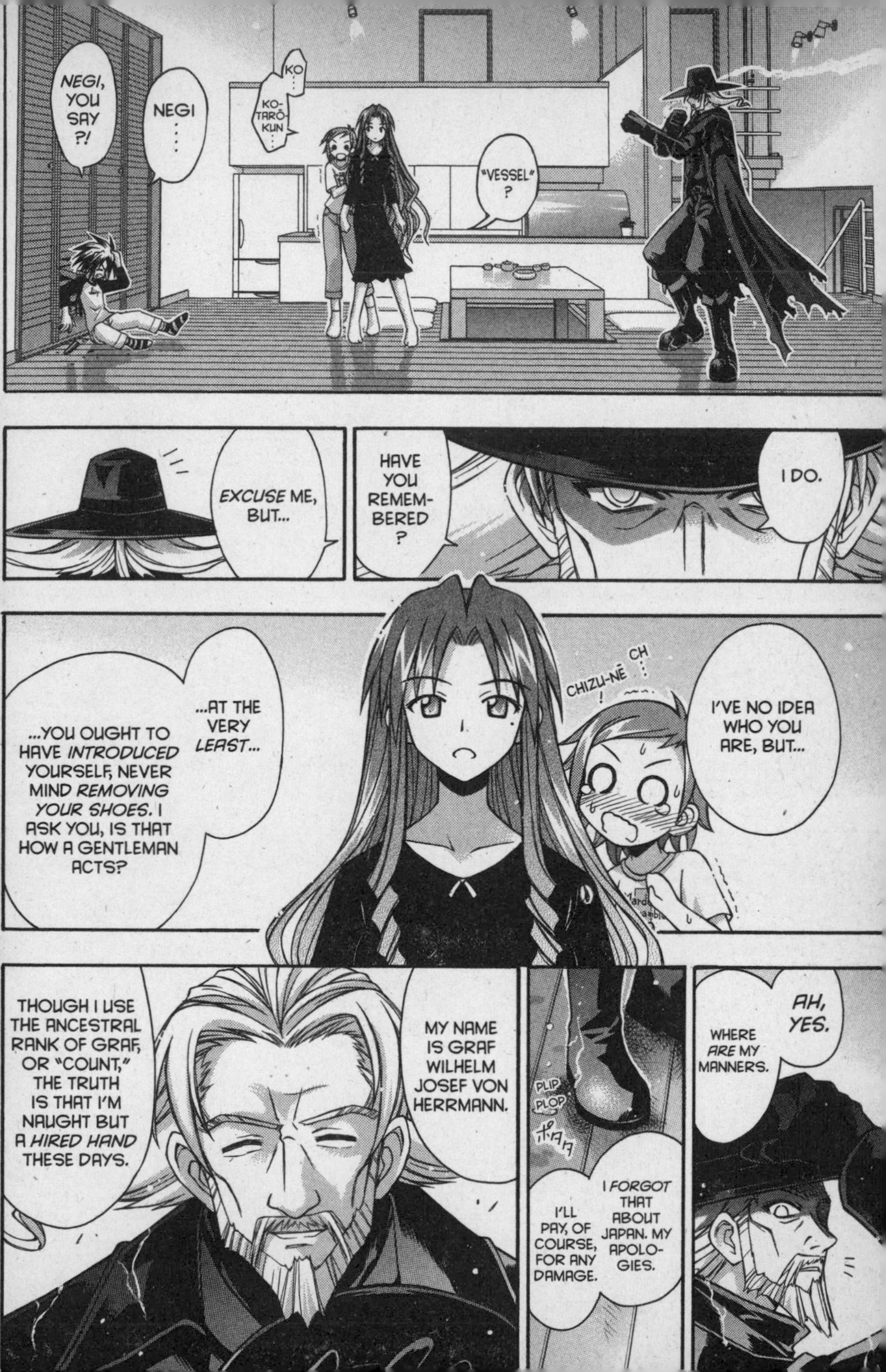
"VESSEL"?
KO... KO-TARŌ-KUN...
NEGI....
NEGI, YOU SAY?!
HAVE YOU REMEMBERED?
I DO.
EXCUSE ME, BUT...
I'VE NO IDEA WHO YOU ARE, BUT...
CH... CHIZU-NĒ!
...AT THE VERY LEAST...
...YOU OUGHT TO HAVE INTRODUCED YOURSELF, NEVER MIND REMOVING YOUR SHOES. I ASK YOU, IS THAT HOW A GENTLEMAN ACTS?
AH, YES.
WHERE ARE MY MANNERS.
I FORGOT THAT ABOUT JAPAN. MY APOLOGIES.
I'LL PAY, OF COURSE, FOR ANY DAMAGE.
PLIP PLOP
MY NAME IS GRAF WILHELM JOSEF VON HERRMANN.
THOUGH I USE THE ANCESTRAL RANK OF GRAF, OR "COUNT," THE TRUTH IS THAT I'M NAUGHT BUT A HIRED HAND THESE DAYS.

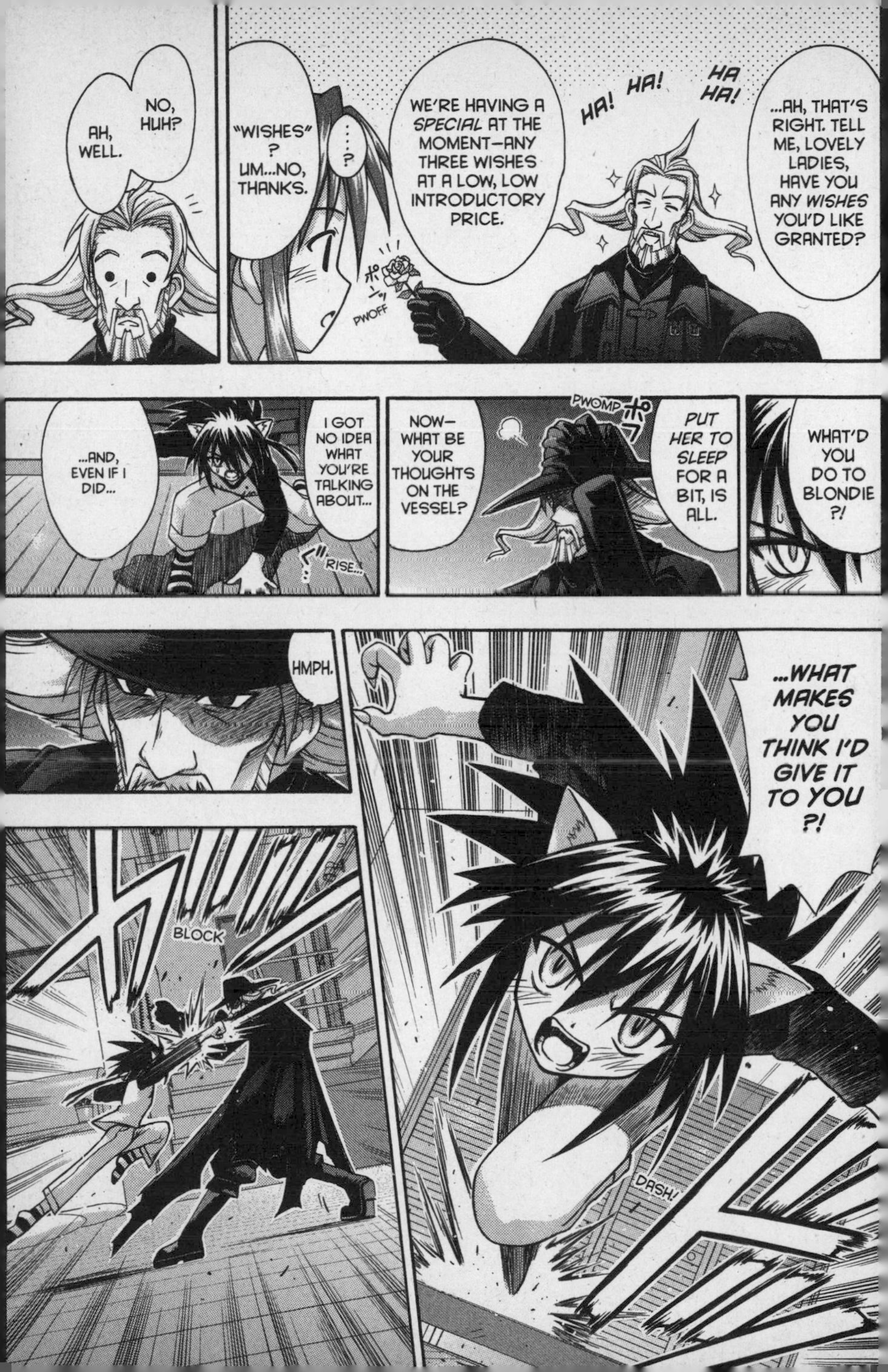
...AH, THAT'S RIGHT. TELL ME, LOVELY LADIES, HAVE YOU ANY *WISHES* YOU'D LIKE GRANTED?
HA! HA! HA HA!
WE'RE HAVING A *SPECIAL* AT THE MOMENT—ANY THREE WISHES AT A LOW, LOW INTRODUCTORY PRICE.
PWOFF
...?
"WISHES"? UM...NO, THANKS.
NO, HUH?
AH, WELL.
WHAT'D YOU DO TO BLONDIE?!
PUT HER TO SLEEP FOR A BIT, IS ALL.
PWOMP
NOW—WHAT BE YOUR THOUGHTS ON THE VESSEL?
I GOT NO IDEA WHAT YOU'RE TALKING ABOUT...
...AND, EVEN IF I DID...
RISE...
...WHAT MAKES YOU THINK I'D GIVE IT TO YOU?!
DASH!
HMPH.
BLOCK

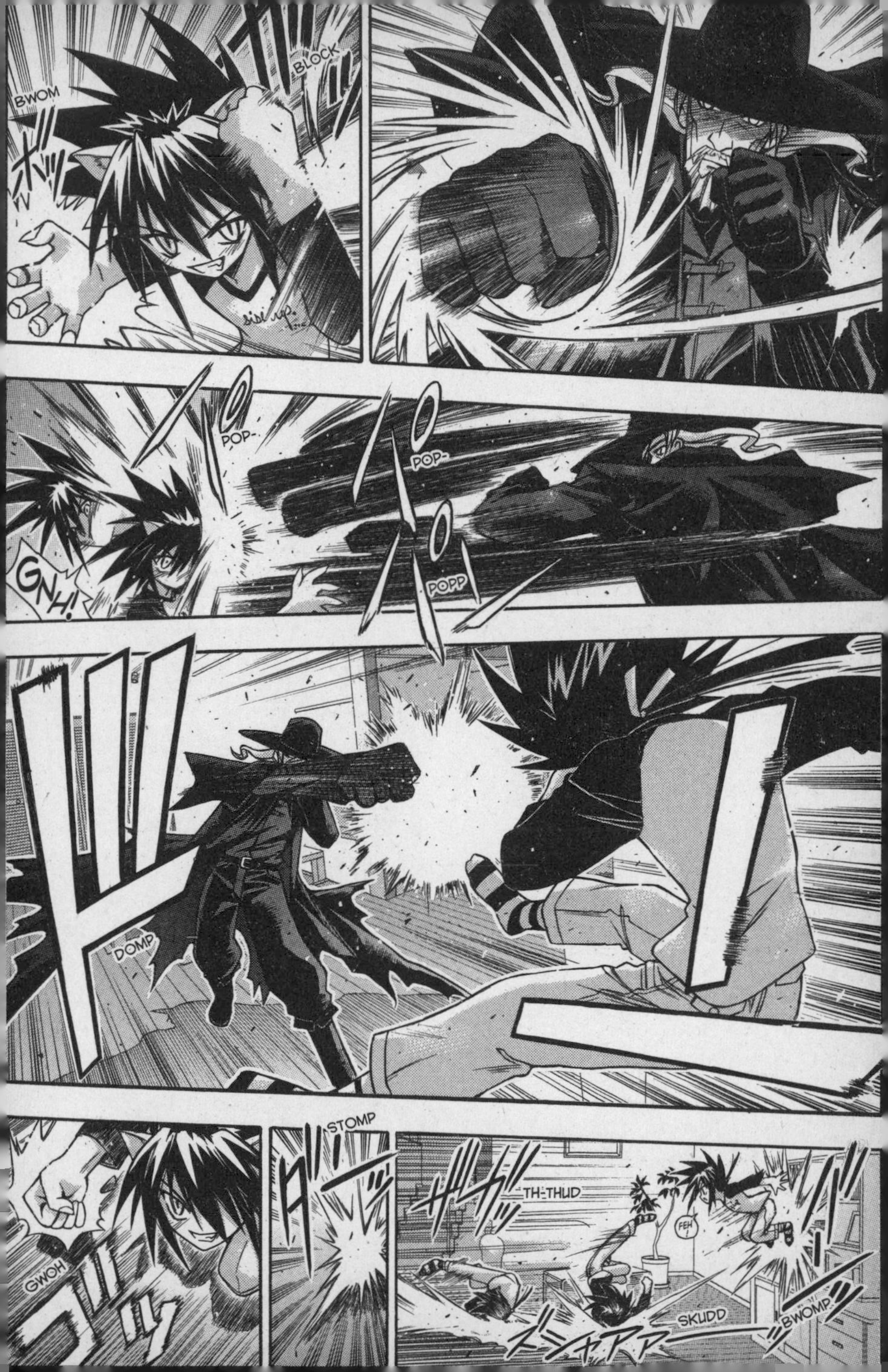
BLOCK
BWOM
POPP
POP-
POP-
GNH!
DOMP
TH-THUD
FEH!
BWOMP
SKUDD
STOMP
GWOH

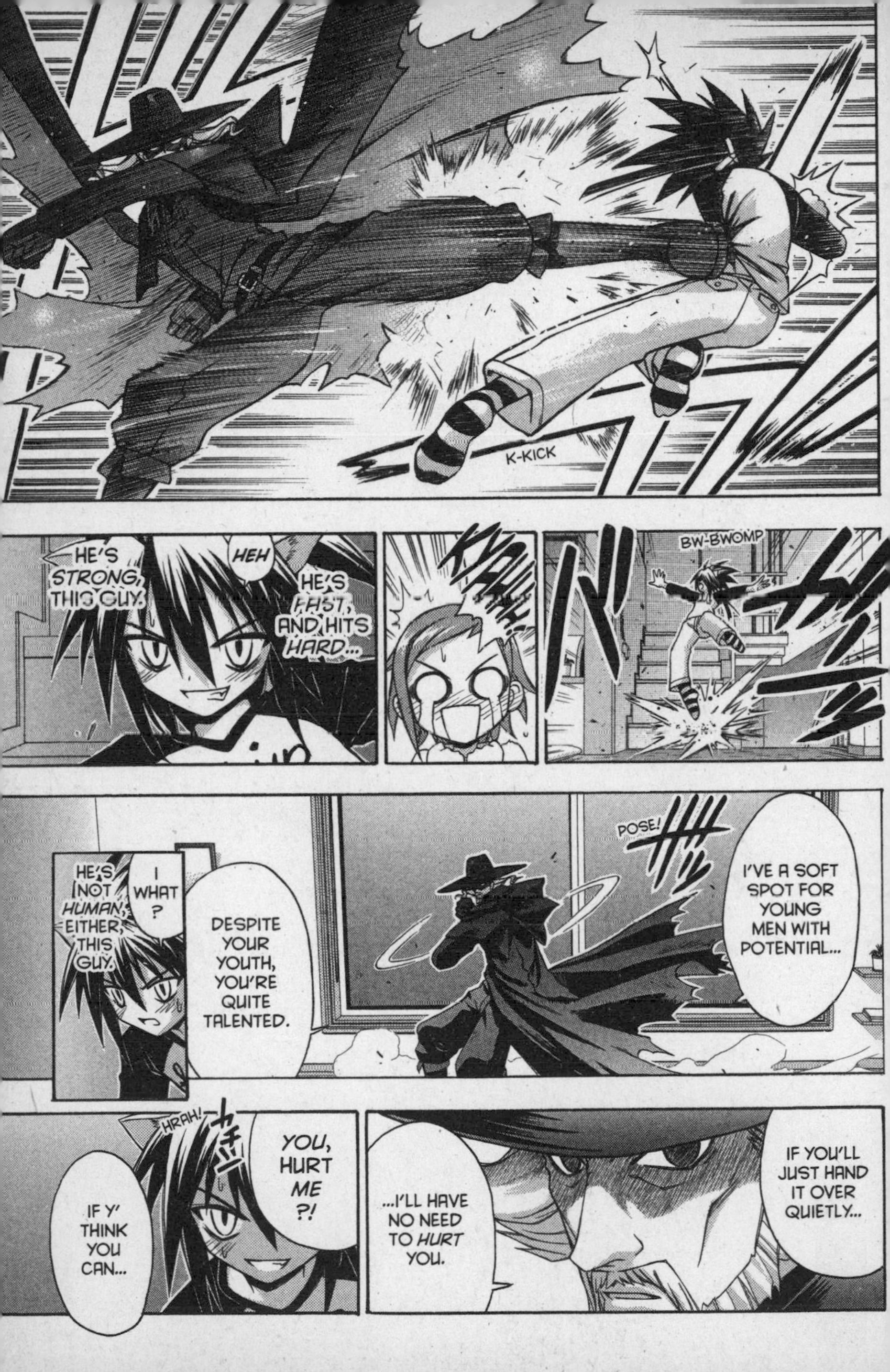

K-KICK
BW-BWOMP
HEH
HE'S FAST, AND HITS HARD...
HE'S STRONG, THIS GUY.
POSE!
I'VE A SOFT SPOT FOR YOUNG MEN WITH POTENTIAL...
DESPITE YOUR YOUTH, YOU'RE QUITE TALENTED.
I WHAT?
HE'S NOT HUMAN, EITHER, THIS GUY.
IF YOU'LL JUST HAND IT OVER QUIETLY...
...I'LL HAVE NO NEED TO HURT YOU.
HRAH!
YOU, HURT ME?!
IF Y' THINK YOU CAN...

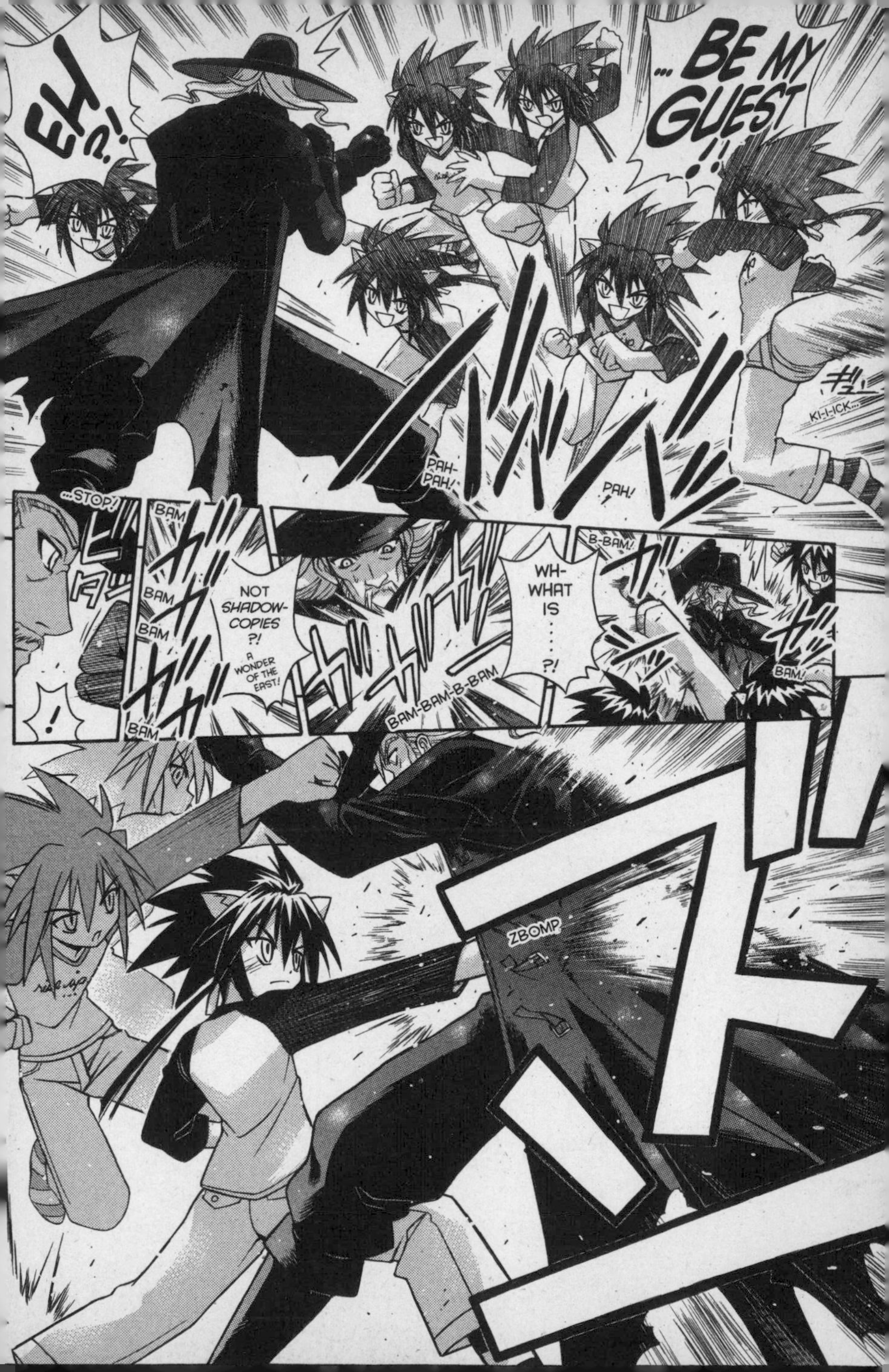
...BE MY GUEST!!
EH?!!
KI-I-ICK...
PAH!
PAH-PAH!
B-BAM!
BAM!
WH-WHAT IS.....?!
NOT SHADOW-COPIES?!
A WONDER OF THE EAST!
BAM-BAM-B-BAM
BAM
BAM
BAM
BAM
...STOP!
!
ZBOMP

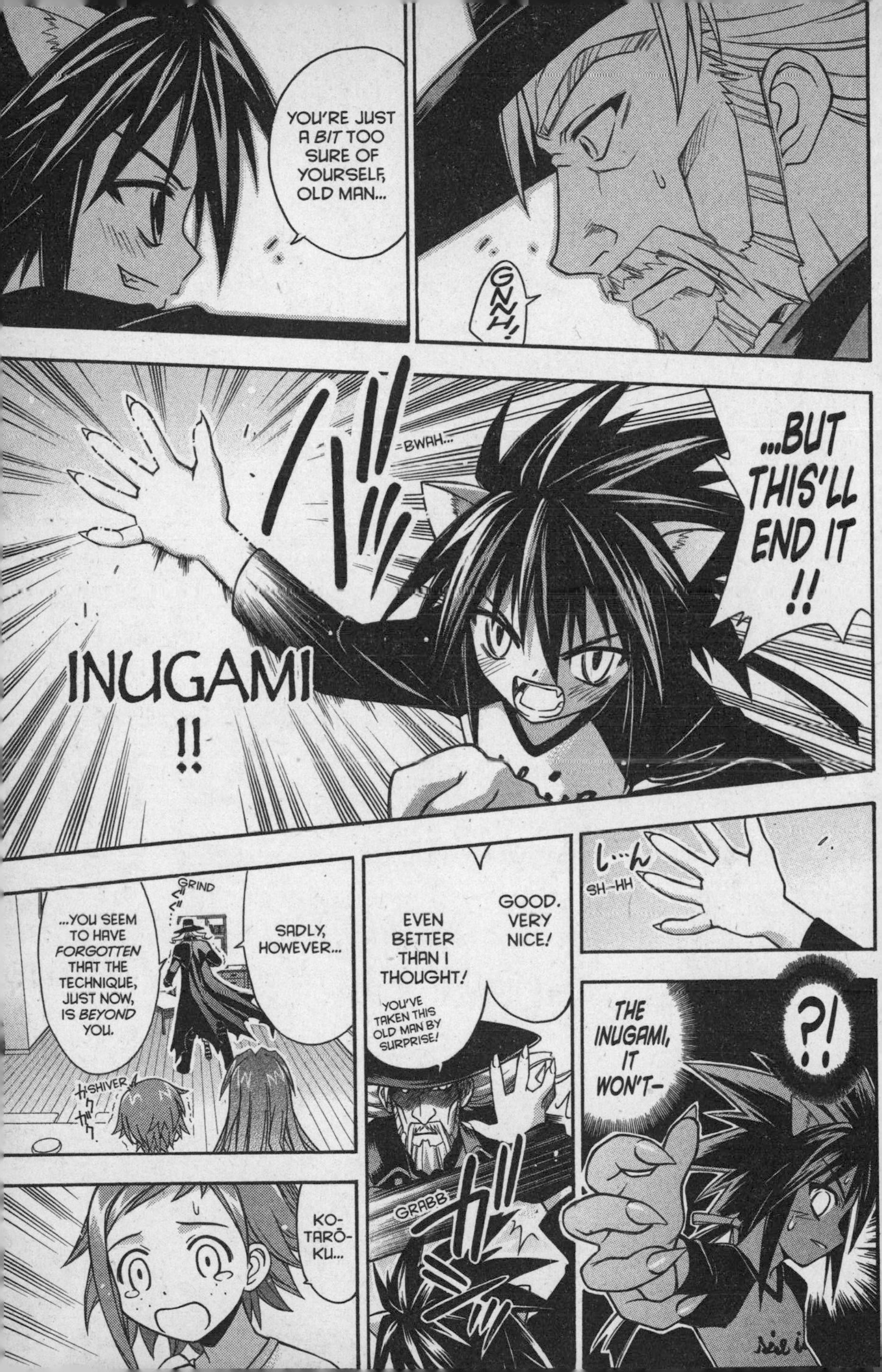
GNNH!
YOU'RE JUST A *BIT* TOO SURE OF YOURSELF, OLD MAN...
...BUT THIS'LL END IT !!
BWAH...
INUGAMI !!
SH--HH
?!
THE INUGAMI, IT WON'T-
GOOD. VERY NICE!
EVEN BETTER THAN I THOUGHT!
YOU'VE TAKEN THIS OLD MAN BY SURPRISE!
GRABB
SADLY, HOWEVER...
...YOU SEEM TO HAVE *FORGOTTEN* THAT THE TECHNIQUE, JUST NOW, IS *BEYOND* YOU.
GRIND
SHIVER
KO-TARŌ-KU...

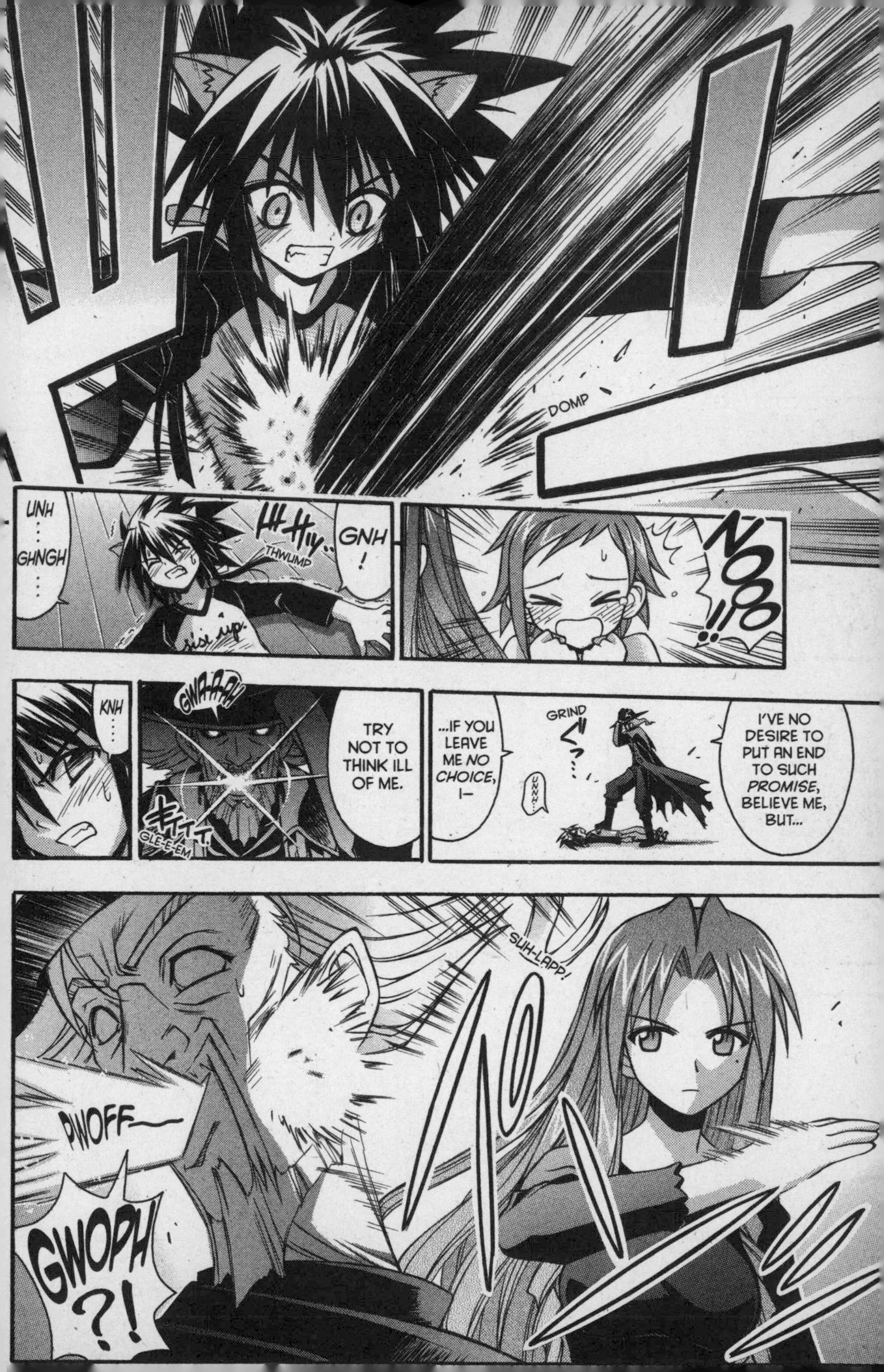
DOMP
NOOOO!!!
GNH!
THWUMP
UNH... GHNGH...
I'VE NO DESIRE TO PUT AN END TO SUCH *PROMISE*, BELIEVE ME, BUT...
GRIND
UNNH...
...IF YOU LEAVE ME *NO CHOICE*, I—
TRY NOT TO THINK ILL OF ME.
GLE-E-EM
KNH...
SUH-LAPP!
PWOFF~~
GWOPH?!

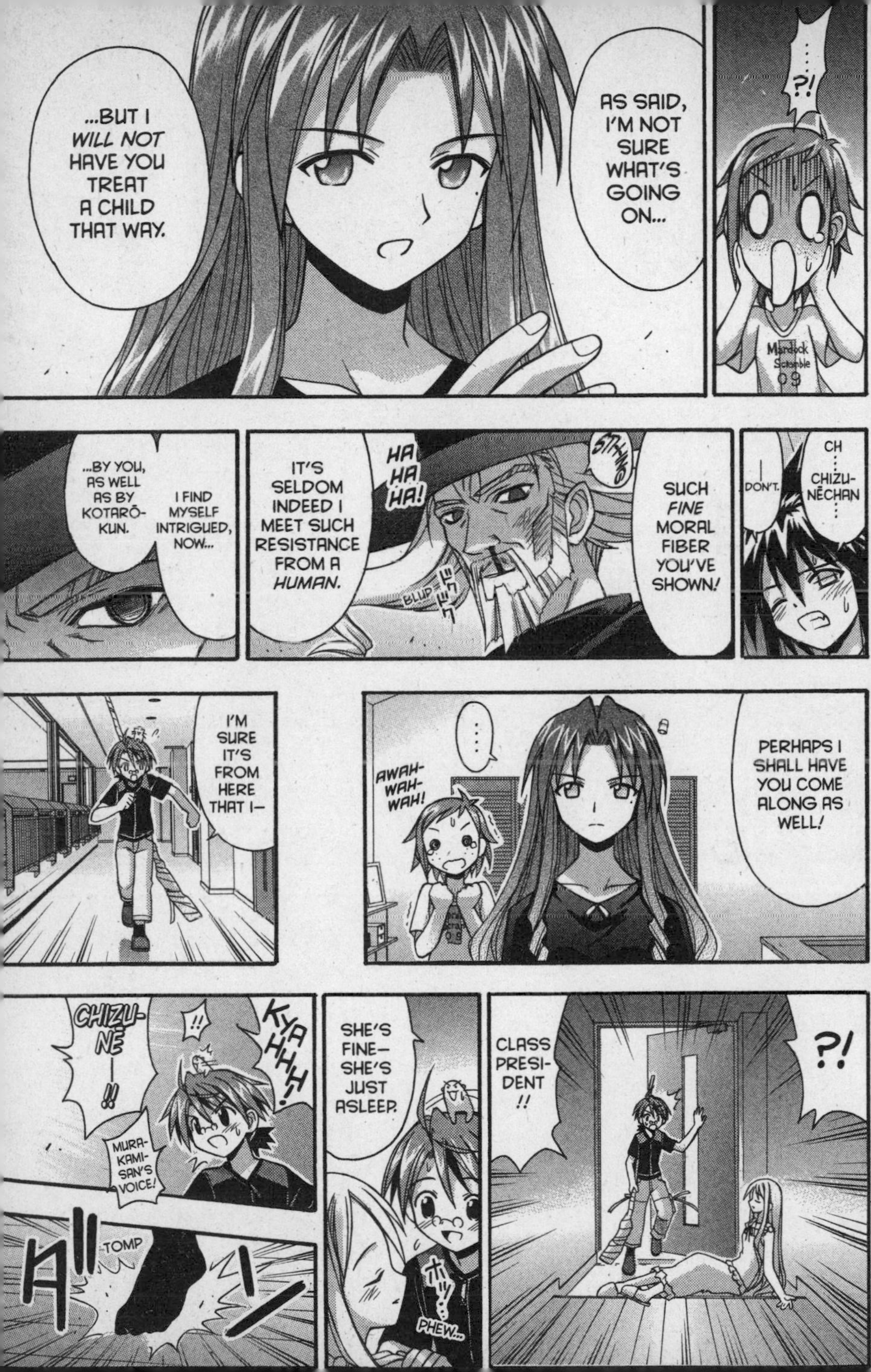
...?!
AS SAID, I'M NOT SURE WHAT'S GOING ON...
...BUT I *WILL NOT* HAVE YOU TREAT A CHILD THAT WAY.
CH... CHIZU-NĒCHAN...
I DON'T.
SUCH *FINE* MORAL FIBER YOU'VE SHOWN!
HA HA HA!
IT'S SELDOM INDEED I MEET SUCH RESISTANCE FROM A *HUMAN*.
BLUP
I FIND MYSELF INTRIGUED, NOW...
...BY YOU, AS WELL AS BY KOTARŌ-KUN.
PERHAPS I SHALL HAVE YOU COME ALONG AS WELL!
....
AWAH-WAH-WAH!
I'M SURE IT'S FROM HERE THAT I—
?!
CLASS PRESIDENT!!
SHE'S FINE—SHE'S JUST ASLEEP.
PHEW...
KYAHHH!
!!
CHIZU-NĒ—!!
MURAKAMI-SAN'S VOICE!
TOMP

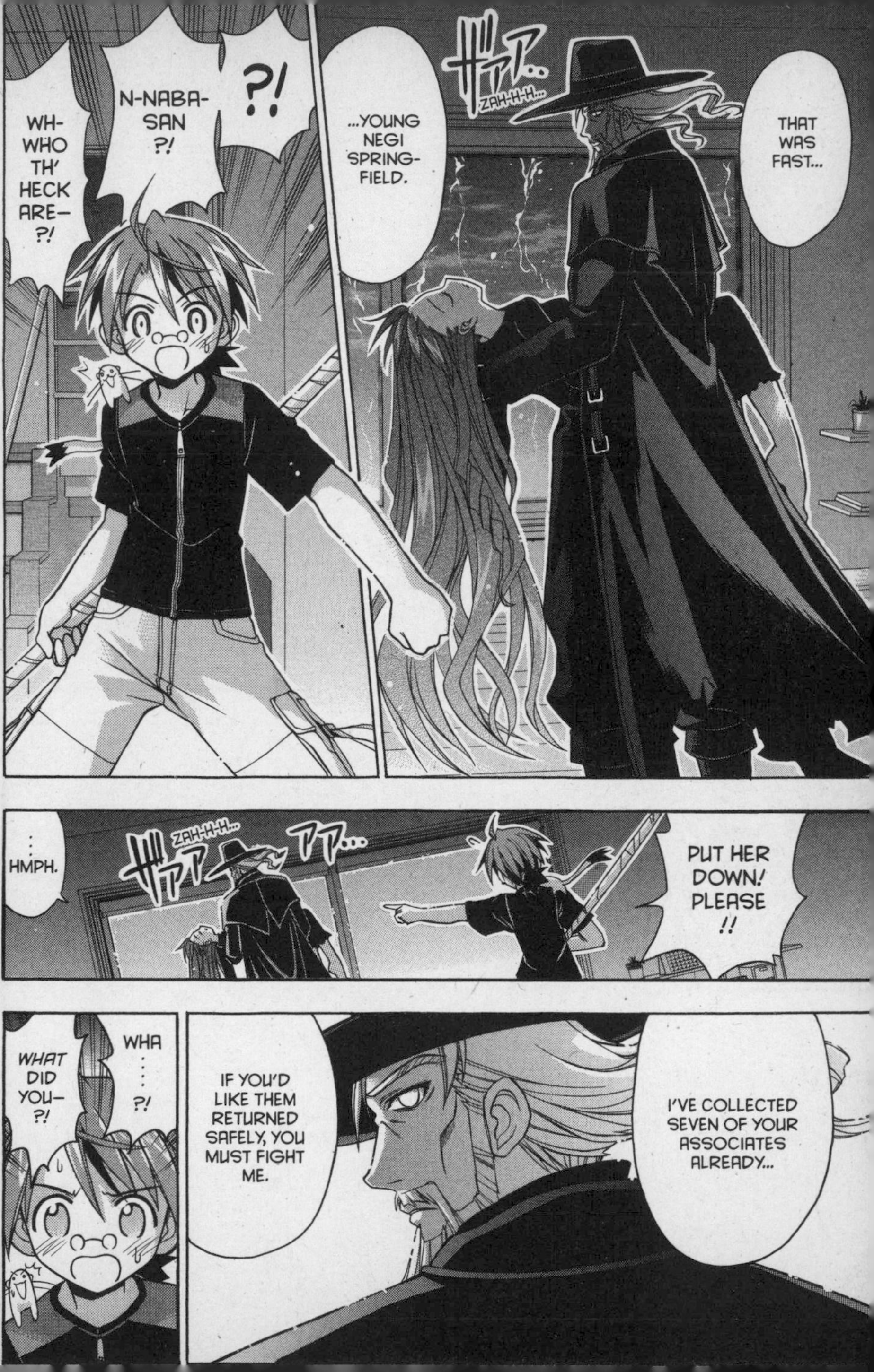
ZAH-H-H...
THAT WAS FAST...
...YOUNG NEGI SPRING-FIELD.
?!
N-NABA-SAN ?!
WH-WHO TH' HECK ARE—?!
PUT HER DOWN! PLEASE !!
ZAH-H-H...
...HMPH.
I'VE COLLECTED SEVEN OF YOUR ASSOCIATES ALREADY...
IF YOU'D LIKE THEM RETURNED SAFELY, YOU MUST FIGHT ME.
WHA...?!
WHAT DID YOU—?!

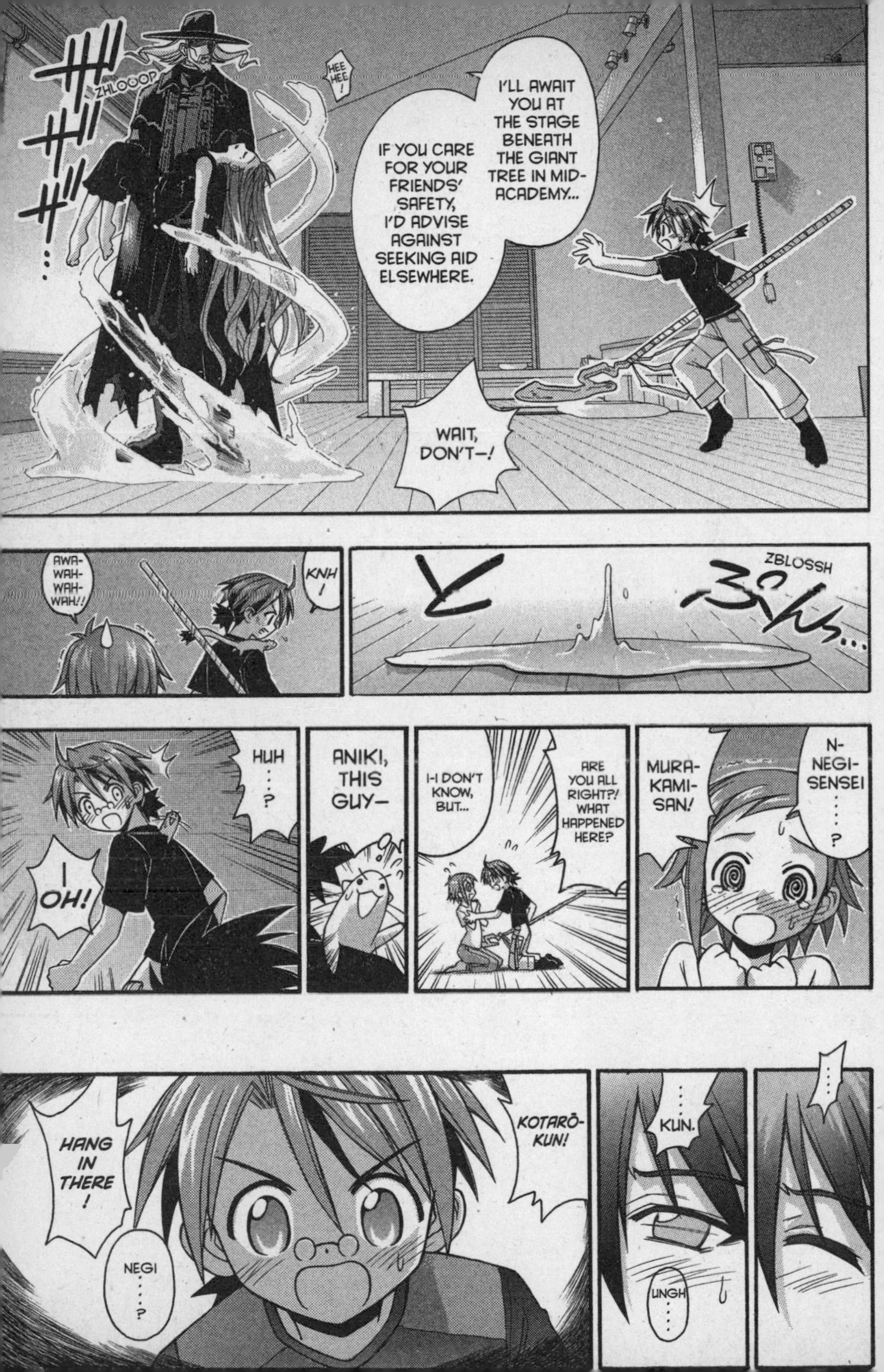
I'LL AWAIT YOU AT THE STAGE BENEATH THE GIANT TREE IN MID-ACADEMY...
IF YOU CARE FOR YOUR FRIENDS' SAFETY, I'D ADVISE AGAINST SEEKING AID ELSEWHERE.
HEE HEE!
ZHLOOOP
WAIT, DON'T—!
ZBLOSSH
KNH!
AWA-WAH-WAH-WAH!!
N-NEGI-SENSEI.....?
MURA-KAMI-SAN!
ARE YOU ALL RIGHT?! WHAT HAPPENED HERE?
I-I DON'T KNOW, BUT...
ANIKI, THIS GUY—
HUH...?
OH!
...!
....KUN.
UNGH.....
KOTARŌ-KUN!
HANG IN THERE!
NEGI.....?

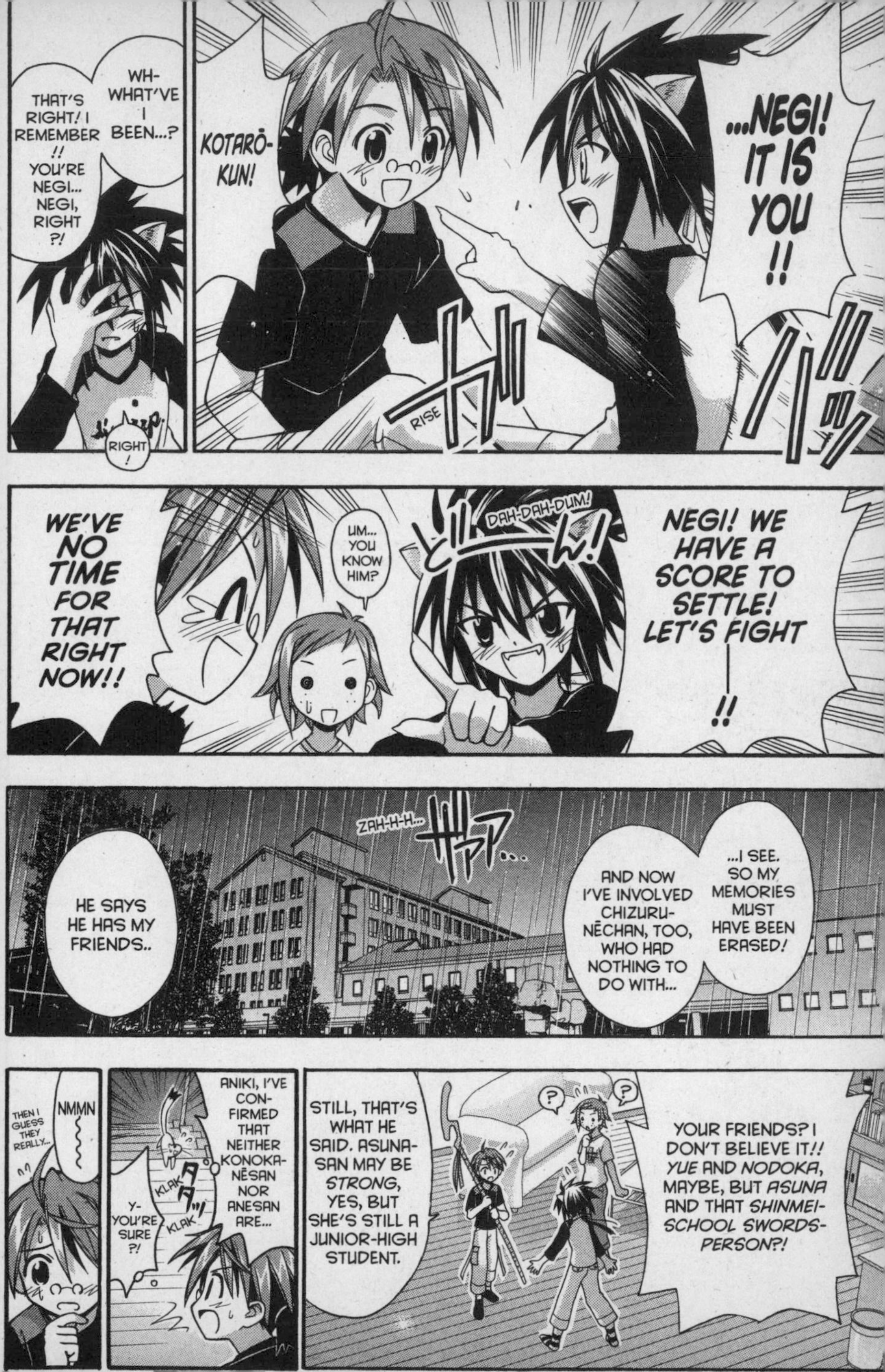
...NEGI! IT IS YOU!!
KOTARŌ-KUN!
RISE
WH- WHAT'VE I BEEN...?
THAT'S RIGHT! I REMEMBER!! YOU'RE NEGI... NEGI, RIGHT?!
RIGHT!
NEGI! WE HAVE A SCORE TO SETTLE! LET'S FIGHT—!!
DAH-DAH-DUM!
UM... YOU KNOW HIM?
WE'VE NO TIME FOR THAT RIGHT NOW!!
...I SEE. SO MY MEMORIES MUST HAVE BEEN ERASED!
AND NOW I'VE INVOLVED CHIZURU-NĒCHAN, TOO, WHO HAD NOTHING TO DO WITH...
ZAH-H-H...
HE SAYS HE HAS MY FRIENDS..
YOUR FRIENDS? I DON'T BELIEVE IT!! YUE AND NODOKA, MAYBE, BUT ASUNA AND THAT SHINMEI-SCHOOL SWORDS-PERSON?!
STILL, THAT'S WHAT HE SAID. ASUNA-SAN MAY BE STRONG, YES, BUT SHE'S STILL A JUNIOR-HIGH STUDENT.
ANIKI, I'VE CONFIRMED THAT NEITHER KONOKA-NĒSAN NOR ANESAN ARE...
KLAK KLAK
Y-YOU'RE SURE?!
NMMN
THEN I GUESS THEY REALLY...

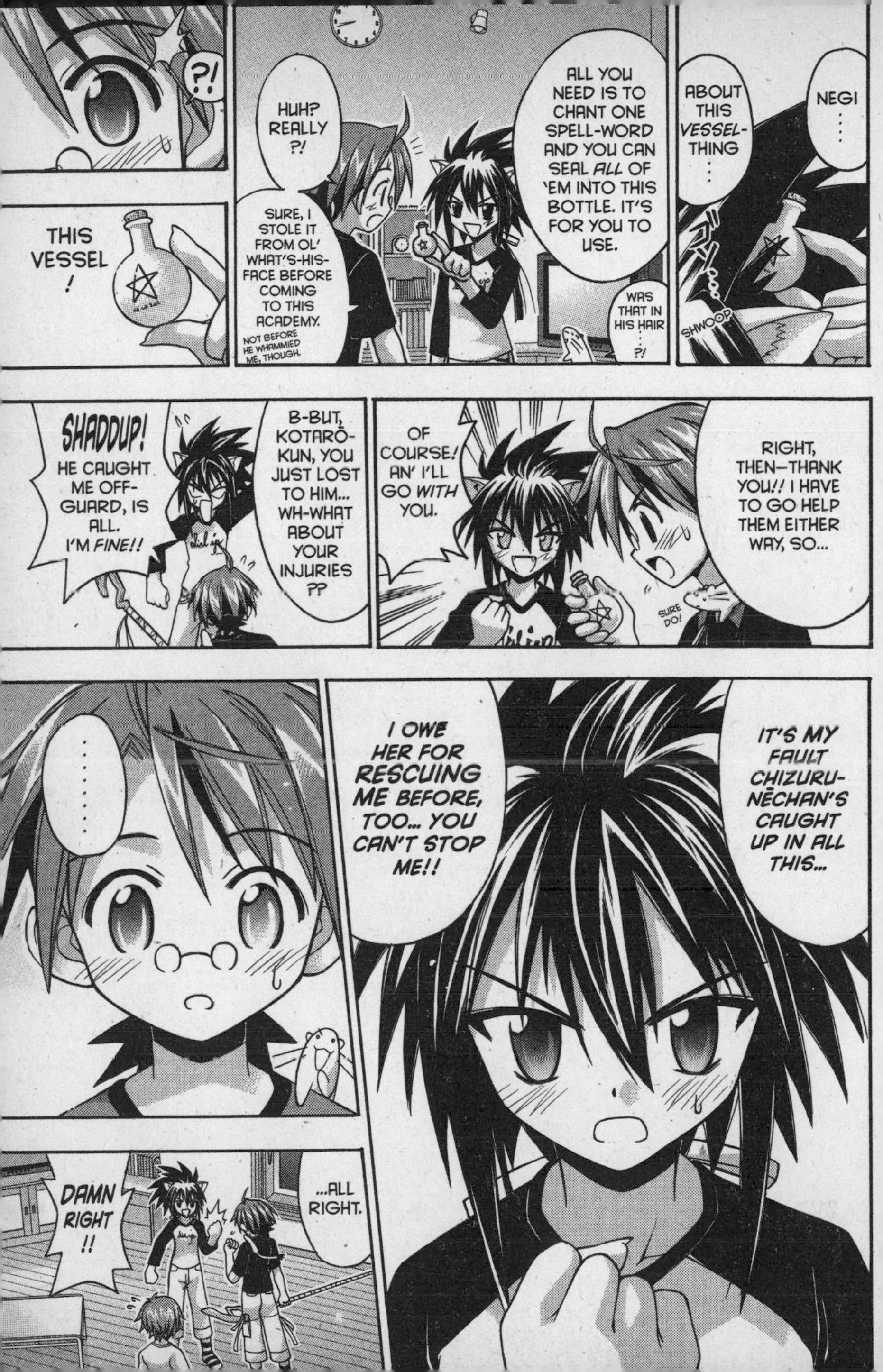

NEGI ......
ABOUT THIS VESSEL-THING ...
SHWOOP
ALL YOU NEED IS TO CHANT ONE SPELL-WORD AND YOU CAN SEAL ALL OF 'EM INTO THIS BOTTLE. IT'S FOR YOU TO USE.
HUH? REALLY ?!
WAS THAT IN HIS HAIR ...?!
SURE, I STOLE IT FROM OL' WHAT'S-HIS-FACE BEFORE COMING TO THIS ACADEMY.
NOT BEFORE HE WHAMMIED ME, THOUGH.
?!
THIS VESSEL !
RIGHT, THEN—THANK YOU!! I HAVE TO GO HELP THEM EITHER WAY, SO...
OF COURSE! AN' I'LL GO WITH YOU.
SURE DO!
B-BUT, KOTARŌ-KUN, YOU JUST LOST TO HIM... WH-WHAT ABOUT YOUR INJURIES ??
SHADDUP! HE CAUGHT ME OFF-GUARD, IS ALL. I'M FINE!!
IT'S MY FAULT CHIZURU-NĒCHAN'S CAUGHT UP IN ALL THIS...
I OWE HER FOR RESCUING ME BEFORE, TOO... YOU CAN'T STOP ME!!
......
...ALL RIGHT.
DAMN RIGHT !!

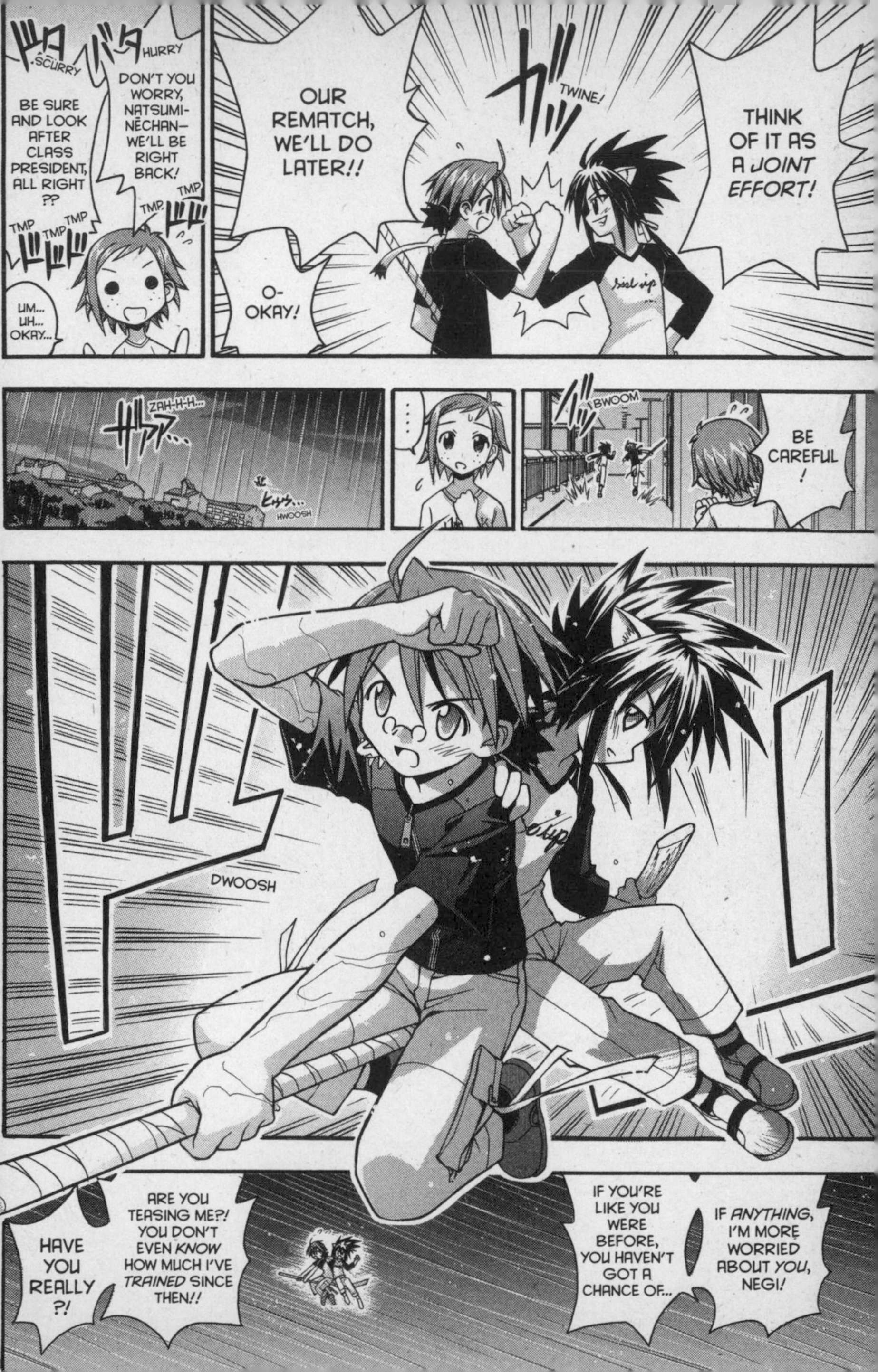
THINK OF IT AS A *JOINT EFFORT!*
TWINE!
OUR REMATCH, WE'LL DO LATER!!
O-OKAY!
HURRY
SCURRY
DON'T YOU WORRY, NATSUMI-NĒCHAN— WE'LL BE RIGHT BACK!
BE SURE AND LOOK AFTER CLASS PRESIDENT, ALL RIGHT ??
TMP TMP
TMP TMP TMP
UM... UH... OKAY...
BE CAREFUL!
BWOOM
.....
ZAH-H-H...
HWOOSH
DWOOSH
IF *ANYTHING,* I'M MORE WORRIED ABOUT *YOU,* NEGI!
IF YOU'RE LIKE YOU WERE BEFORE, YOU HAVEN'T GOT A CHANCE OF...
ARE YOU TEASING ME?! YOU DON'T EVEN *KNOW* HOW MUCH I'VE *TRAINED* SINCE THEN!!
HAVE YOU REALLY ?!

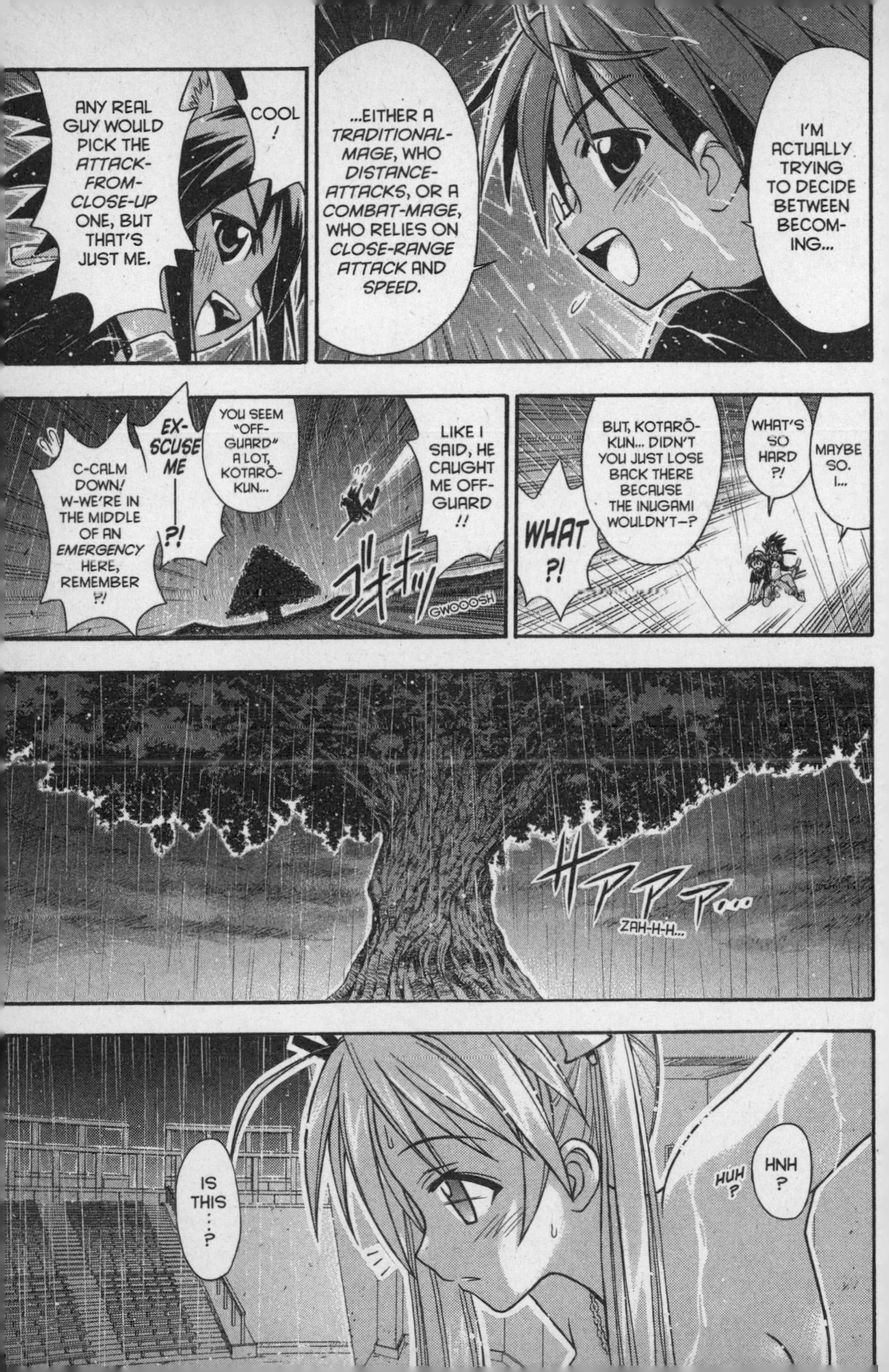
I'M ACTUALLY TRYING TO DECIDE BETWEEN BECOMING...
...EITHER A *TRADITIONAL-MAGE*, WHO *DISTANCE-ATTACKS*, OR A *COMBAT-MAGE*, WHO RELIES ON *CLOSE-RANGE ATTACK* AND *SPEED*.
COOL!
ANY REAL GUY WOULD PICK THE *ATTACK-FROM-CLOSE-UP* ONE, BUT THAT'S JUST ME.
MAYBE SO. I...
WHAT'S SO HARD?!
BUT, KOTARŌ-KUN... DIDN'T YOU JUST LOSE BACK THERE BECAUSE THE INUGAMI WOULDN'T—?
WHAT?!
LIKE I SAID, HE CAUGHT ME OFF-GUARD!!
GWOOOSH
YOU SEEM "OFF-GUARD" A LOT, KOTARŌ-KUN...
EX-SCUSE ME—?!
C-CALM DOWN! W-WE'RE IN THE MIDDLE OF AN *EMERGENCY* HERE, REMEMBER?!
ZAH-H-H...
HNH?
HUH?
IS THIS...?

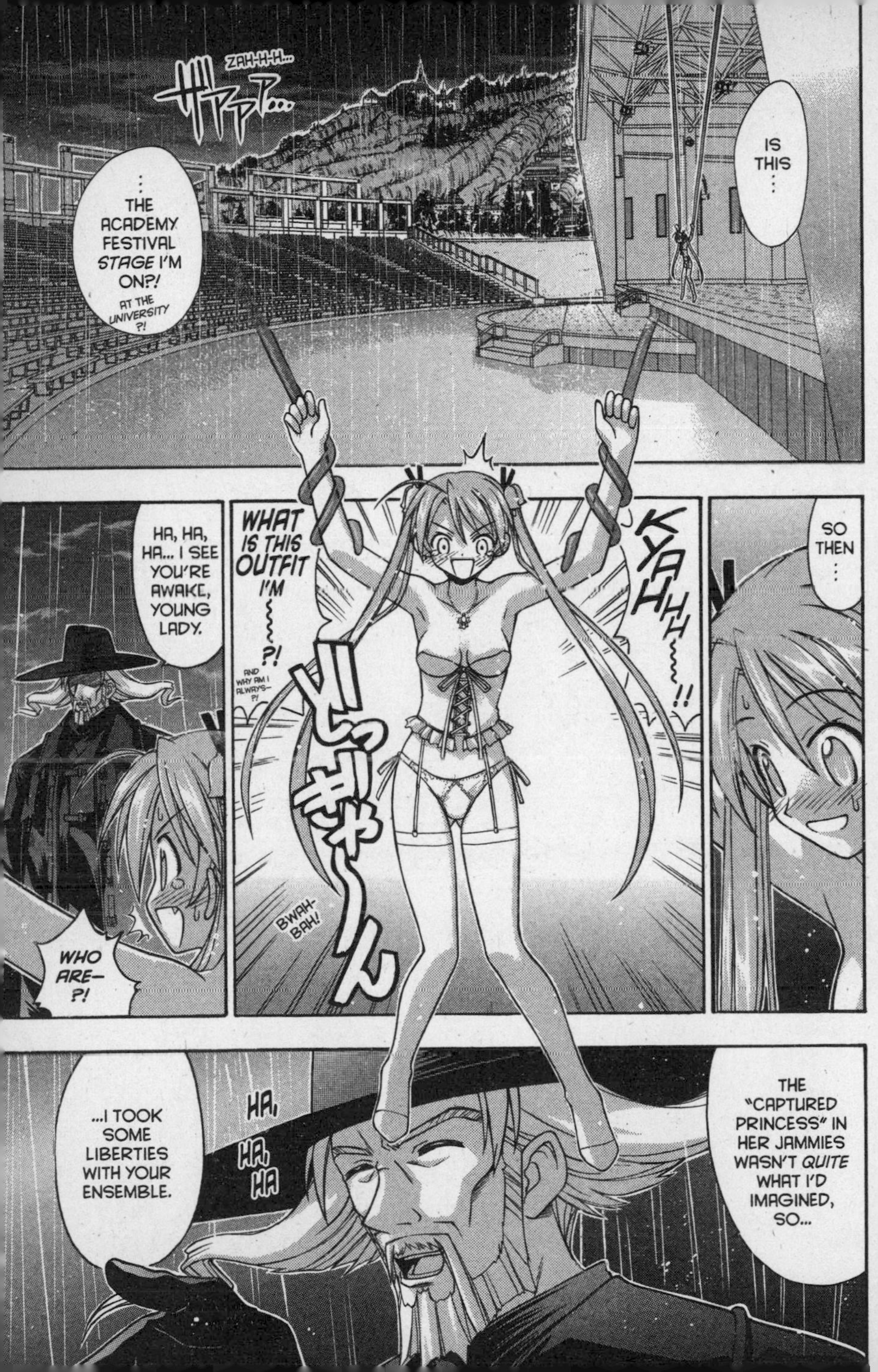
ZAH-H-H...
ザァァァ...
IS THIS...
...THE ACADEMY FESTIVAL STAGE I'M ON?!
AT THE UNIVERSITY?!
SO THEN...
KYAHHH~~!!
WHAT IS THIS OUTFIT I'M~~?!
AND WHY AM I ALWAYS—?!
どっきゃ〜ん
BWAH-BAH!
HA, HA, HA... I SEE YOU'RE AWAKE, YOUNG LADY.
WHO ARE—?!
THE "CAPTURED PRINCESS" IN HER JAMMIES WASN'T *QUITE* WHAT I'D IMAGINED, SO...
HA, HA, HA
...I TOOK SOME LIBERTIES WITH YOUR ENSEMBLE.

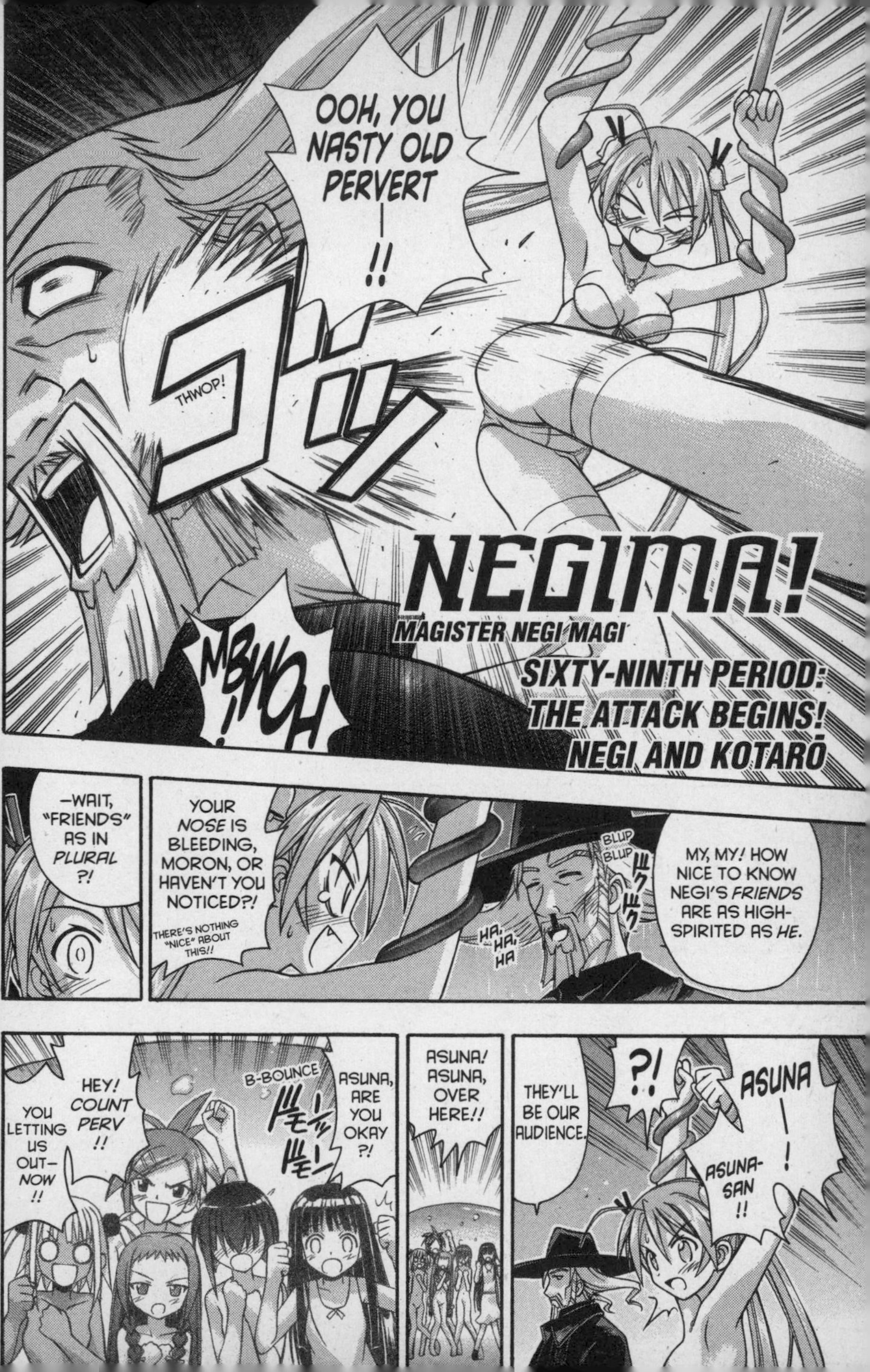
OOH, YOU NASTY OLD PERVERT—!!
THWOP!
NEGIMA!
MAGISTER NEGI MAGI
SIXTY-NINTH PERIOD: THE ATTACK BEGINS! NEGI AND KOTARŌ
MBWOH!
MY, MY! HOW NICE TO KNOW NEGI'S FRIENDS ARE AS HIGH-SPIRITED AS HE.
BLUP BLUP
HA, HA, HA
YOUR NOSE IS BLEEDING, MORON, OR HAVEN'T YOU NOTICED?!
THERE'S NOTHING "NICE" ABOUT THIS!!
—WAIT, "FRIENDS" AS IN PLURAL?!
?!
ASUNA—!
ASUNA-SAN!!
THEY'LL BE OUR AUDIENCE.
ASUNA! ASUNA, OVER HERE!!
B-BOUNCE
ASUNA, ARE YOU OKAY?!
HEY! COUNT PERV!!
YOU LETTING US OUT—NOW!!

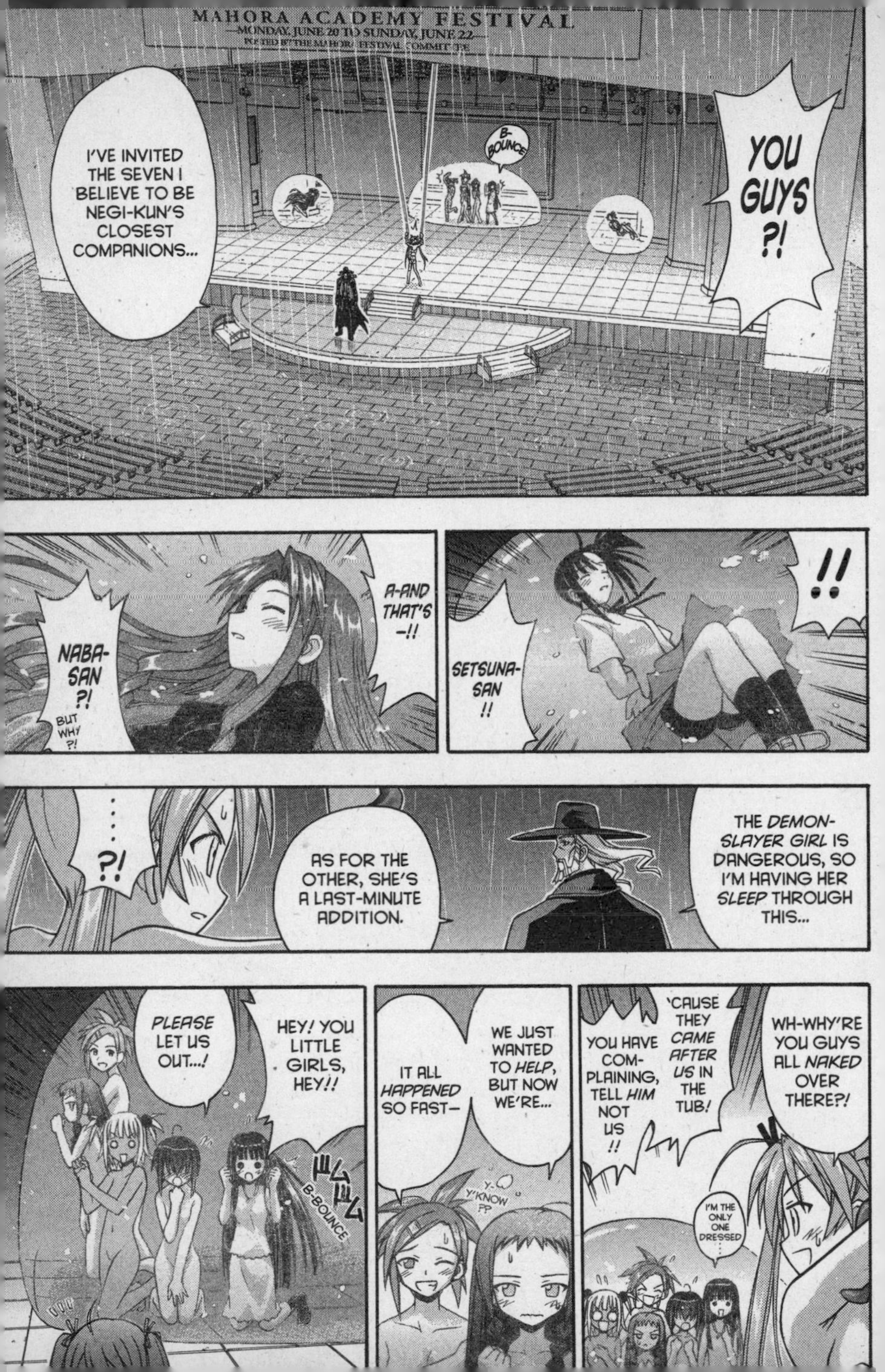
MAHORA ACADEMY FESTIVAL
—MONDAY, JUNE 20 TO SUNDAY, JUNE 22—
YOU GUYS ?!
B-BOUNCE
I'VE INVITED THE SEVEN I BELIEVE TO BE NEGI-KUN'S CLOSEST COMPANIONS...
!!
SETSUNA-SAN !!
A-AND THAT'S—!!
NABA-SAN ?!
BUT WHY ?!
THE *DEMON-SLAYER GIRL* IS DANGEROUS, SO I'M HAVING HER *SLEEP* THROUGH THIS...
AS FOR THE OTHER, SHE'S A LAST-MINUTE ADDITION.
...?!
WH-WHY'RE YOU GUYS ALL *NAKED* OVER THERE?!
'CAUSE THEY *CAME AFTER US* IN THE TUB!
YOU HAVE COM-PLAINING, TELL *HIM* NOT US!!
I'M THE ONLY ONE DRESSED...
WE JUST WANTED TO *HELP*, BUT NOW WE'RE...
IT ALL *HAPPENED* SO FAST—
Y-Y'KNOW ?!
HEY! YOU LITTLE GIRLS, HEY!!
PLEASE LET US OUT...!
B-BOUNCE

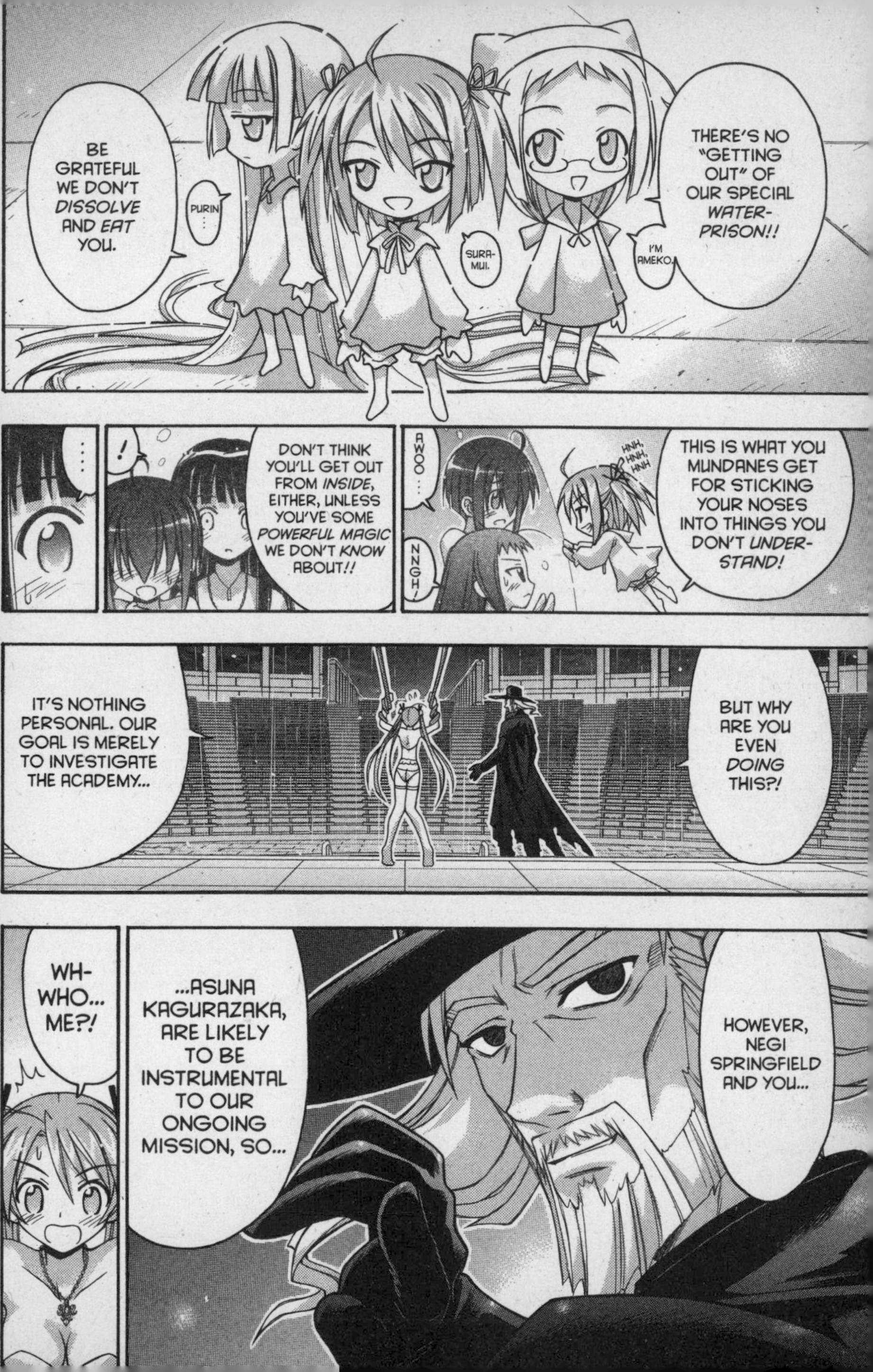
THERE'S NO "GETTING OUT" OF OUR SPECIAL *WATER-PRISON!!*
I'M AMEKO.
SURA-MUI.
PURIN...
BE GRATEFUL WE DON'T *DISSOLVE* AND *EAT* YOU.
THIS IS WHAT YOU MUNDANES GET FOR STICKING YOUR NOSES INTO THINGS YOU DON'T *UNDER-STAND!*
HNH, HNH, HNH
AWOO...
NNGH!
DON'T THINK YOU'LL GET OUT FROM *INSIDE,* EITHER, UNLESS YOU'VE SOME *POWERFUL MAGIC* WE DON'T *KNOW* ABOUT!!
!
...
BUT WHY ARE YOU EVEN *DOING* THIS?!
IT'S NOTHING PERSONAL. OUR GOAL IS MERELY TO INVESTIGATE THE ACADEMY...
HOWEVER, NEGI SPRINGFIELD AND YOU...
...ASUNA KAGURAZAKA, ARE LIKELY TO BE INSTRUMENTAL TO OUR ONGOING MISSION, SO...
WH-WHO... ME?!

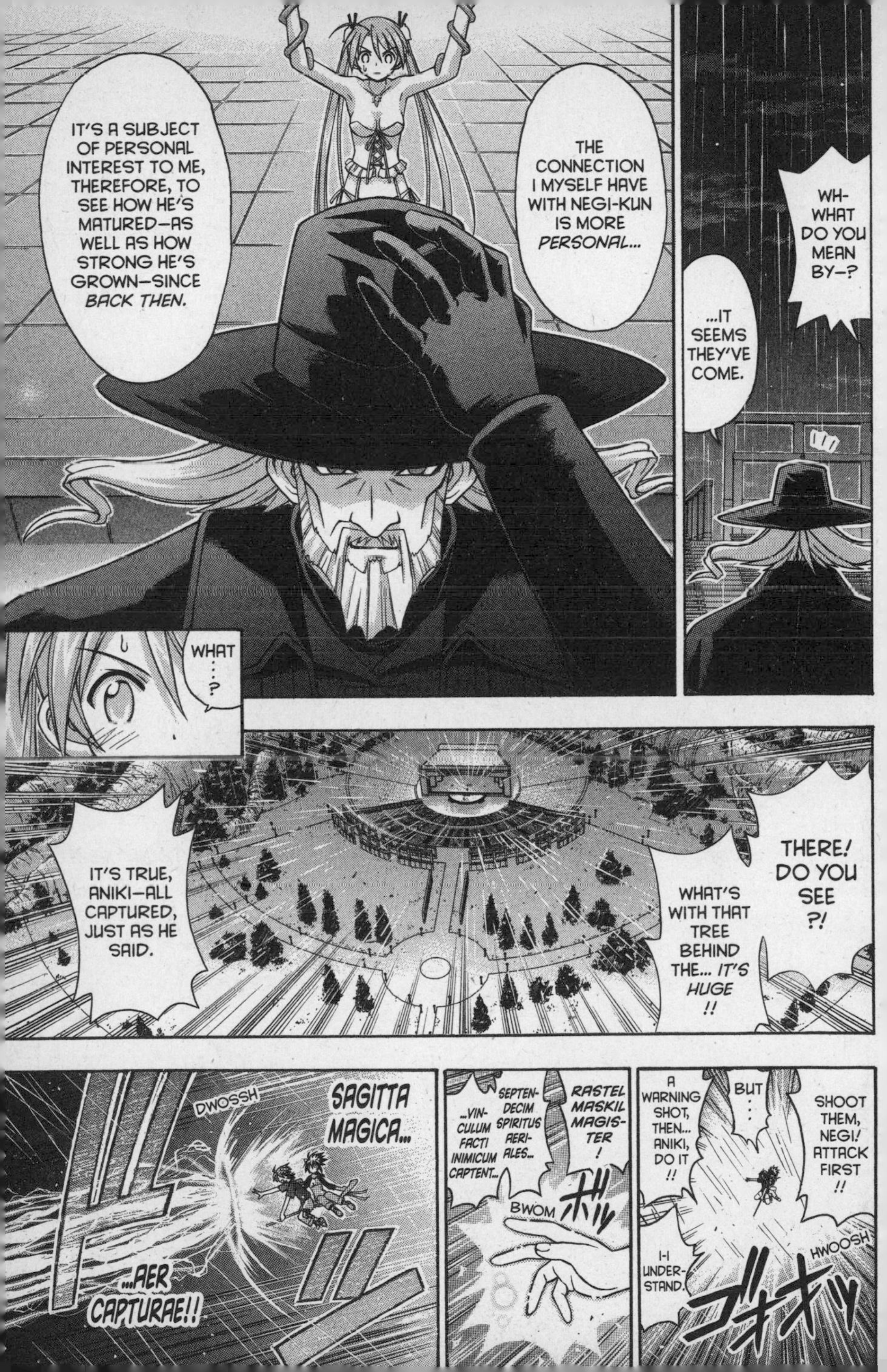
WH-WHAT DO YOU MEAN BY–?
...IT SEEMS THEY'VE COME.
THE CONNECTION I MYSELF HAVE WITH NEGI-KUN IS MORE *PERSONAL*...
IT'S A SUBJECT OF PERSONAL INTEREST TO ME, THEREFORE, TO SEE HOW HE'S MATURED—AS WELL AS HOW STRONG HE'S GROWN—SINCE *BACK THEN*.
WHAT ...?
THERE! DO YOU SEE ?!
WHAT'S WITH THAT TREE BEHIND THE... *IT'S HUGE* !!
IT'S TRUE, ANIKI—ALL CAPTURED, JUST AS HE SAID.
SHOOT THEM, NEGI! ATTACK FIRST !!
BUT ...
A WARNING SHOT, THEN... ANIKI, DO IT !!
I-I UNDERSTAND.
HWOOSH
ゴオォッ
RASTEL MASKIL MAGISTER !
SEPTENDECIM SPIRITUS AERIALES...
...VINCULUM FACTI INIMICUM CAPTENT...
BWOM
ボッ
SAGITTA MAGICA...
DWOSSH
...AER CAPTURAE!!

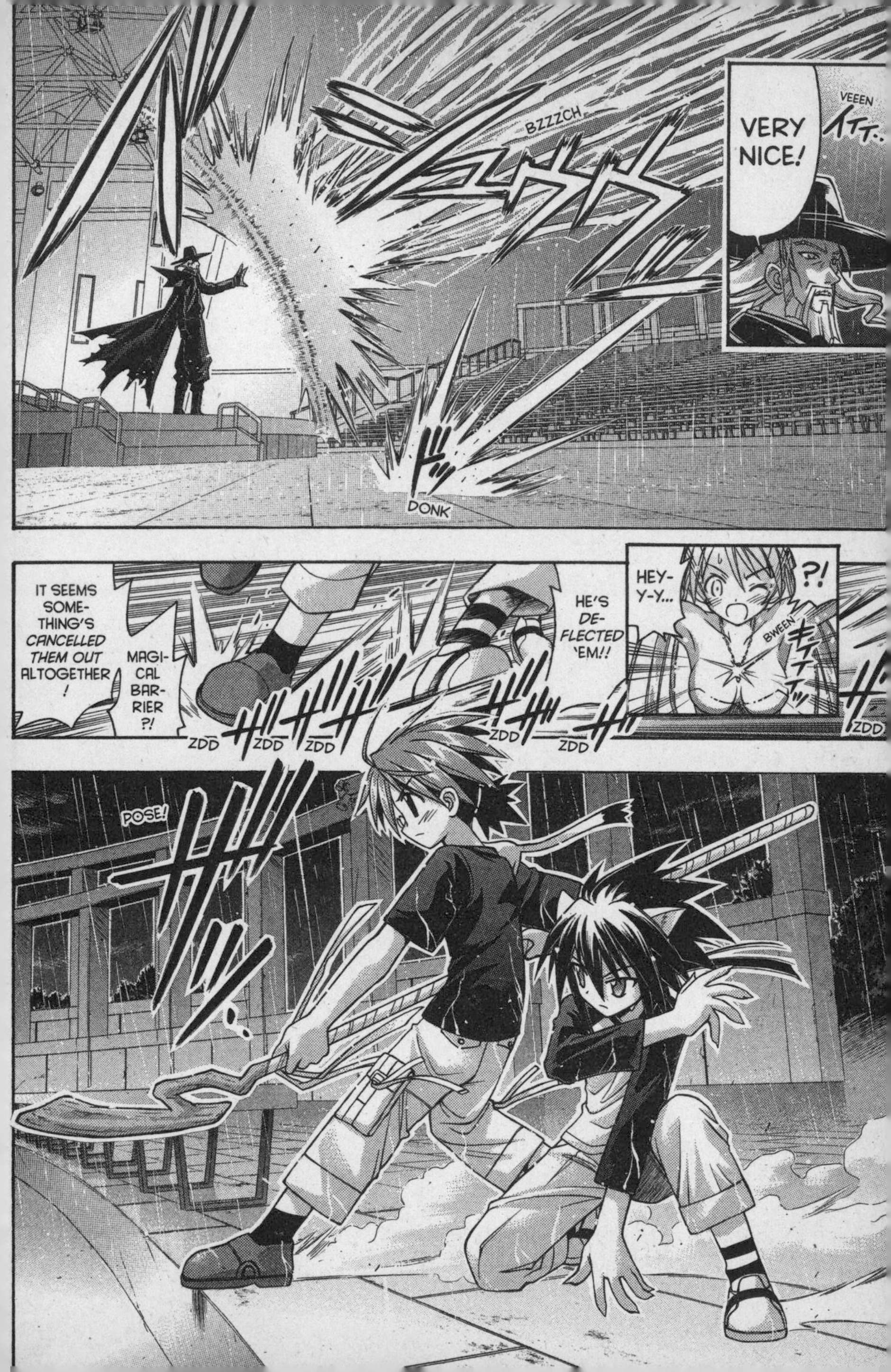

VERY NICE!
VEEEN
BZZZCH
DONK
HEY-Y-Y...
?!
BWEEN
ZDD
HE'S DE-FLECTED 'EM!!
MAGI-CAL BAR-RIER ?!
IT SEEMS SOME-THING'S *CANCELLED* THEM OUT ALTOGETHER!
ZDD
ZDD
ZDD
ZDD
ZDD
POSE!

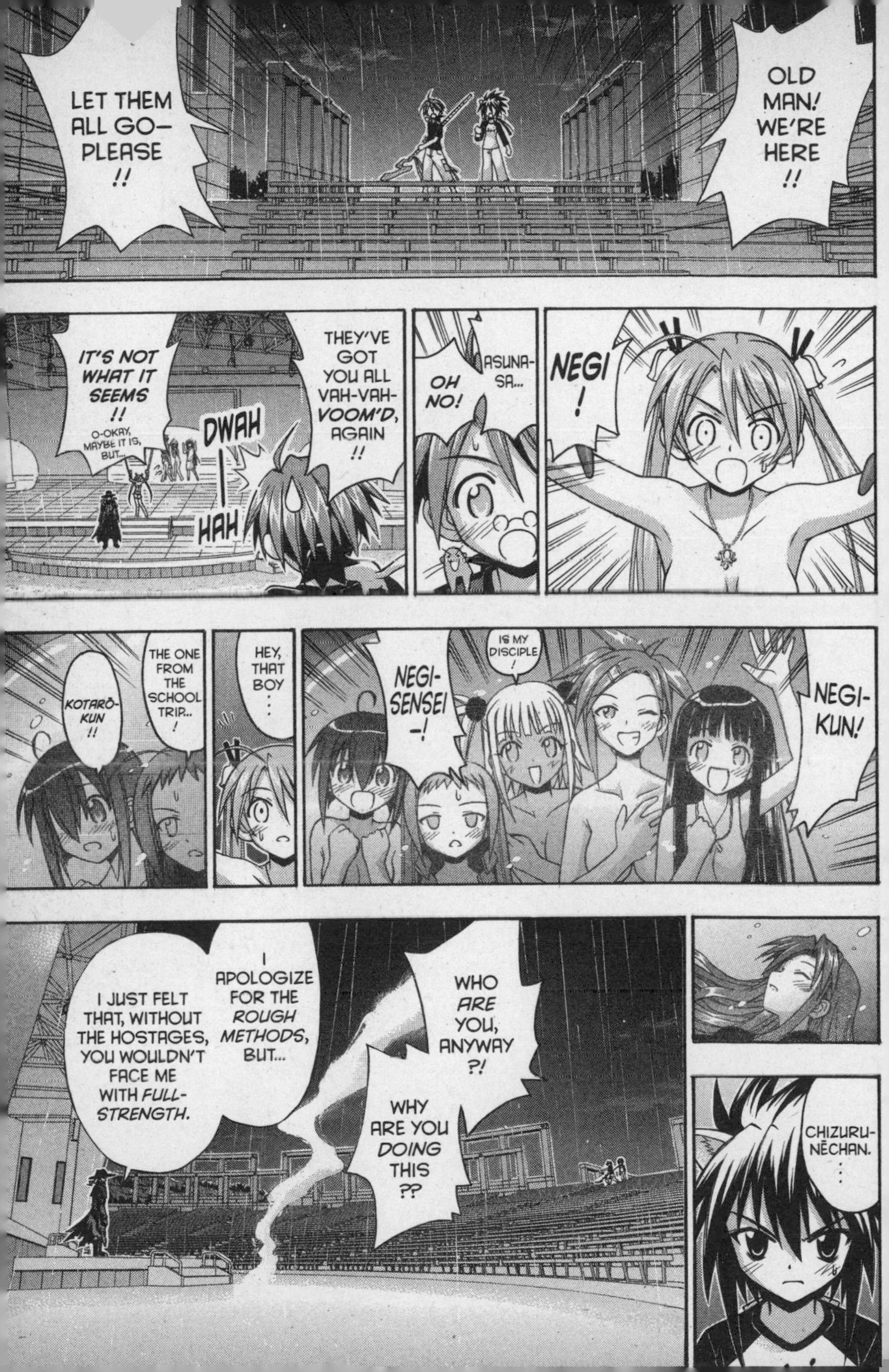
OLD MAN! WE'RE HERE!!
LET THEM ALL GO—PLEASE!!
NEGI!
ASUNA-SA...
OH NO!
THEY'VE GOT YOU ALL VAH-VAH-VOOM'D, AGAIN!!
DWAH-HAH
IT'S NOT WHAT IT SEEMS!!
O-OKAY, MAYBE IT IS, BUT...
NEGI-KUN!
IS MY DISCIPLE!
NEGI-SENSEI—!
HEY, THAT BOY...
THE ONE FROM THE SCHOOL TRIP...!
KOTARŌ-KUN!!
CHIZURU-NĒCHAN...
WHO ARE YOU, ANYWAY?!
WHY ARE YOU DOING THIS??
I APOLOGIZE FOR THE ROUGH METHODS, BUT...
I JUST FELT THAT, WITHOUT THE HOSTAGES, YOU WOULDN'T FACE ME WITH FULL-STRENGTH.

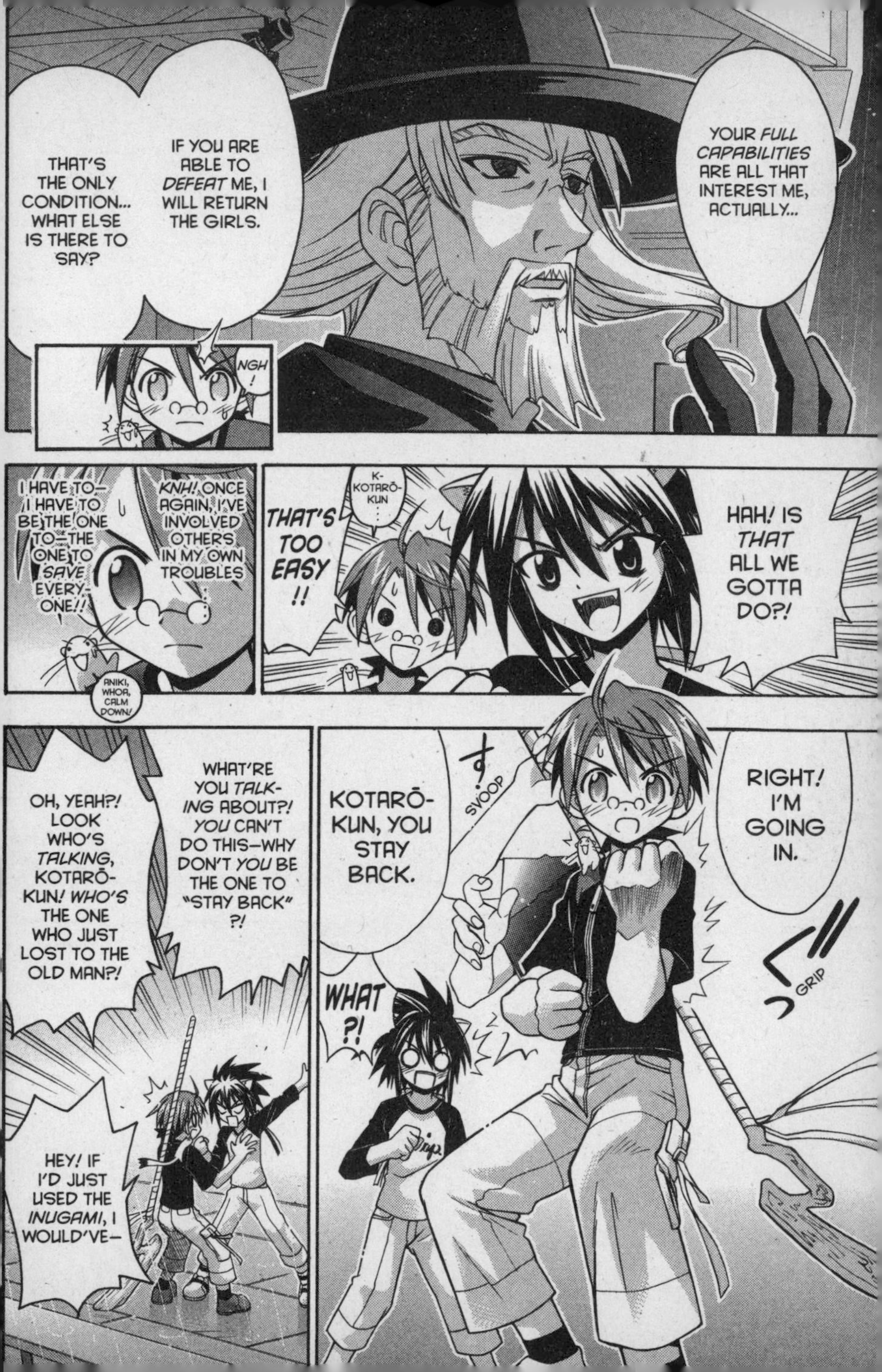
YOUR FULL CAPABILITIES ARE ALL THAT INTEREST ME, ACTUALLY...
IF YOU ARE ABLE TO DEFEAT ME, I WILL RETURN THE GIRLS.
THAT'S THE ONLY CONDITION... WHAT ELSE IS THERE TO SAY?
NGH!
HAH! IS THAT ALL WE GOTTA DO?!
THAT'S TOO EASY!!
K-KOTARŌ-KUN...
KNH! ONCE AGAIN, I'VE INVOLVED OTHERS IN MY OWN TROUBLES
I HAVE TO— I HAVE TO BE THE ONE TO—THE ONE TO SAVE EVERY-ONE!!
ANIKI, WHOA, CALM DOWN!
RIGHT! I'M GOING IN.
GRIP
す SVOOP
KOTARŌ-KUN, YOU STAY BACK.
WHAT?!
WHAT'RE YOU TALKING ABOUT?! YOU CAN'T DO THIS—WHY DON'T YOU BE THE ONE TO "STAY BACK"?!
OH, YEAH?! LOOK WHO'S TALKING, KOTARŌ-KUN! WHO'S THE ONE WHO JUST LOST TO THE OLD MAN?!
HEY! IF I'D JUST USED THE INUGAMI, I WOULD'VE—

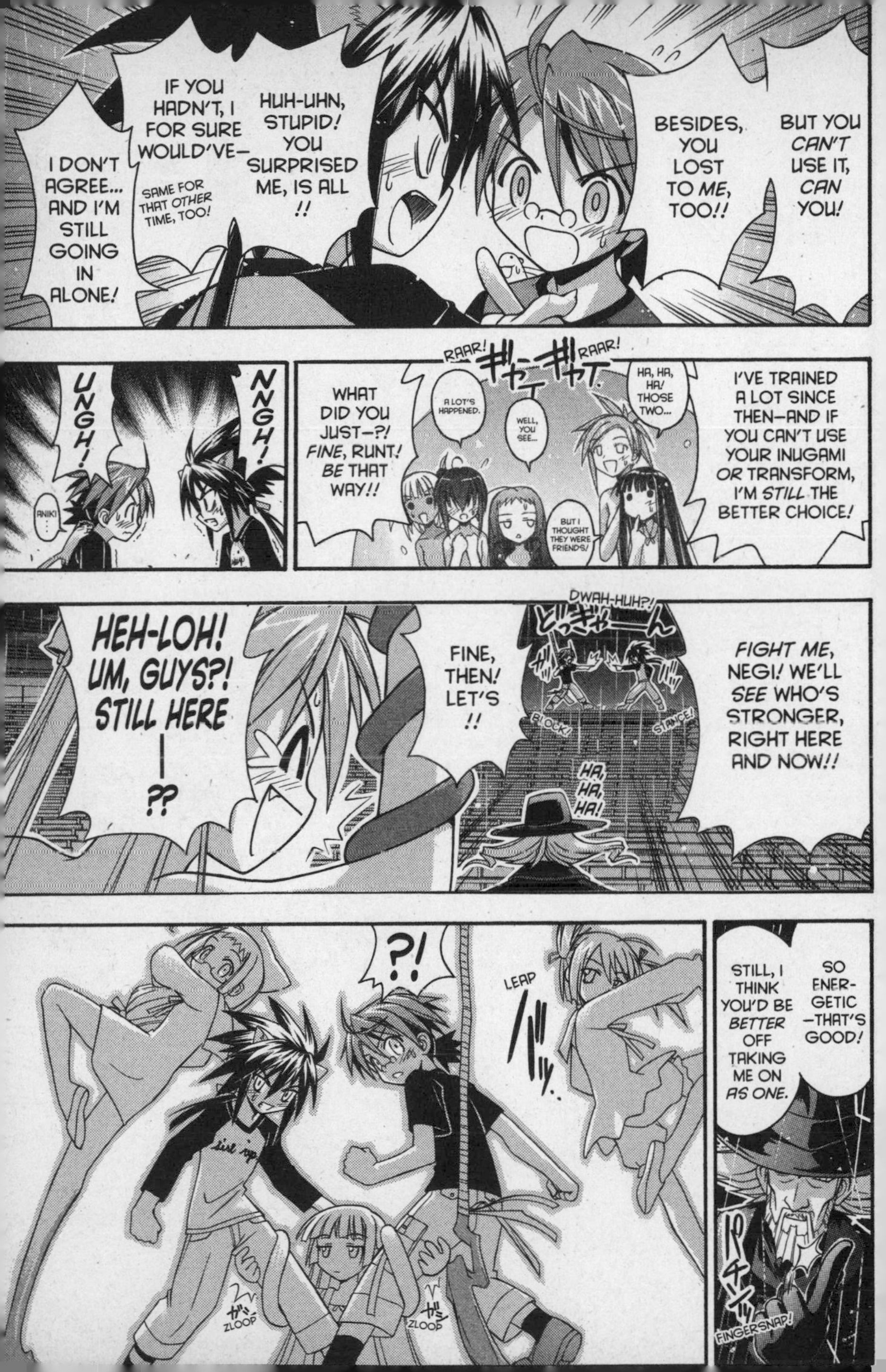
BUT YOU CAN'T USE IT, CAN YOU!
BESIDES, YOU LOST TO ME, TOO!!
HUH-UHN, STUPID! YOU SURPRISED ME, IS ALL!!
IF YOU HADN'T, I FOR SURE WOULD'VE—
SAME FOR THAT OTHER TIME, TOO!
I DON'T AGREE... AND I'M STILL GOING IN ALONE!
I'VE TRAINED A LOT SINCE THEN—AND IF YOU CAN'T USE YOUR INUGAMI OR TRANSFORM, I'M STILL THE BETTER CHOICE!
RAAR!
RAAR!
HA, HA, HA! THOSE TWO...
WELL, YOU SEE...
A LOT'S HAPPENED.
BUT I THOUGHT THEY WERE FRIENDS!
WHAT DID YOU JUST—?! FINE, RUNT! BE THAT WAY!!
NNGH!
UNGH!
ANIKI ...
FIGHT ME, NEGI! WE'LL SEE WHO'S STRONGER, RIGHT HERE AND NOW!!
DWAH-HUH?!
STANCE!
BLOCK!
HA, HA, HA!
FINE, THEN! LET'S!!
HEH-LOH! UM, GUYS?! STILL HERE—??
SO ENERGETIC—THAT'S GOOD!
STILL, I THINK YOU'D BE BETTER OFF TAKING ME ON AS ONE.
FINGERSNAP!
LEAP
?!
ZLOOP
ZLOOP

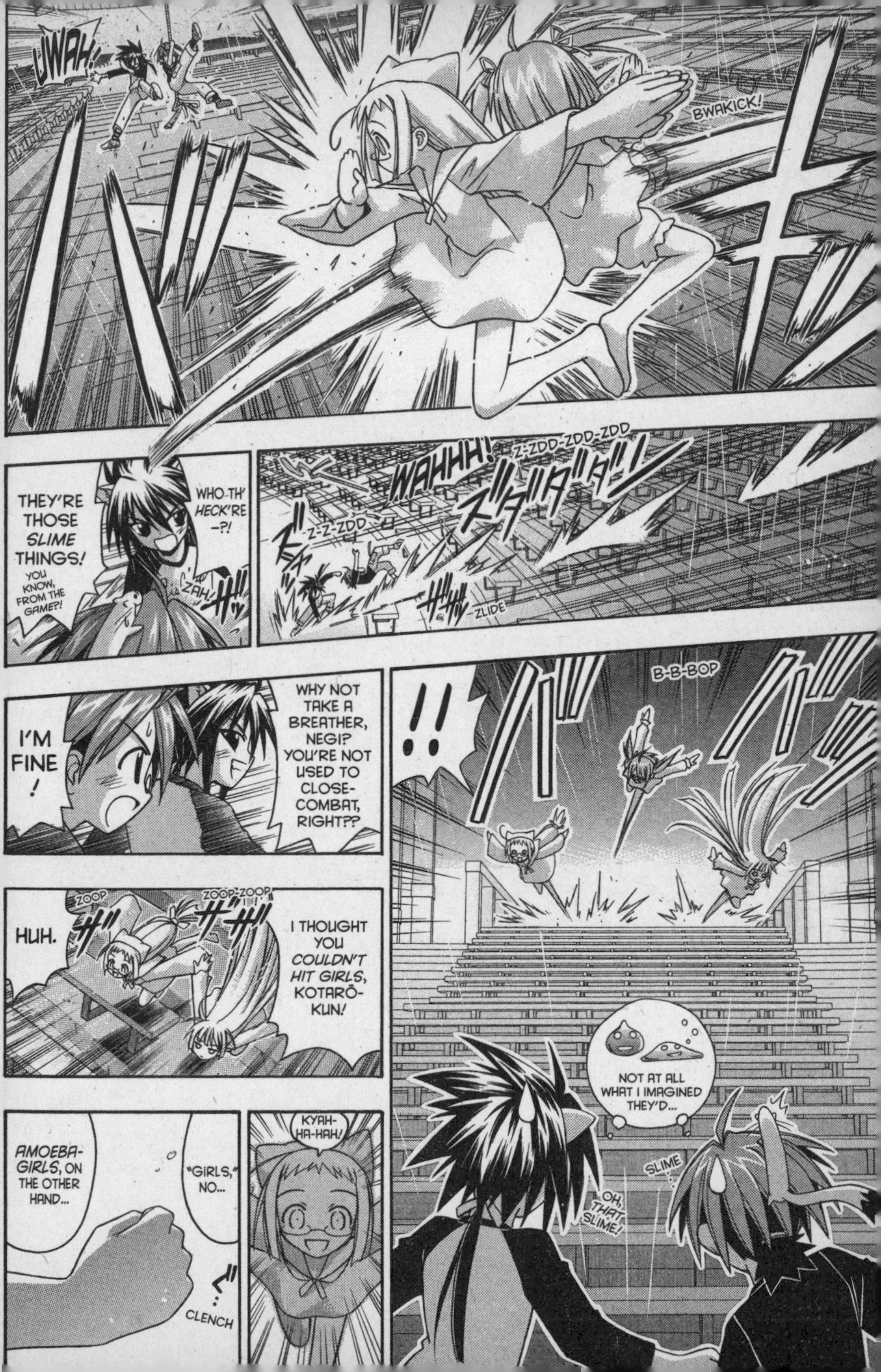
UWAH!
BWAKICK!
WAHHH!
Z-ZDD-ZDD-ZDD
Z-Z-ZDD
ZLIDE
WHO TH' HECK'RE —?!
THEY'RE THOSE *SLIME* THINGS!
YOU KNOW, FROM THE GAME?!
ZAH!
B-B-BOP
!!
NOT AT ALL WHAT I IMAGINED THEY'D...
SLIME
OH, THAT SLIME!
WHY NOT TAKE A BREATHER, NEGI? YOU'RE NOT USED TO CLOSE-COMBAT, RIGHT??
I'M FINE!
ZOOP-ZOOP
ZOOP
I THOUGHT YOU *COULDN'T HIT GIRLS*, KOTARŌ-KUN!
HUH.
KYAH-HA-HAH!
"GIRLS," NO...
AMOEBA-GIRLS, ON THE OTHER HAND...
CLENCH

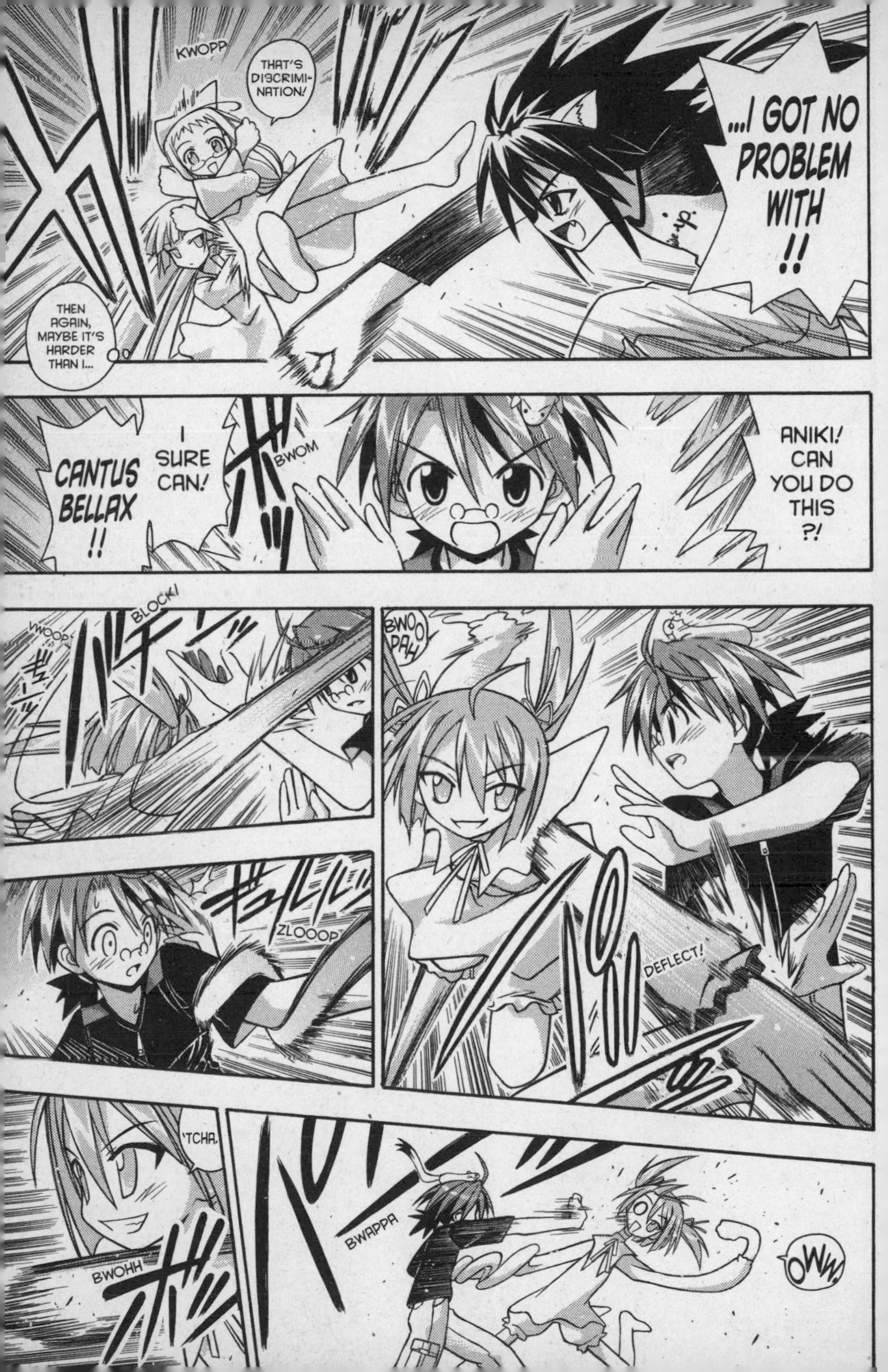

...I GOT NO PROBLEM WITH !!
THAT'S DISCRIMI-NATION!
KWOPP
THEN AGAIN, MAYBE IT'S HARDER THAN I...
ANIKI! CAN YOU DO THIS ?!
BWOM
I SURE CAN!
CANTUS BELLAX !!
BWOOPAH
DEFLECT!
BLOCK!
VWOOP
ZLOOOP
OWW!
BWAPPA
'TCHA.
BWOHH

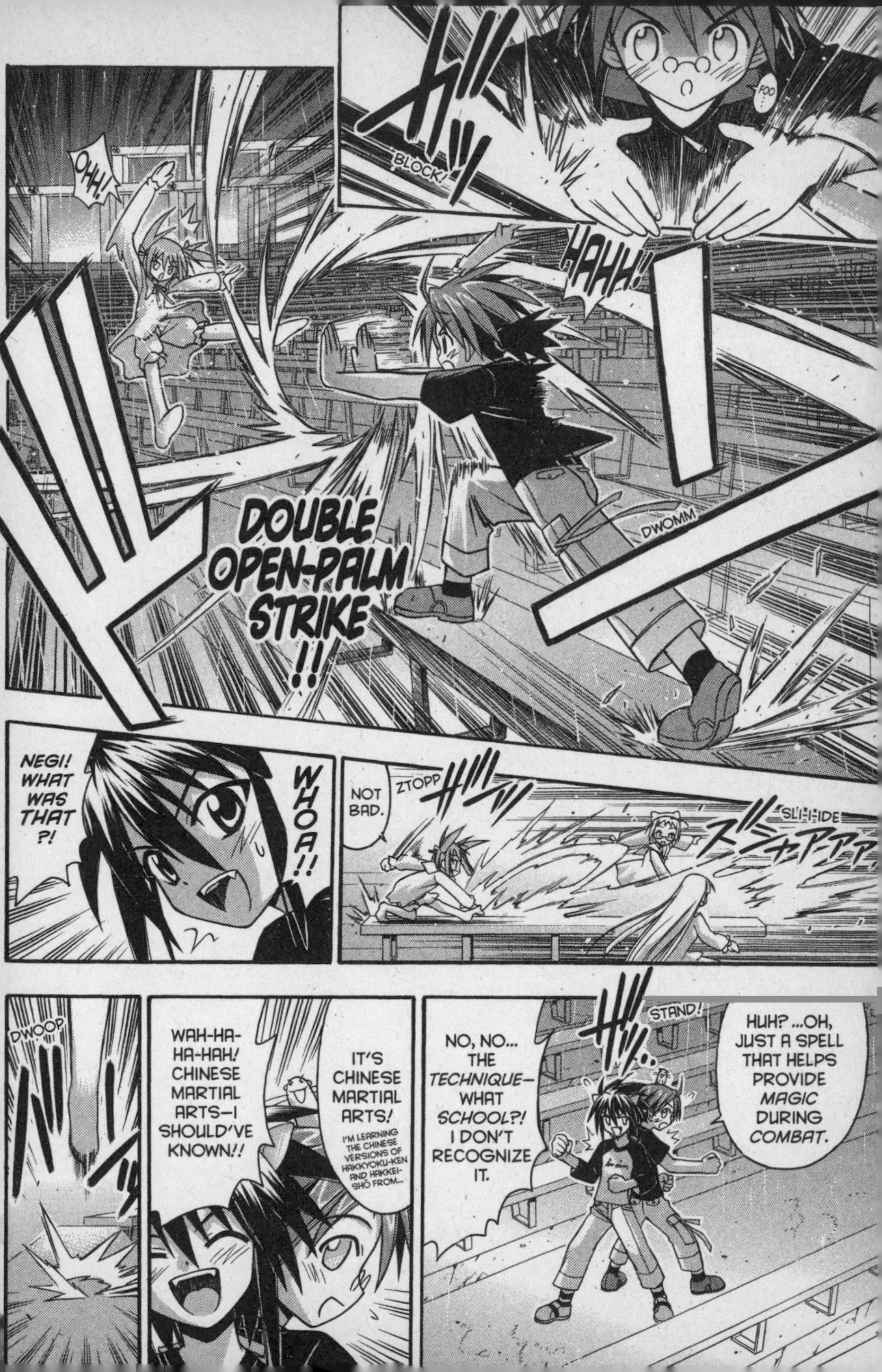
FOO...
BLOCK!
HAHH!!
OHH!
DOUBLE OPEN-PALM STRIKE!!
DWOMM
NOT BAD.
ZTOPP
SLIHHIDE
WHOA!!
NEGI! WHAT WAS THAT?!
STAND!
HUH? ...OH, JUST A SPELL THAT HELPS PROVIDE *MAGIC* DURING *COMBAT*.
NO, NO... THE *TECHNIQUE*—WHAT *SCHOOL?!* I DON'T RECOGNIZE IT.
IT'S CHINESE MARTIAL ARTS!
I'M LEARNING THE CHINESE VERSIONS OF HAKKYOKU-KEN AND HAKKEI-SHŌ FROM...
WAH-HA-HA-HAH! CHINESE MARTIAL ARTS—I SHOULD'VE KNOWN!!
DWOOP

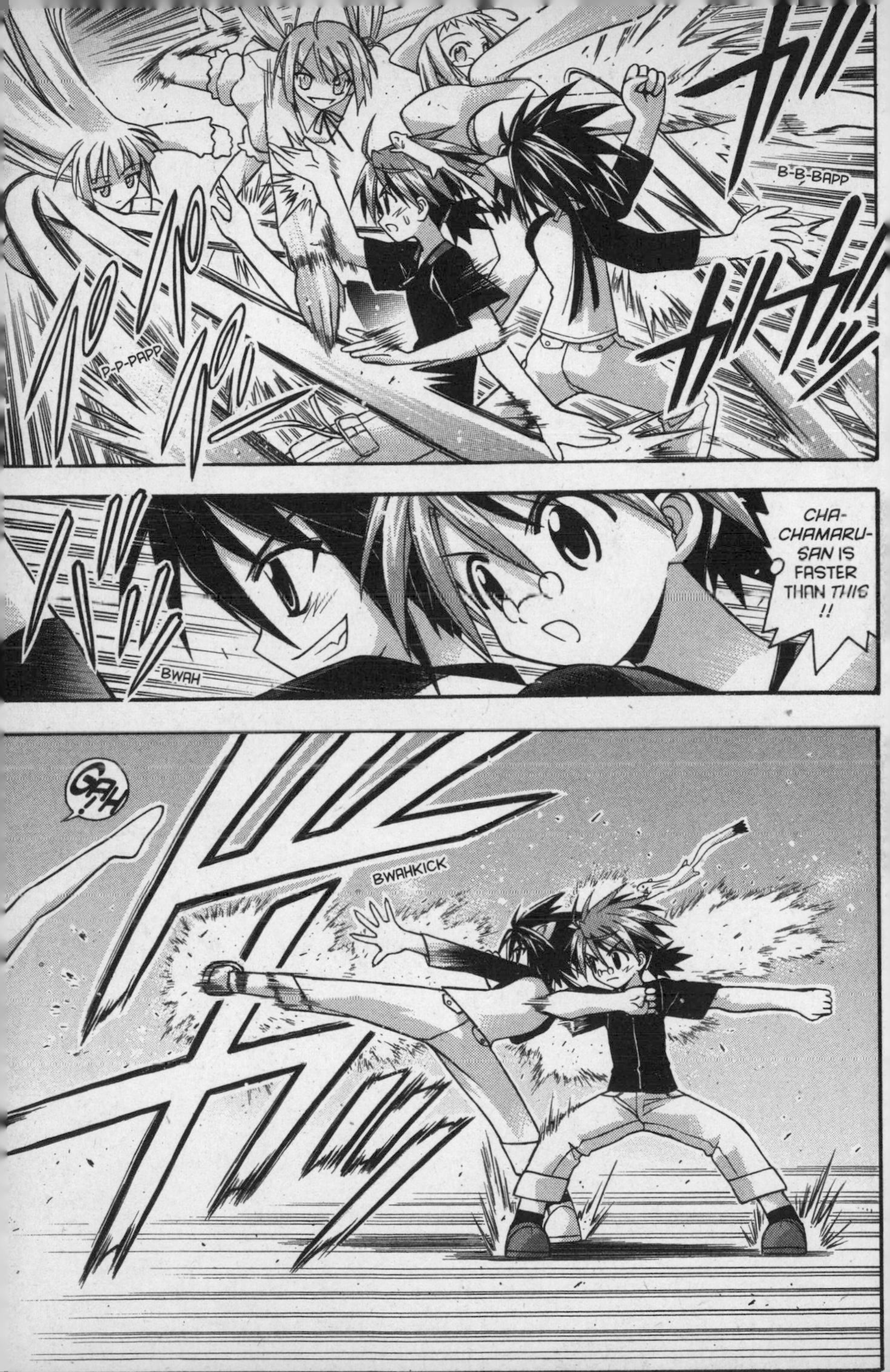
B-B-BAPP
P-P-PAPP
CHA-CHAMARU-SAN IS FASTER THAN THIS!!
BWAH
BWAHKICK
GAH!?

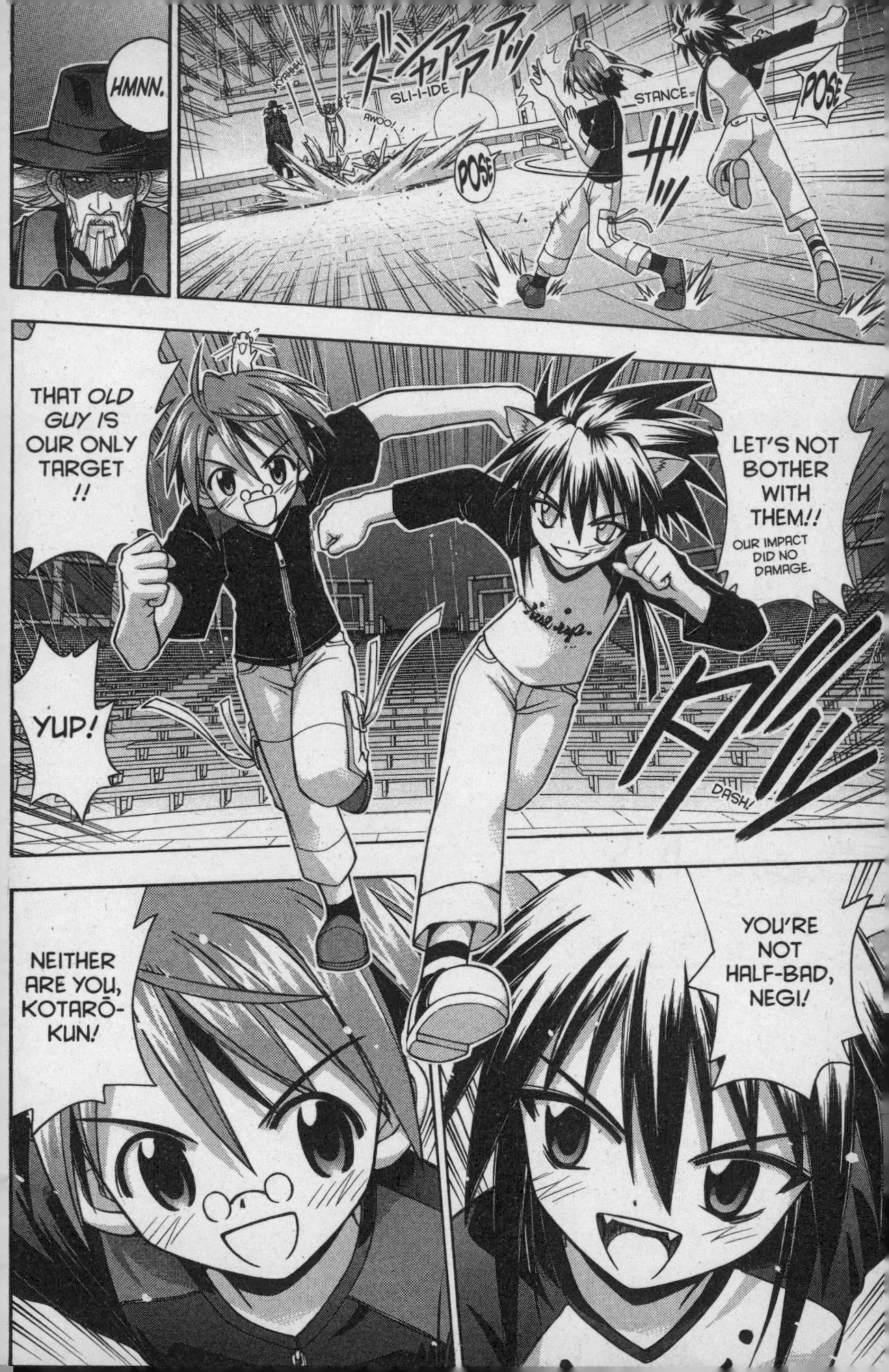

POSE
STANCE
ズシャアアッ
SLI-I-IDE
AWOO!
POSE
HMNN.
LET'S NOT BOTHER WITH THEM!!
OUR IMPACT DID NO DAMAGE.
THAT OLD GUY IS OUR ONLY TARGET!!
YUP!
DASH!
YOU'RE NOT HALF-BAD, NEGI!
NEITHER ARE YOU, KOTARŌ-KUN!

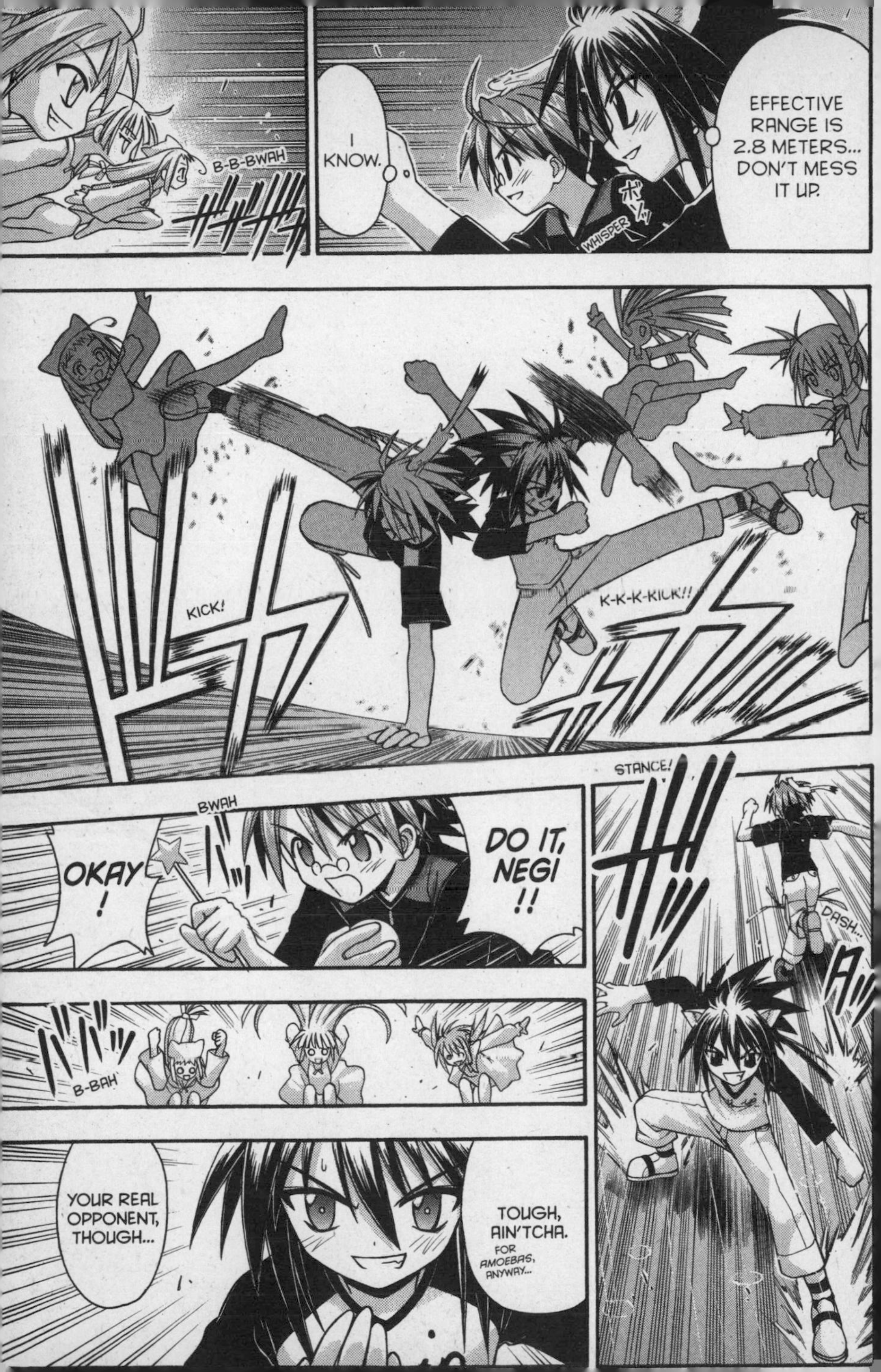
EFFECTIVE RANGE IS 2.8 METERS... DON'T MESS IT UP.
WHISPER
I KNOW.
B-B-BWAH
K-K-K-KICK!!
KICK!
STANCE!
DASH...
DO IT, NEGI!!
BWAH
OKAY!
B-BAH
TOUGH, AIN'TCHA.
FOR AMOEBAS, ANYWAY...
YOUR REAL OPPONENT, THOUGH...

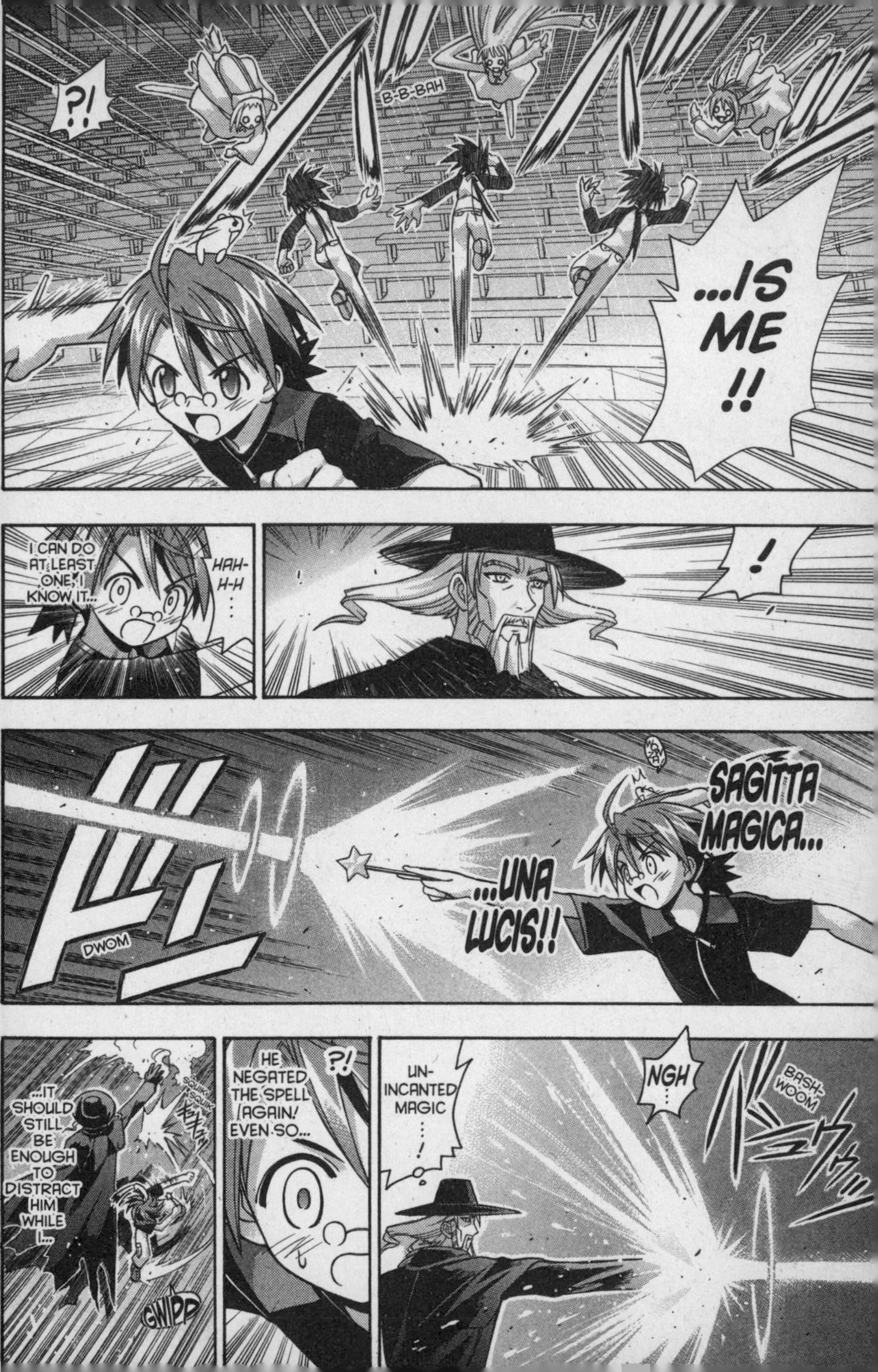
...IS ME!!
B-B-BAH
?!
!
HAH-H-H...
I CAN DO AT LEAST ONE, I KNOW IT...
SAGITTA MAGICA...
...UNA LUCIS!!
DWOM
BASH-WOOM
NGH...
UN-INCANTED MAGIC...!
?!
HE NEGATED THE SPELL AGAIN! EVEN SO...
SQUIK SQUIK
...IT SHOULD STILL BE ENOUGH TO DISTRACT HIM WHILE I...
GWIPP

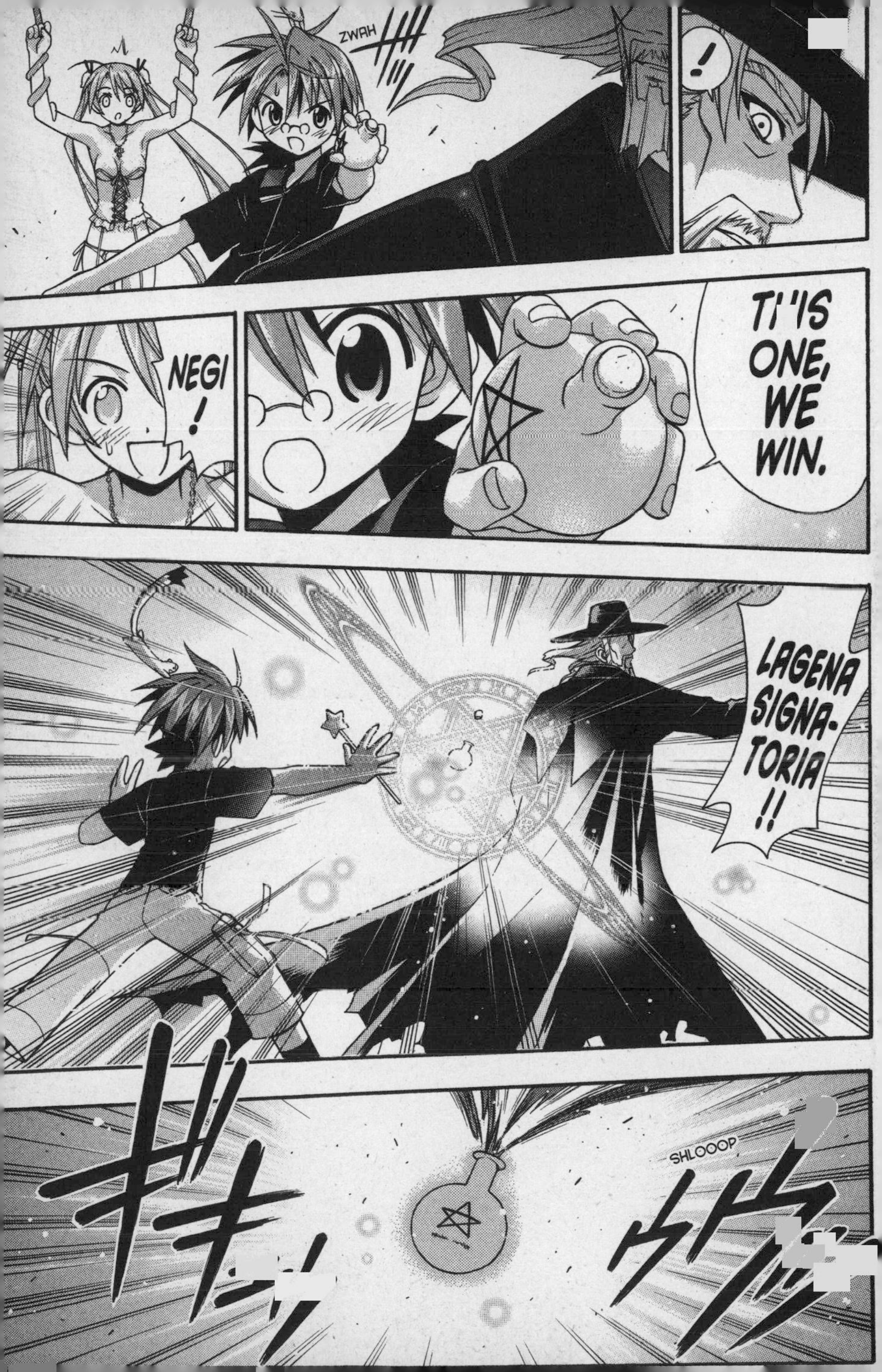
!
ZWAH
THIS ONE, WE WIN.
NEGI!
LAGENA SIGNATORIA!!
SHLOOOP

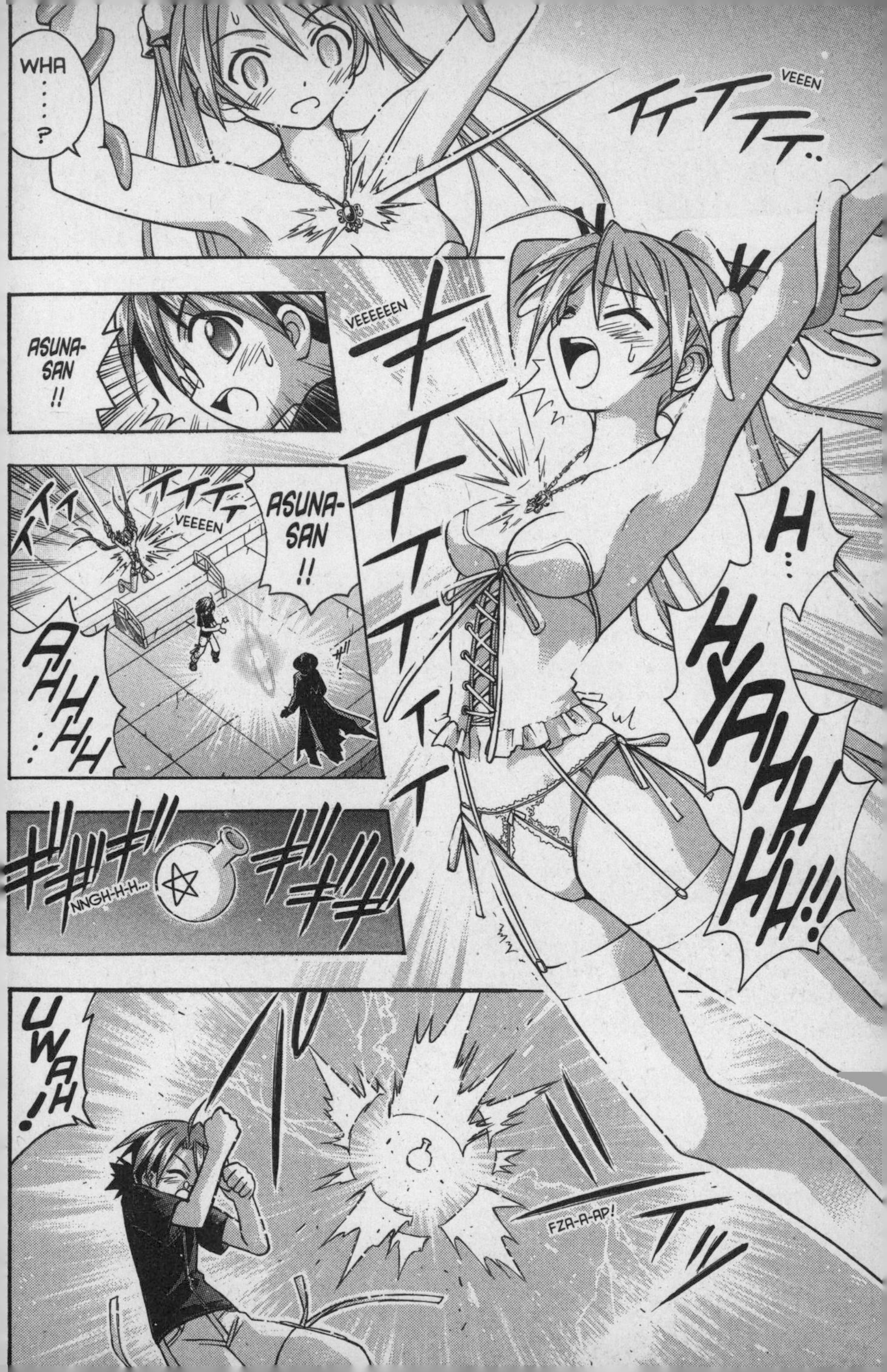
WHA.....?
VEEEN
VEEEEEEN
H... HYAHHHH!!
ASUNA-SAN!!
ASUNA-SAN!!
VEEEEN
AHHHH...
NNGH-H-H...
FZA-A-AP!
UWAH!

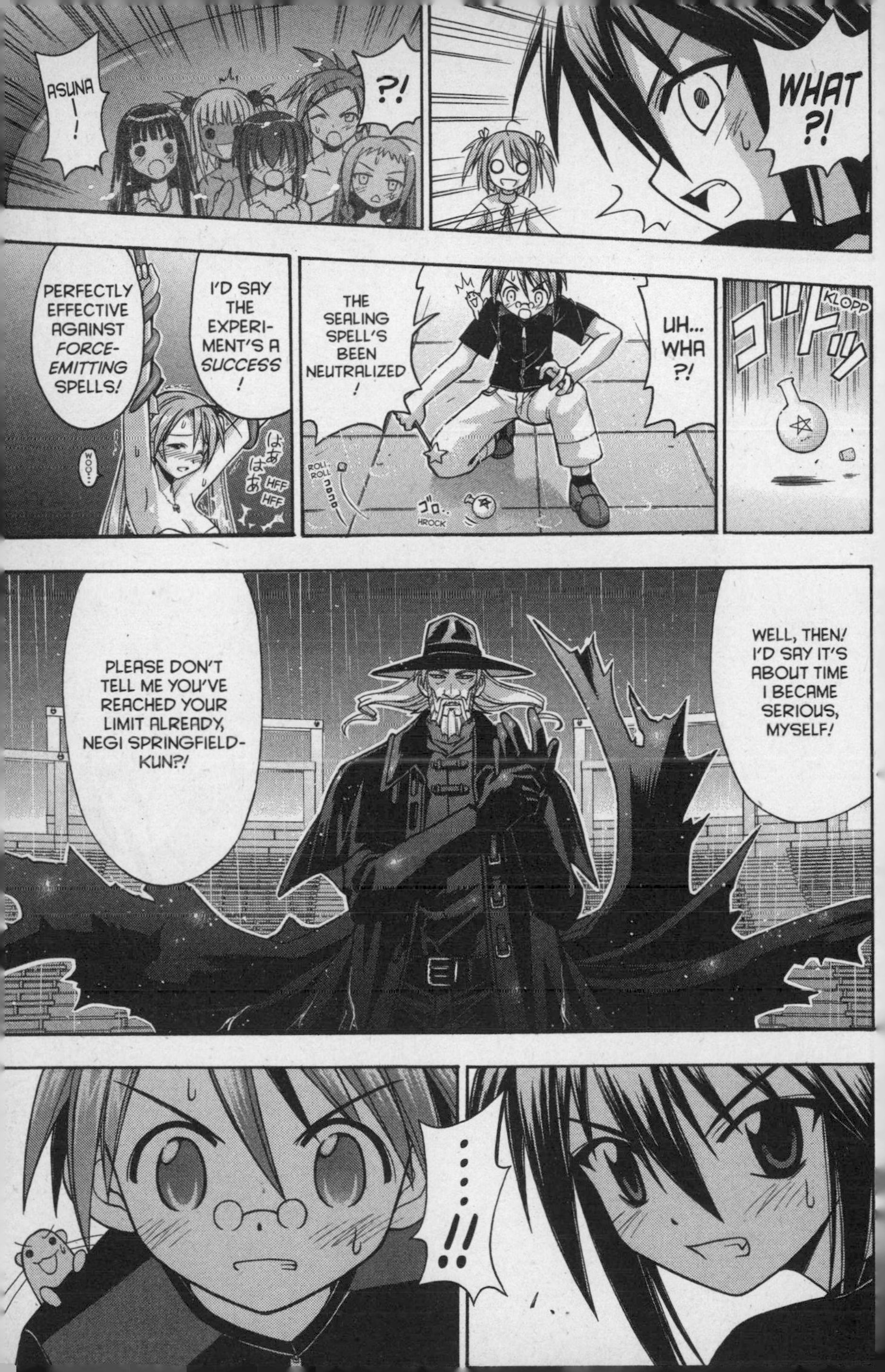
WHAT ?!
?!
ASUNA—!
KLOPP
UH... WHA ?!
THE SEALING SPELL'S BEEN NEUTRALIZED!
ROLL ROLL
HROCK
I'D SAY THE EXPERIMENT'S A SUCCESS!
PERFECTLY EFFECTIVE AGAINST FORCE-EMITTING SPELLS!
HFF HFF
WELL, THEN! I'D SAY IT'S ABOUT TIME I BECAME SERIOUS, MYSELF!
PLEASE DON'T TELL ME YOU'VE REACHED YOUR LIMIT ALREADY, NEGI SPRINGFIELD-KUN?!
......!!

NEGIMA!
MAGISTER NEGI MAGI

SIXTY-NINTH PERIOD: "MAGIC WORD" LEXICON

■「『戦いの歌』」
CANTUS BELLAX

From Latin to Japanese and then to English, "Cantus Bellax" may be transliterated as "Song of Battle," and is a high-level spell typically cast by a mage immediately before entering physical battle. In addition to surrounding the mage's body with a powerful barrier that protects from physical attack, the physical attributes of the caster are enhanced (muscle expansion, power, speed, endurance), while the body is magically spared damage from overexertion (pulled muscles, sprains, torn ligaments). Further, the spell also has the ability to increase reaction time by heightening the sensitivity of the nervous system.

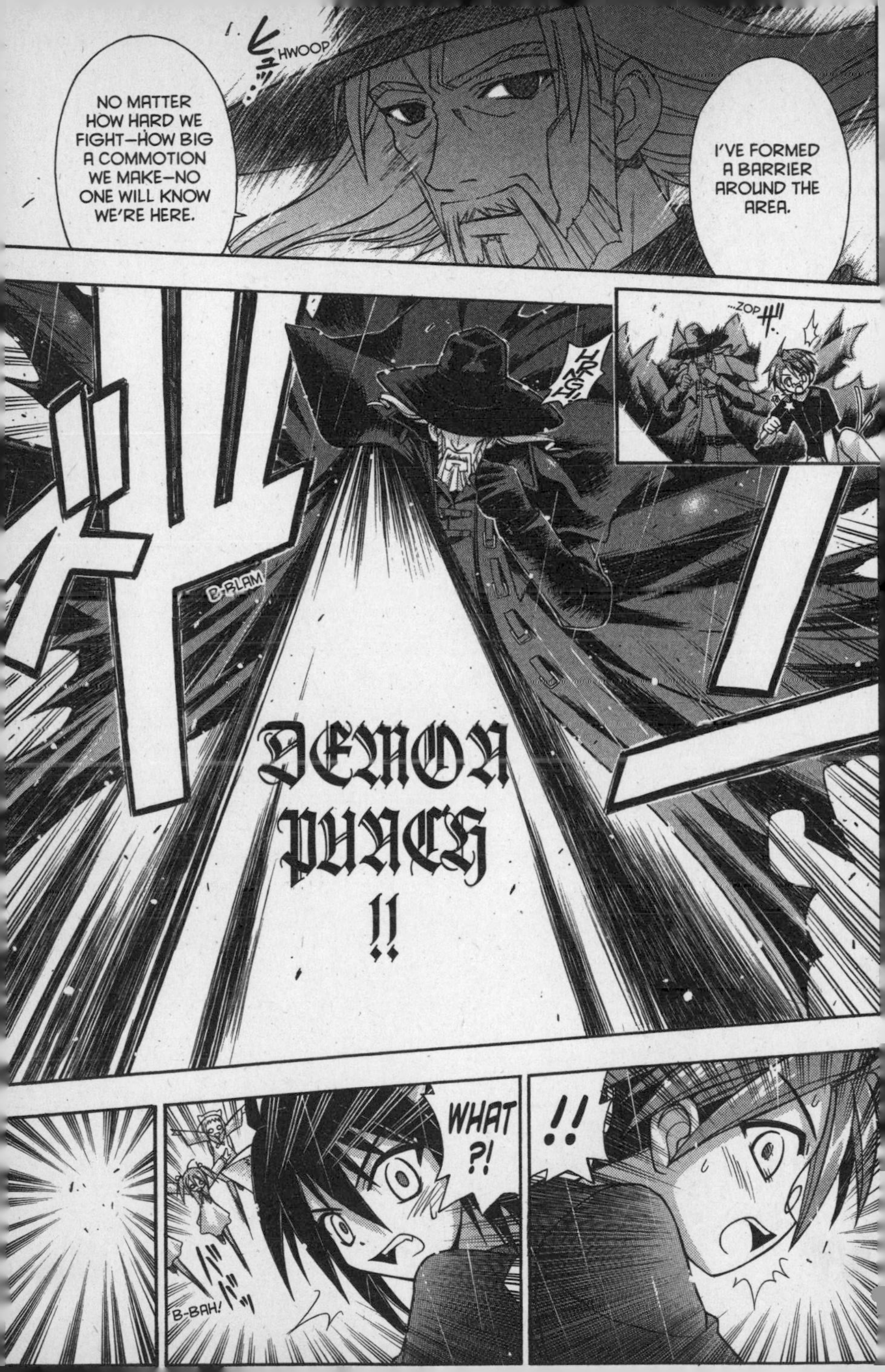
I'VE FORMED A BARRIER AROUND THE AREA.
HWOOP
NO MATTER HOW HARD WE FIGHT—HOW BIG A COMMOTION WE MAKE—NO ONE WILL KNOW WE'RE HERE.
...ZOP
HRNGH!
B-BLAM
DEMON PUNCH !!
!!
WHAT ?!
B-BAH!

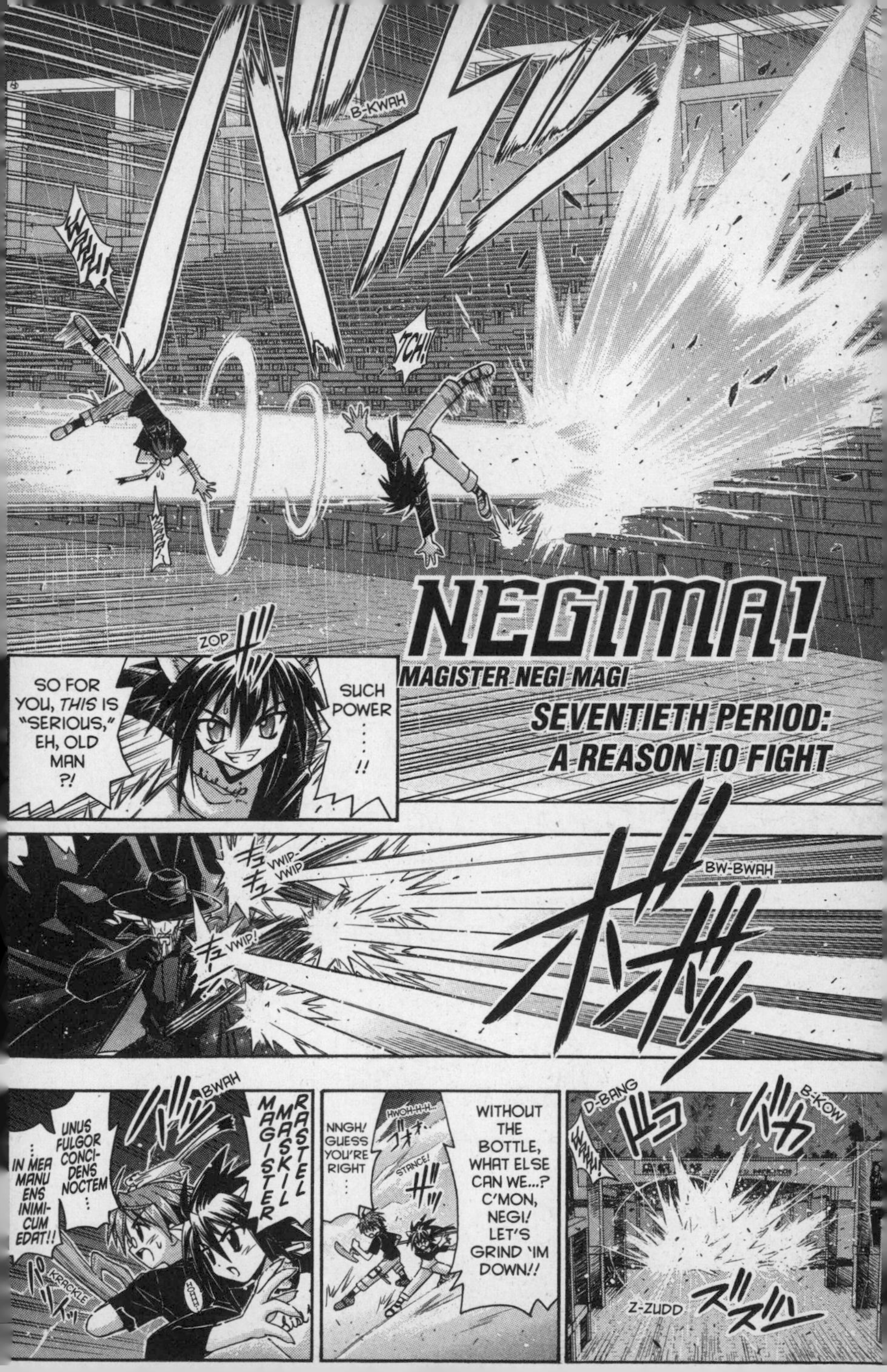
B-KWAH
TCH!
WAAH!
NEGIMA!
MAGISTER NEGI MAGI
SEVENTIETH PERIOD: A REASON TO FIGHT
ZOP
SUCH POWER ... !!
SO FOR YOU, THIS IS "SERIOUS," EH, OLD MAN ?!
BW-BWAH
VWIP-VWIP
VWIP!
B-KOW
D-BANG
WAAH!
Z-ZUDD
WITHOUT THE BOTTLE, WHAT ELSE CAN WE...? C'MON, NEGI! LET'S GRIND 'IM DOWN!!
HWOH-H-H...
NNGH! GUESS YOU'RE RIGHT ...
STANCE!
RASTEL MASKIL MAGISTER
ABWAH
UNUS FULGOR CONCIDENS NOCTEM ...
... IN MEA MANU ENS INIMICUM EDAT!!
KRACKLE

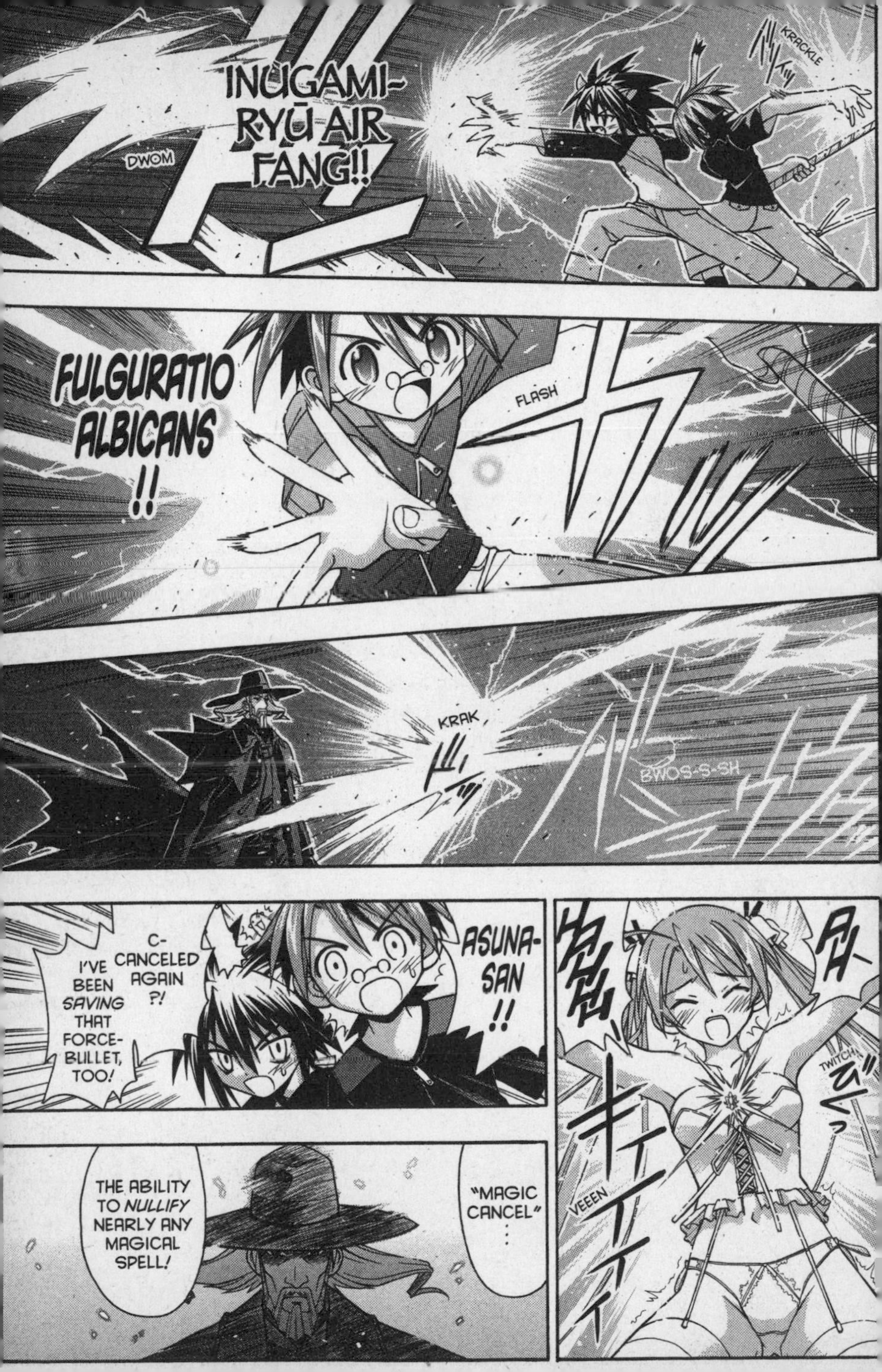
KRACKLE
INUGAMI-RYŪ AIR FANG!!
DWOM
FLASH
FULGURATIO ALBICANS!!
KRAK
BWOS-S-SH
AH-
TWITCH
VEEEN
ASUNA-SAN!!
C-CANCELED AGAIN?!
I'VE BEEN *SAVING* THAT FORCE-BULLET, TOO!
"MAGIC CANCEL"...
THE ABILITY TO *NULLIFY* NEARLY ANY MAGICAL SPELL!

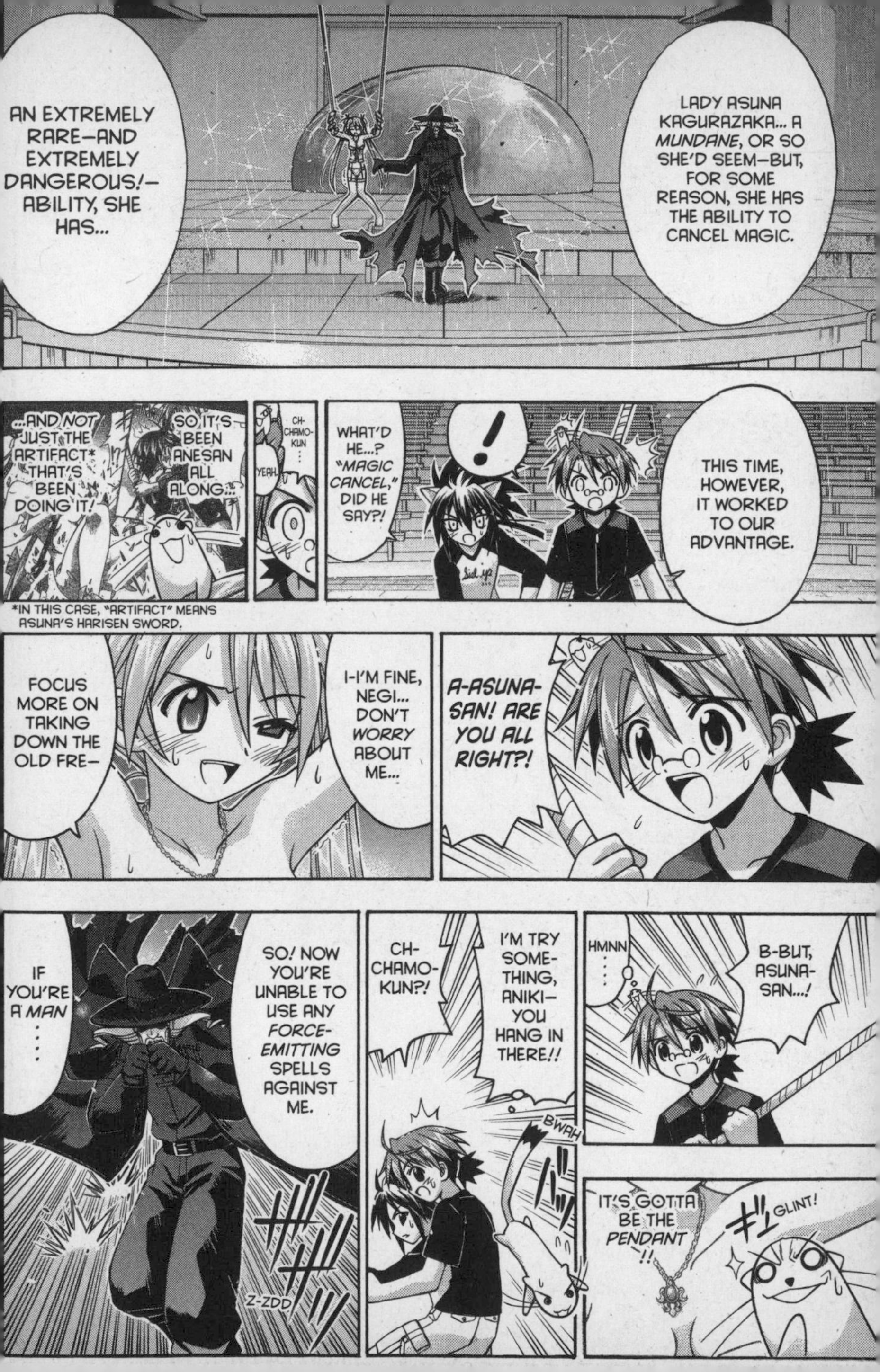
LADY ASUNA KAGURAZAKA... A *MUNDANE*, OR SO SHE'D SEEM—BUT, FOR SOME REASON, SHE HAS THE ABILITY TO CANCEL MAGIC.
AN EXTREMELY RARE—AND EXTREMELY DANGEROUS!—ABILITY, SHE HAS...
THIS TIME, HOWEVER, IT WORKED TO OUR ADVANTAGE.
!
WHAT'D HE...? "*MAGIC CANCEL*," DID HE SAY?!
CH-CHAMO-KUN...
YEAH.
SO IT'S BEEN ANESAN ALL ALONG...
...AND *NOT* JUST THE ARTIFACT* THAT'S BEEN DOING IT!
A-ASUNA-SAN! ARE YOU ALL RIGHT?!
I-I'M FINE, NEGI... DON'T *WORRY* ABOUT ME...
FOCUS MORE ON TAKING DOWN THE OLD FRE—
B-BUT, ASUNA-SAN...!
HMNN...
GLINT!
IT'S GOTTA BE THE *PENDANT*—!!
I'M TRY SOME-THING, ANIKI—YOU HANG IN THERE!!
CH-CHAMO-KUN?!
BWAH
SO! NOW YOU'RE UNABLE TO USE ANY *FORCE-EMITTING* SPELLS AGAINST ME.
IF YOU'RE A *MAN*...
Z-ZDD
*IN THIS CASE, "ARTIFACT" MEANS ASUNA'S HARISEN SWORD.

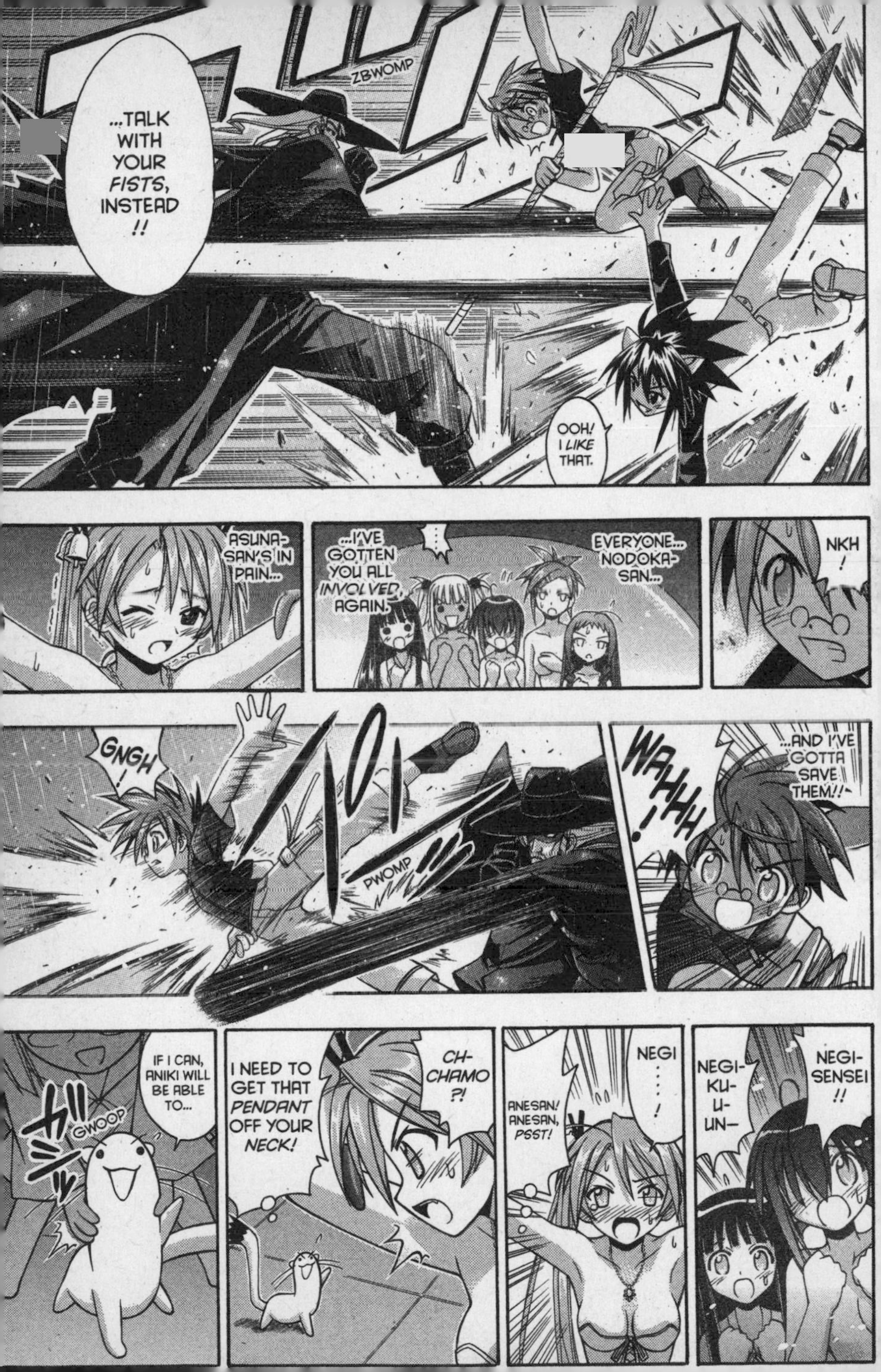
ZBWOMP
...TALK WITH YOUR *FISTS*, INSTEAD!!
OOH! I *LIKE* THAT.
NKH!
EVERYONE... NODOKA-SAN...
...I'VE GOTTEN YOU ALL *INVOLVED* AGAIN.
ASUNA-SAN'S IN PAIN...
...AND I'VE GOTTA SAVE THEM!!
WAHHH!
PWOMP
GNGH!
NEGI-SENSEI!!
NEGI-KU-U-UN—
NEGI...!
ANESAN! ANESAN, *PSST!*
CH-CHAMO?!
I NEED TO GET THAT *PENDANT* OFF YOUR *NECK!*
IF I CAN, ANIKI WILL BE ABLE TO...
GWOOP

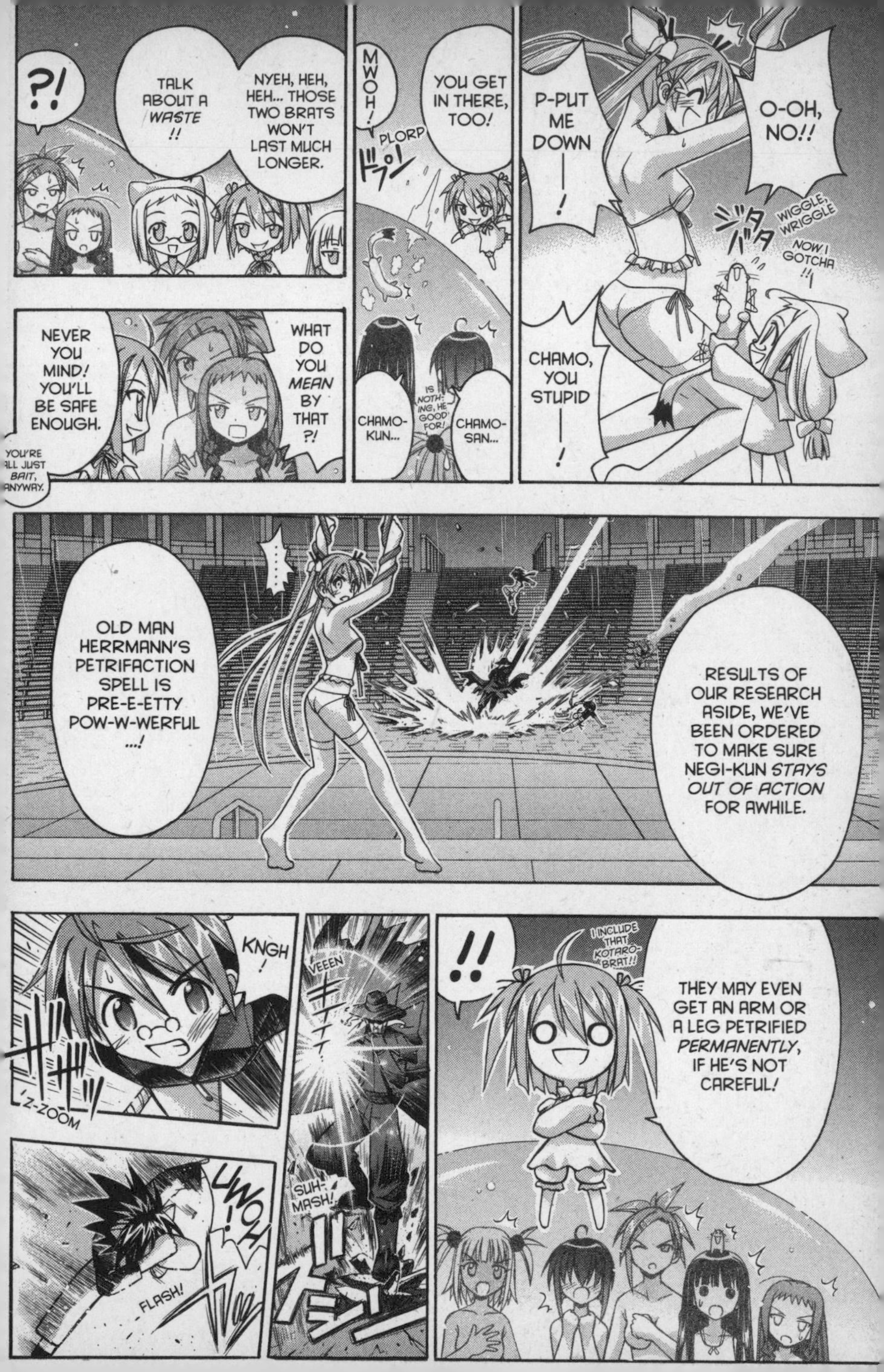

O-OH, NO!!
P-PUT ME DOWN—!
WIGGLE, WRIGGLE
NOW I GOTCHA!!
CHAMO, YOU STUPID—!
YOU GET IN THERE, TOO!
MWOH!
PLORP
CHAMO-SAN...
IS NOTHING HE GOOD FOR!
CHAMO-KUN...
NYEH, HEH, HEH... THOSE TWO BRATS WON'T LAST MUCH LONGER.
TALK ABOUT A WASTE!!
?!
WHAT DO YOU MEAN BY THAT?!
NEVER YOU MIND! YOU'LL BE SAFE ENOUGH.
YOU'RE ALL JUST BAIT, ANYWAY.
RESULTS OF OUR RESEARCH ASIDE, WE'VE BEEN ORDERED TO MAKE SURE NEGI-KUN STAYS OUT OF ACTION FOR AWHILE.
......!
OLD MAN HERRMANN'S PETRIFACTION SPELL IS PRE-E-ETTY POW-W-WERFUL ...!
THEY MAY EVEN GET AN ARM OR A LEG PETRIFIED PERMANENTLY, IF HE'S NOT CAREFUL!
I INCLUDE THAT KOTARŌ-BRAT!!
!!
VEEEN
SUH-MASH!
KNGH!
Z-ZOOM
UWOH!
FLASH!

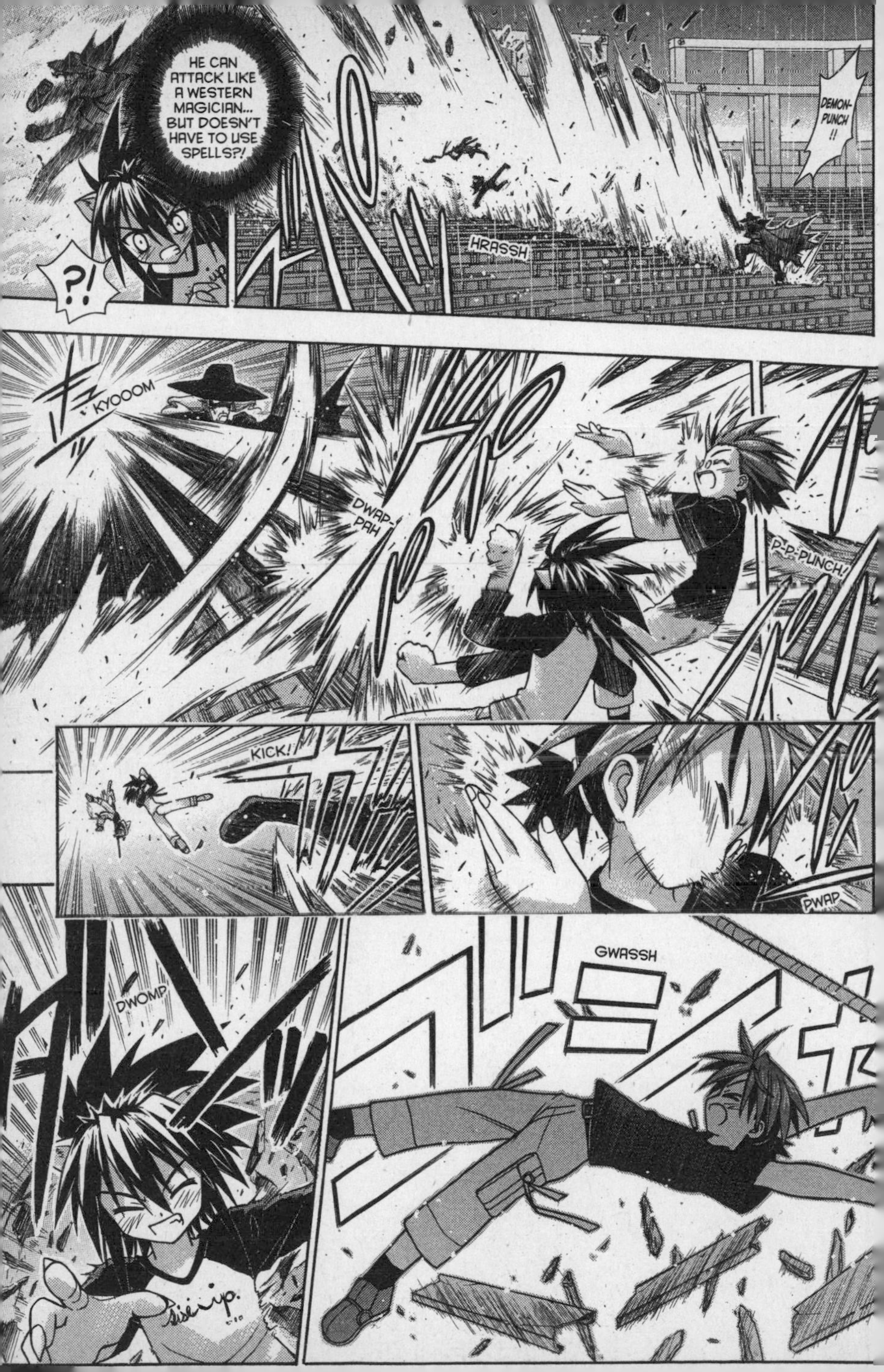
DEMON-PUNCH!!
HRASSH
HE CAN ATTACK LIKE A WESTERN MAGICIAN... BUT DOESN'T HAVE TO USE SPELLS?!
?!
P-P-PUNCH!
DWAP-PAH
KYOOOM
PWAP
KICK!
GWASSH
DWOMP

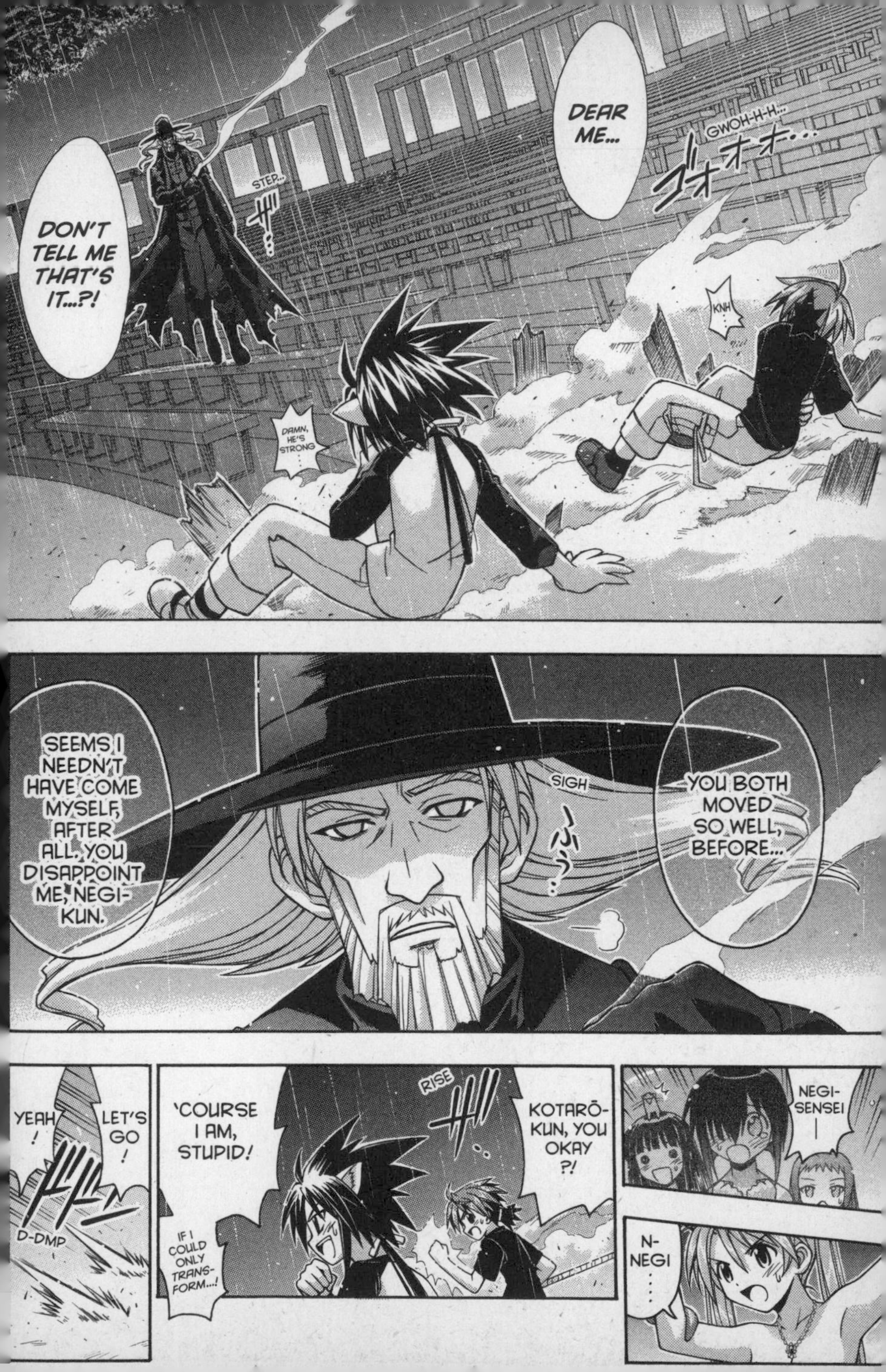
DEAR ME...
GWOH-H-H...
ゴオオオ...
KNH
...
STEP...
DON'T TELL ME THAT'S IT...?!
DAMN, HE'S STRONG...
YOU BOTH MOVED SO WELL, BEFORE...
SIGH
ふぅ...
SEEMS I NEEDN'T HAVE COME MYSELF, AFTER ALL. YOU DISAPPOINT ME, NEGI-KUN.
NEGI-SENSEI—
N-NEGI.....
KOTARŌ-KUN, YOU OKAY?!
RISE
'COURSE I AM, STUPID!
IF I COULD ONLY TRANSFORM...!
LET'S GO!
YEAH!
D-DMP

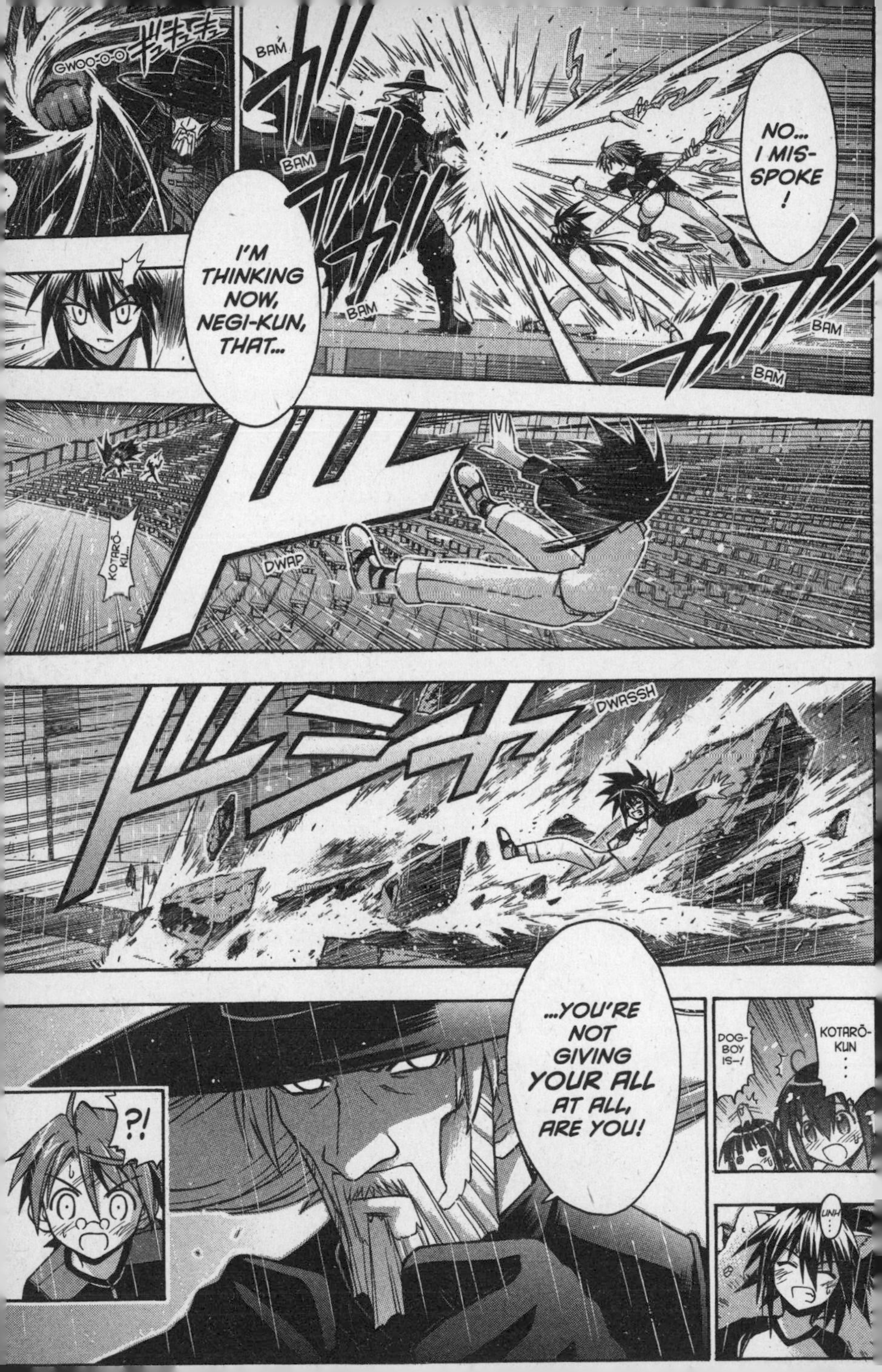
NO... I MIS-SPOKE!
BAM
BAM
BAM
BAM
BAM
BAM
GWOO-O-O
I'M THINKING NOW, NEGI-KUN, THAT...
DWAP
KOTARŌ-KU...
DWASSH
KOTARŌ-KUN...
DOG-BOY IS-!
UNH...
...YOU'RE NOT GIVING YOUR ALL AT ALL, ARE YOU!
?!

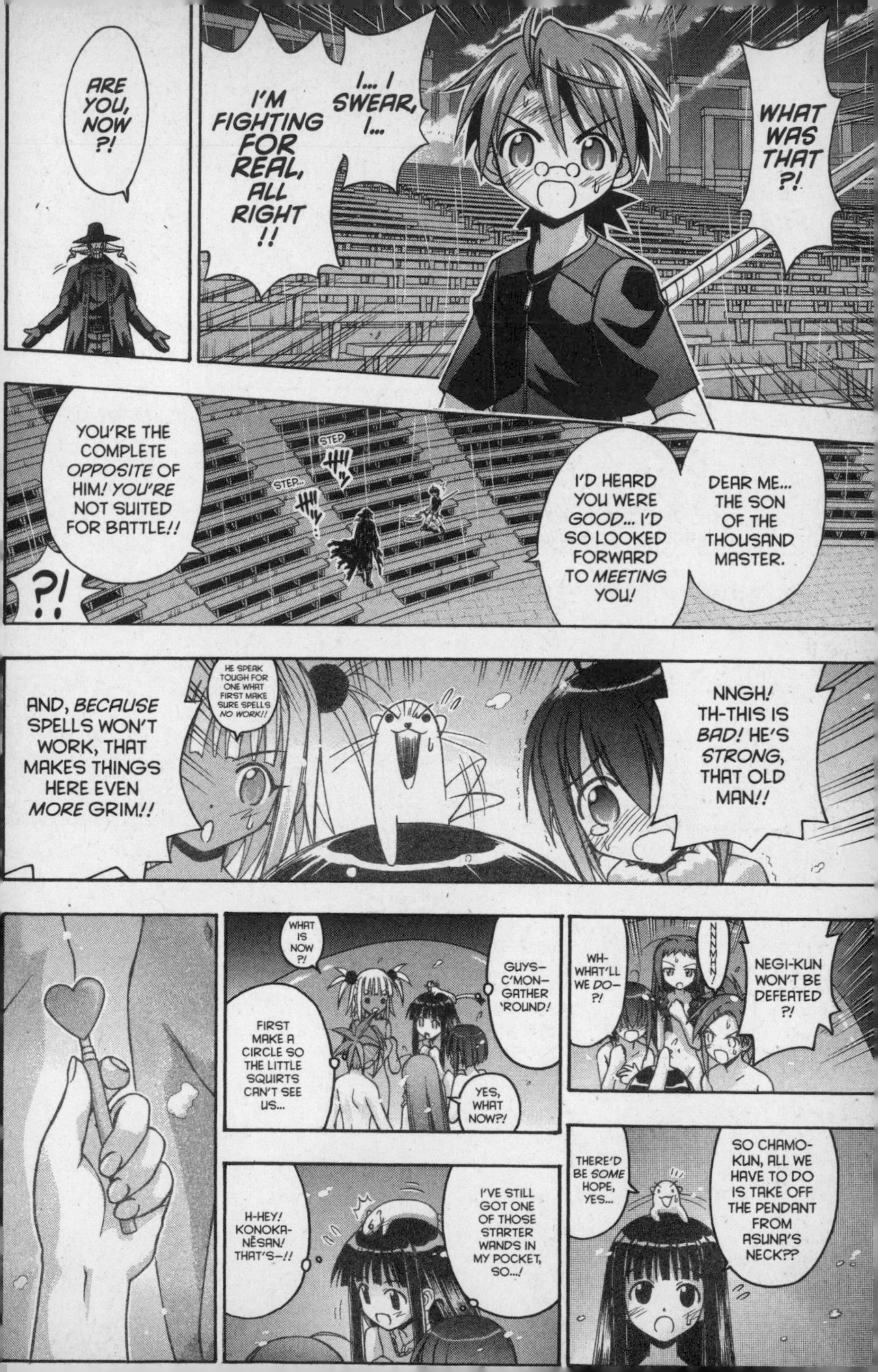
WHAT WAS THAT?!
I... I SWEAR, I...
I'M FIGHTING FOR REAL, ALL RIGHT!!
ARE YOU, NOW?!
DEAR ME... THE SON OF THE THOUSAND MASTER.
I'D HEARD YOU WERE GOOD... I'D SO LOOKED FORWARD TO MEETING YOU!
STEP
STEP..
YOU'RE THE COMPLETE OPPOSITE OF HIM! YOU'RE NOT SUITED FOR BATTLE!!
?!
NNGH! TH-THIS IS BAD! HE'S STRONG, THAT OLD MAN!!
HE SPEAK TOUGH FOR ONE WHAT FIRST MAKE SURE SPELLS NO WORK!!
AND, BECAUSE SPELLS WON'T WORK, THAT MAKES THINGS HERE EVEN MORE GRIM!!
NNNMMH!
NEGI-KUN WON'T BE DEFEATED?!
WH-WHAT'LL WE DO-?!
SO CHAMO-KUN, ALL WE HAVE TO DO IS TAKE OFF THE PENDANT FROM ASUNA'S NECK??
THERE'D BE SOME HOPE, YES...
GUYS—C'MON—GATHER 'ROUND!
WHAT IS NOW?!
YES, WHAT NOW?!
FIRST MAKE A CIRCLE SO THE LITTLE SQUIRTS CAN'T SEE US...
I'VE STILL GOT ONE OF THOSE STARTER WANDS IN MY POCKET, SO...!
H-HEY! KONOKA-NĒSAN! THAT'S—!!

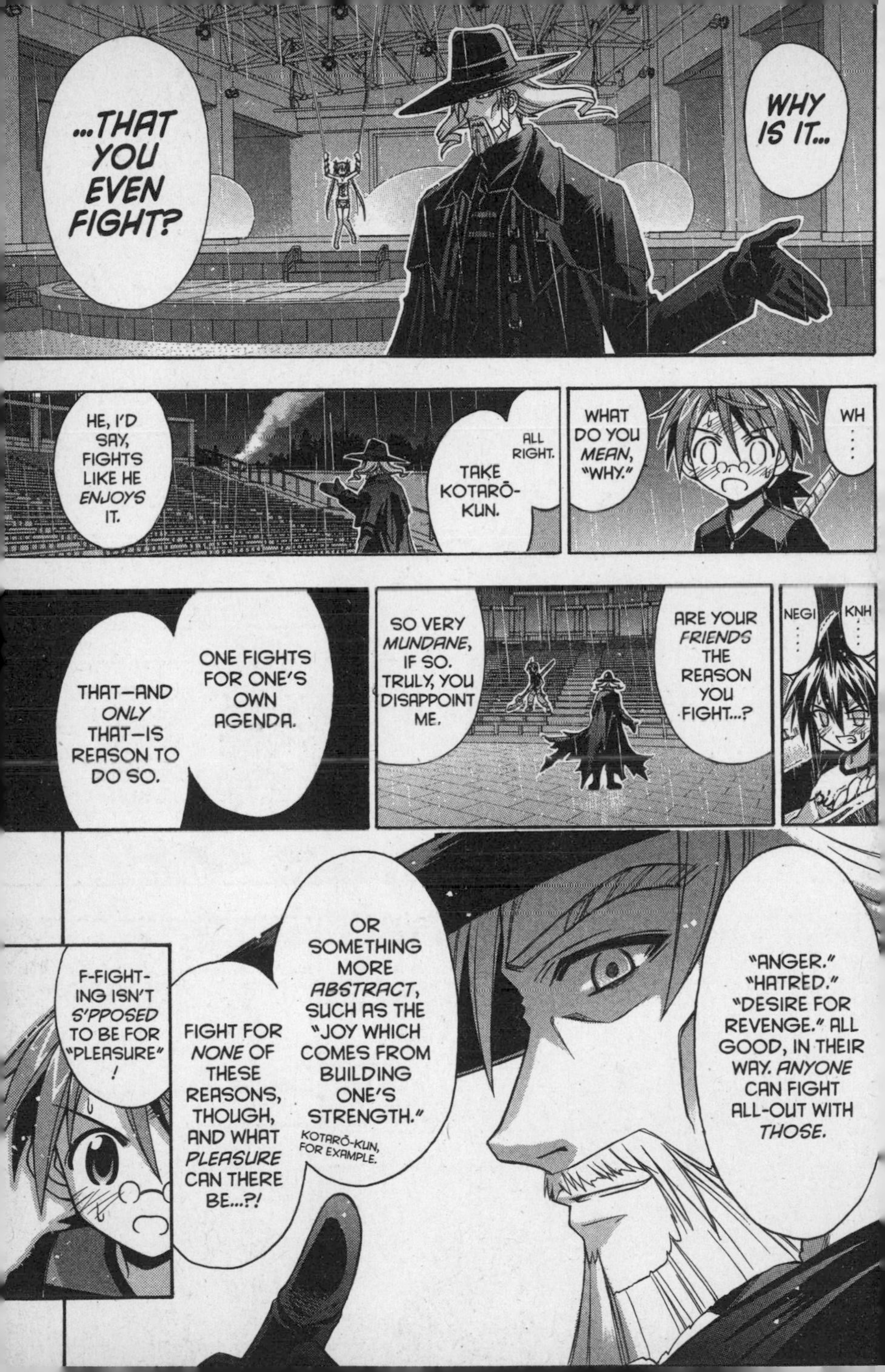
WHY IS IT...
...THAT YOU EVEN FIGHT?
WH...
WHAT DO YOU MEAN, "WHY."
ALL RIGHT.
TAKE KOTARŌ-KUN.
HE, I'D SAY, FIGHTS LIKE HE ENJOYS IT.
KNH...
NEGI...
ARE YOUR FRIENDS THE REASON YOU FIGHT...?
SO VERY MUNDANE, IF SO. TRULY, YOU DISAPPOINT ME.
ONE FIGHTS FOR ONE'S OWN AGENDA.
THAT—AND ONLY THAT—IS REASON TO DO SO.
"ANGER." "HATRED." "DESIRE FOR REVENGE." ALL GOOD, IN THEIR WAY. ANYONE CAN FIGHT ALL-OUT WITH THOSE.
OR SOMETHING MORE ABSTRACT, SUCH AS THE "JOY WHICH COMES FROM BUILDING ONE'S STRENGTH."
KOTARŌ-KUN, FOR EXAMPLE.
FIGHT FOR NONE OF THESE REASONS, THOUGH, AND WHAT PLEASURE CAN THERE BE...?!
F-FIGHTING ISN'T S'PPOSED TO BE FOR "PLEASURE"!

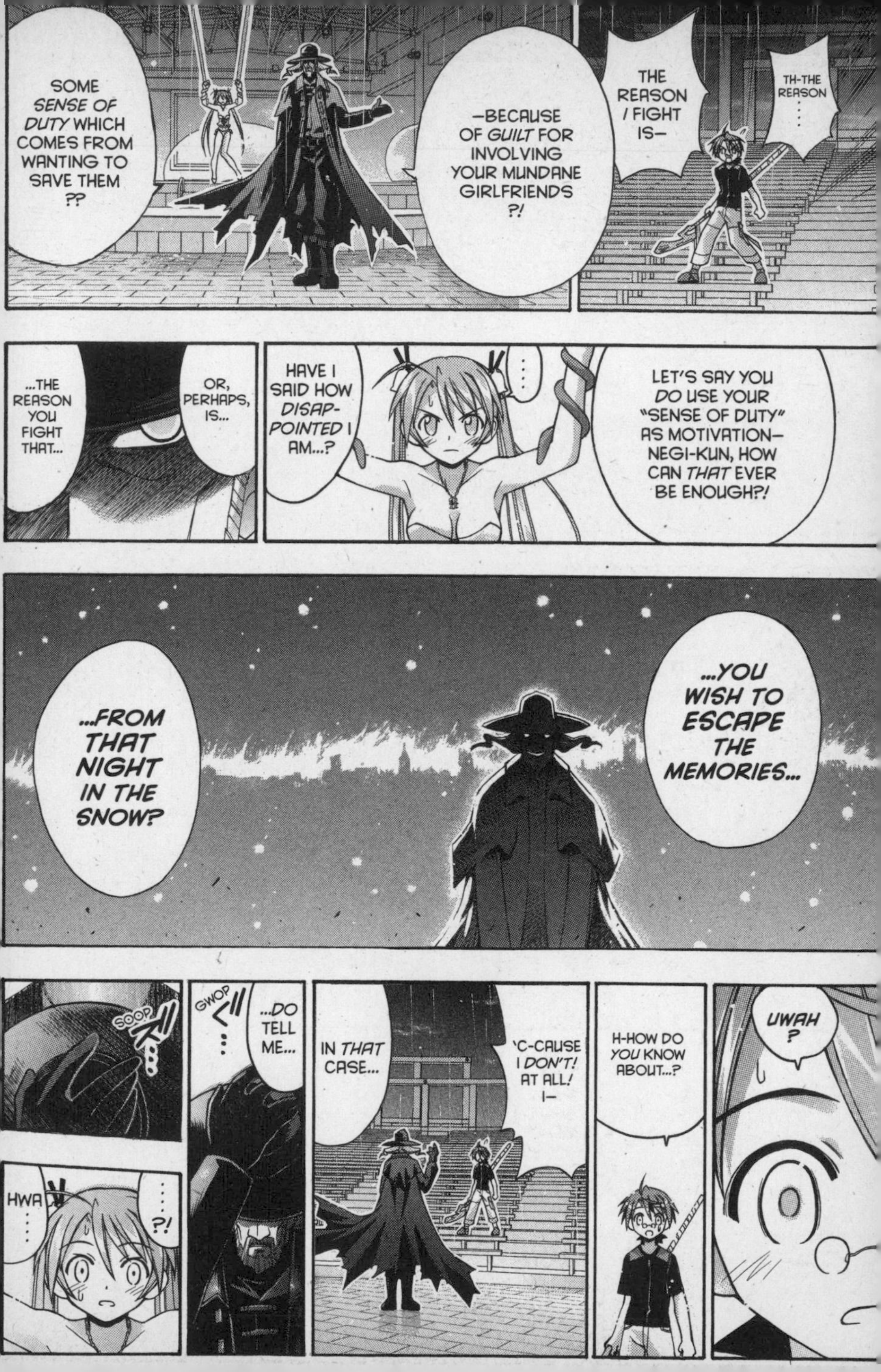
TH-THE REASON ....
THE REASON I FIGHT IS—
—BECAUSE OF GUILT FOR INVOLVING YOUR MUNDANE GIRLFRIENDS ?!
SOME SENSE OF DUTY WHICH COMES FROM WANTING TO SAVE THEM ??
LET'S SAY YOU DO USE YOUR "SENSE OF DUTY" AS MOTIVATION— NEGI-KUN, HOW CAN THAT EVER BE ENOUGH?!
....
HAVE I SAID HOW DISAP-POINTED I AM...?
OR, PERHAPS, IS...
...THE REASON YOU FIGHT THAT...
...YOU WISH TO ESCAPE THE MEMORIES...
...FROM THAT NIGHT IN THE SNOW?
UWAH ?
H-HOW DO YOU KNOW ABOUT...?
'C-CAUSE I DON'T! AT ALL! I—
IN THAT CASE...
...DO TELL ME...
GWOP
...
SOOP
...
....?!
HWA ...

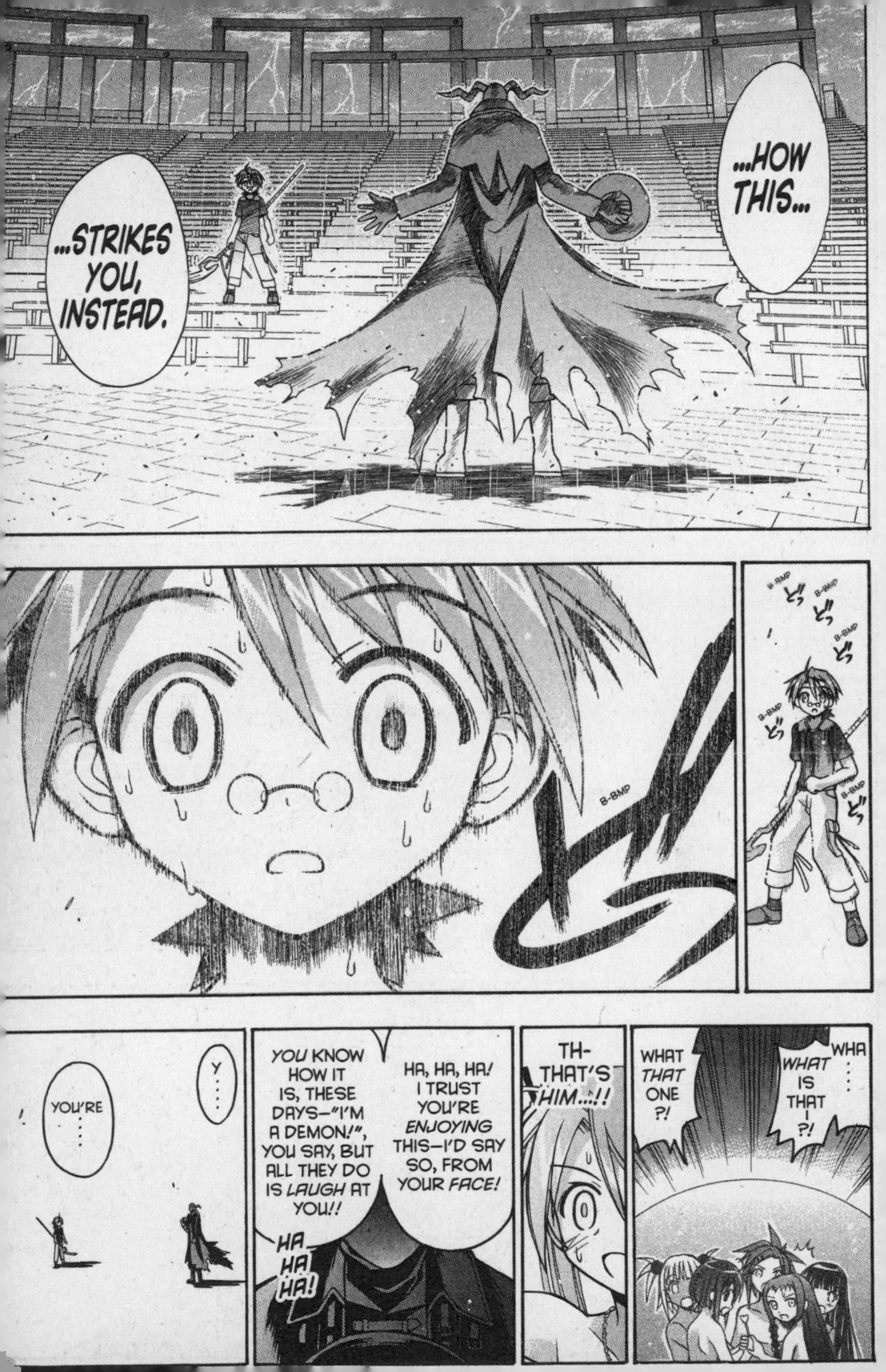
...HOW THIS...
...STRIKES YOU, INSTEAD.
B-BMP どっ
B-BMP どっ
B-BMP どっ
B-BMP どっ
B-BMP どっ
B-BMP
WHA...
WHAT IS THAT I ?!
WHAT THAT ONE ?!
TH- THAT'S HIM...!!
HA, HA, HA! I TRUST YOU'RE ENJOYING THIS—I'D SAY SO, FROM YOUR FACE!
YOU KNOW HOW IT IS, THESE DAYS—"I'M A DEMON!", YOU SAY, BUT ALL THEY DO IS LAUGH AT YOU!!
HA HA HA!
Y.....
YOU'RE ....

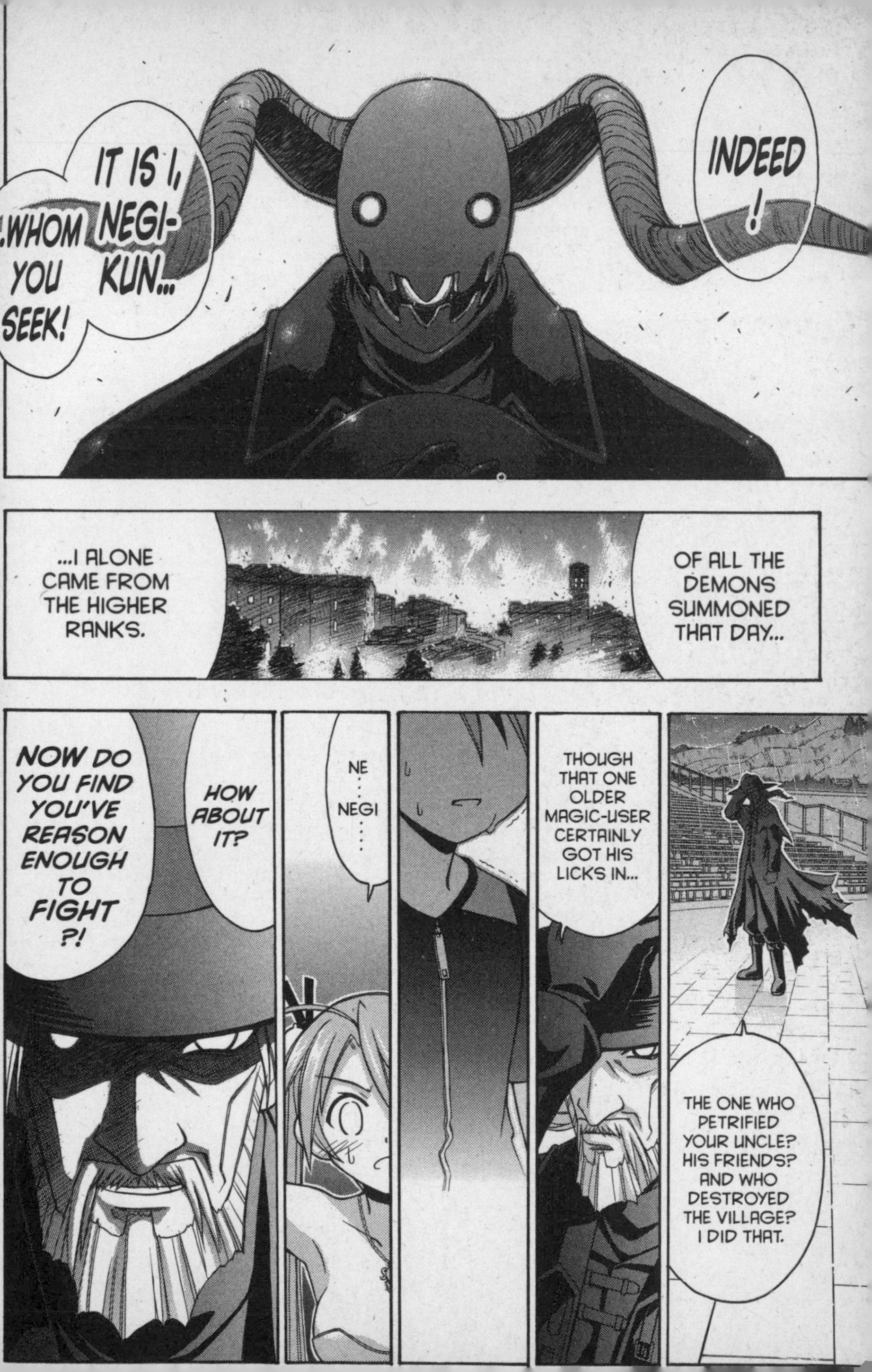
INDEED!
IT IS I, NEGI-KUN...
...WHOM YOU SEEK!
OF ALL THE DEMONS SUMMONED THAT DAY...
...I ALONE CAME FROM THE HIGHER RANKS.
THE ONE WHO PETRIFIED YOUR UNCLE? HIS FRIENDS? AND WHO DESTROYED THE VILLAGE? I DID THAT.
THOUGH THAT ONE OLDER MAGIC-USER CERTAINLY GOT HIS LICKS IN...
NE... NEGI......
HOW ABOUT IT?
NOW DO YOU FIND YOU'VE REASON ENOUGH TO FIGHT?!

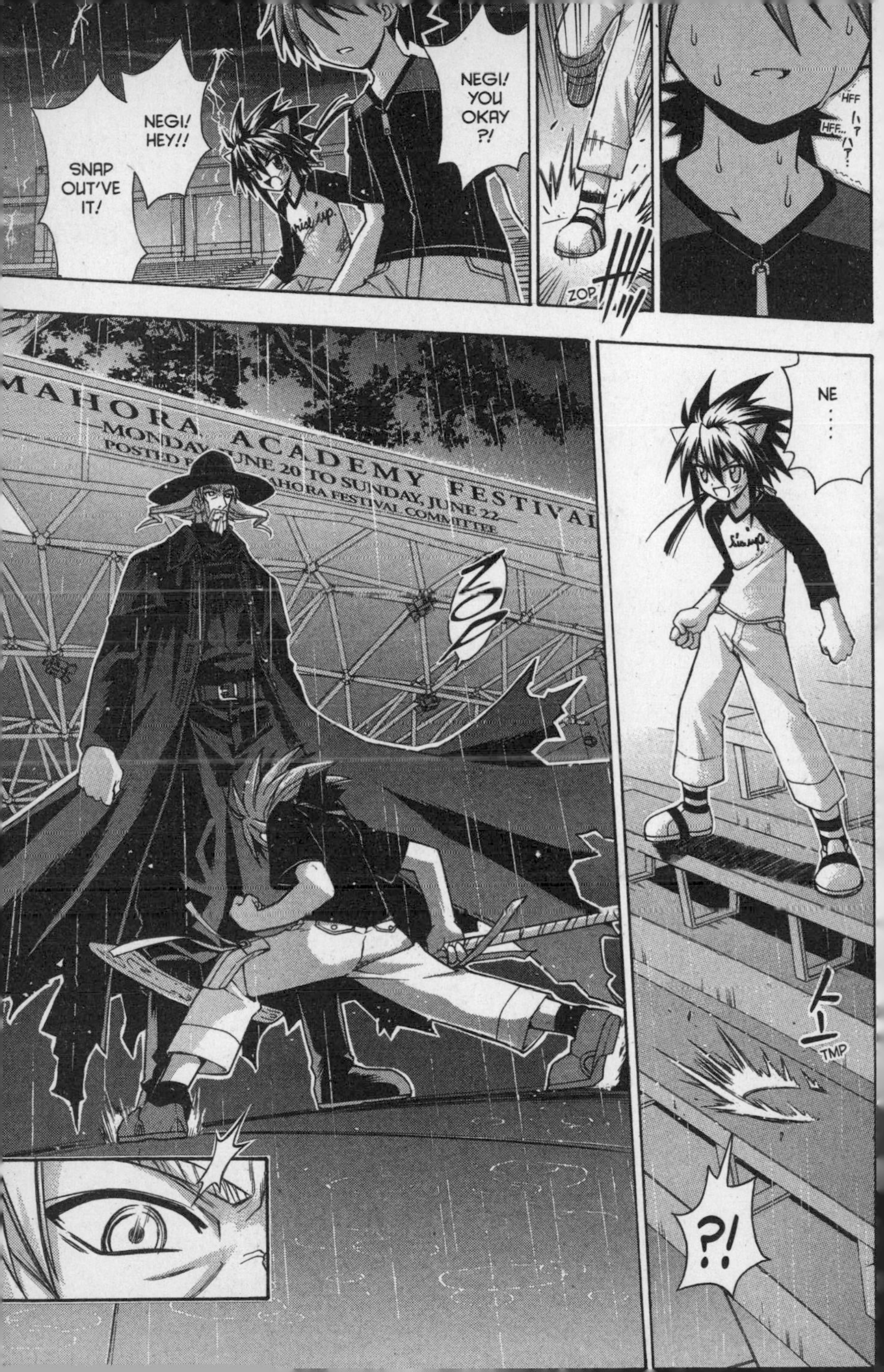
HFF
HFF...
ZOP
NEGI! YOU OKAY ?!
NEGI! HEY!!
SNAP OUT'VE IT!
NE ....
TMP
?!
MAHORA ACADEMY FESTIVAL

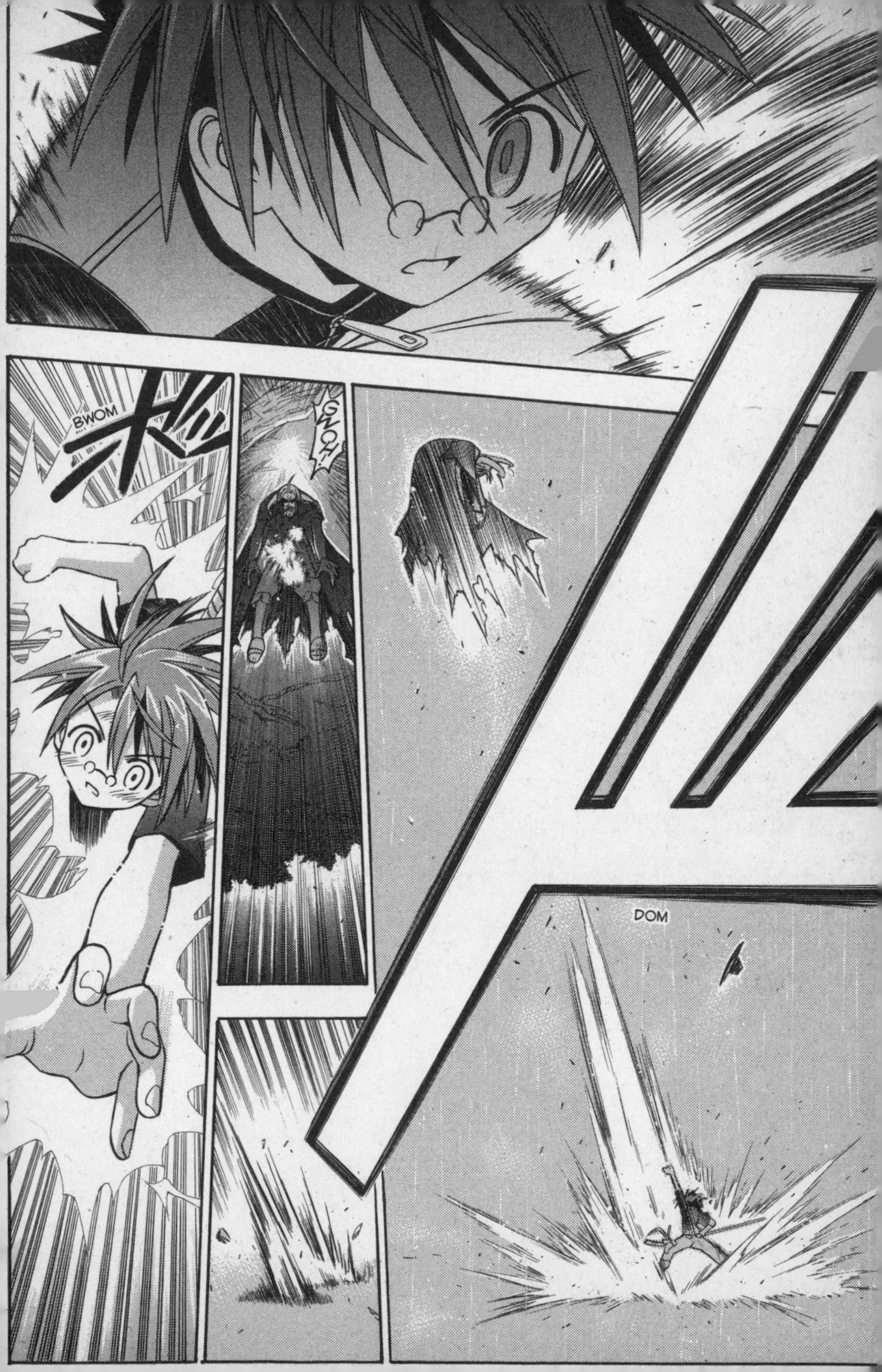
GWCH!
BWOM
DOM

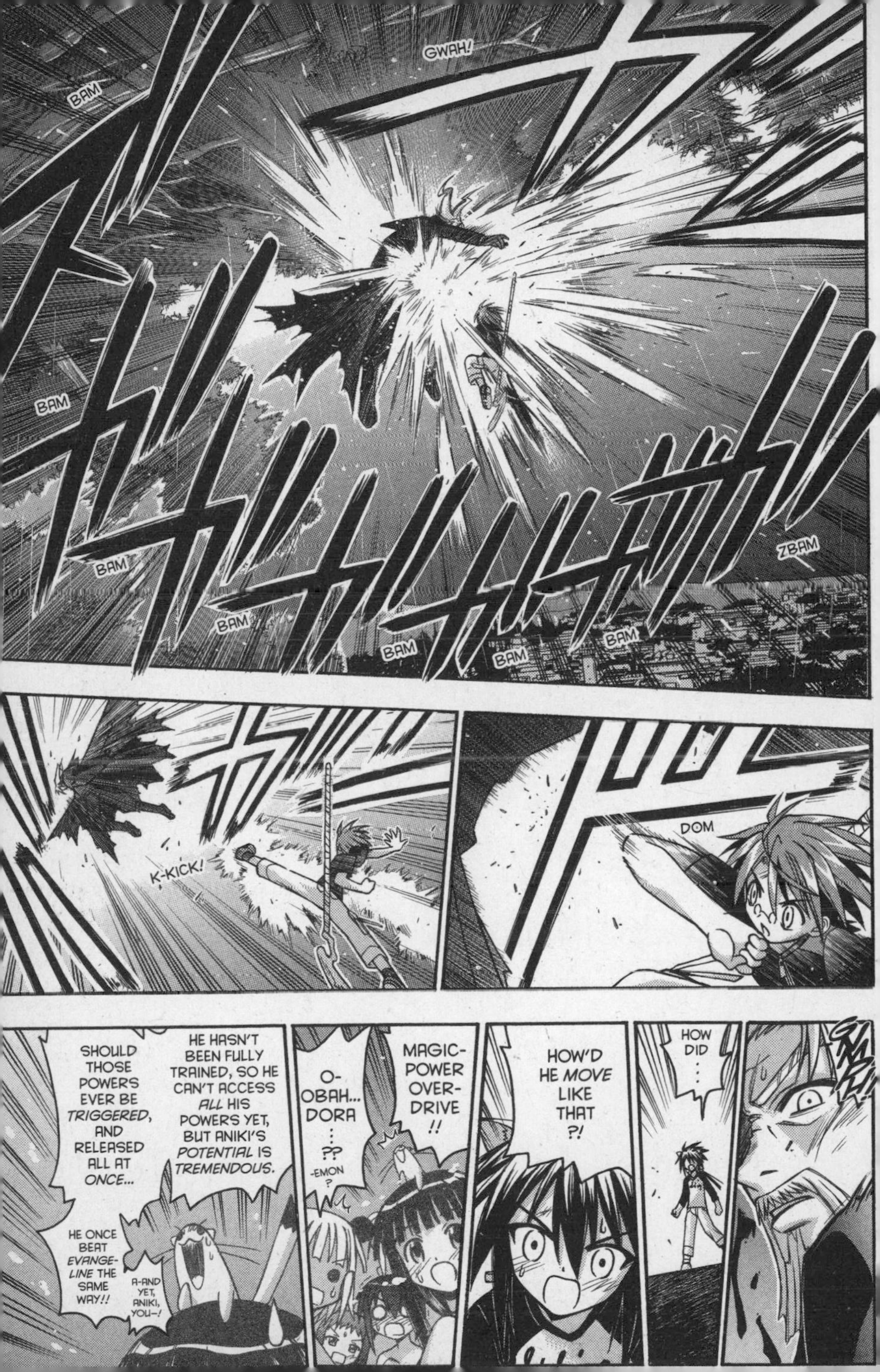
GWAH!
ZBAM
BAM
BAM
BAM
BAM
BAM
BAM
BAM
DOM
K-KICK!
HOW DID . . .
HOW'D HE *MOVE* LIKE THAT ?!
MAGIC-POWER OVER-DRIVE!!
O-OBAH... DORA . . . ??
-EMON ?
HE HASN'T BEEN FULLY TRAINED, SO HE CAN'T ACCESS *ALL* HIS POWERS YET, BUT ANIKI'S *POTENTIAL* IS *TREMENDOUS*.
SHOULD THOSE POWERS EVER BE *TRIGGERED*, AND RELEASED ALL AT *ONCE*...
HE ONCE BEAT *EVANGE-LINE* THE SAME WAY!!
A-AND YET, ANIKI, YOU—!

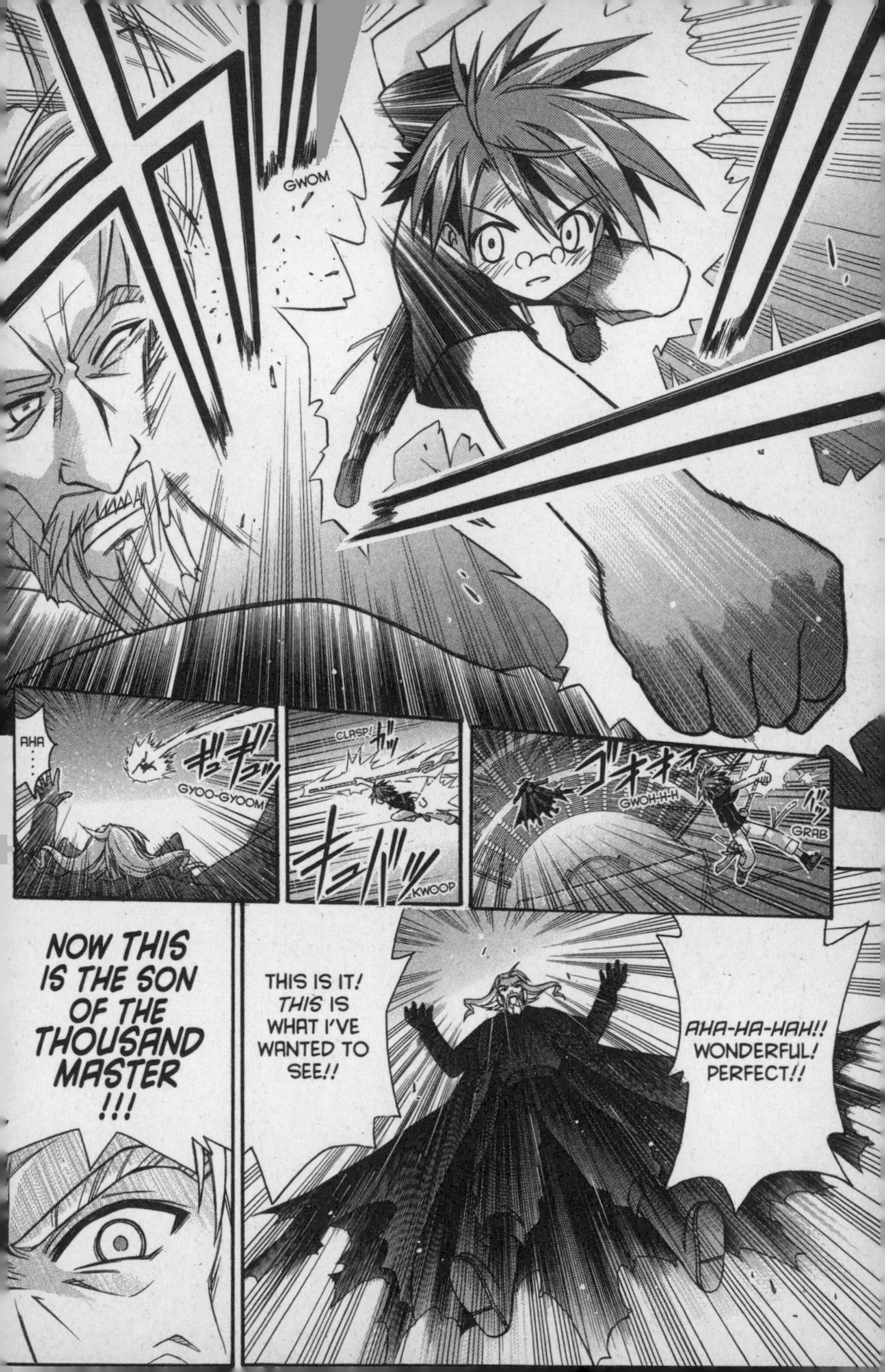
GWOM
GWOH-H-H
GRAB
CLASP!
KWOOP
AHA......
GYOO-GYOOM
AHA-HA-HAH!! WONDERFUL! PERFECT!!
THIS IS IT! *THIS* IS WHAT I'VE WANTED TO SEE!!
NOW THIS IS THE SON OF THE THOUSAND MASTER !!!

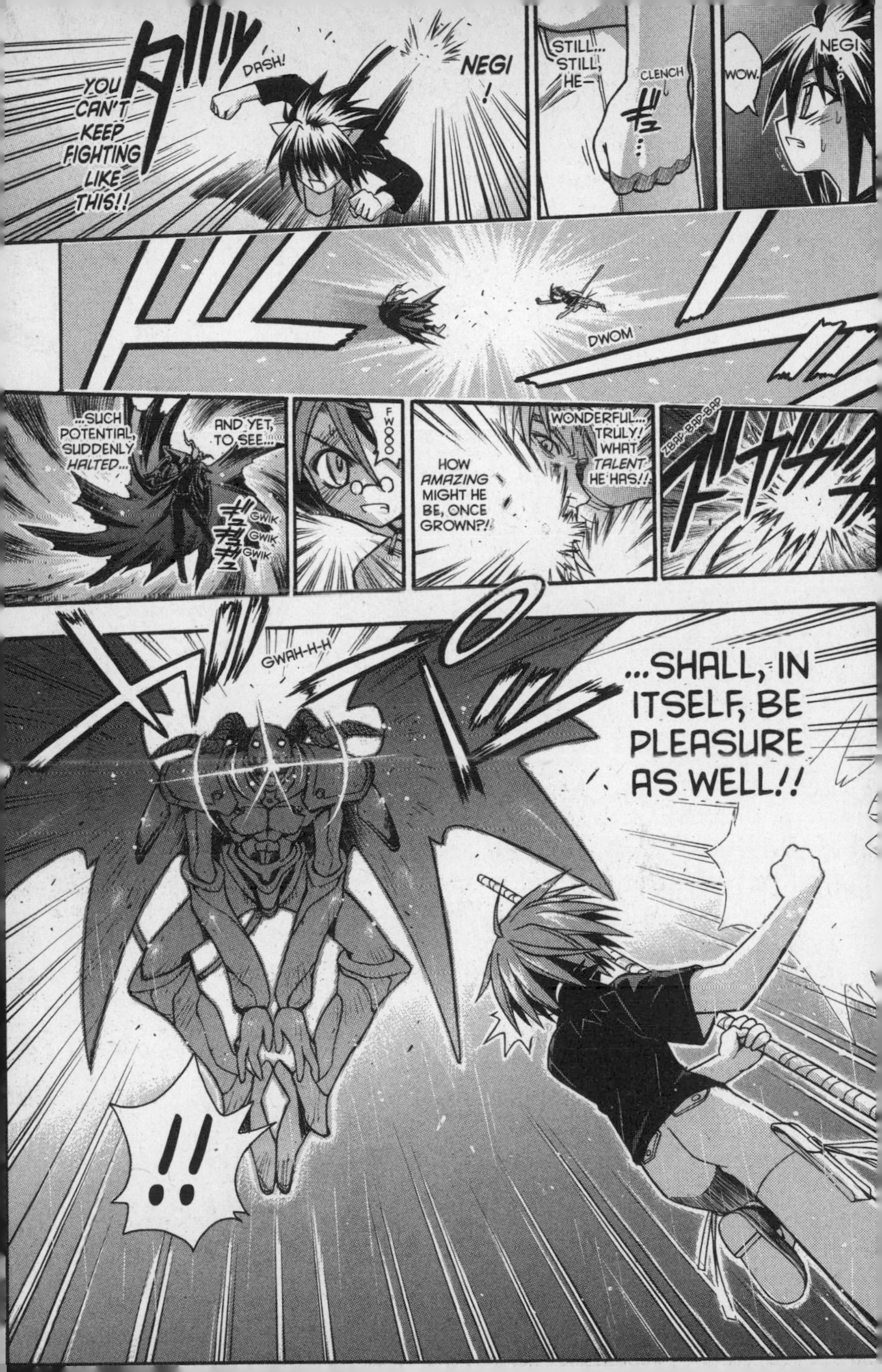
NEGI...
WOW.
STILL... STILL, HE—
CLENCH
NEGI!
DASH!
YOU CAN'T KEEP FIGHTING LIKE THIS!!
DWOM
ZBAP-BAP-BAP
WONDERFUL... TRULY! WHAT TALENT HE HAS!!
HOW AMAZING MIGHT HE BE, ONCE GROWN?!
FWOOO
AND YET, TO SEE...
...SUCH POTENTIAL, SUDDENLY HALTED...
GWIK GWIK GWIK
...SHALL, IN ITSELF, BE PLEASURE AS WELL!!
GWAH-H-H
!!

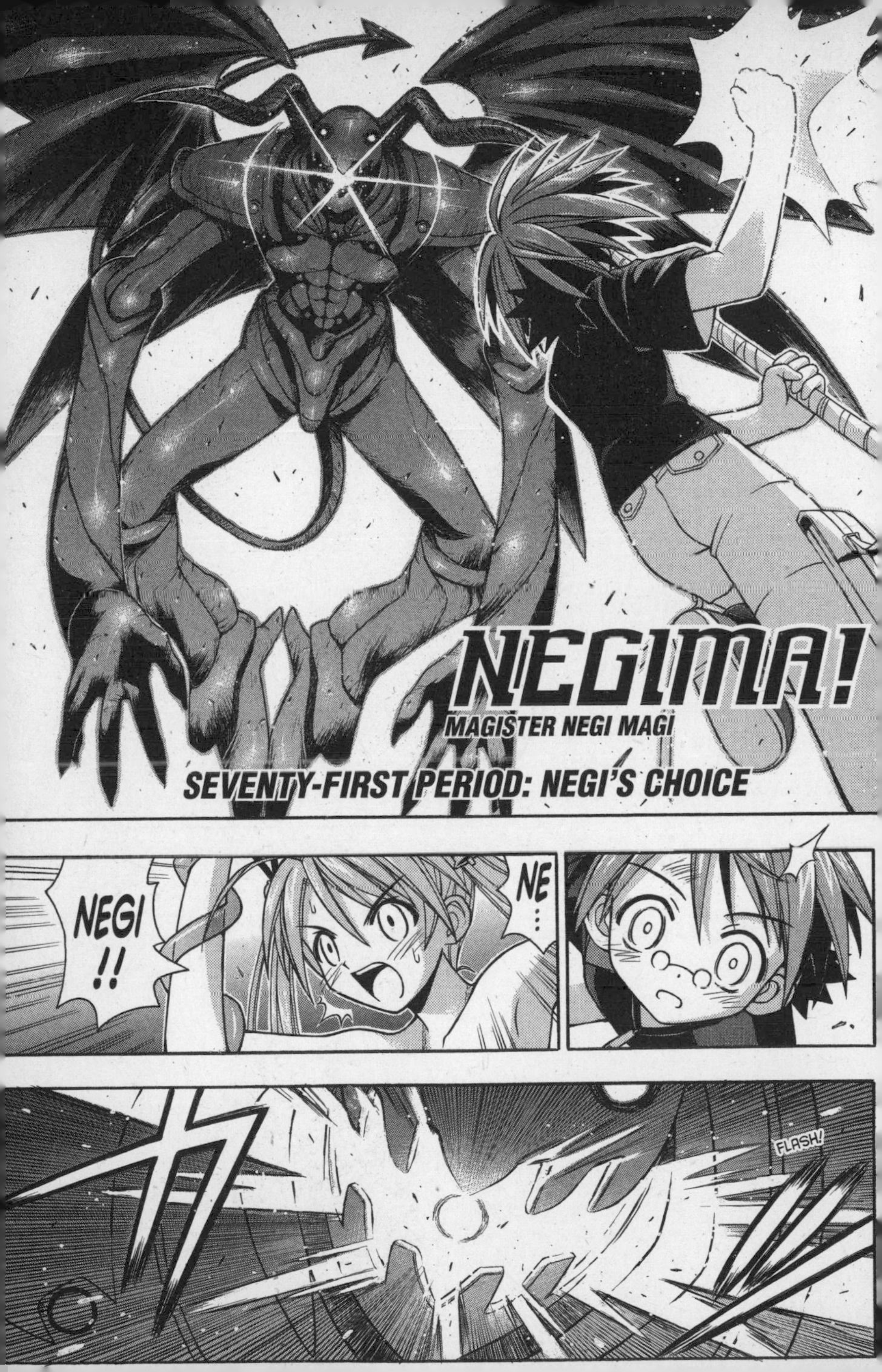
NEGIMA!
MAGISTER NEGI MAGI
SEVENTY-FIRST PERIOD: NEGI'S CHOICE
NE...
NEGI!!
FLASH!

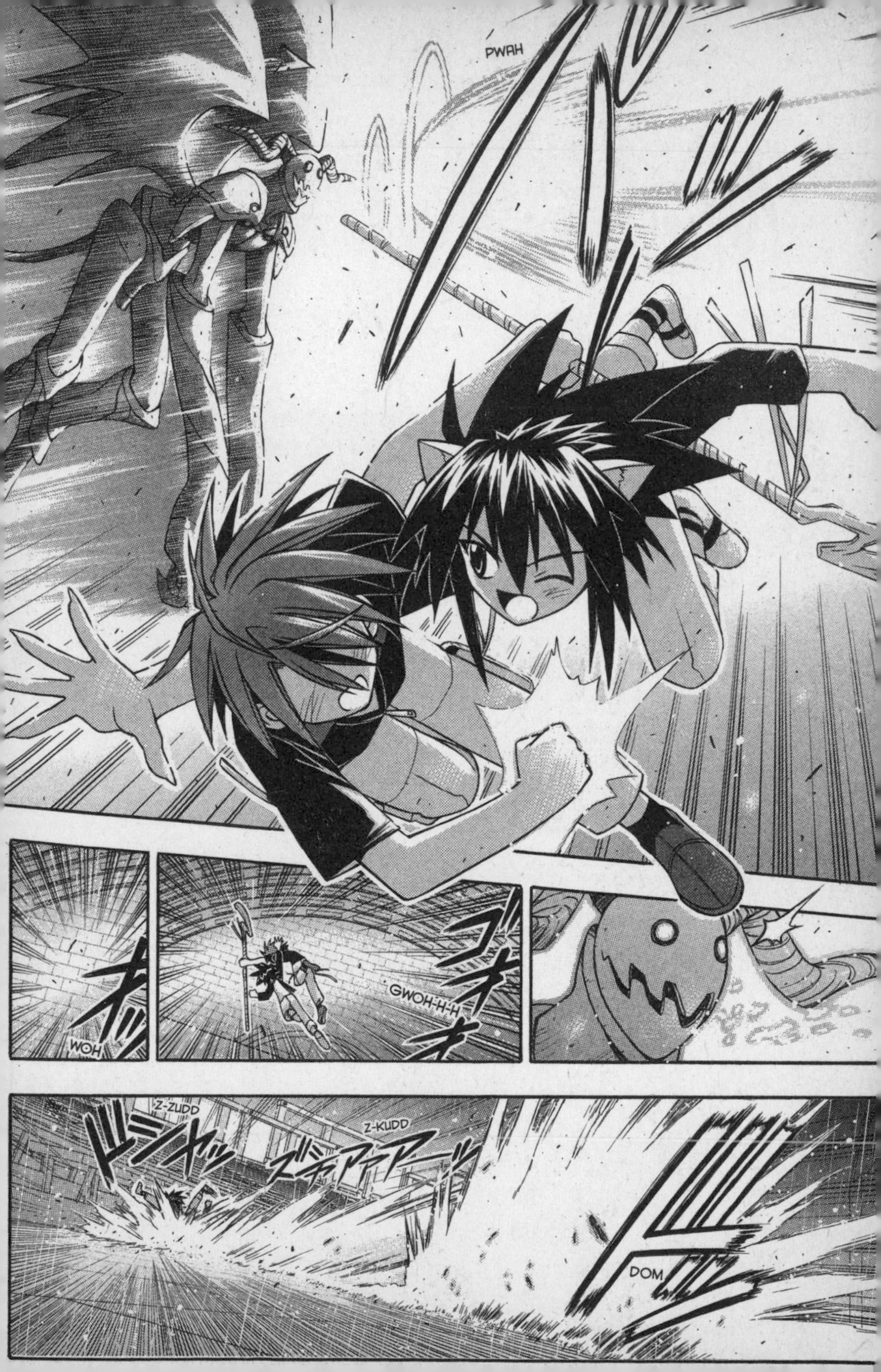
PWAH
GWOH-H-H
WOH
Z-KUDD
Z-ZUDD
DOM

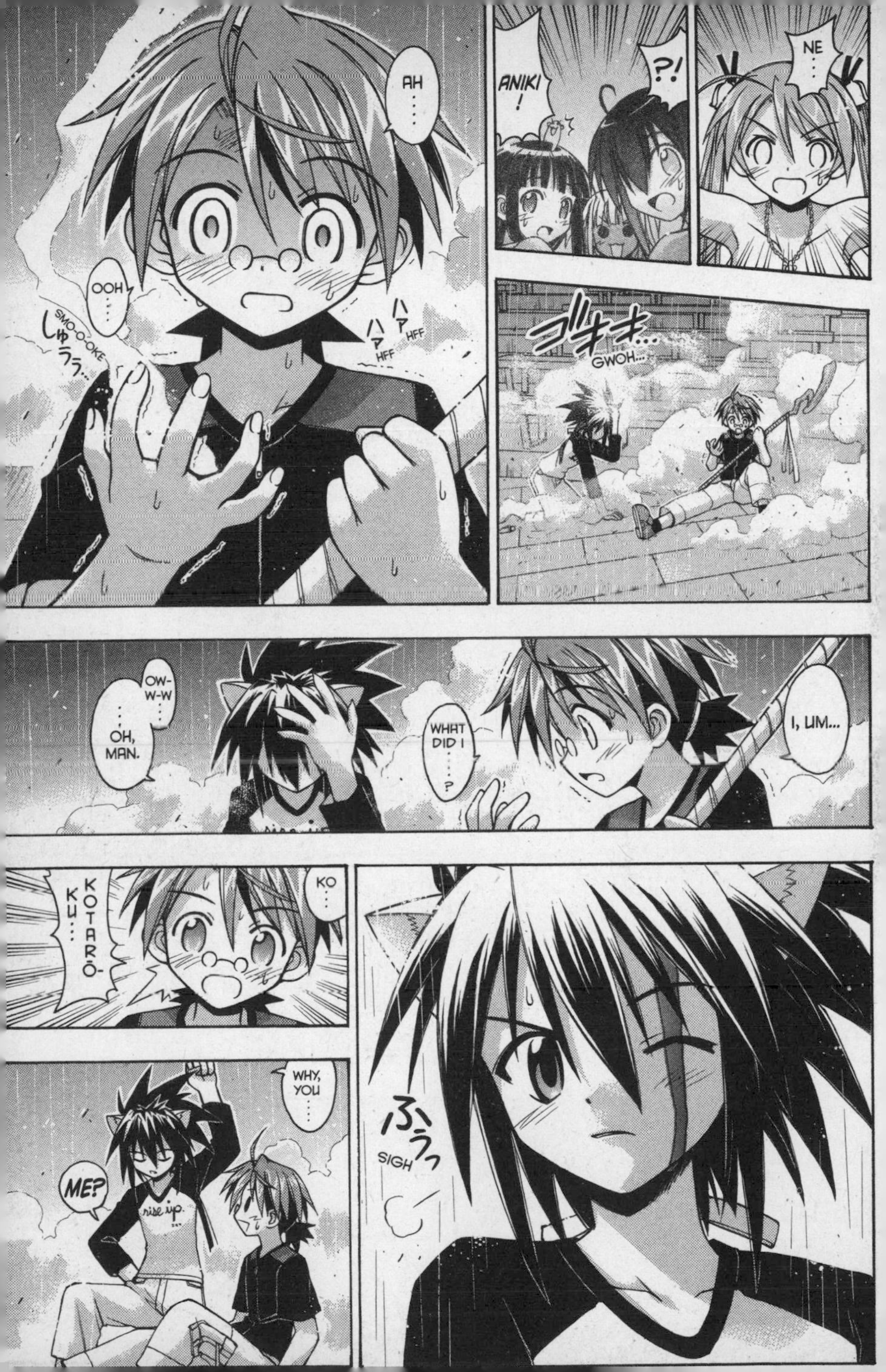
NE...
?!
ANIKI!
GWOH...
AH...
OOH...
SMO-O-OKE
HFF HFF
I, UM...
WHAT DID I ...?
OW-W-W... OH, MAN.
SIGH
KO...
KOTARŌ-KUN...
WHY, YOU...
ME?

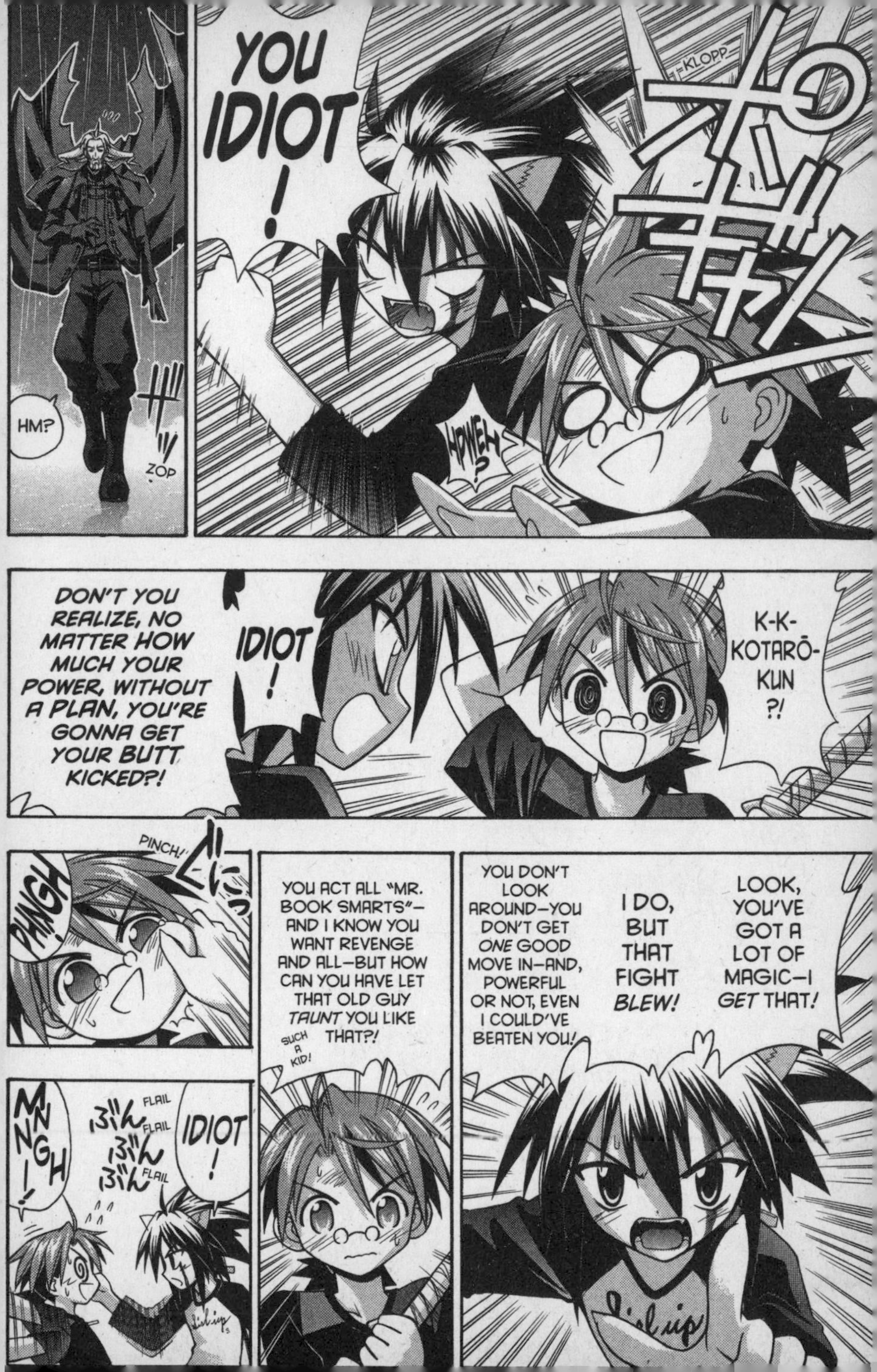
-KLOPP
YOU IDIOT!
HOWEH?
HM?
ZOP
K-K-KOTARŌ-KUN?!
IDIOT!
DON'T YOU REALIZE, NO MATTER HOW MUCH YOUR POWER, WITHOUT A PLAN, YOU'RE GONNA GET YOUR BUTT KICKED?!
LOOK, YOU'VE GOT A LOT OF MAGIC—I *GET* THAT!
I DO, BUT THAT FIGHT *BLEW!*
YOU DON'T LOOK AROUND—YOU DON'T GET *ONE* GOOD MOVE IN—AND, POWERFUL OR NOT, EVEN I COULD'VE BEATEN YOU!
YOU ACT ALL "MR. BOOK SMARTS"—AND I KNOW YOU WANT REVENGE AND ALL—BUT HOW CAN YOU HAVE LET THAT OLD GUY *TAUNT* YOU LIKE THAT?!
SUCH A KID!
PINCH!
PHNGH
IDIOT!
ぶん FLAIL
ぶん FLAIL
ぶん FLAIL
MNNGH!

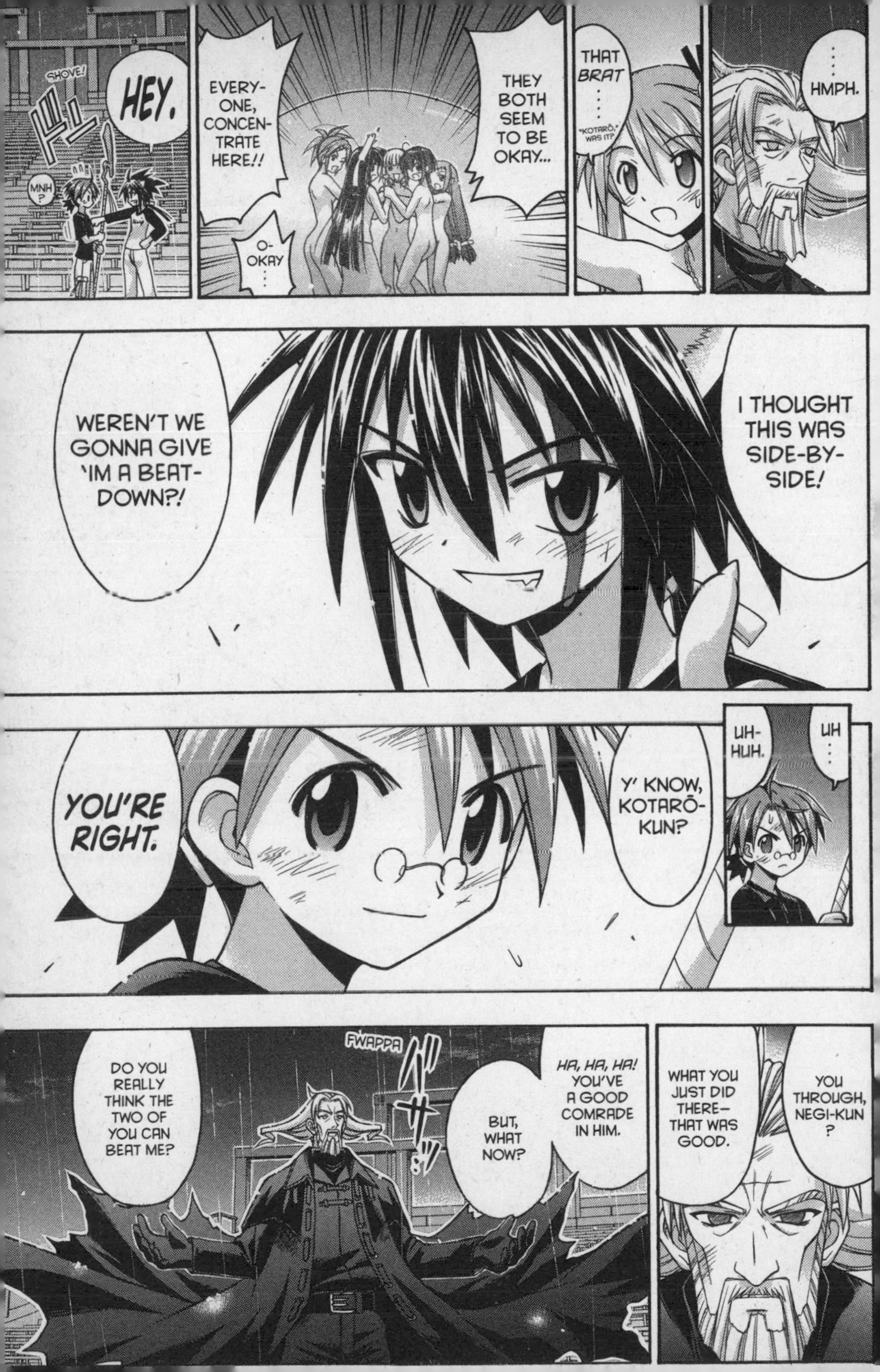
......
HMPH.
THAT BRAT ......
"KOTARŌ," WAS IT?
THEY BOTH SEEM TO BE OKAY...
EVERY-ONE, CONCEN-TRATE HERE!!
O-OKAY ...
SHOVE!
HEY.
MNH ?
I THOUGHT THIS WAS SIDE-BY-SIDE!
WEREN'T WE GONNA GIVE 'IM A BEAT-DOWN?!
UH ...
UH-HUH.
Y' KNOW, KOTARŌ-KUN?
YOU'RE RIGHT.
YOU THROUGH, NEGI-KUN ?
WHAT YOU JUST DID THERE— THAT WAS GOOD.
HA, HA, HA! YOU'VE A GOOD COMRADE IN HIM.
BUT, WHAT NOW?
FWAPPA
DO YOU REALLY THINK THE TWO OF YOU CAN BEAT ME?

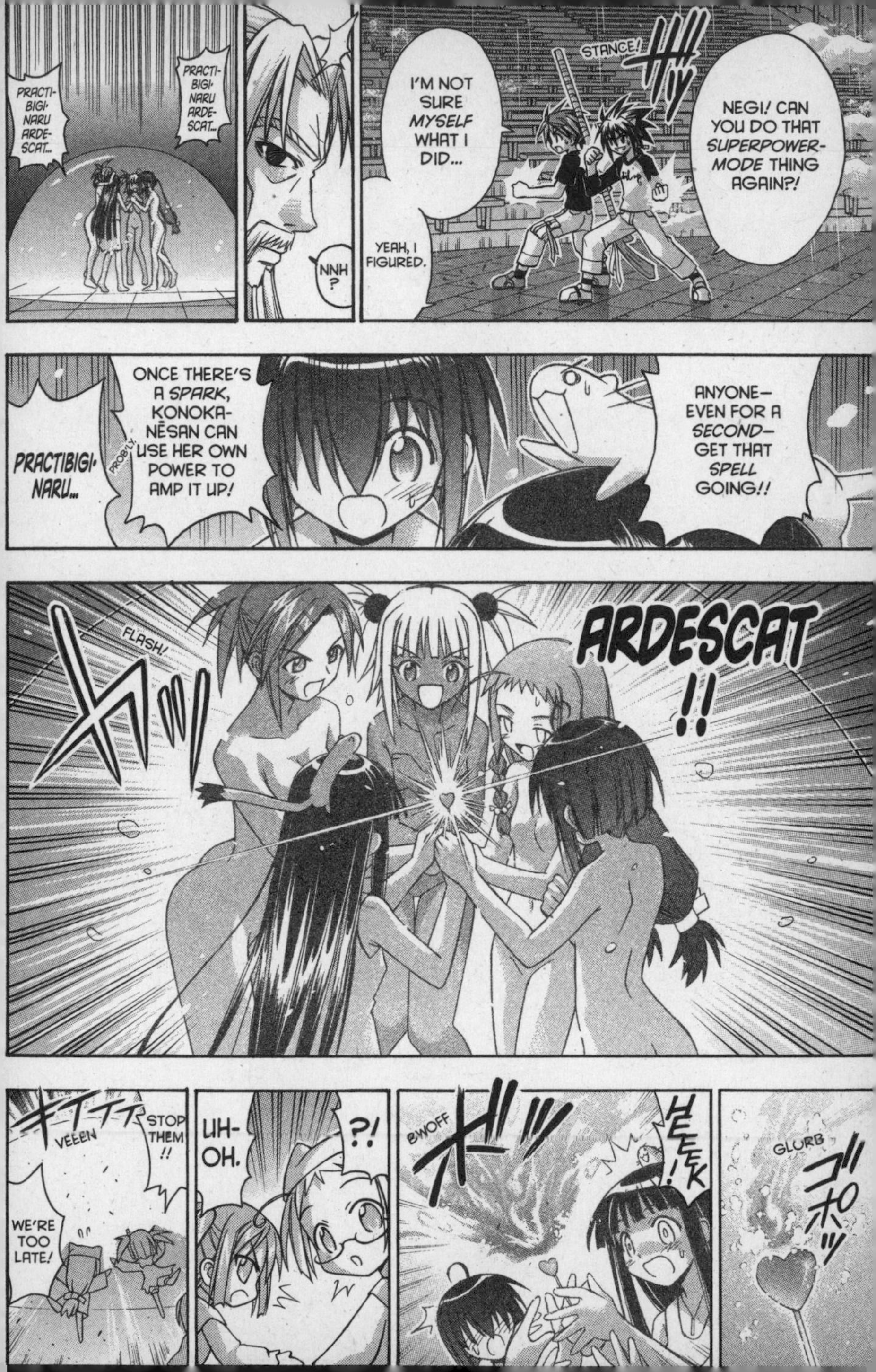
STANCE!
NEGI! CAN YOU DO THAT SUPERPOWER-MODE THING AGAIN?!
I'M NOT SURE MYSELF WHAT I DID...
YEAH, I FIGURED.
PRACTI-BIGI-NARU ARDE-SCAT...
NNH?
PRACTI-BIGI-NARU ARDE-SCAT...
ANYONE— EVEN FOR A SECOND— GET THAT SPELL GOING!!
ONCE THERE'S A SPARK, KONOKA-NĒSAN CAN USE HER OWN POWER TO AMP IT UP!
PROBLY
PRACTIBIGI-NARU...
ARDESCAT!!
FLASH!
GLURB
HEEEK!
BWOFF
?!
UH-OH.
STOP THEM!!
VEEEN
WE'RE TOO LATE!

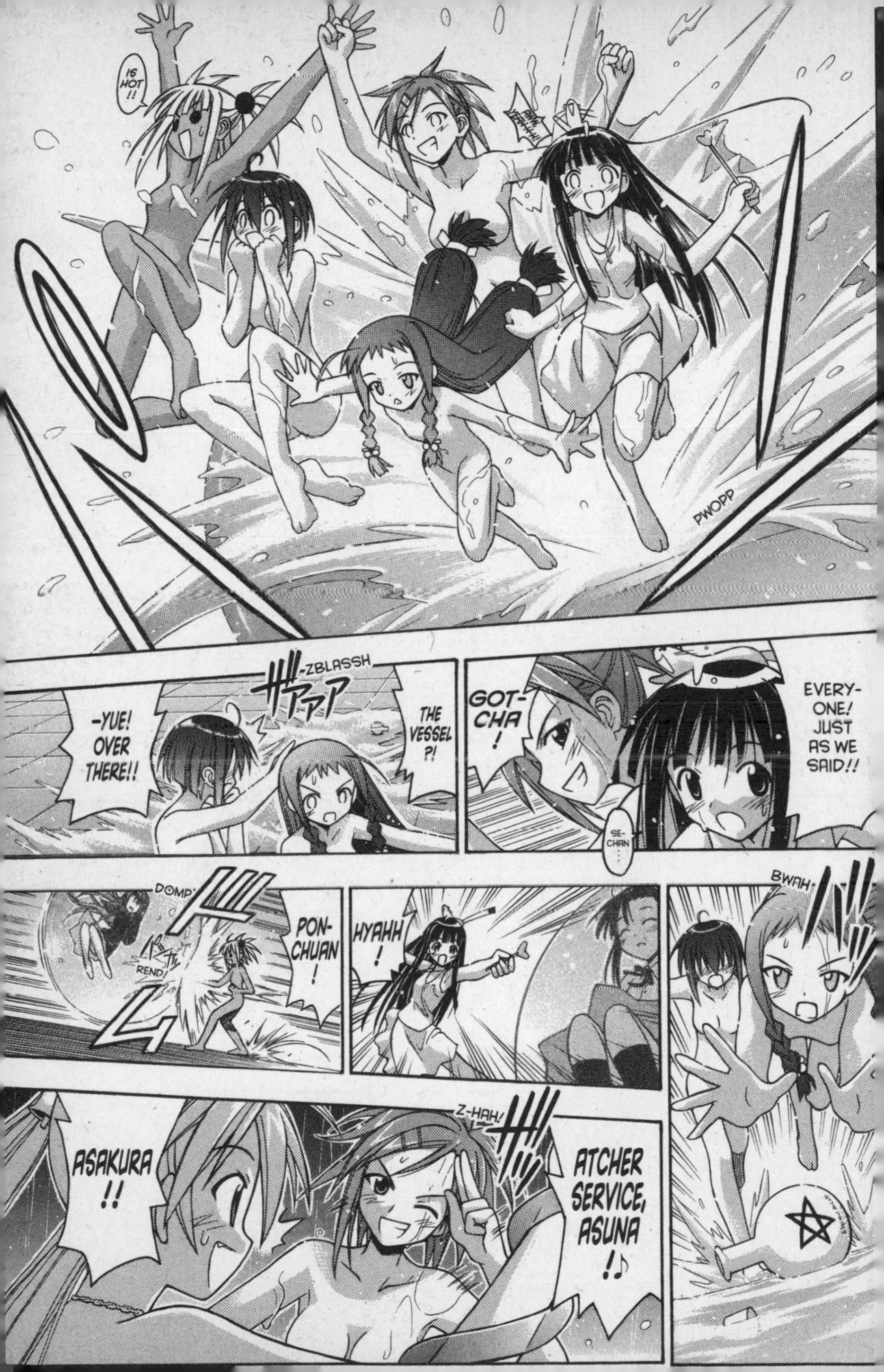

AWW, YEAH!!!
IS HOT!!
PWOPP
EVERY-ONE! JUST AS WE SAID!!
GOT-CHA!
SE-CHAN...
-ZBLASSH
THE VESSEL?!
-YUE! OVER THERE!!
BWAH
HYAHH!
PON-CHUAN!
DOMP
REND!
Z-HAH!
ATCHER SERVICE, ASUNA!♪
ASAKURA!!

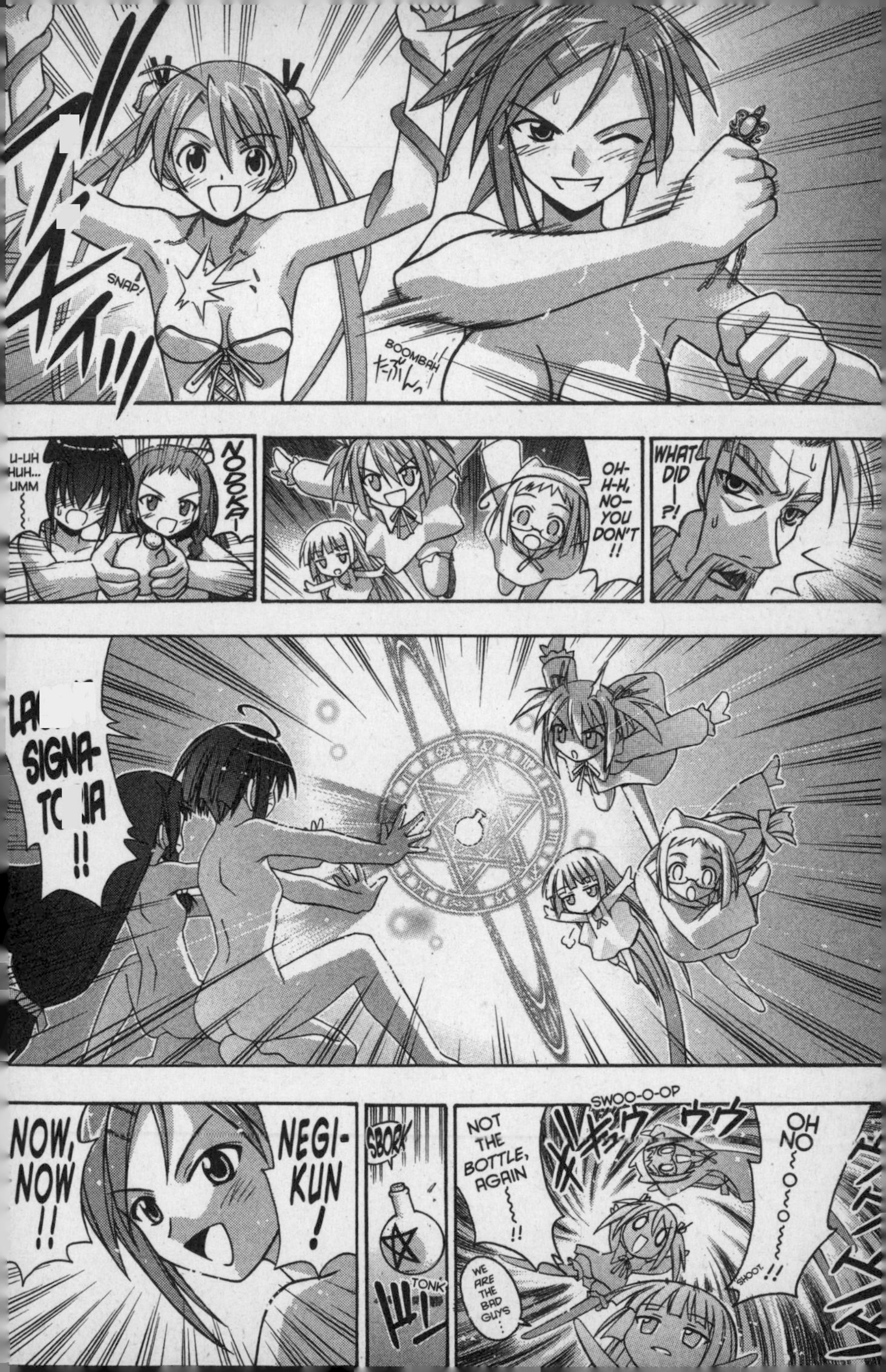
SNAP!
BOOMBAH
WHAT DID I-?!
OH-H-H, NO-YOU DON'T!!
NODOKA!
U-UH HUH... UMM
SIGNA-
!!
OH NO~O~O~!!
SWOO-O-OP
NOT THE BOTTLE, AGAIN~!!
WE ARE THE BAD GUYS...
SHOOT.
SBORK
TONK
NEGI-KUN!
NOW, NOW!!

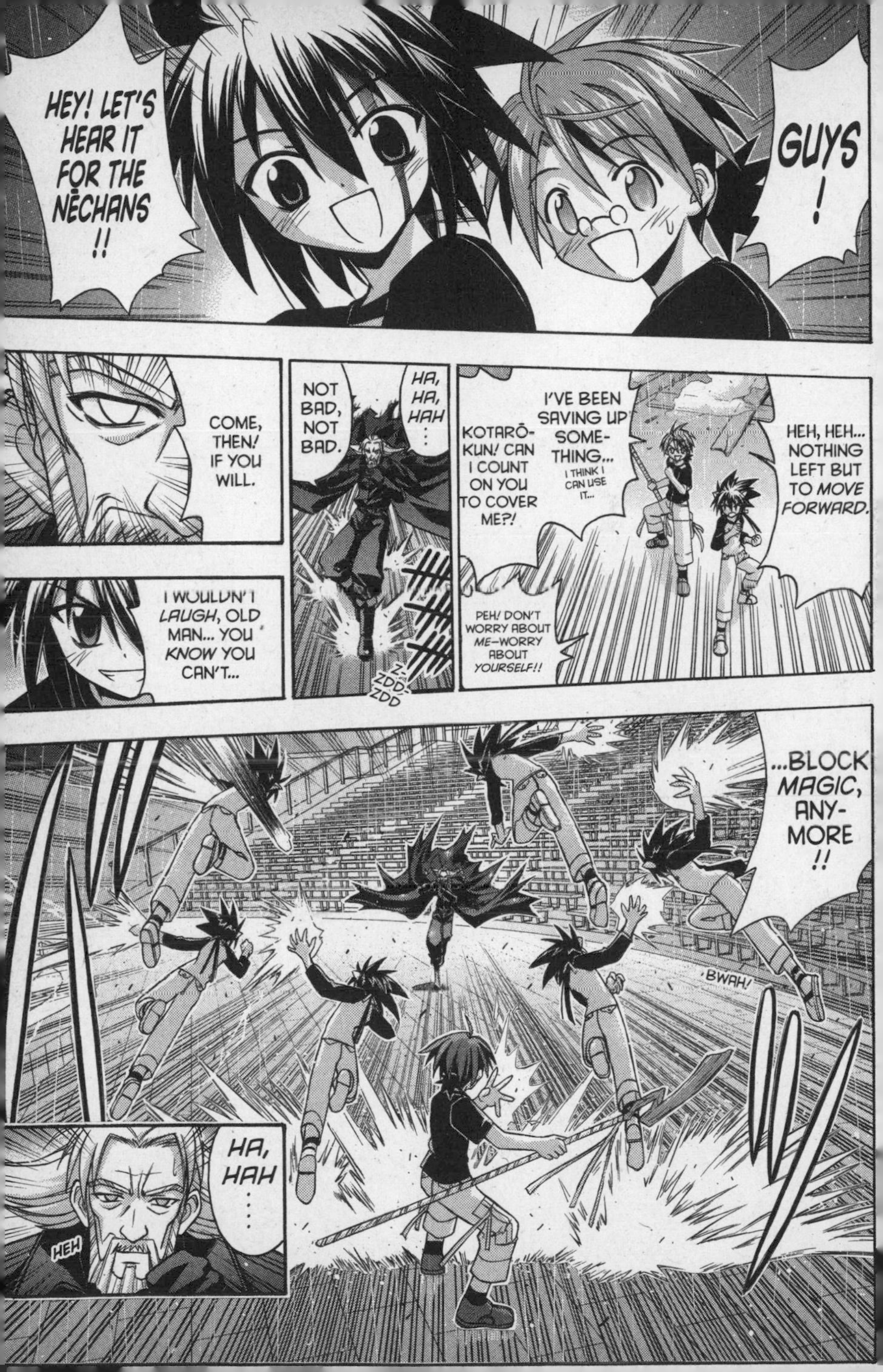
GUYS !
HEY! LET'S HEAR IT FOR THE NECHANS !!
HEH, HEH... NOTHING LEFT BUT TO *MOVE FORWARD*.
I'VE BEEN SAVING UP SOME-THING...
I THINK I CAN USE IT...
KOTARŌ-KUN! CAN I COUNT ON YOU TO COVER ME?!
PEH! DON'T WORRY ABOUT *ME*—WORRY ABOUT *YOURSELF*!!
HA, HA, HAH . . .
NOT BAD, NOT BAD.
Z-ZDD-ZDD
COME, THEN! IF YOU WILL.
I WOULDN'T *LAUGH*, OLD MAN... YOU *KNOW* YOU CAN'T...
...BLOCK *MAGIC*, ANY-MORE !!
BWAH!
HA, HAH . . .
HEH

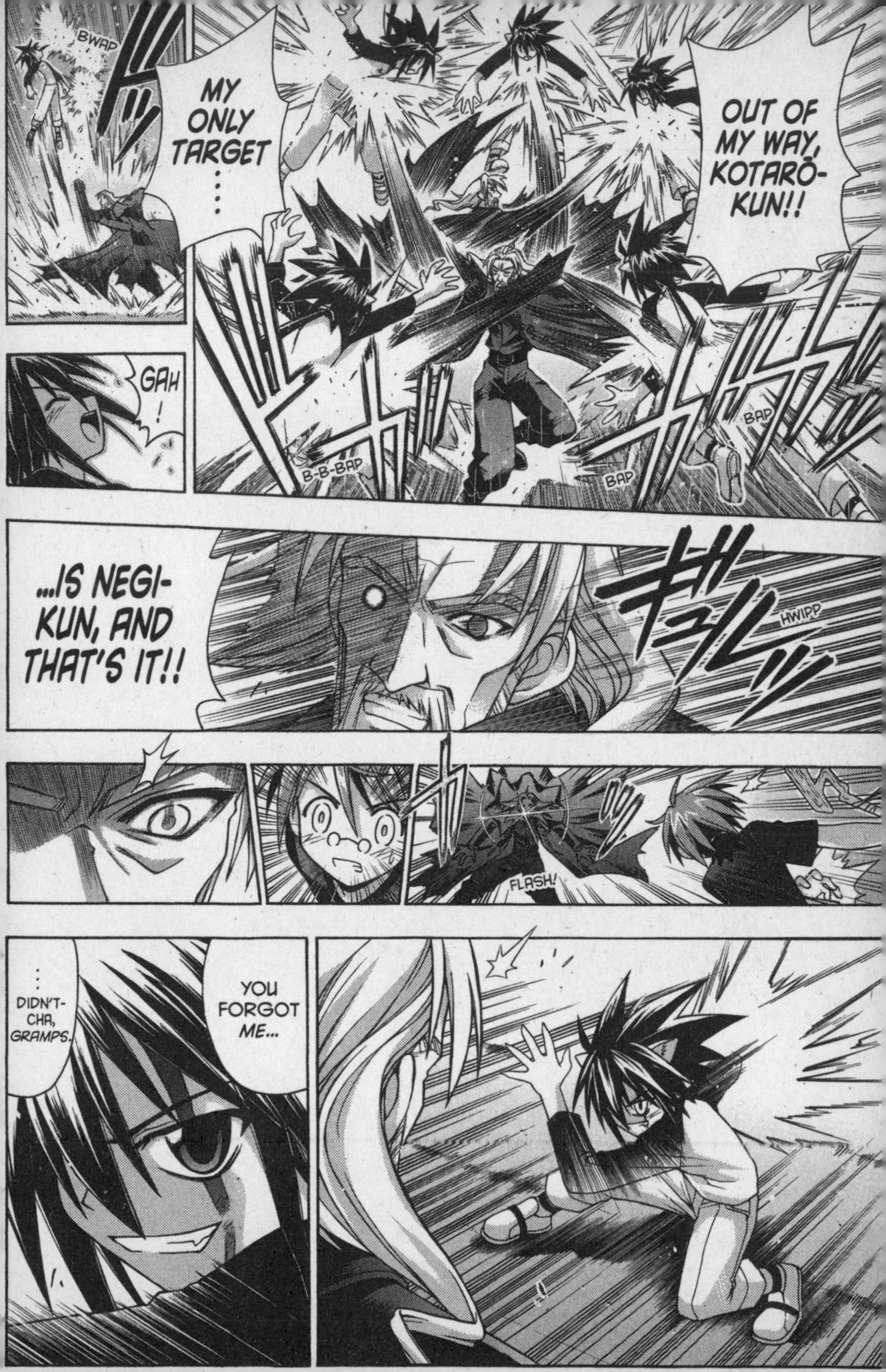
OUT OF MY WAY, KOTARŌ-KUN!!
MY ONLY TARGET . . .
BAP
BAP
B-B-BAP
BWAP
GAH!
...IS NEGI-KUN, AND THAT'S IT!!
HWIPP
FLASH!
YOU FORGOT ME...
...DIDN'T-CHA, GRAMPS.

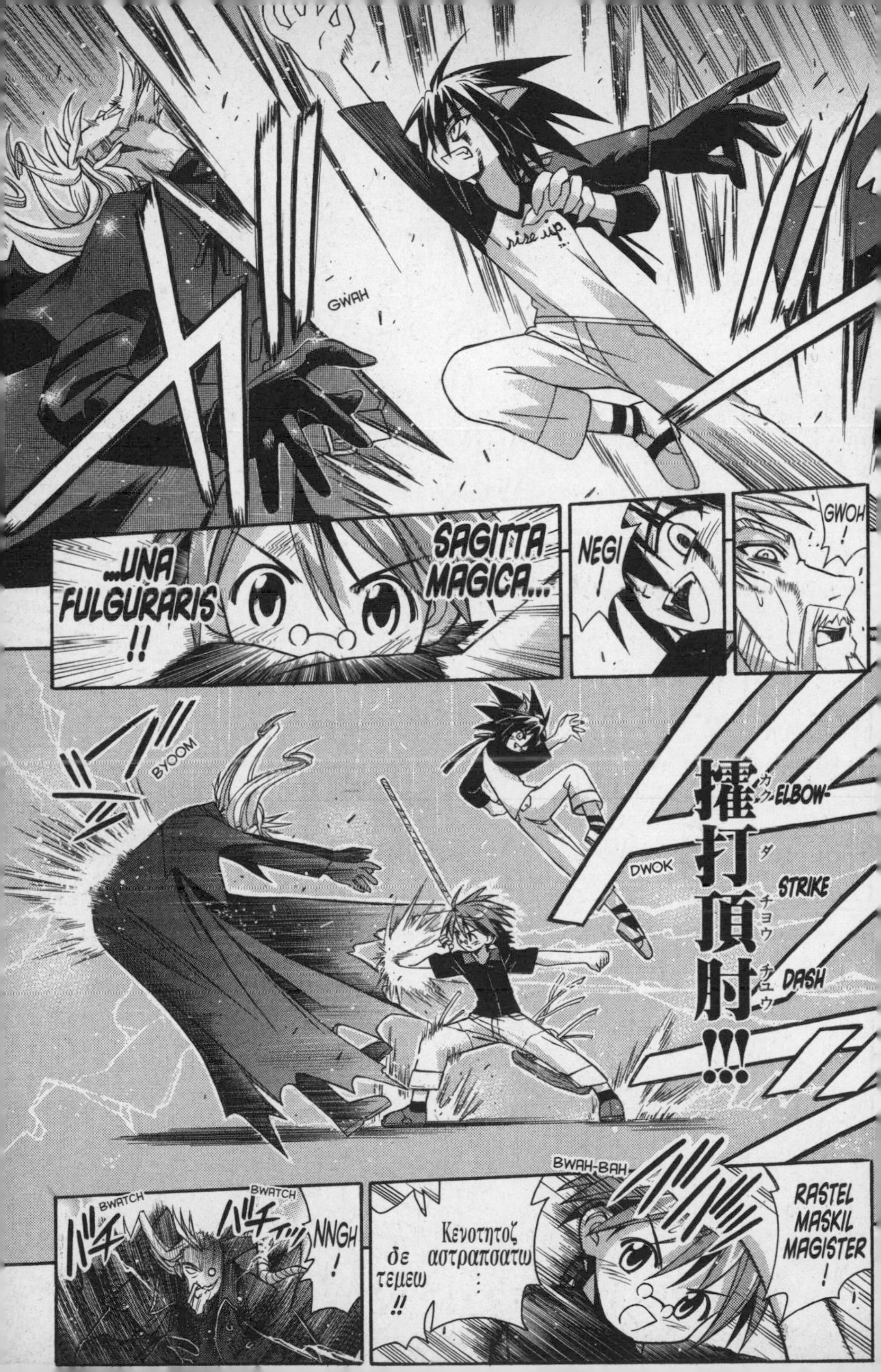
GWAH
GWOH!
NEGI!
SAGITTA MAGICA...
...UNA FULGURARIS!!
攉打頂肘!!!
カク ダ チョウ チュウ
ELBOW-STRIKE DASH
DWOK
BYOOM
BWAH-BAH
RASTEL MASKIL MAGISTER!
Κενοτητος αστραπσατω...
δε τεμεω!!
NNGH!
バチィッ
BWATCH
バチ
BWATCH

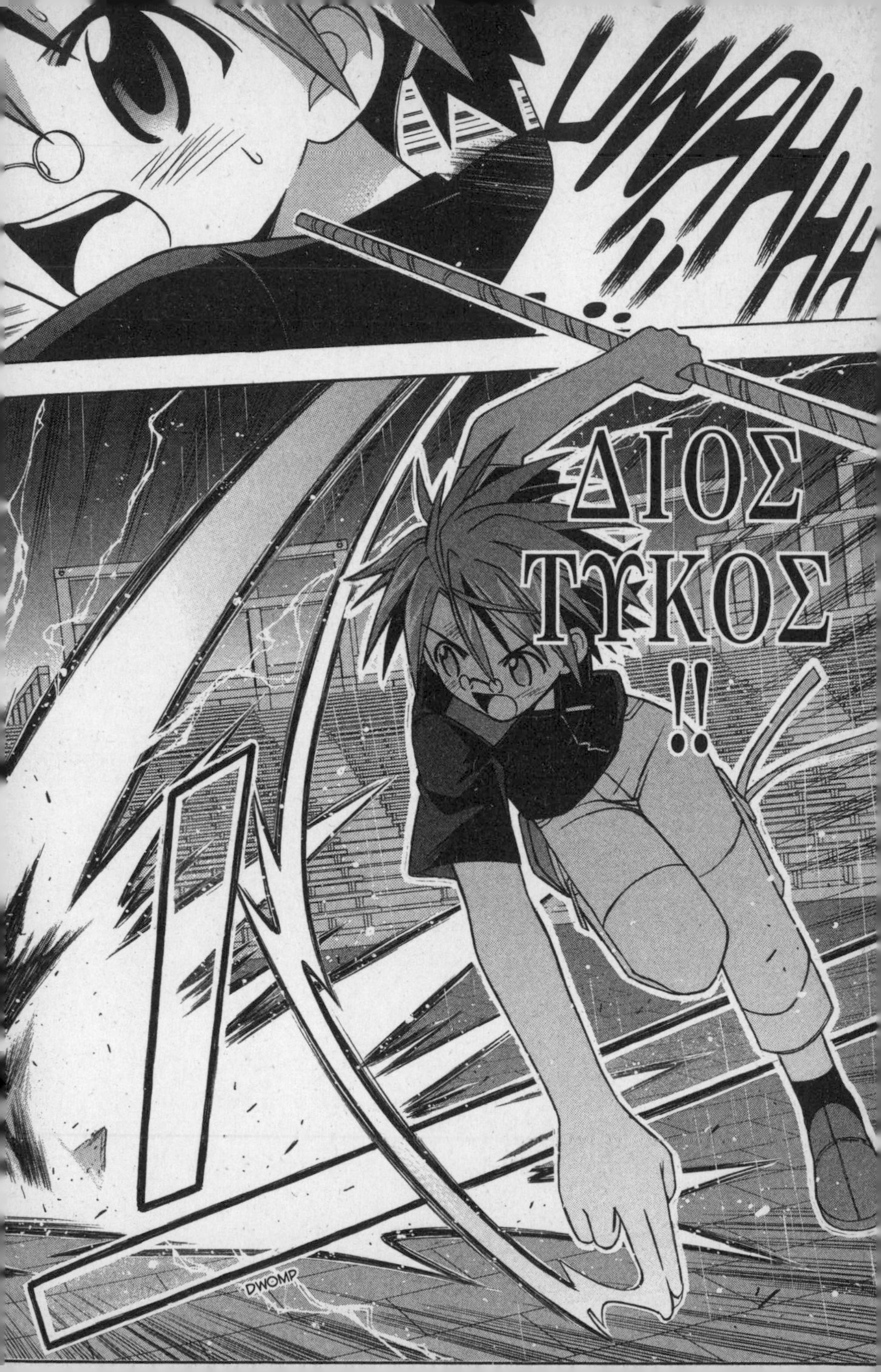
UWAAHH...
ΔΙΟΣ ΤΥΚΟΣ!!
DWOMP

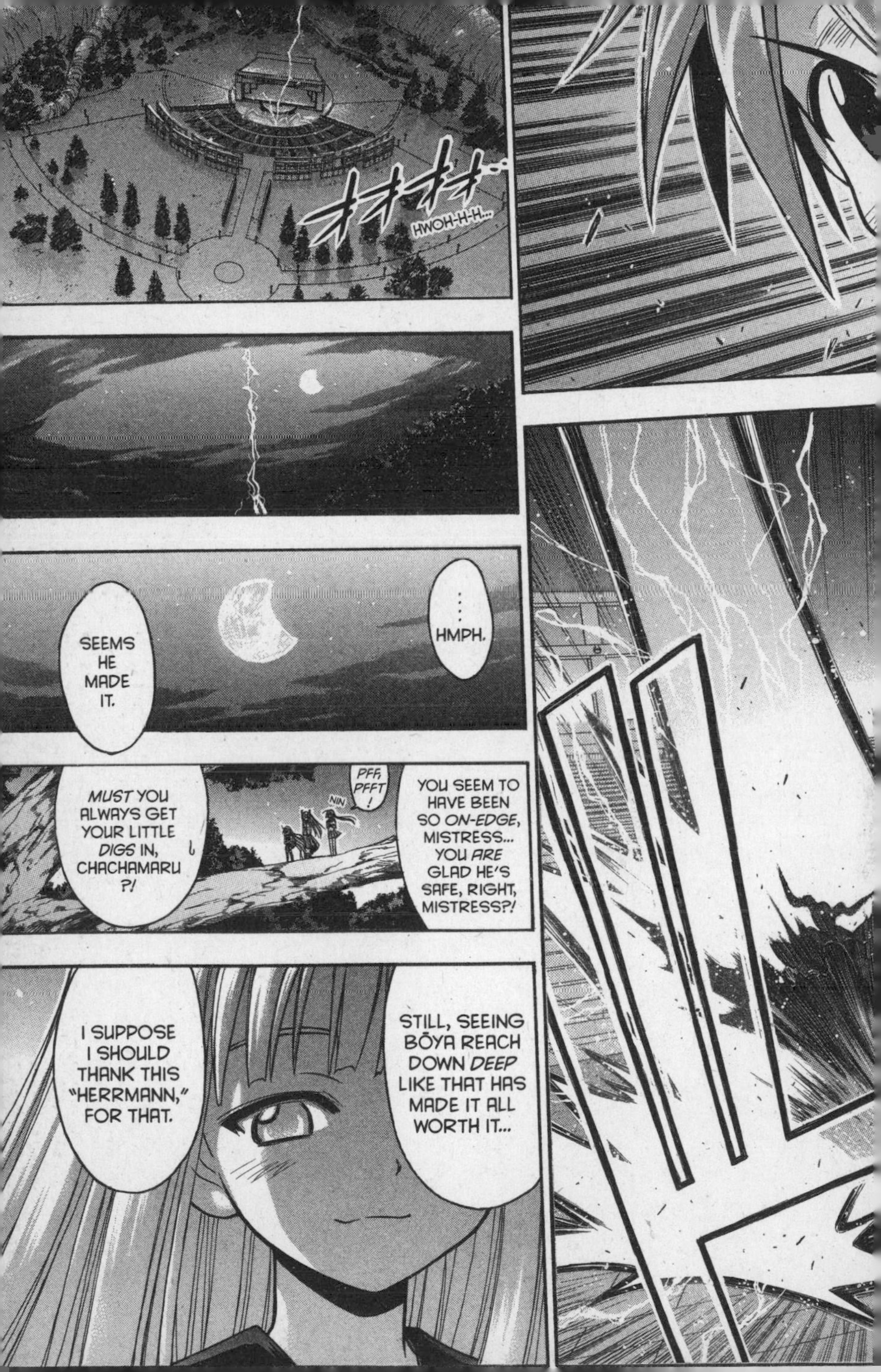

HWOH-H-H...
. . . . HMPH.
SEEMS HE MADE IT.
YOU SEEM TO HAVE BEEN SO *ON-EDGE*, MISTRESS... YOU *ARE* GLAD HE'S SAFE, RIGHT, MISTRESS?!
PFF, PFFT!
NIN
MUST YOU ALWAYS GET YOUR LITTLE *DIGS* IN, CHACHAMARU?!
STILL, SEEING BŌYA REACH DOWN *DEEP* LIKE THAT HAS MADE IT ALL WORTH IT...
I SUPPOSE I SHOULD THANK THIS "HERRMANN," FOR THAT.

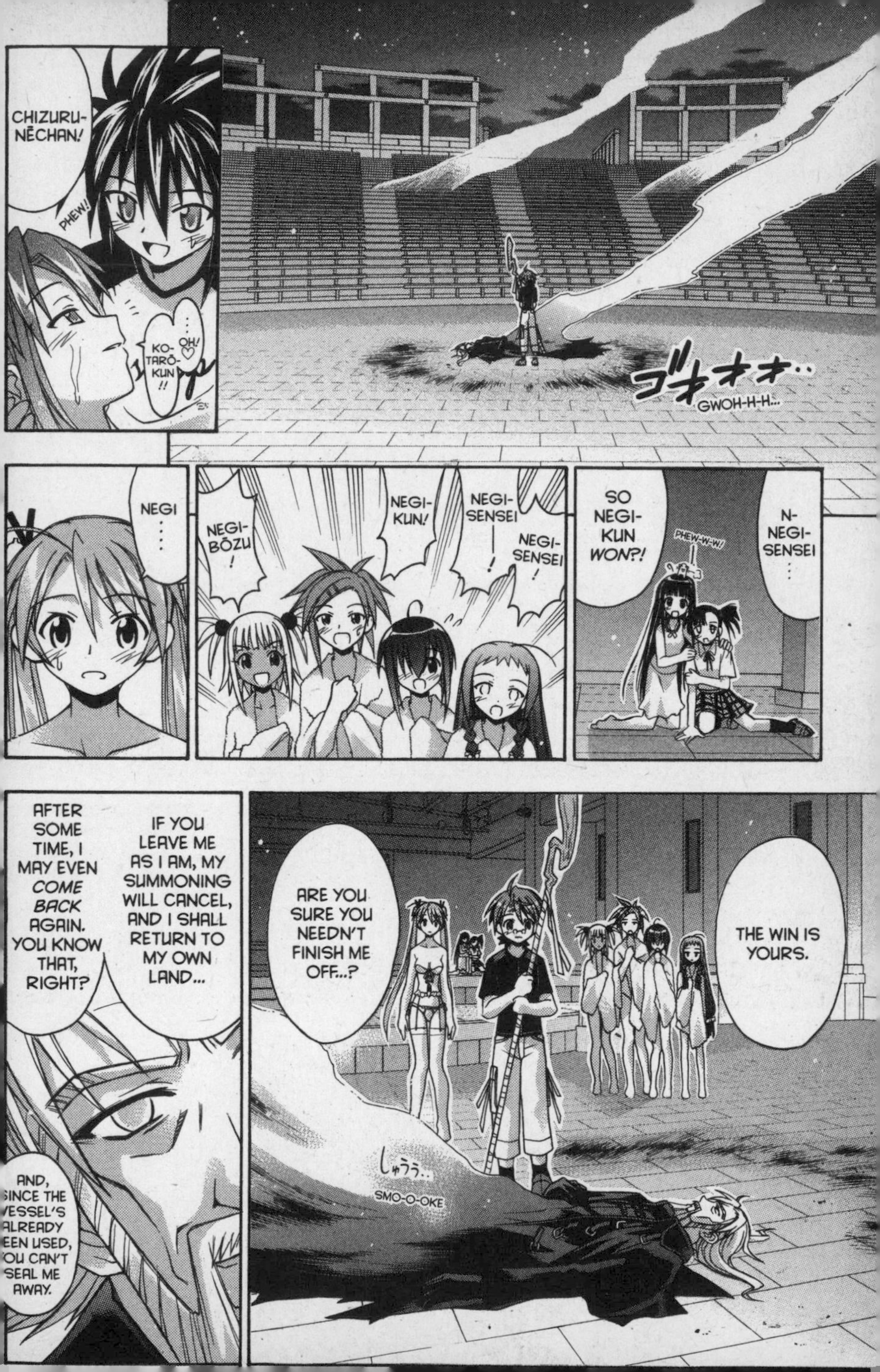
ゴオオオ‥
GWOH-H-H...
CHIZURU-NĒCHAN!
PHEW!
...OH! ♡ KO-TARŌ-KUN!!
N-NEGI-SENSEI...
SO NEGI-KUN WON?!
PHEW-W-W!
NEGI-SENSEI!
NEGI-SENSEI!
NEGI-KUN!
NEGI-BŌZU!
NEGI....
THE WIN IS YOURS.
ARE YOU SURE YOU NEEDN'T FINISH ME OFF...?
しゅうう‥
SMO-O-OKE
IF YOU LEAVE ME AS I AM, MY SUMMONING WILL CANCEL, AND I SHALL RETURN TO MY OWN LAND...
AFTER SOME TIME, I MAY EVEN *COME BACK* AGAIN. YOU KNOW THAT, RIGHT?
AND, SINCE THE VESSEL'S ALREADY EEN USED, OU CAN'T SEAL ME AWAY.

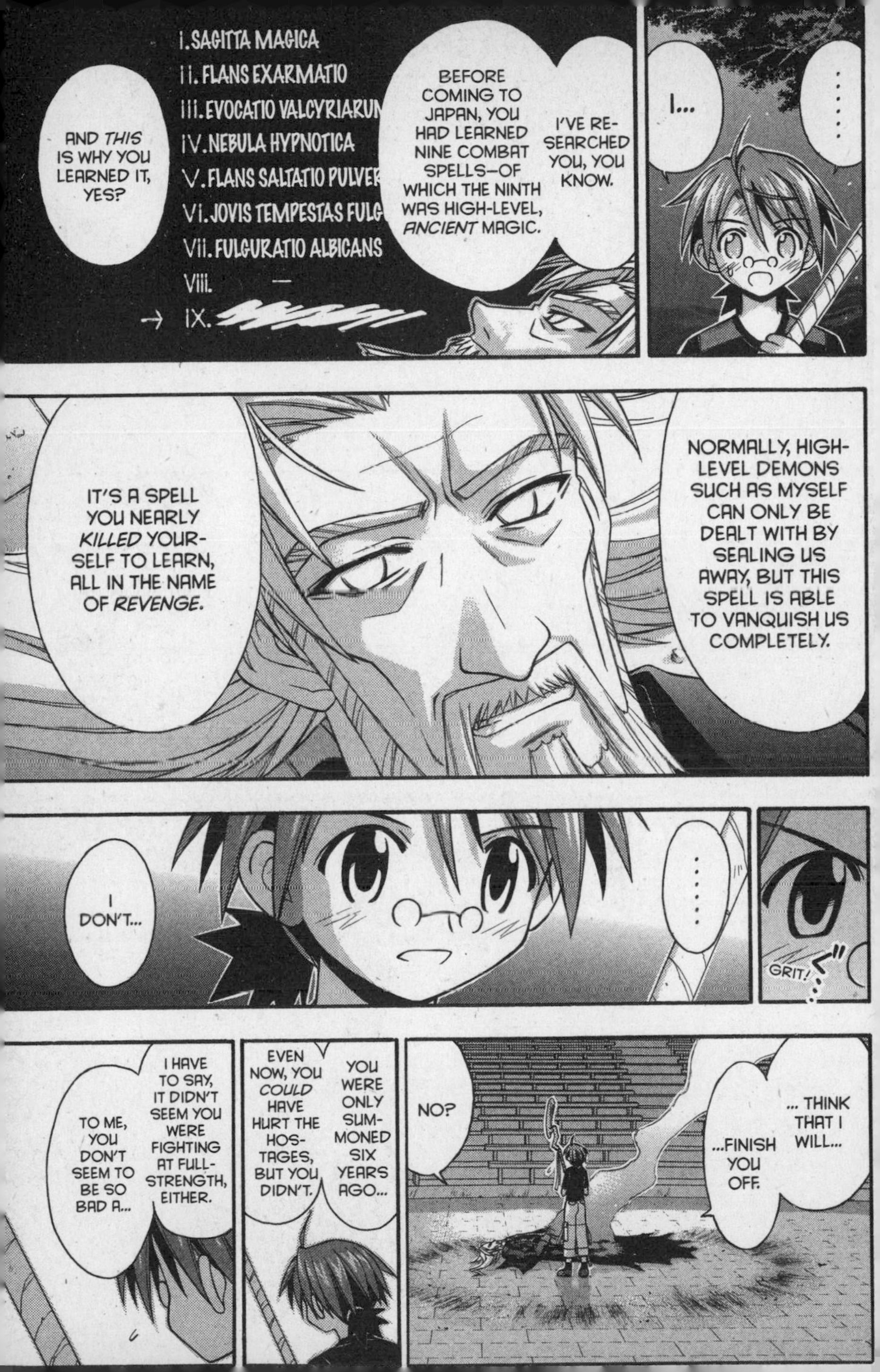

......
I...
I'VE RESEARCHED YOU, YOU KNOW.
BEFORE COMING TO JAPAN, YOU HAD LEARNED NINE COMBAT SPELLS—OF WHICH THE NINTH WAS HIGH-LEVEL, *ANCIENT* MAGIC.
I. SAGITTA MAGICA
II. FLANS EXARMATIO
III. EVOCATIO VALCYRIARU
IV. NEBULA HYPNOTICA
V. FLANS SALTATIO PULVER
VI. JOVIS TEMPESTAS FULG
VII. FULGURATIO ALBICANS
VIII. —
→ IX.
AND *THIS* IS WHY YOU LEARNED IT, YES?
NORMALLY, HIGH-LEVEL DEMONS SUCH AS MYSELF CAN ONLY BE DEALT WITH BY SEALING US AWAY, BUT THIS SPELL IS ABLE TO VANQUISH US COMPLETELY.
IT'S A SPELL YOU NEARLY *KILLED* YOURSELF TO LEARN, ALL IN THE NAME OF *REVENGE*.
GRIT!
......
I DON'T...
... THINK THAT I WILL...
...FINISH YOU OFF.
NO?
YOU WERE ONLY SUMMONED SIX YEARS AGO...
EVEN NOW, YOU *COULD* HAVE HURT THE HOSTAGES, BUT YOU DIDN'T.
I HAVE TO SAY, IT DIDN'T SEEM YOU WERE FIGHTING AT FULL-STRENGTH, EITHER.
TO ME, YOU DON'T SEEM TO BE SO BAD A...

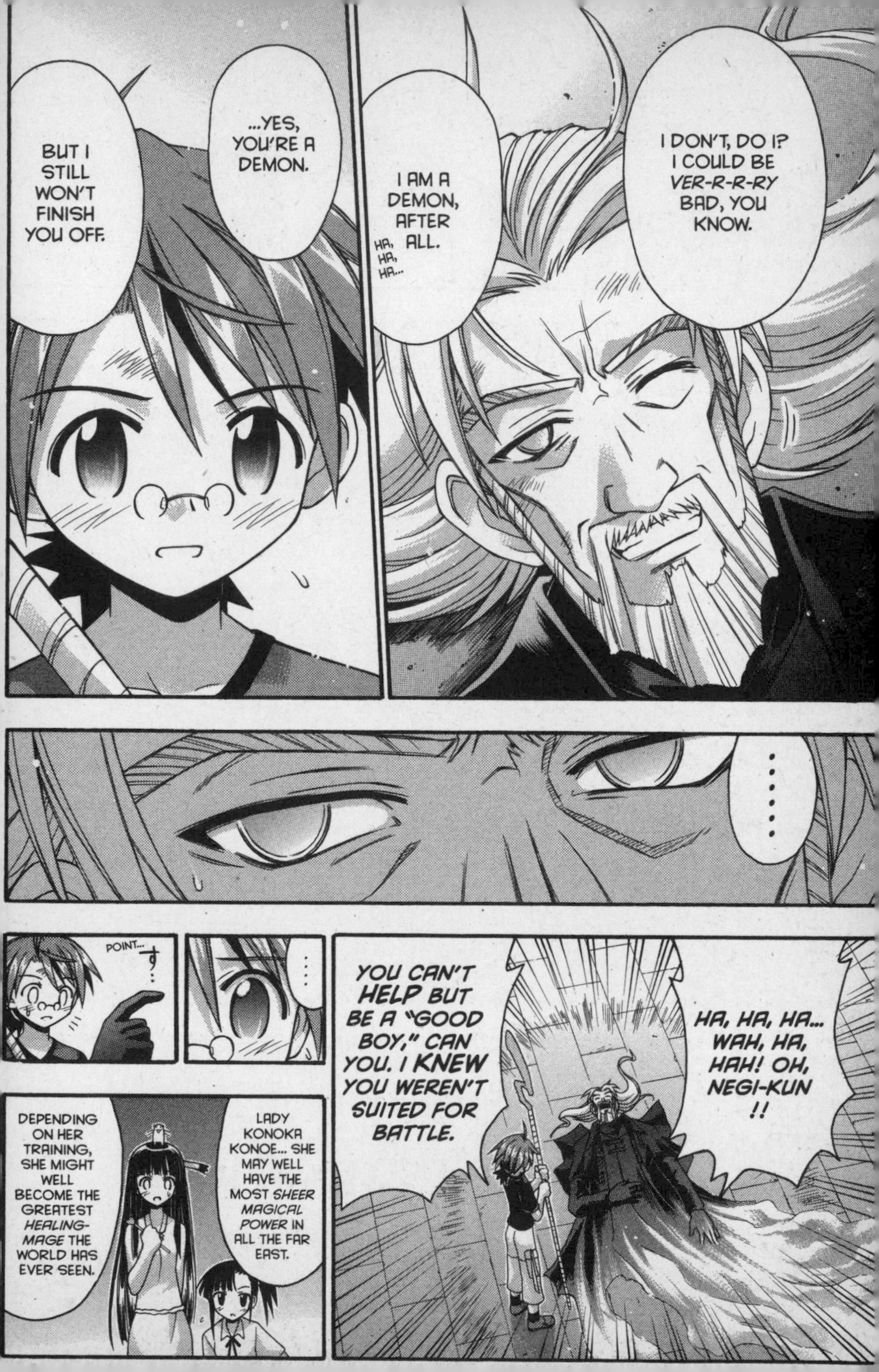
I DON'T, DO I? I COULD BE VER-R-R-RY BAD, YOU KNOW.
I AM A DEMON, AFTER ALL.
HA, HA, HA...
...YES, YOU'RE A DEMON.
BUT I STILL WON'T FINISH YOU OFF.
......
HA, HA, HA... WAH, HA, HAH! OH, NEGI-KUN!!
YOU CAN'T HELP BUT BE A "GOOD BOY," CAN YOU. I KNEW YOU WEREN'T SUITED FOR BATTLE.
....
POINT... す
LADY KONOKA KONOE... SHE MAY WELL HAVE THE MOST SHEER MAGICAL POWER IN ALL THE FAR EAST.
DEPENDING ON HER TRAINING, SHE MIGHT WELL BECOME THE GREATEST HEALING-MAGE THE WORLD HAS EVER SEEN.

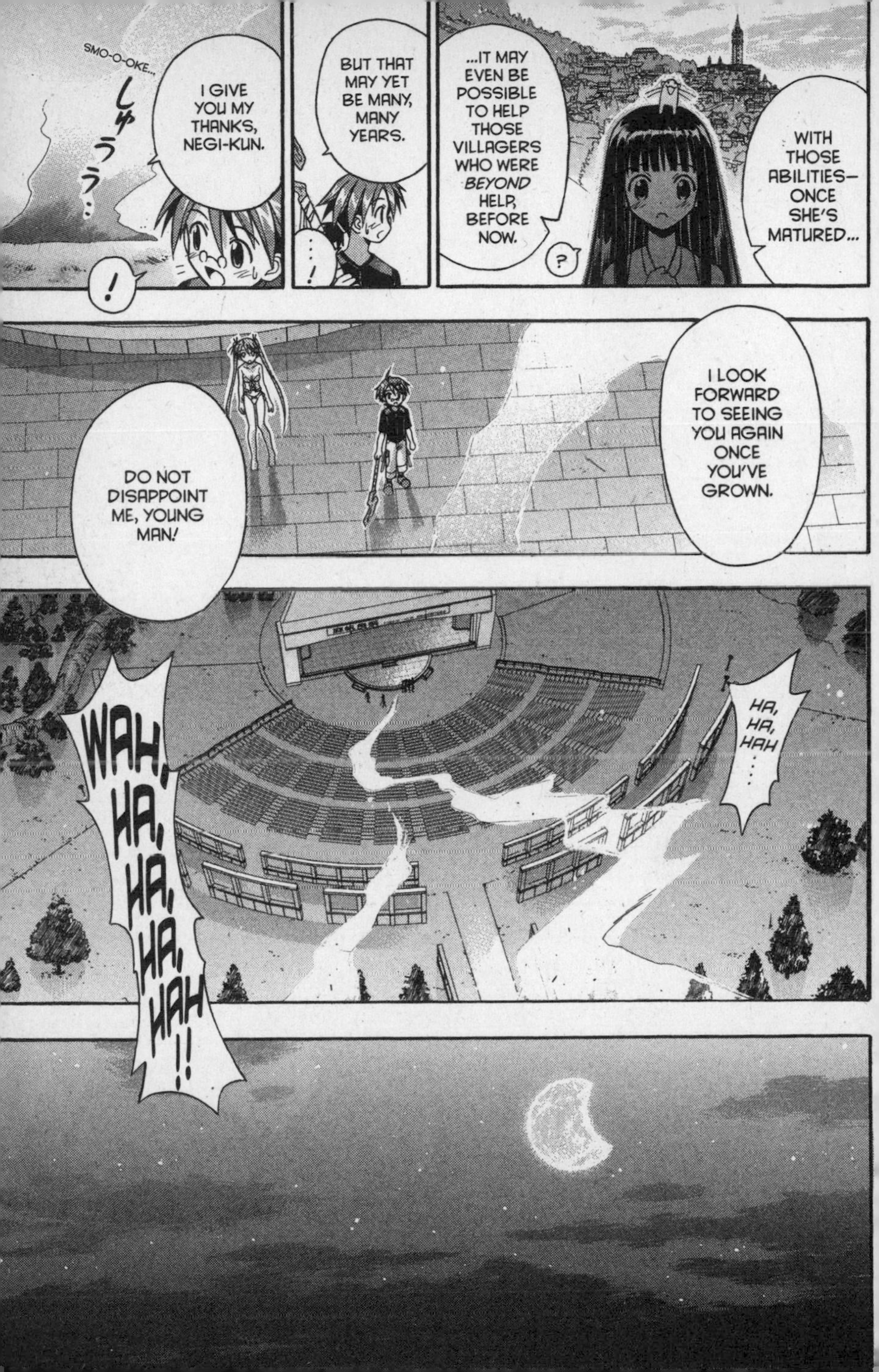
WITH THOSE ABILITIES— ONCE SHE'S MATURED...
?
...IT MAY EVEN BE POSSIBLE TO HELP THOSE VILLAGERS WHO WERE *BEYOND* HELP, BEFORE NOW.
BUT THAT MAY YET BE MANY, MANY YEARS.
...!
I GIVE YOU MY THANKS, NEGI-KUN.
SMO-O-OKE...
しゅララ‥
!
I LOOK FORWARD TO SEEING YOU AGAIN ONCE YOU'VE GROWN.
DO NOT DISAPPOINT ME, YOUNG MAN!
HA, HA, HAH...
WAH, HA, HA, HA, HAH!!

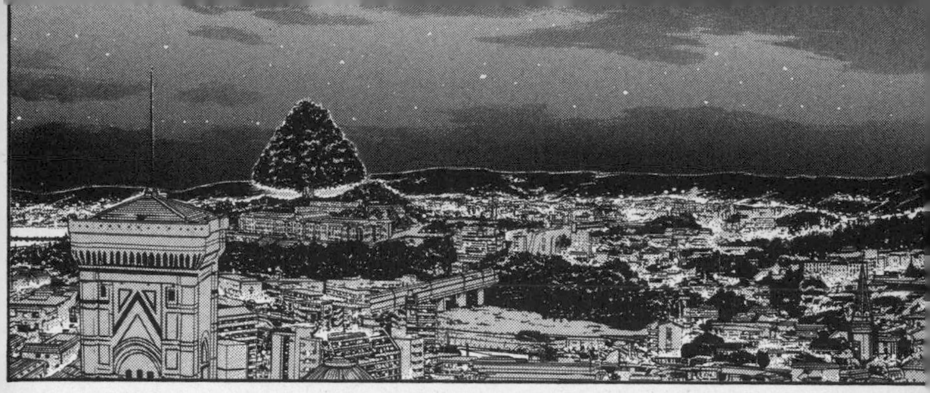

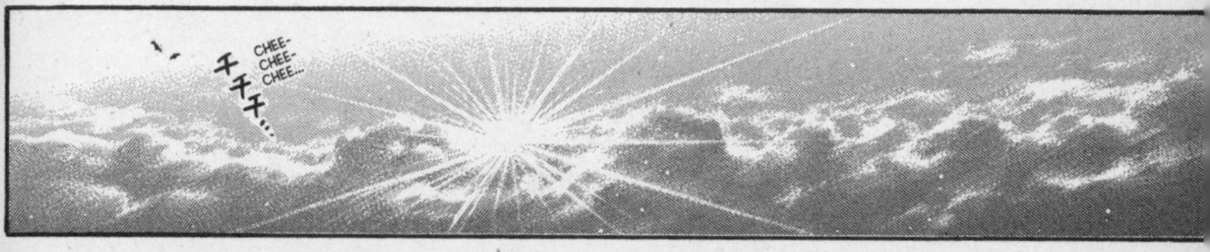
チチチ…
CHEE-
CHEE-
CHEE...

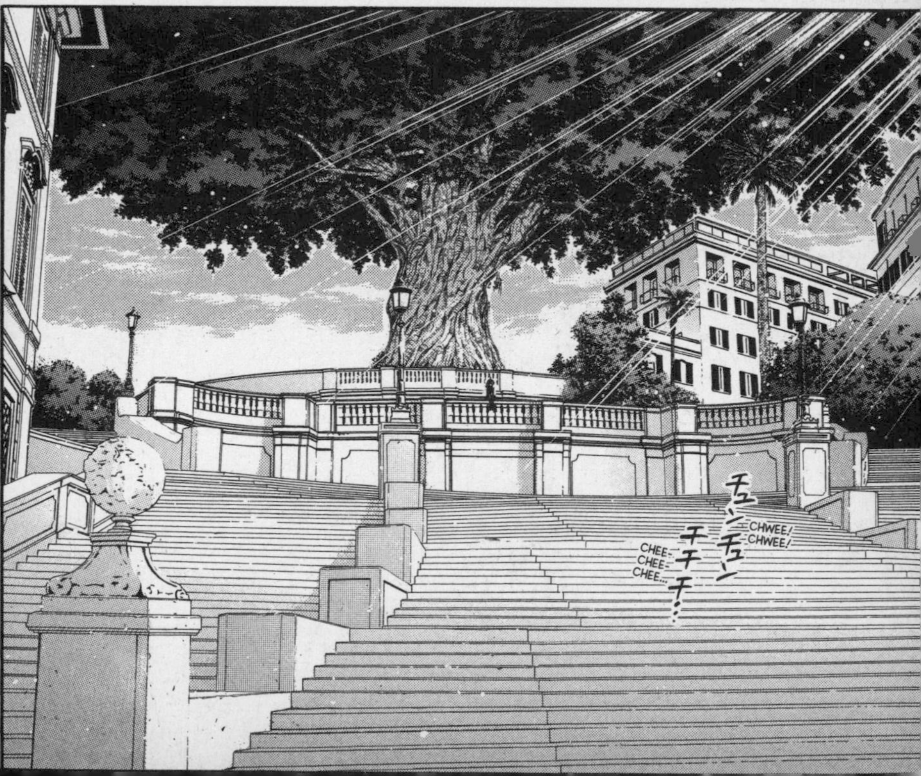
チュンチュン
CHWEE!
CHWEE!
チチチ…
CHEE-
CHEE-
CHEE...

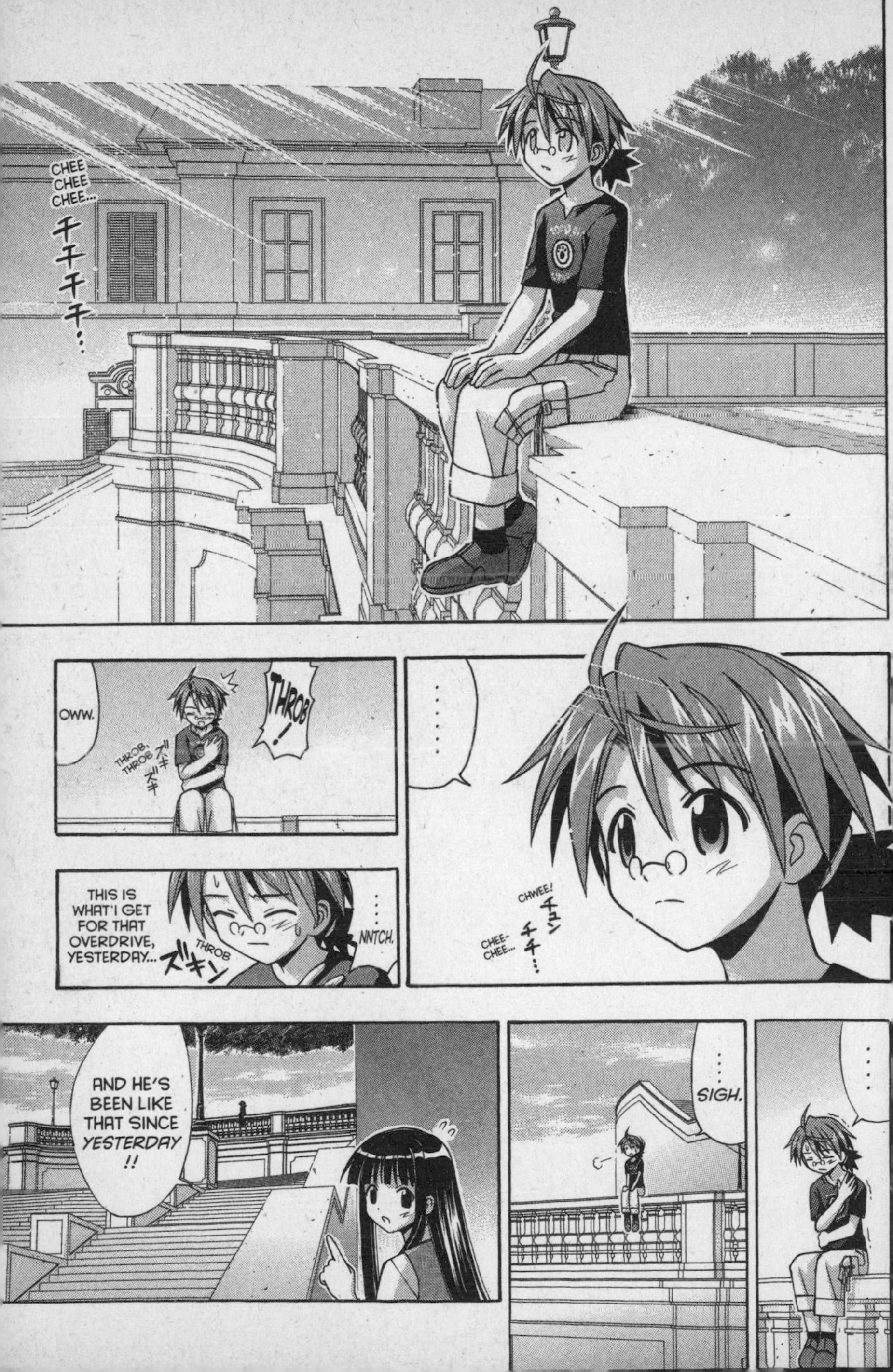
CHEE CHEE CHEE...
チチチチ…
.....
CHWEE! チュン
CHEE-CHEE... チチ…
THROB!
THROB, THROB ズキズキ
OWW.
.....
NNTCH.
THIS IS WHAT I GET FOR THAT OVERDRIVE, YESTERDAY...
THROB ズキン
....
.... SIGH.
AND HE'S BEEN LIKE THAT SINCE *YESTERDAY* !!

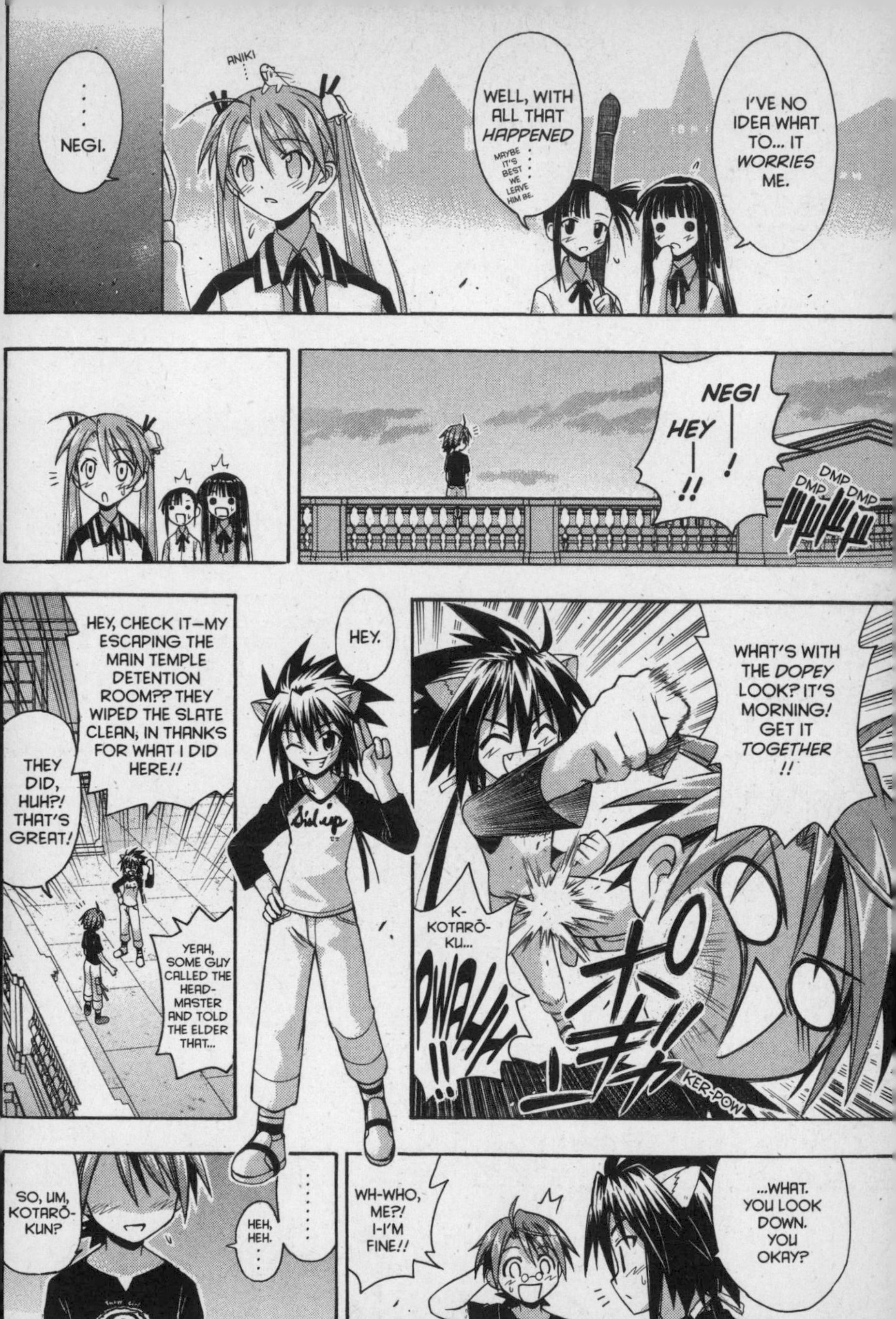
I'VE NO IDEA WHAT TO... IT WORRIES ME.
WELL, WITH ALL THAT HAPPENED
MAYBE IT'S BEST WE LEAVE HIM BE.
ANIKI ...
.... NEGI.
NEGI—!
HEY—!!
DMP DMP DMP
WHAT'S WITH THE DOPEY LOOK? IT'S MORNING! GET IT TOGETHER!!
K-KOTARŌ-KU...
PWAHH!!
KER-POW
HEY.
HEY, CHECK IT—MY ESCAPING THE MAIN TEMPLE DETENTION ROOM?? THEY WIPED THE SLATE CLEAN, IN THANKS FOR WHAT I DID HERE!!
THEY DID, HUH?! THAT'S GREAT!
YEAH, SOME GUY CALLED THE HEAD-MASTER AND TOLD THE ELDER THAT...
...WHAT. YOU LOOK DOWN. YOU OKAY?
WH-WHO, ME?! I-I'M FINE!!
......
HEH, HEH. ...
SO, UM, KOTARŌ-KUN?

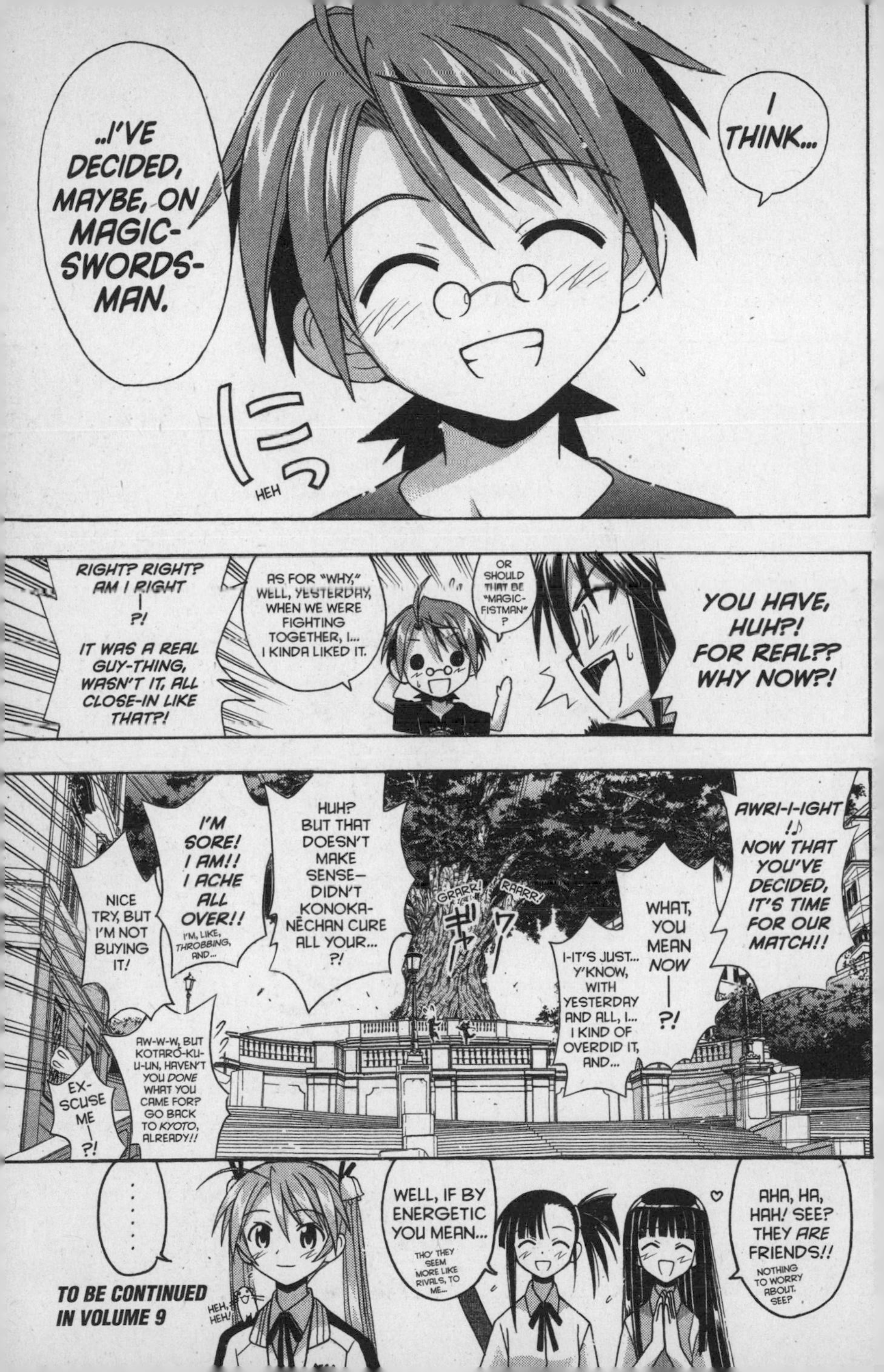
I THINK...
..I'VE DECIDED, MAYBE, ON MAGIC-SWORDSMAN.
HEH
YOU HAVE, HUH?! FOR REAL?? WHY NOW?!
OR SHOULD THAT BE "MAGIC-FISTMAN"?
AS FOR "WHY," WELL, YESTERDAY, WHEN WE WERE FIGHTING TOGETHER, I... I KINDA LIKED IT.
RIGHT? RIGHT? AM I RIGHT—?!
IT WAS A REAL GUY-THING, WASN'T IT, ALL CLOSE-IN LIKE THAT?!
AWRI-I-IGHT!♪ NOW THAT YOU'VE DECIDED, IT'S TIME FOR OUR MATCH!!
WHAT, YOU MEAN NOW—?!
I-IT'S JUST... Y'KNOW, WITH YESTERDAY AND ALL, I... I KIND OF OVERDID IT, AND...
HUH? BUT THAT DOESN'T MAKE SENSE—DIDN'T KONOKA-NĒCHAN CURE ALL YOUR...?!
RAAARR!
GRARR!
I'M SORE! I AM!! I ACHE ALL OVER!!
I'M, LIKE, THROBBING, AND...
NICE TRY, BUT I'M NOT BUYING IT!
AW-W-W, BUT KOTARŌ-KU-U-UN, HAVEN'T YOU DONE WHAT YOU CAME FOR? GO BACK TO KYOTO, ALREADY!!
EX-SCUSE ME—?!
AHA, HA, HAH! SEE? THEY ARE FRIENDS!!
NOTHING TO WORRY ABOUT. SEE?
WELL, IF BY ENERGETIC YOU MEAN...
THO' THEY SEEM MORE LIKE RIVALS, TO ME...
......
HEH, HEH!
TO BE CONTINUED IN VOLUME 9

- STAFF -

Ken Akamatsu
Takashi Takemoto
Kenichi Nakamura
Masaki Ohyama
Keiichi Yamashita
Chigusa Amagasaki
Takaaki Miyahara

Thanks To

Ran Ayanaga

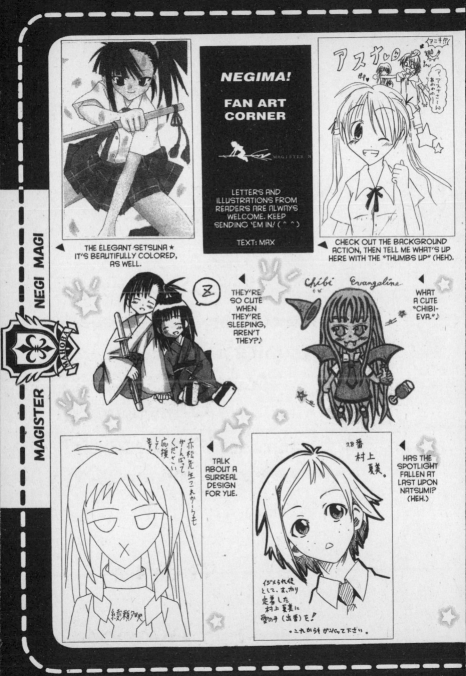

NEGIMA!

FAN ART CORNER

LETTERS AND ILLUSTRATIONS FROM READERS ARE ALWAYS WELCOME. KEEP SENDING 'EM IN! (^ ^)

TEXT: MAX

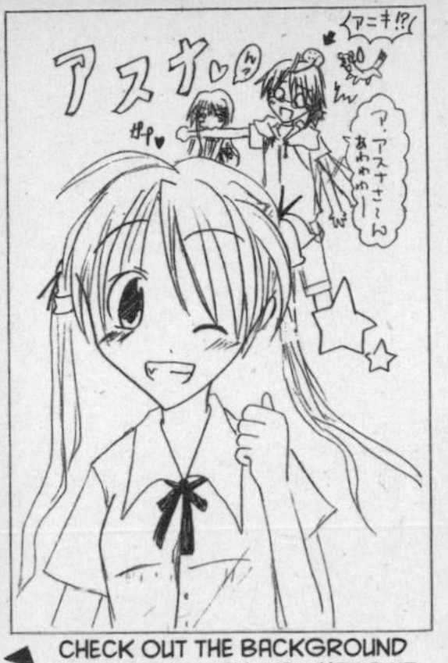
アスナ♡
ア、アスナさ〜ん あわわわ〜!

CHECK OUT THE BACKGROUND ACTION, THEN TELL ME WHAT'S UP HERE WITH THE "THUMBS UP" (HEH).

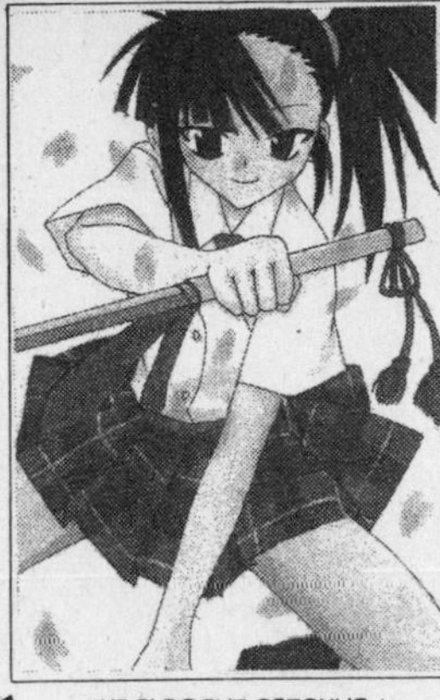

THE ELEGANT SETSUNA ★ IT'S BEAUTIFULLY COLORED, AS WELL.

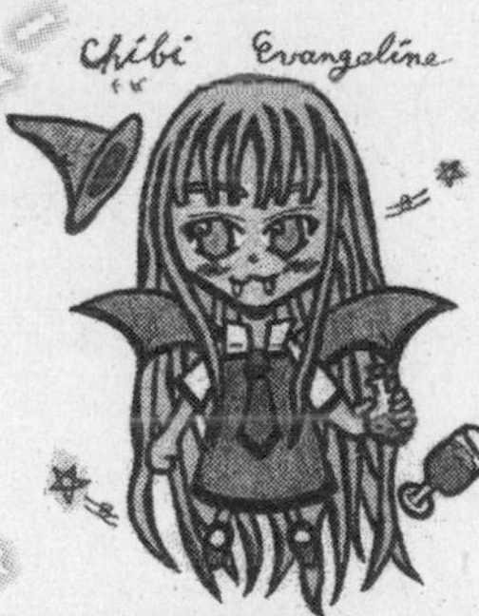
Chibi Evangeline

WHAT A CUTE "CHIBI-EVA."♪

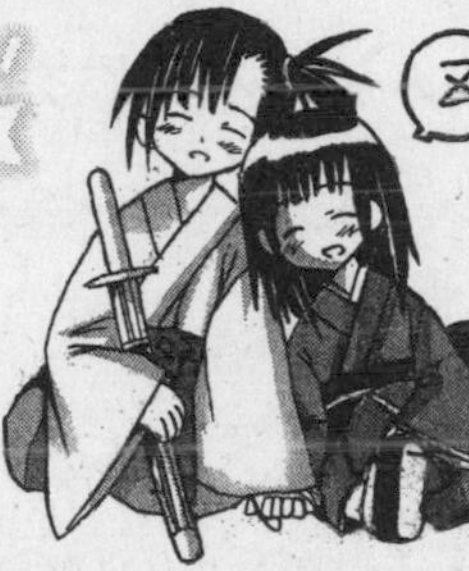
Z

THEY'RE SO CUTE WHEN THEY'RE SLEEPING, AREN'T THEY?♪

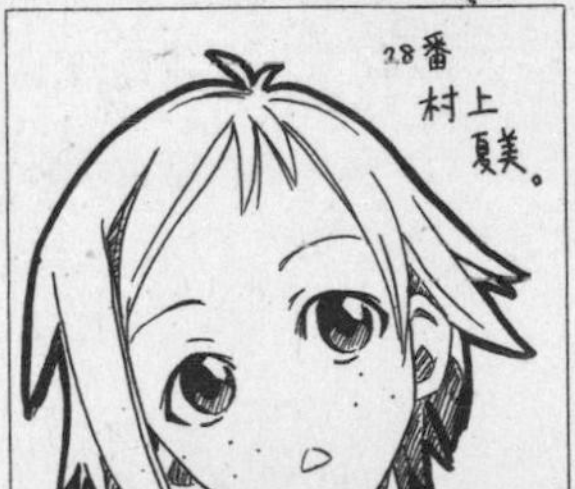
28番
村上夏美。
イジメられ役として、すっかり定着した村上夏美に愛の手(出番)を!
これからもガンバッて下さい。

HAS THE SPOTLIGHT FALLEN AT LAST UPON NATSUMI? (HEH.)

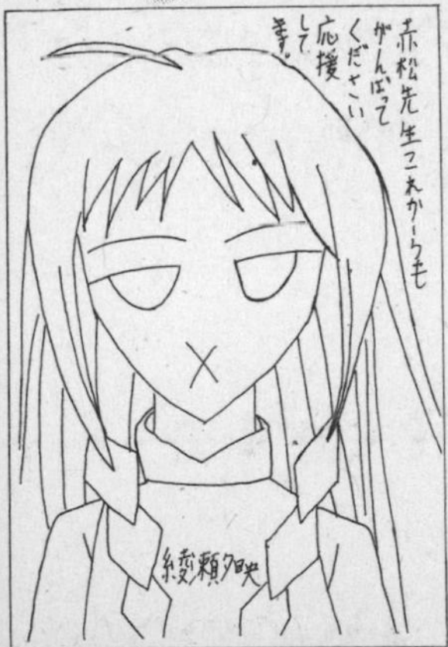
赤松先生これからもがんばってください応援してます。
綾瀬夕映

TALK ABOUT A SURREAL DESIGN FOR YUE.

EVANGELINE'S RESORT
—PRELIMINARY SKETCHES—

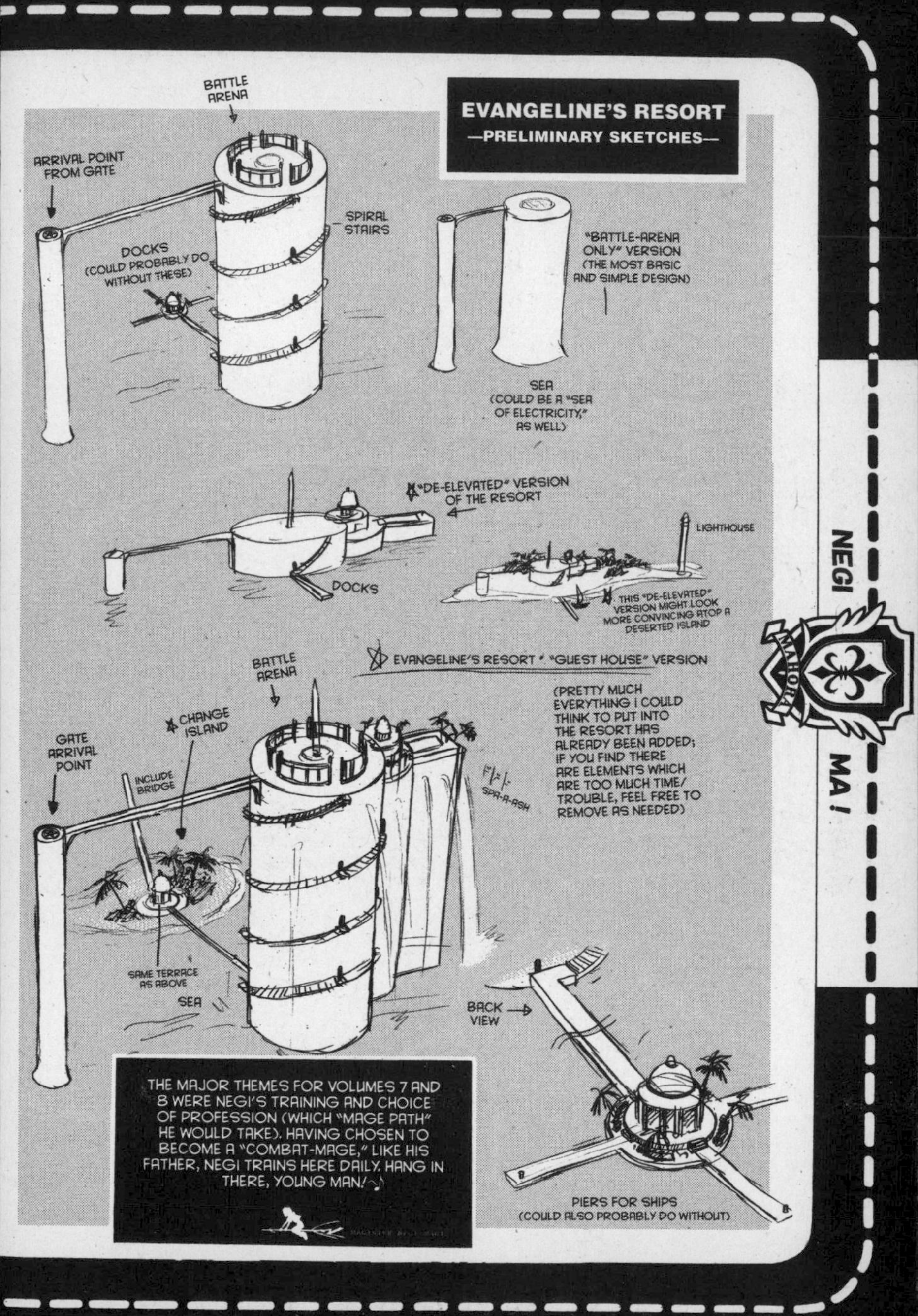
BATTLE ARENA
ARRIVAL POINT FROM GATE
SPIRAL STAIRS
DOCKS (COULD PROBABLY DO WITHOUT THESE)
"BATTLE-ARENA ONLY" VERSION (THE MOST BASIC AND SIMPLE DESIGN)
SEA (COULD BE A "SEA OF ELECTRICITY," AS WELL)
"DE-ELEVATED" VERSION OF THE RESORT
LIGHTHOUSE
DOCKS
THIS "DE-ELEVATED" VERSION MIGHT LOOK MORE CONVINCING ATOP A DESERTED ISLAND
EVANGELINE'S RESORT * "GUEST HOUSE" VERSION
BATTLE ARENA
CHANGE ISLAND
GATE ARRIVAL POINT
INCLUDE BRIDGE
(PRETTY MUCH EVERYTHING I COULD THINK TO PUT INTO THE RESORT HAS ALREADY BEEN ADDED; IF YOU FIND THERE ARE ELEMENTS WHICH ARE TOO MUCH TIME/ TROUBLE, FEEL FREE TO REMOVE AS NEEDED)
SPA-A-ASH
SAME TERRACE AS ABOVE
SEA
BACK VIEW
PIERS FOR SHIPS (COULD ALSO PROBABLY DO WITHOUT)

THE MAJOR THEMES FOR VOLUMES 7 AND 8 WERE NEGI'S TRAINING AND CHOICE OF PROFESSION (WHICH "MAGE PATH" HE WOULD TAKE). HAVING CHOSEN TO BECOME A "COMBAT-MAGE," LIKE HIS FATHER, NEGI TRAINS HERE DAILY. HANG IN THERE, YOUNG MAN!♪

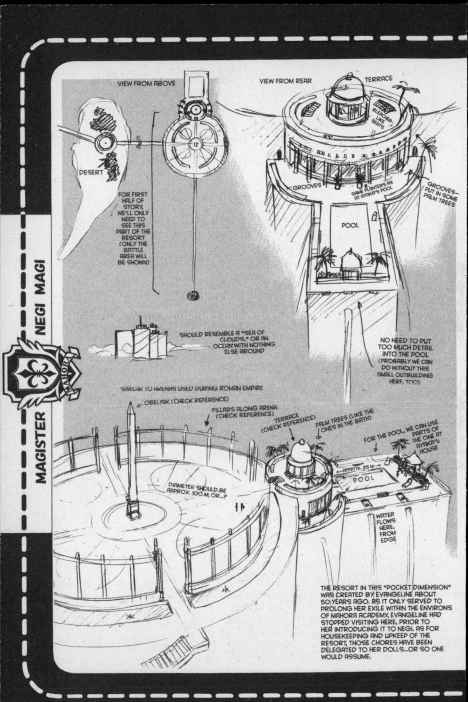

VIEW FROM ABOVE
DESERT
FOR FIRST HALF OF STORY, WE'LL ONLY NEED TO SEE THIS PART OF THE RESORT (ONLY THE BATTLE AREA WILL BE SHOWN)
VIEW FROM REAR
TERRACE
BLEACHER-LIKE SEATS
GROOVES
SAME PLANTERS AS AT AYAKA'S POOL
GROOVES—PUT IN SOME PALM TREES
POOL
SHOULD RESEMBLE A "SEA OF CLOUDS," OR AN OCEAN WITH NOTHING ELSE AROUND
NO NEED TO PUT TOO MUCH DETAIL INTO THE POOL (PROBABLY WE CAN DO WITHOUT THIS SMALL OUTBUILDING HERE, TOO)
SIMILAR TO ARENAS USED DURING ROMAN EMPIRE
OBELISK (CHECK REFERENCE)
PILLARS ALONG ARENA (CHECK REFERENCE)
TERRACE (CHECK REFERENCE)
PALM TREES (LIKE THE ONES IN THE BATH)
FOR THE POOL, WE CAN USE PARTS OF THE ONE AT AYAKA'S HOUSE
APPROX. 25 M
POOL
DIAMETER SHOULD BE APPROX. 100 M, OR...?
WATER FLOWS HERE, FROM EDGE

THE RESORT IN THIS "POCKET DIMENSION" WAS CREATED BY EVANGELINE ABOUT 50 YEARS AGO. AS IT ONLY SERVED TO PROLONG HER EXILE WITHIN THE ENVIRONS OF MAHORA ACADEMY, EVANGELINE HAD STOPPED VISITING HERE, PRIOR TO HER INTRODUCING IT TO NEGI. AS FOR HOUSEKEEPING AND UPKEEP OF THE RESORT, THOSE CHORES HAVE BEEN DELEGATED TO HER DOLLS...OR SO ONE WOULD ASSUME.

NEGIMA!
—ABOUT THE CG BACKGROUNDS—

YOU SEE THEM ALL OVER THE PLACE IN VIDEO GAMES AND MOVIES—NOW COMPUTER GRAPHICS ARE A PART OF THE BACKGROUND FOR NEGIMA!, TOO. YOU MAY OR MAY NOT HAVE NOTICED THAT THE VARIOUS LOCATIONS NEGI AND ASUNA VISIT AT MAHORA ACADEMY HAVE ACTUALLY BEEN CREATED NOT WITH A PEN, BUT ON A COMPUTER. FOR THIS INSTALLMENT, WE'LL USE EVANGELINE'S ROOM AS AN EXAMPLE OF HOW ONE GOES ABOUT CREATING A 3-D, COMPUTER GRAPHICS OR "CG" BACKGROUND.

STEP 1: GATHER REFERENCE MATERIALS

THE VERY FIRST THING IS TO GATHER PHOTOS FOR REFERENCE, EITHER BY TAKING PHOTOS MYSELF, OR BY FINDING THEM ONLINE. IN SOME CASES, WE'LL START FROM A ROUGH SKETCH.

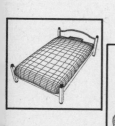 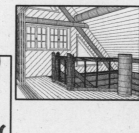

STEP 2: MODEL BUILDING

USING THE CG APPLICATION "LIGHTWAVE 3D," WE CREATE OR BUILD MODELS OF WHAT WE WANT FOR BACKGROUNDS (MODELS ARE COMPRISED OF POLYGONS). THE IMAGES TO THE LEFT ARE A FEW, REPRESENTATIVE SAMPLES: A BED, A HANGING KETTLE, STAIRS LEADING UP TO A ROOM.

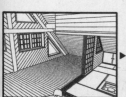 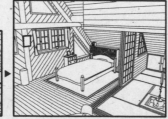

STEP 3: SCENE COMPOSITION

ONCE THE ROOM AND THE FURNITURE HAVE BEEN CREATED, EVERYTHING IS PUT INTO PLACE AND THE BACKGROUND IS COMPLETE. ONE SIDE NOTE: WE REUSE AN AWFUL LOT OF FURNITURE FROM VARIOUS PEOPLE'S ROOMS. (^_^;)

STEP 4: SCAN ROUGH SKETCH

NOW THAT THE BACKGROUND MODELS ARE COMPLETE, WE CAN BEGIN ACTUAL PRODUCTION OF THE COMIC PANEL. WE'LL START BY SCANNING IN A ROUGH SKETCH.

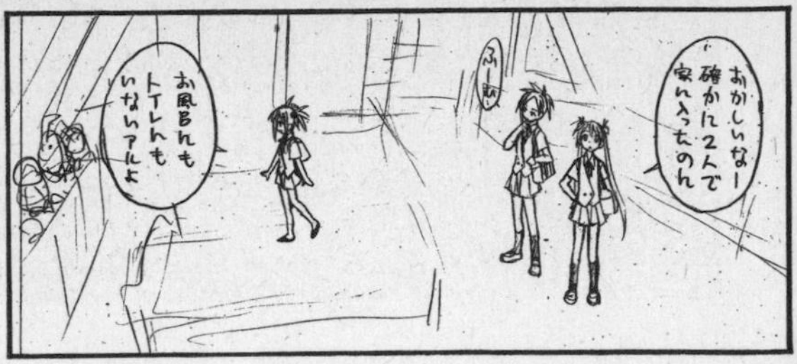
おかしいなー確かに2人で寝入ったのに
ふーん
お風呂にもトイレにもいないアルよ

STEP 5: IMAGE-CREATION TEST

A TEST IMAGE IS CREATED USING THE SCANNED IMAGE AS A GUIDE TO SET CAMERA ANGLES. THE IMAGE TO THE RIGHT SHOWS THE OVERLAPPING OF THE SCANNED ROUGH SKETCH, AS WELL AS THE BACKGROUND MODELS BEING LINED UP AGAINST IT.

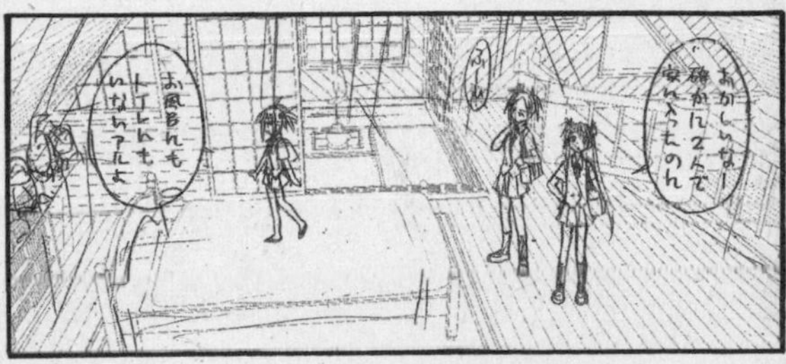
おかしいなー確かに2人で寝入ったのに
ふーん
お風呂にもトイレにもいないアルよ

STEP 6: BACKGROUND CREATION

WITH CAMERA ANGLES DECIDED UPON, A HIGH-RESOLUTION VERSION OF THE MODEL IS CREATED FOR PRINTING PURPOSES. ONCE IT'S PRINTED OUT, WE HAVE A NEARLY COMPLETED PANEL, READY FOR FINISHING.

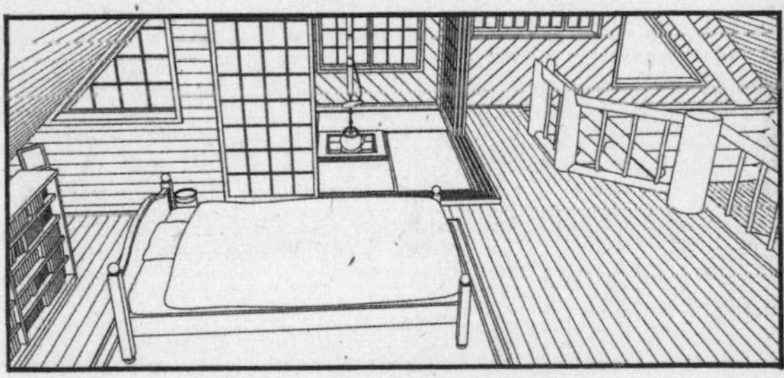

STEP 7: FINISHING

IN COMPLETING THE PANEL, TONE AND ADDITIONAL INK (IF NEEDED) IS ADDED TO THE PRINT OF THE BACKGROUND. NEXT ARE CHARACTERS AND WORD BALLOONS, AND THEN THE PANEL IS DONE. THAT WASN'T SO BAD, WAS IT? (^_^)

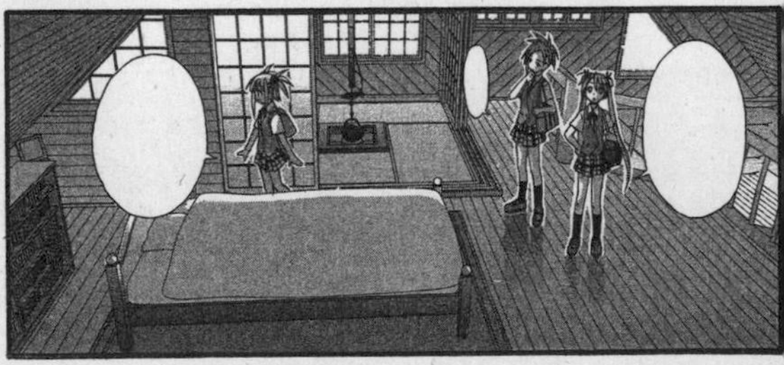

CG BACKGROUNDS LINE-ART GALLERY

A SELECTION OF VARIOUS LOCATIONS AND ITEMS THAT HAVE SHOWN UP OVER THE COURSE OF THE STORY—WITH COMMENTARY!

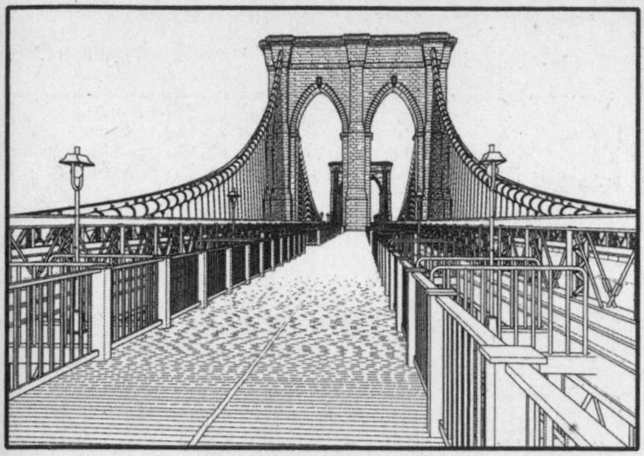

SCENE NAME: BRIDGE
(POLYGON COUNT: 814,856)

THIS IS THE BRIDGE WHERE, IN VOLUME 3, THE BATTLE AGAINST EVANGELINE TAKES PLACE. ALTHOUGH IT'S MODELED AFTER THE BROOKLYN BRIDGE IN MANHATTAN, UNLIKE THE TWO-LEVEL ORIGINAL, OUR VERSION HAS BEEN FORCED TO SINGLE-LEVEL PERSPECTIVE, EXPLAINING WHY IT MAY LOOK A BIT "OFF." (^_^;) OF ALL THE COMPUTER GRAPHICS CREATED, THIS STRUCTURE IS BY FAR THE LARGEST BOTH IN SIZE, AND IN POLYGON COUNT.

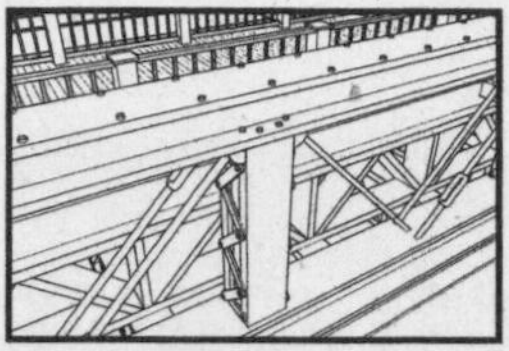

EVEN THE INDIVIDUAL BOLTS OF THE BRIDGE WERE DONE.

AS HAS NO DOUBT (?) BECOME FAMILIAR, HERE'S THE ROOM SHARED BY AYAKA, CHIZURU, AND NATSUMI. AS FOR WHY IT LOOKS SO DIFFERENT FROM ASUNA'S ROOM—BECAUSE THEY ARE BOTH STILL ONLY DORM ROOMS—THE VAST WEALTH OF AYAKA'S FAMILY IS SAID TO HAVE FUNDED THE REMODELING. THAT THE RAISED-FLOOR BEDROOMS ARE SEPARATE FROM THE REST OF THE SPACE IS EVIDENCE ENOUGH OF THE EXTRAVAGANCE; OF ALL THE BEDROOMS, AYAKA'S, OF COURSE, IS THE LARGEST. (HEH.)

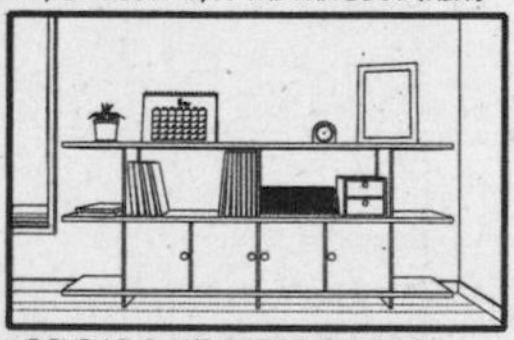

WE EVEN DID THE OFFICE SUPPLIES.

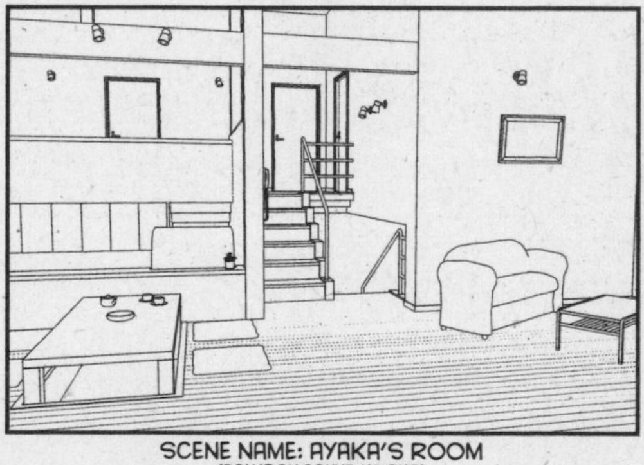

SCENE NAME: AYAKA'S ROOM
(POLYGON COUNT: 49,840)

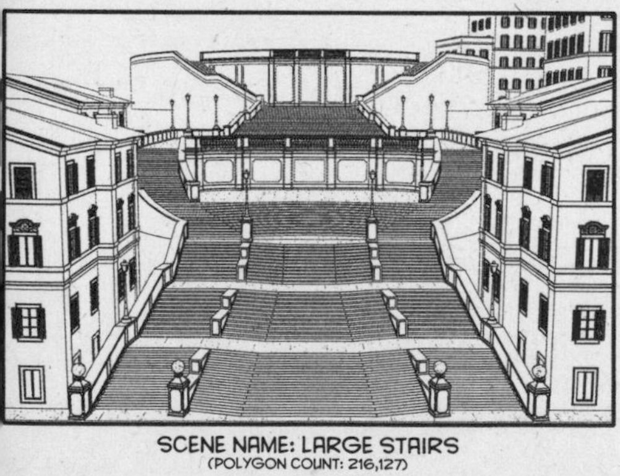

SCENE NAME: LARGE STAIRS
(POLYGON COUNT: 216,127)

OF ALL THE MODELING WE DID, THE GREAT STEPS THAT LEAD UP TO THE WORLD TREE TOOK LONGEST. ORIGINALLY MODELED AFTER A PUBLIC SQUARE IN SPAIN, THE WEEK WE HAD BEFORE THE PUBLISHING DEADLINE TO COMPLETE IT WASN'T NEARLY ENOUGH TIME, SO, AS THE SERIES HAS PROGRESSED, WE'VE SLO-O-OWLY ADDED TO IT. (^_^;) THE WORLD TREE ITSELF, OF COURSE, IS HAND-DRAWN, MEANING IT'S TRULY A BLEND OF DIGITAL AND ANALOG ART THAT GOES INTO CREATING THE BACKGROUNDS OF *NEGIMA!*.

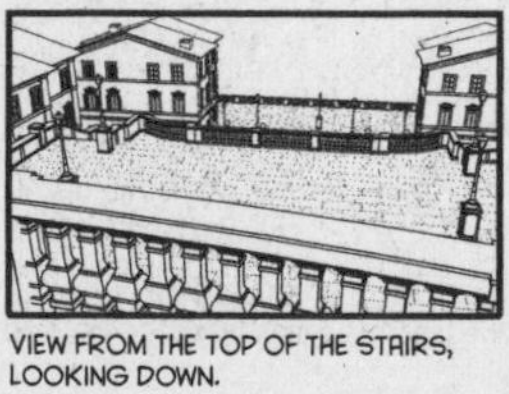

VIEW FROM THE TOP OF THE STAIRS, LOOKING DOWN.

SCENE NAME: ASUNA'S ROOM
(POLYGON COUNT: 80,013)

AS I'M SURE YOU RECOGNIZE RIGHT OFF, THIS IS ASUNA AND KONOKA'S ROOM. ALTHOUGH IT'S NOT OFTEN SEEN, WE'VE CREATED A KITCHEN FOR THEM, AS WELL.

SCENE NAME: LARGE BATH
(POLYGON COUNT: 203,212)

PLANTS ARE NORMALLY DRAWN BY HAND BUT, IN THIS CASE, THE PALM TREES ARE POLYGONAL, TOO.

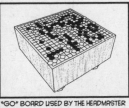

SCENE NAME: BOWLING ALLEY
(POLYGON COUNT: 313,720)

THE BOWLING ALLEY FROM VOLUME 7. IT'LL NEVER SHOW UP AGAIN, SO I THOUGHT I MAY AS WELL GIVE IT ONE LAST SHOWING.

SCENE NAME: ALTAR
(POLYGON COUNT: 171,493)

THIS IS THE LARGE STRUCTURE YOU SEE IN THE BACKGROUND ON THE OTHER SIDE OF THE LARGE ROCK WHICH IS THE SEAL OF SUKUNA IN VOLUME 6. THE CHARACTERS NEVER GOT CLOSE TO IT IN THE STORY, BUT HERE'S A MORE DETAILED SHOT OF WHAT IT LOOKED LIKE.

AS FOR THE FIRST TIME WE USED 3-D COMPUTER GRAPHICS IN THE SERIES, THAT WOULD HAVE BEEN THE CLASSROOM AND THE SPIRAL STAIRCASE, BACK IN VOLUME 2. FOR ANY BACKGROUND WITH INTERCHANGEABLE ELEMENTS, OR THAT REPEATS, I HAVE TO SAY, CG IS IDEAL. (AND DON'T FORGET THOSE CIRCULAR PILLARS!)

AS OF VOLUME 9, THE SCHOOL FESTIVAL BEGINS! THE CLASSMATES WILL ALL BE A PART OF THE ACTION, SO BE SURE AND LOOK FORWARD TO IT. ...OH, AND DON'T FORGET TO WATCH THE ANIME, EITHER!

"GO" BOARD USED BY THE HEADMASTER AND EVA

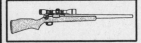

TATSUMIYA'S RIFLE, THE REMINGTON M700

—BONUS—

BET YOU DIDN'T REALIZE THAT ALL THIS STUFF WAS CG, TOO!!

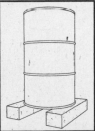

DRUM-CAN IN WHICH NEGI AND KAEDE TAKE A BATH

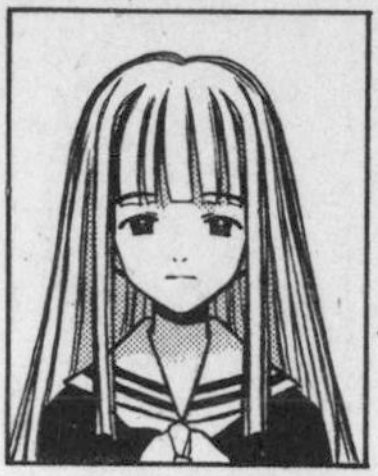

1. SAYO AISAKA

1940~
DON'T CHANGE HER SEATING

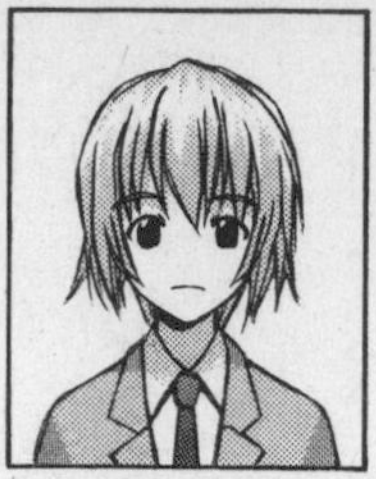

5. AKO IZUMI

NURSE'S OFFICE
SOCCER TEAM
(NON-SCHOOL ACTIVITY)

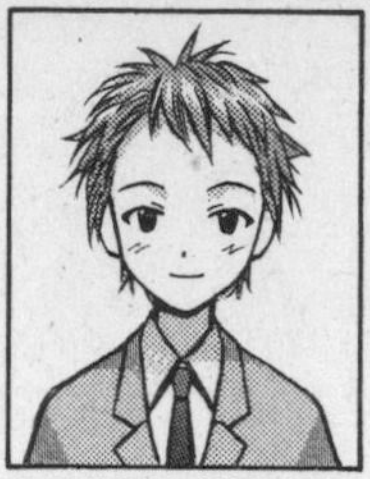

9. MISORA KASUGA

TRACK & FIELD

GRANDDAUGHTER OF SCHOOL DEAN

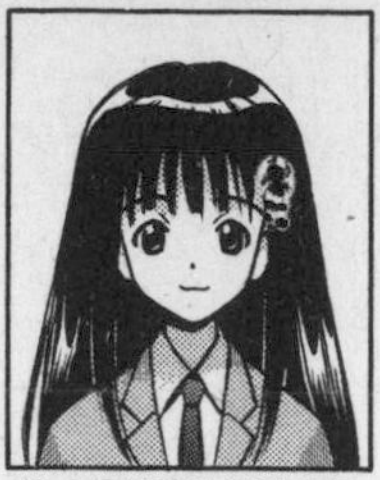

13. KONOKA KONOE

SECRETARY
FORTUNE-TELLING CLUB
LIBRARY EXPLORATION CLUB

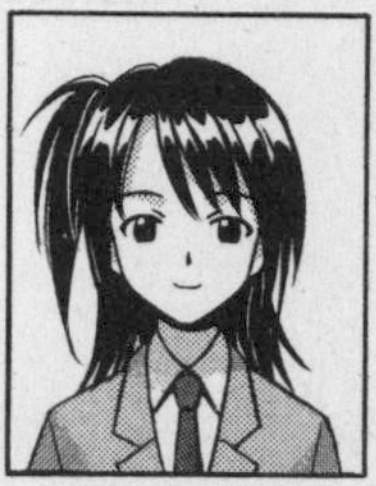

2. YUNA AKASHI

BASKETBALL TEAM

PROFESSOR AKASHI'S DAUGHTER

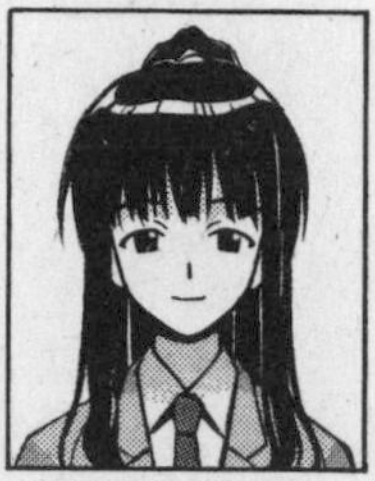

6. AKIRA OKOCHI

SWIM TEAM

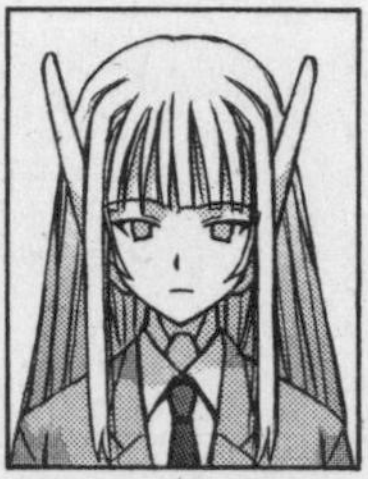

10. CHACHAMARU KARAKURI

TEA CEREMONY CLUB
GO CLUB

CALL ENGINEERING (ext. A08-7796)
IN CASE OF EMERGENCY

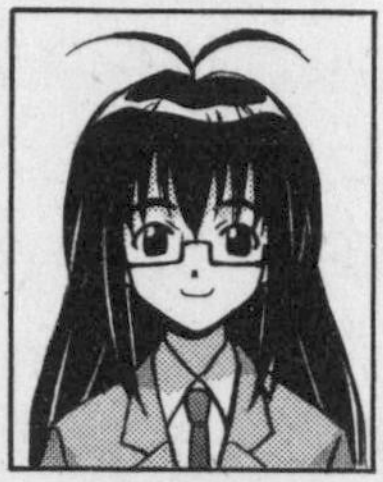

14. HARUNA SAOTOME

MANGA CLUB
LIBRARY EXPLORATION CLUB

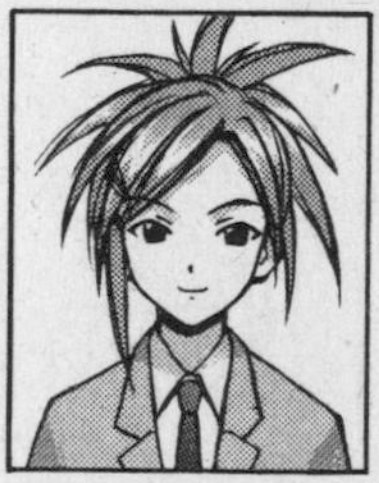

3. KAZUMI ASAKURA

SCHOOL NEWSPAPER

MAHORA NEWS (ext. 809-3780)

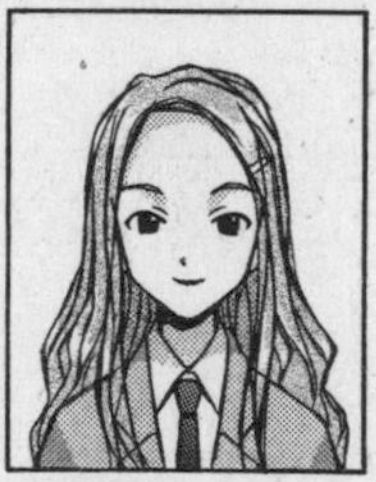

7. MISA KAKIZAKI

CHEERLEADER
CHORUS

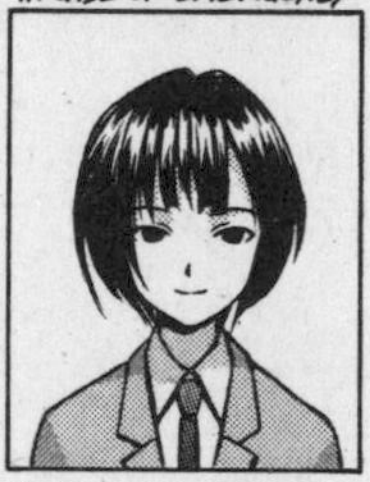

11. MADOKA KUGIMIYA

CHEERLEADER

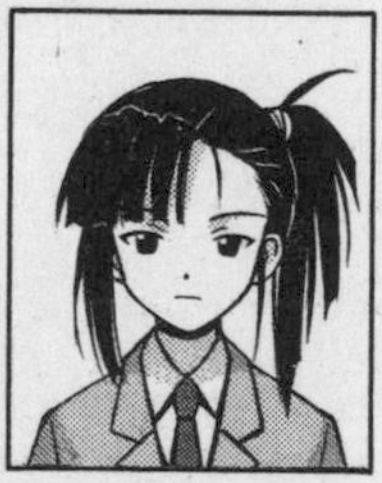

15 SETSUNA SAKURAZAKI

JAPANESE FENCING

KYOTO SHINMEI STYLE

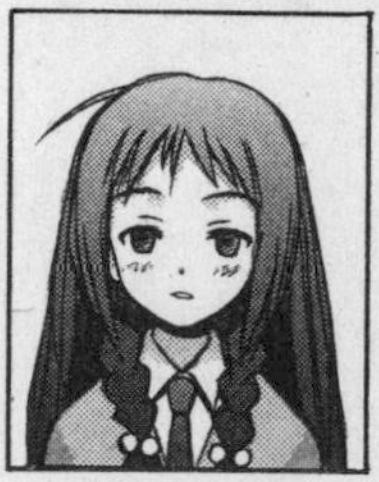

4. YUE AYASE

KID'S LIT CLUB
PHILOSOPHY CLUB
LIBRARY EXPLORATION CLUB

A GOOD PERSON JUST
AS I THOUGHT.

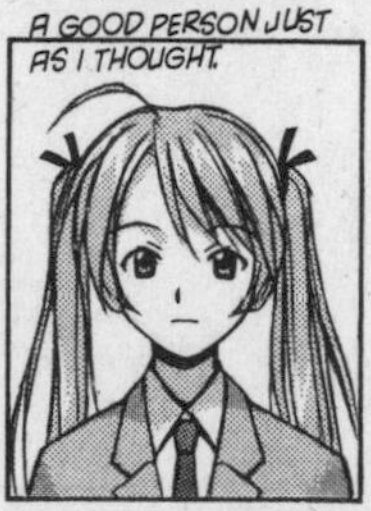

8. ASUNA KAGURAZAKA

ART CLUB

HAS A TERRIBLE KICK

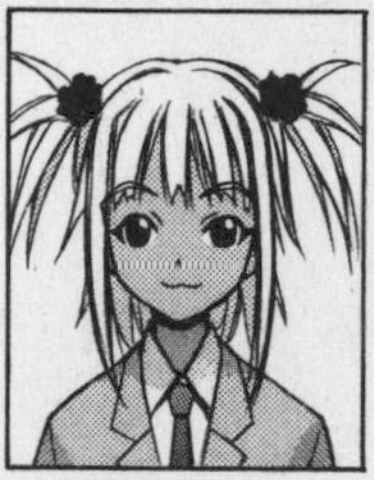

12. KŪ FEI

CHINESE MARTIAL ARTS
GROUP

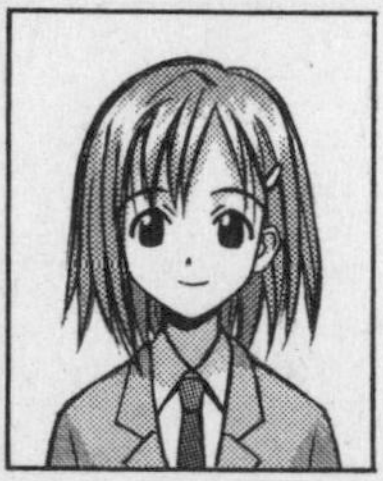

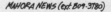

16. MAKIE SASAKI

GYMNASTICS

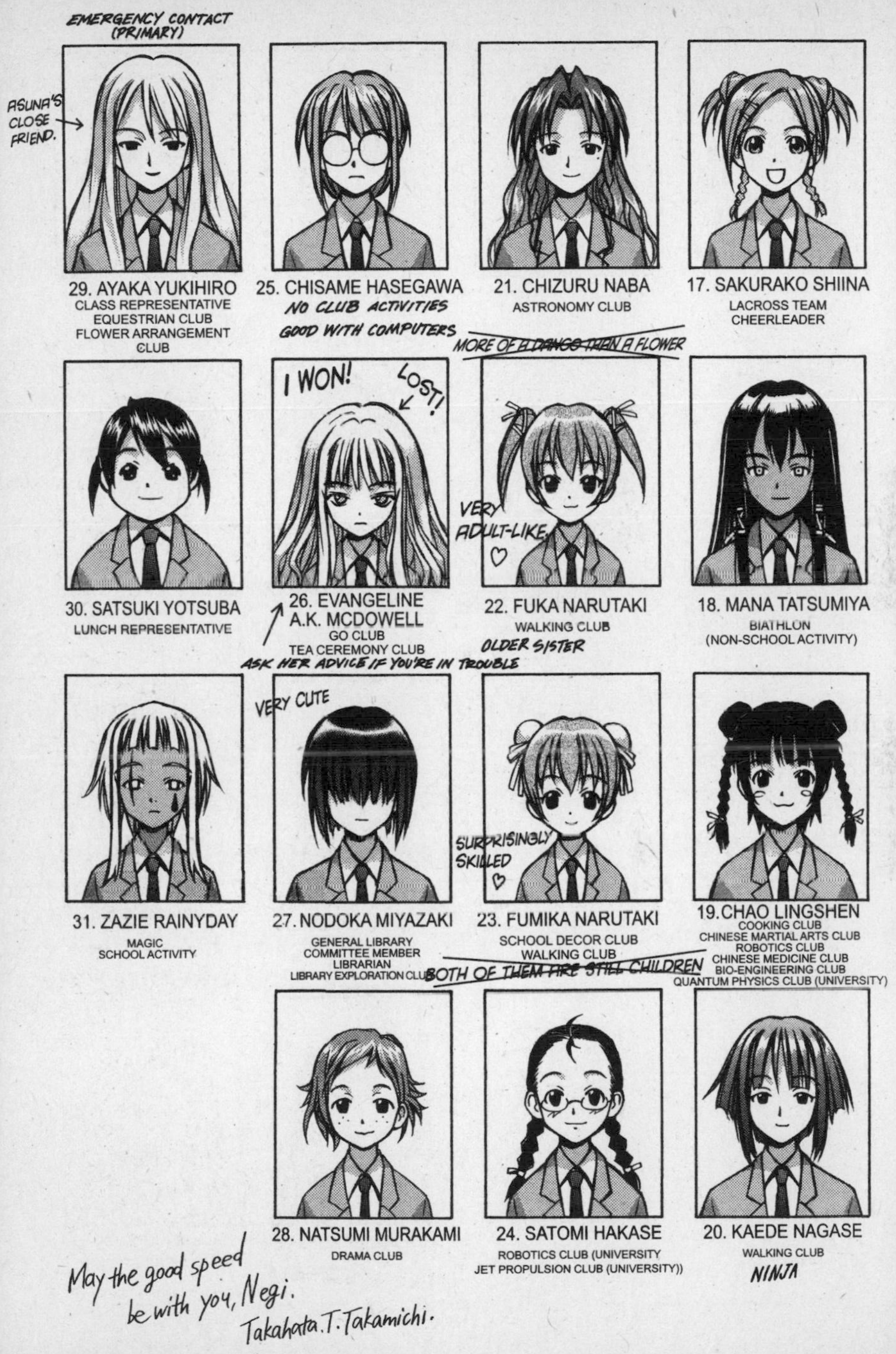
17. SAKURAKO SHIINA
LACROSS TEAM
CHEERLEADER
21. CHIZURU NABA
ASTRONOMY CLUB
MORE OF A DANGO THAN A FLOWER
25. CHISAME HASEGAWA
NO CLUB ACTIVITIES
GOOD WITH COMPUTERS
EMERGENCY CONTACT (PRIMARY)
ASUNA'S CLOSE FRIEND.
29. AYAKA YUKIHIRO
CLASS REPRESENTATIVE
EQUESTRIAN CLUB
FLOWER ARRANGEMENT CLUB
18. MANA TATSUMIYA
BIATHLON
(NON-SCHOOL ACTIVITY)
VERY ADULT-LIKE ♡
22. FUKA NARUTAKI
WALKING CLUB
OLDER SISTER
LOST!
I WON!
26. EVANGELINE A.K. MCDOWELL
GO CLUB
TEA CEREMONY CLUB
ASK HER ADVICE IF YOU'RE IN TROUBLE
30. SATSUKI YOTSUBA
LUNCH REPRESENTATIVE
19. CHAO LINGSHEN
COOKING CLUB
CHINESE MARTIAL ARTS CLUB
ROBOTICS CLUB
CHINESE MEDICINE CLUB
BIO-ENGINEERING CLUB
QUANTUM PHYSICS CLUB (UNIVERSITY)
SURPRISINGLY SKILLED ♡
23. FUMIKA NARUTAKI
SCHOOL DECOR CLUB
WALKING CLUB
BOTH OF THEM ARE STILL CHILDREN
VERY CUTE
27. NODOKA MIYAZAKI
GENERAL LIBRARY
COMMITTEE MEMBER
LIBRARIAN
LIBRARY EXPLORATION CLUB
31. ZAZIE RAINYDAY
MAGIC
SCHOOL ACTIVITY
20. KAEDE NAGASE
WALKING CLUB
NINJA
24. SATOMI HAKASE
ROBOTICS CLUB (UNIVERSITY
JET PROPULSION CLUB (UNIVERSITY))
28. NATSUMI MURAKAMI
DRAMA CLUB
May the good speed be with you, Negi.
Takahata.T.Takamichi.

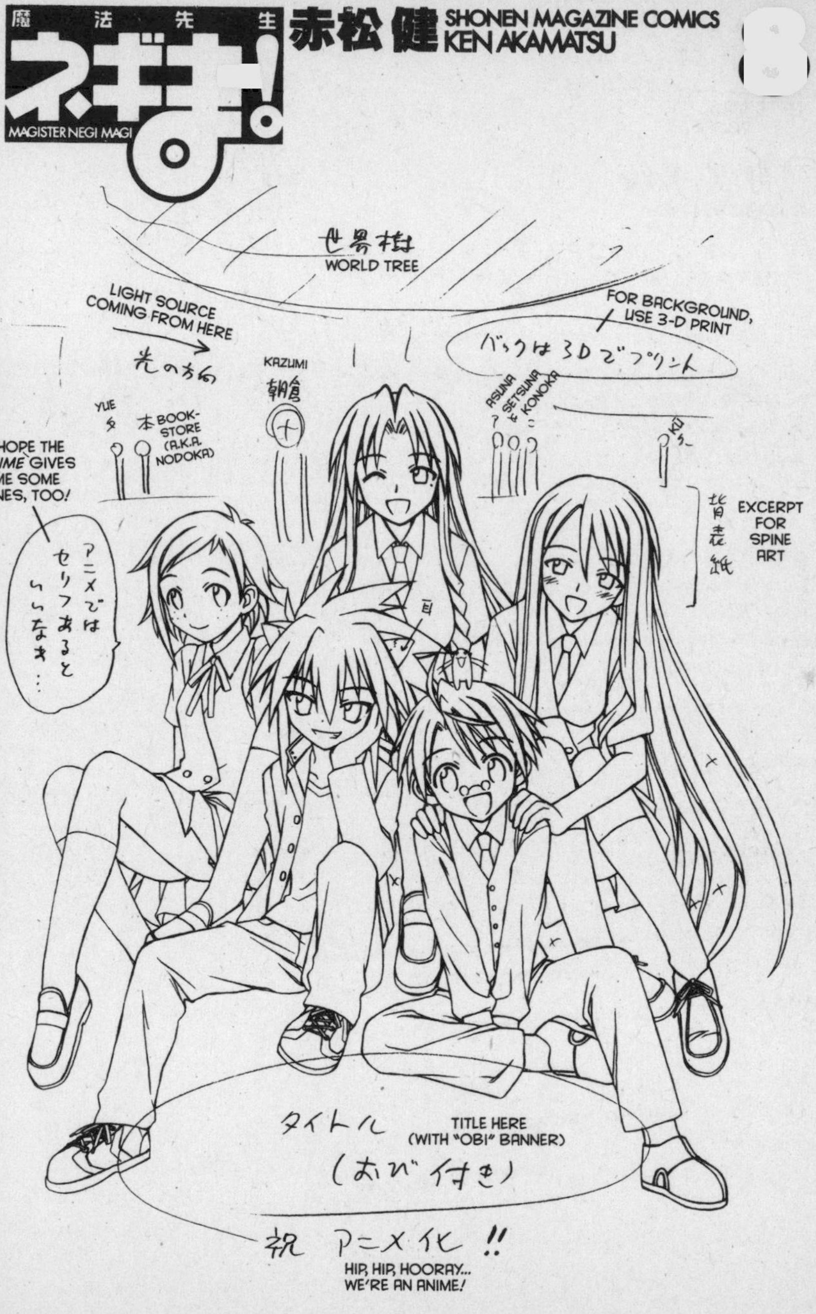
魔法先生
ネギま!
MAGISTER NEGI MAGI
赤松健
SHONEN MAGAZINE COMICS
KEN AKAMATSU
8
世界樹
WORLD TREE
LIGHT SOURCE COMING FROM HERE
光の方向
FOR BACKGROUND, USE 3-D PRINT
バックは3Dでプリント
KAZUMI
朝倉
YUE
夕
本
BOOK-STORE (A.K.A. NODOKA)
ASUNA
SETSUNA
& KONOKA
ア
せ
こ
背表紙
EXCERPT FOR SPINE ART
I HOPE THE ANIME GIVES ME SOME LINES, TOO!
アニメではセリフあるといいなぁ…
タイトル
(おび付き)
TITLE HERE (WITH "OBI" BANNER)
祝 アニメ化!!
HIP, HIP, HOORAY... WE'RE AN ANIME!

キャラ解説
CHARACTER PROFILE

㉑ 那波千鶴
㉑ CHIZURU NABA

ちづ姉はクラスNo.1の巨乳で
ENDOWED (PERHAPS NOT UNCOINCIDENTALLY) WITH THE
母性あふれるキャラなのですが
BIGGEST BREASTS OF THE ENTIRE CLASS, "CHIZU-NĒ" IS A
ラブひなのむつみと違っているのは
CHARACTER...UM...OVERFLOWING WITH MATERNAL INSTINCTS. THE
押しが強いところですね。
BIGGEST DIFFERENCE BETWEEN
この辺は、
HER AND "MUTSUMI" IN *LOVE HINA*
保母さんの手伝いをしていて
IS THAT, IN COMPARISON, CHIZURU IS FAR MORE ASSERTIVE. (THIS
身についたようです。
MAY IN FACT COME FROM HER WORK AS AN

アニメ版での活躍は…
ASSISTANT CHILDCARE PROVIDER.) AS FOR HOW OFTEN SHE'LL
ちょっとむずかしいかも…?!
APPEAR IN THE ANIME VERSION...WE'LL HAVE TO WAIT AND SEE.
でも小太郎の扱いによっては
NOW, IF KOTARO WERE TO GFT LOTS OF SCREEN
あるいは?!
TIME, WHO KNOWS?!

GEE, Y' THINK?!
カモ?!

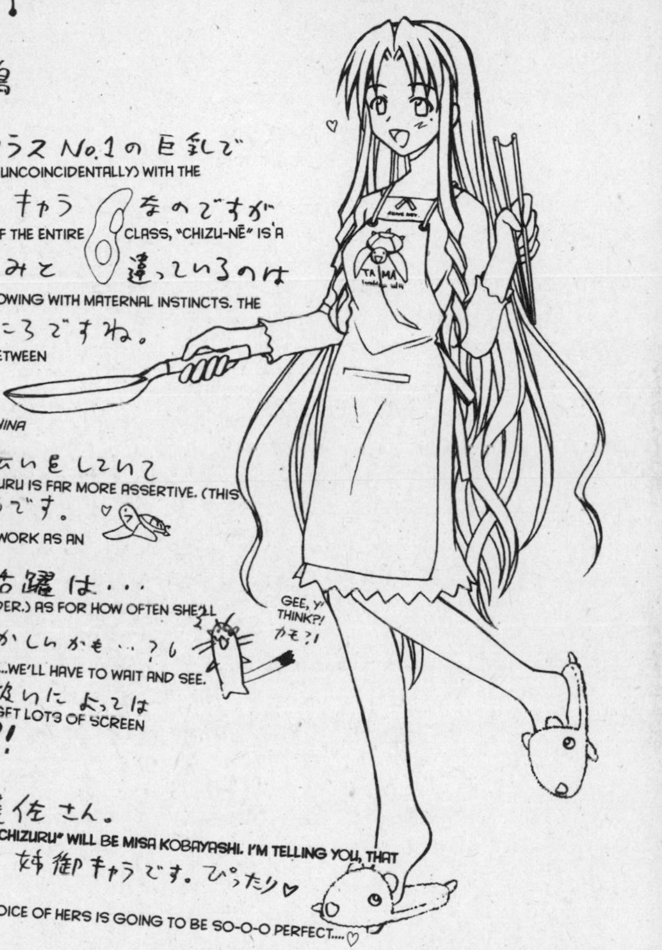

声優は小林美佐さん。
ACTOR-WISE, THE VOICE FOR "CHIZURU" WILL BE MISA KOBAYASHI. I'M TELLING YOU, THAT
面倒見のいい姉御キャラです。ぴったり♡
KIND AND CARING *"ANEGO"* VOICE OF HERS IS GOING TO BE SO-O-O PERFECT....♡

それでは、次の9巻で
THAT'S IT FOR THIS TIME, THEN.
お会いしましょう!
SEE YOU IN VOLUME 9, HUH?!

赤松
AKAMATSU

About the Creator

Negima! is only Ken Akamatsu's third manga, although he started working in the field in 1994 with *AI Ga Tomaranai* (released in the United States with the title *A.I. Love You*). Like all of Akamatsu's work to date, it was published in Kodansha's *Shonen Magazine*. *AI Ga Tomaranai* ran for five years before concluding in 1999. In 1998, however, Akamatsu began the work that would make him one of the most popular manga artists in Japan: *Love Hina*. *Love Hina* ran for four years, and before its conclusion in 2002, it would cause Akamatsu to be granted the prestigious Manga of the Year award from Kodansha, as well as going on to become one of the best-selling manga in the United States.

Translation Notes

Japanese is a tricky language for most westerners, and translation is often more art than science. For your edification and reading pleasure, here are notes on some of the places where we could have gone in a different direction in our translation of the work, or where a Japanese cultural reference is used.

"A Dog, A Day", page 31

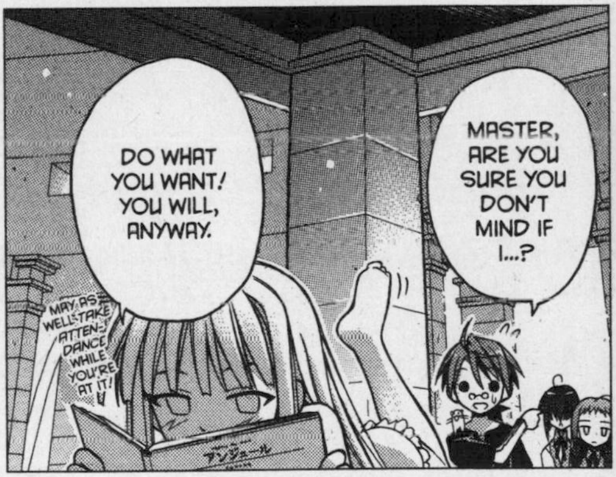
MASTER, ARE YOU SURE YOU DON'T MIND IF I...?
DO WHAT YOU WANT! YOU WILL, ANYWAY.
MAY AS WELL TAKE ATTENDANCE WHILE YOU'RE AT IT!

The book Evangeline is reading on page 31, panel 2 is *A Dog, A Day* by Gabrielle Vincent (author of the "Ernest and Celestine" books). Cited by more than one reviewer as a condemnation of animal cruelty, another remarks that, although the illustrations are worthwhile, the book's "existentialism" may prove confusing to children (which makes the fact that the child-in-body-yet-grown-in-mind Evangeline is reading it even funnier).
[64th Period]

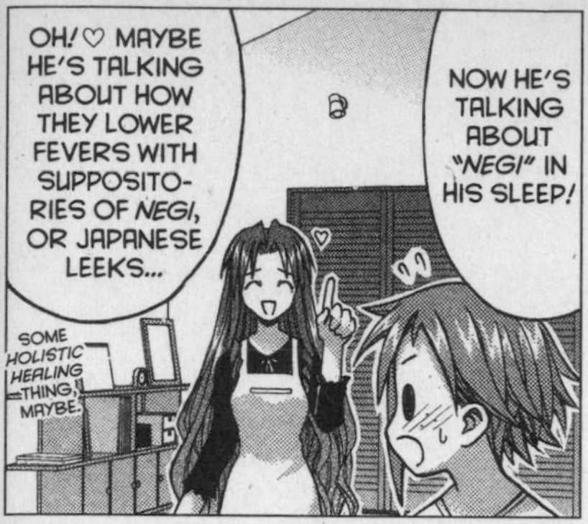
NOW HE'S TALKING ABOUT "NEGI" IN HIS SLEEP!
OH! ♡ MAYBE HE'S TALKING ABOUT HOW THEY LOWER FEVERS WITH SUPPOSITORIES OF NEGI, OR JAPANESE LEEKS...
SOME HOLISTIC HEALING THING, MAYBE.

Onion Suppositories, page 37

When Chizuru claims that sticking a *negi* or Japanese long onion up the... um, *you know*...is a regional Japanese folk remedy for reducing fever, she wasn't kidding. Apparently, it's also a cure for constipation! But don't go rushing to the produce department just yet—the practice is also known for inducing tears in the sphincter muscles, causing hemorrhoids, and even bacterial infections. My goodness. Something new to learn in every volume.
[64th Period]

Ranks of European Nobility, page 104

Because we care, a brief listing of European titles and their German equivalents:

KNIGHT	RITTER
BARON	FREIHERR
COUNT	GRAF
MARQUIS	FURST
DUKE	HERZOG

[68th Period]

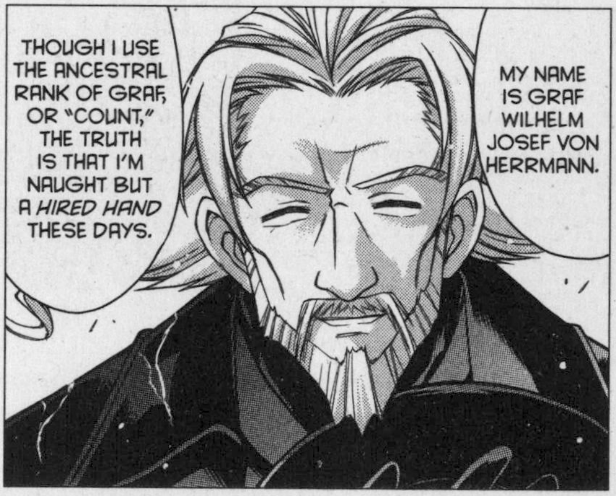
MY NAME IS GRAF WILHELM JOSEF VON HERRMANN.
THOUGH I USE THE ANCESTRAL RANK OF GRAF, OR "COUNT," THE TRUTH IS THAT I'M NAUGHT BUT A HIRED HAND THESE DAYS.

"Slime!", page 128

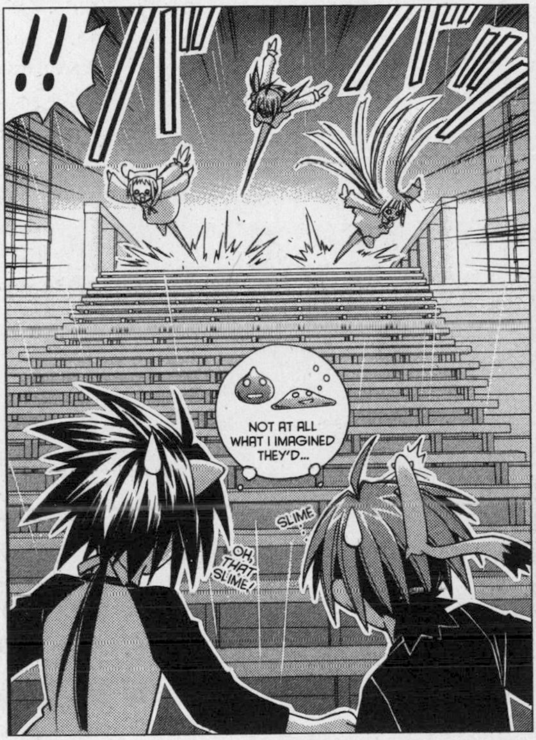
!!
NOT AT ALL WHAT I IMAGINED THEY'D...
SLIME
OH, THAT SLIME!

In their shared word balloon on page 128, panel 4, Kotarō and Negi take a moment to picture their own ideas of what a "slime" might look like. Familiar to gamers everywhere, the illustration of course is an exact representation of an early-level monster encountered in the original "Dragon Quest," an RPG released in the '80s for the Nintendo Famcom (Nintendo Entertainment System or NES in the U.S.). Designed by none other than Akira Toriyama of "Dragon Ball" fame, the cute, turd-like *suraimu* or "slime" character proved so popular in its native Japan it not only became a recurring game element, but also spawned its own line of character goods. ("Suramui," the name of one of the three slime girls in this volume, is Akamatsu's winking reversal of the final two syllables in "*suraimu*.")
[69th Period]

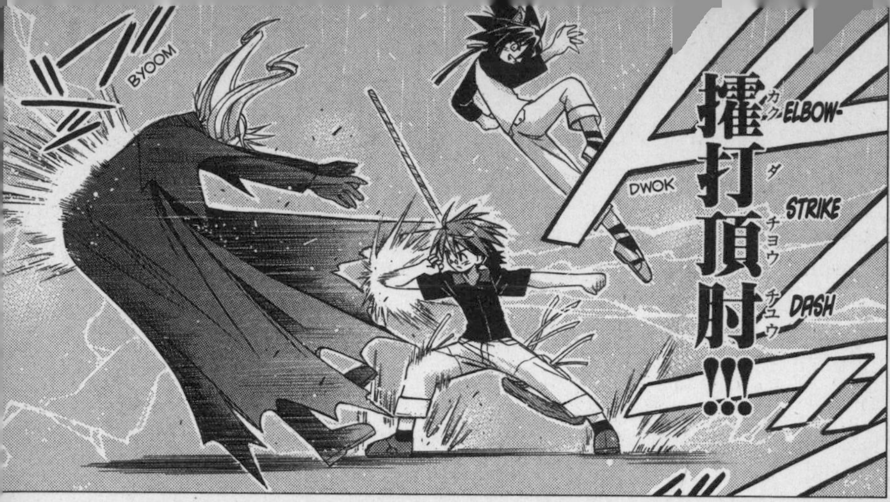
攉打頂肘!!!
カクダチョウチュウ
ELBOW-
STRIKE
DASH
DWOK
BYOOM

Kakudachōchū, page 169

The martial-arts technique Negi uses against Count (or Graf) Herrmann on page 169, panel 5 is—surprised?—a move also used by the character Akira in the 3D polygon fighting game "Virtua Fighter 4." In one translation of the Akira move list printed within the "Virtua Fighter 4" instructions, it's referred to as the "Single Palm—Dashing Elbow," and is executed by pressing down + forward + punch + punch.
[71st Period]

Anego, from the Chizuru sketch on page 191

In the parlance of the Yakuza, an anego is wife or lover to an Oyabun (head or leader of a yakuza group). Can also be used outside yakuza connotations to mean a strong-willed or politically powerful woman who may not, from outward appearances, even seem to be so.
[Back Cover Sketches]

Preview of Volume Nine

Because we're running about one year behind the release of the Japanese *Negima!* manga, we have the opportunity to present to you a preview from volume nine. This volume will be available in English On March 28, 2006.

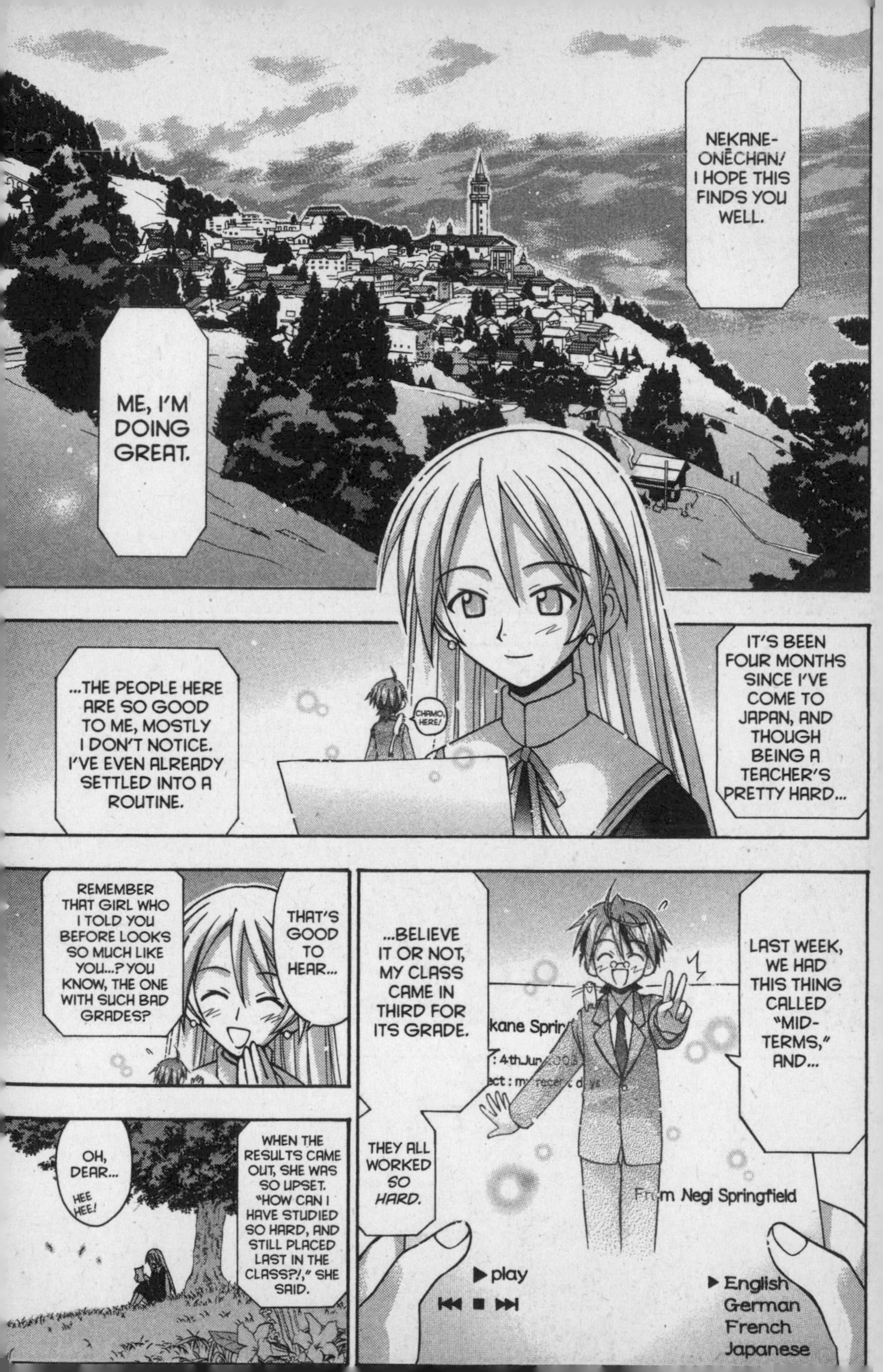
NEKANE-ONĒCHAN! I HOPE THIS FINDS YOU WELL.
ME, I'M DOING GREAT.
IT'S BEEN FOUR MONTHS SINCE I'VE COME TO JAPAN, AND THOUGH BEING A TEACHER'S PRETTY HARD...
CHAMO, HERE!
...THE PEOPLE HERE ARE SO GOOD TO ME, MOSTLY I DON'T NOTICE. I'VE EVEN ALREADY SETTLED INTO A ROUTINE.
LAST WEEK, WE HAD THIS THING CALLED "MID-TERMS," AND...
...BELIEVE IT OR NOT, MY CLASS CAME IN THIRD FOR ITS GRADE.
THEY ALL WORKED SO *HARD.*
From Negi Springfield
play
English
German
French
Japanese
THAT'S GOOD TO HEAR...
REMEMBER THAT GIRL WHO I TOLD YOU BEFORE LOOKS SO MUCH LIKE YOU...? YOU KNOW, THE ONE WITH SUCH BAD GRADES?
WHEN THE RESULTS CAME OUT, SHE WAS SO UPSET. "HOW CAN I HAVE STUDIED SO HARD, AND STILL PLACED LAST IN THE CLASS?!," SHE SAID.
OH, DEAR...
HEE HEE!

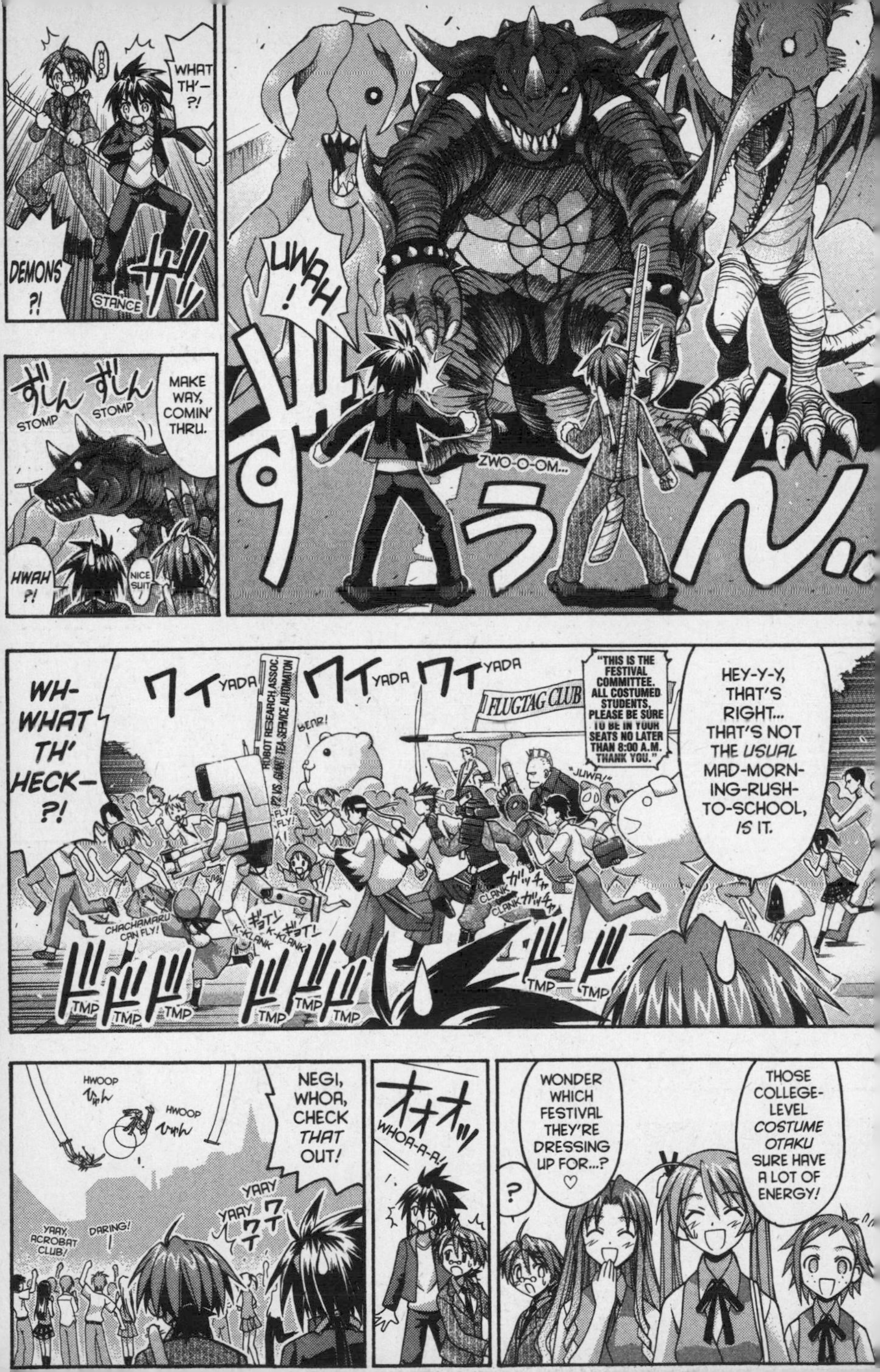
UWAH!
ZWO-O-OM...
ずぅん...
WHOA
WHAT TH'—?!
DEMONS?!
STANCE
ずしん ずしん
STOMP STOMP
MAKE WAY, COMIN' THRU.
HWAH?!
NICE SUIT!
HEY-Y-Y, THAT'S RIGHT... THAT'S NOT THE USUAL MAD-MORNING-ING-RUSH-TO-SCHOOL, IS IT.
"THIS IS THE FESTIVAL COMMITTEE. ALL COSTUMED STUDENTS, PLEASE BE SURE TO BE IN YOUR SEATS NO LATER THAN 8:00 A.M. THANK YOU."
FLUGTAG CLUB
"JUWA!"
ワイ YADA ワイ YADA ワイ YADA
ROBOT RESEARCH ASSOC. P2 VS. GIANT TEA-SERVICE AUTOMATON
BEAR!
FLY! FLY!
WH-WHAT TH' HECK—?!
CLANK CLANK
K-KLANK K-KLANK
CHACHAMARU CAN FLY!
TMP TMP TMP TMP TMP TMP TMP TMP
THOSE COLLEGE-LEVEL COSTUME OTAKU SURE HAVE A LOT OF ENERGY!
WONDER WHICH FESTIVAL THEY'RE DRESSING UP FOR...? ♡
?
オオオッ
WHOA-A-A!
NEGI, WHOA, CHECK THAT OUT!
HWOOP
HWOOP
YAAY ワイ
YAAY ワイ
DARING!
YAAY, ACROBAT CLUB!

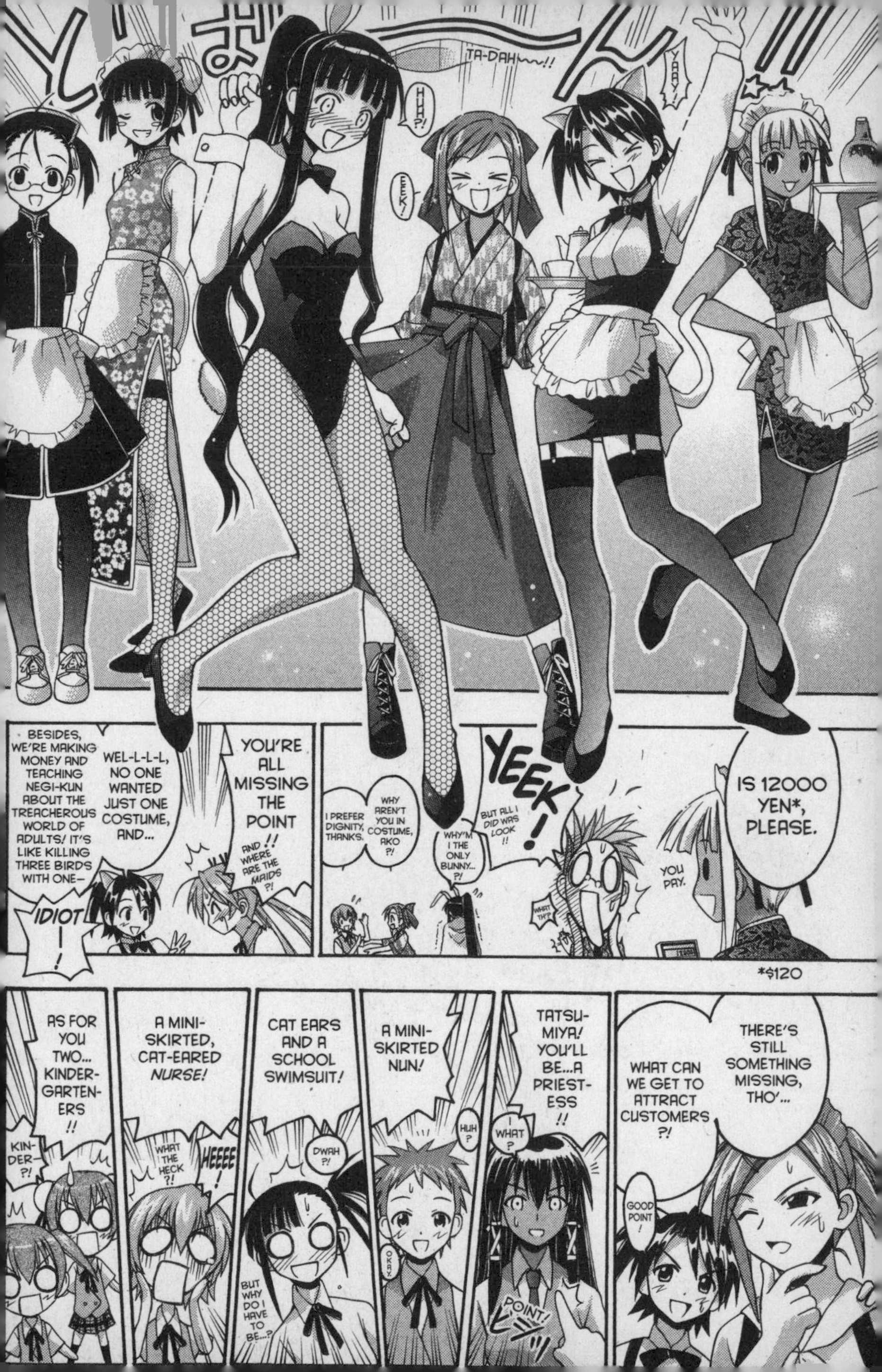
YAAY!
TA-DAH~~!!
HUH?!
EEK!
IS 12000 YEN*, PLEASE.
YOU PAY.
WHAT TH?
YEEK!
BUT ALL I DID WAS LOOK!!
WHY AREN'T YOU IN COSTUME, AKO?!
I PREFER DIGNITY, THANKS.
WHY'M I THE ONLY BUNNY...?!
YOU'RE ALL MISSING THE POINT!!
AND WHERE ARE THE MAIDS?!
WEL-L-L-L, NO ONE WANTED JUST ONE COSTUME, AND...
BESIDES, WE'RE MAKING MONEY AND TEACHING NEGI-KUN ABOUT THE TREACHEROUS WORLD OF ADULTS! IT'S LIKE KILLING THREE BIRDS WITH ONE—
IDIOT!!
*$120
THERE'S STILL SOMETHING MISSING, THO'...
WHAT CAN WE GET TO ATTRACT CUSTOMERS?!
GOOD POINT!
TATSUMIYA! YOU'LL BE...A PRIESTESS!!
I WHAT?
POINT!
A MINI-SKIRTED NUN!
HUH?
OKAY
CAT EARS AND A SCHOOL SWIMSUIT!
DWAH?!
BUT WHY DO I HAVE TO BE...?
A MINI-SKIRTED, CAT-EARED NURSE!
WHAT THE HECK?!
HEEEE!
AS FOR YOU TWO... KINDERGARTENERS!!
KINDER-?!

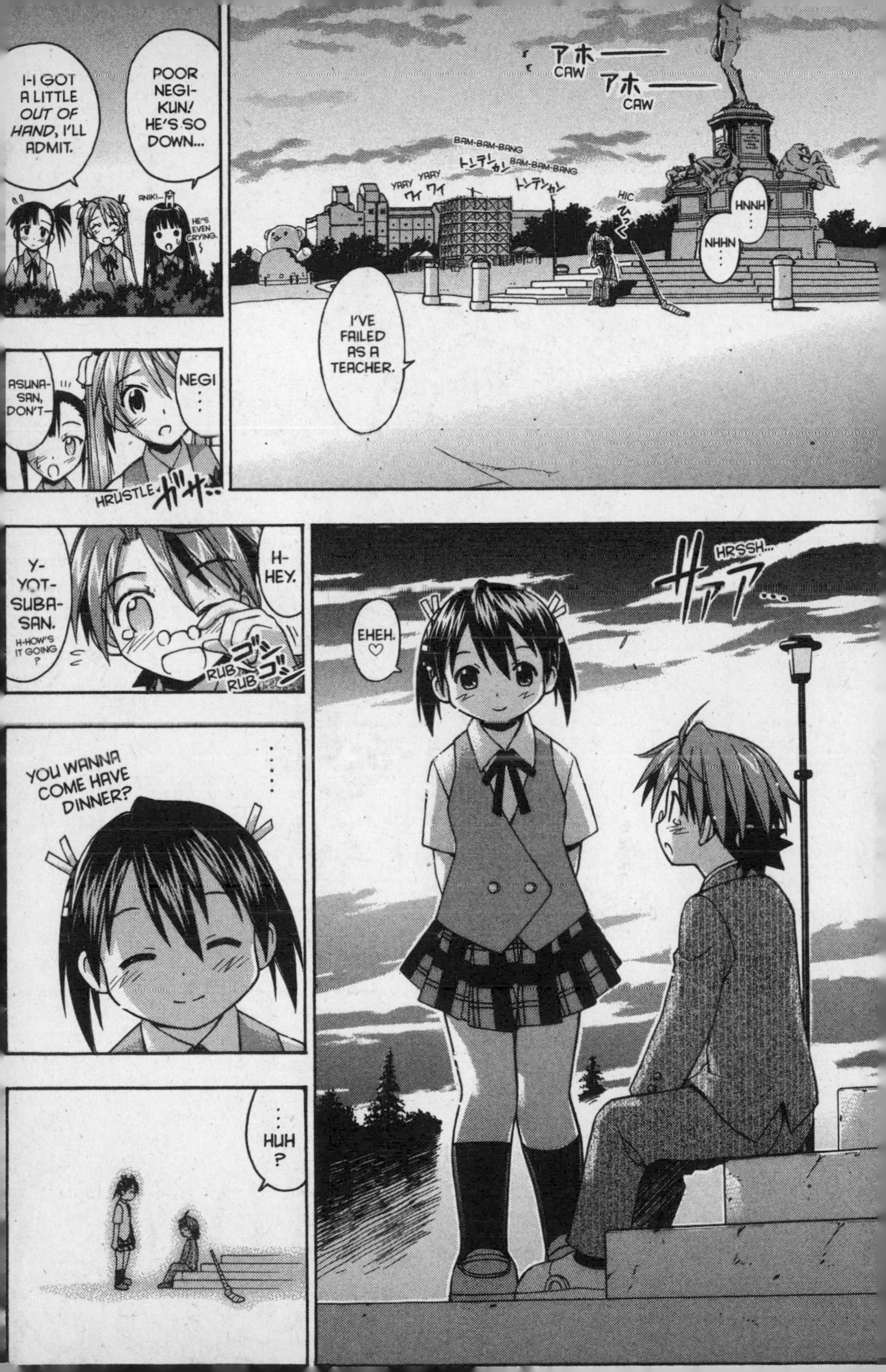

アホー
CAW
アホー
CAW
BAM-BAM-BANG
トンテンカン
BAM-BAM-BANG
トンテンカン
YAAY YAAY
ワイワイ
HIC
ひっく
HNNH...
NHHN...
I'VE FAILED AS A TEACHER.
POOR NEGI-KUN! HE'S SO DOWN...
I-I GOT A LITTLE OUT OF HAND, I'LL ADMIT.
ANIKI...
HE'S EVEN CRYING.
NEGI...
ASUNA-SAN, DON'T—
HRUSTLE
ガサ
HRSSH...
サァア...
EHEH. ♡
H-HEY.
Y-YOTSUBA-SAN.
H-HOW'S IT GOING?
RUB RUB
ゴシゴシ
......
YOU WANNA COME HAVE DINNER?
...HUH?

TOMARE!

[STOP!]

You're going the wrong way!

Manga is a completely different type of reading experience.

To start at the *beginning*, go to the *end*!

That's right! Authentic manga is read the traditional Japanese way—from right to left. Exactly the *opposite* of how American books are read. It's easy to follow: Just go to the other end of the book, and read each page—and each panel—from right side to left side, starting at the top right. Now you're experiencing manga as it was meant to be.